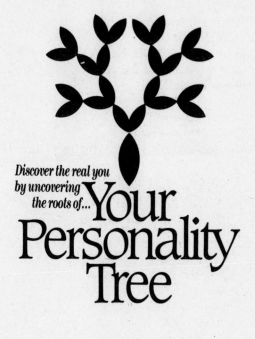

*Discover the real you
by uncovering
the roots of...* Your
Personality
Tree

OTHER BOOKS BY FLORENCE LITTAUER

Lives on the Mend
After Every Wedding Comes a Marriage
Blow Away the Black Clouds
How to Get Along with Difficult People
It Takes So Little to Be Above Average
Out of the Cabbage Patch
Personality Plus
The Pursuit of Happiness
Say It with CLASS
Shades of Beauty (co-authored with Marita Littauer)

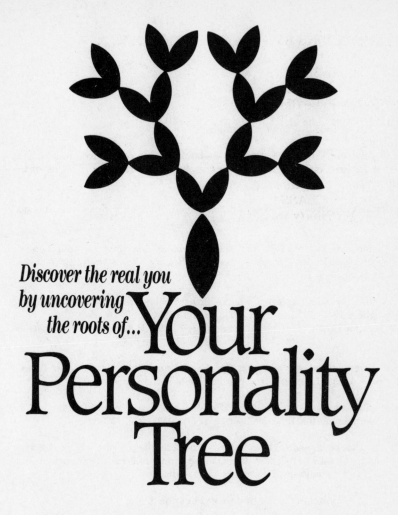

*Discover the real you
by uncovering
the roots of...* Your
Personality
Tree

Florence Littauer

With suggestions for individual and group activities

WORD BOOKS
PUBLISHER
WACO, TEXAS
A DIVISION OF
WORD, INCORPORATED

YOUR PERSONALITY TREE

Scripture quotations marked KJV are from the Authorized or King James Version of the Bible.

Quotations marked NIV are from the Holy Bible, New International Version. Copyright © 1973, 1978, International Bible Society. Used by permission of Zondervan Bible Publishers.

Quotations marked RSV are from the Revised Standard Version of the Bible, copyrighted 1946, 1952, © 1971, 1973 by the Division of Christian Education of the National Council of the Churches of Christ in the U.S.A., and used by permission.

Quotations marked TEV are from *The Good News Bible,* the Bible in Today's English Version. Copyright © American Bible Society, 1976.

Quotations marked NASB are from *The New American Standard Bible,* © The Lockman Foundation 1960, 1962, 1971, 1972, 1973, 1975, 1977.

An effort has been made to locate sources and obtain permission where necessary for quotations used in this book. In the event of any unintended omission, modifications will be gladly incorporated in future editions.

Library of Congress Cataloging-in-Publication Data

Littauer, Florence, 1928–
  Your personality tree.

  Bibliography: p.
  1. Personality.   2. Typology (Psychology)
I. Title.
BF698.3.L57   1986   155.2′6   86–18972
ISBN 0–8499–0571–0

Printed in the United States of America

  898   RRD   9876543

This book is dedicated to Lana Bateman whose addition to our CLASS staff started my search into the different personalities on a much deeper level than I had ever done before. Her godly wisdom has challenged us all to examine ourselves, to get right with the Lord, and to take off any masks or pretenses we might have worn in the past.

I am deeply indebted to her for allowing me to develop her concept of masking in this book and to quote some of her case histories. The chapter on children's personalities is based on her material in *Personality Patterns*, a book on how to use the temperaments in counseling. Some of the parenting pointers are hers also, and I have quoted her frequently throughout this book. She is the author of *God's Crippled Children*, founder of Philippian Ministries, and a CLASS speaker.

With Gratitude,
Florence Littauer
President, CLASS Speakers

Contents

7

8 ❦ **CONTENTS** ❦

Foreword

When sin entered the world it brought with it a splintering or fracturing of the human personality. What was once whole and perfect is now pieced and flawed. People must now learn to live with the strengths and weaknesses of those who are totally different from themselves.

How can we understand another when we have never experienced feelings and needs so common to him or her and yet totally alien to us? How shall we then love?

Florence and I spent a week together during the summer of 1985 in Estes Park, Colorado, asking ourselves that very question. We desired to put together our thoughts and concepts on the personality temperaments in a way that would enable the body of Christ to develop a deeper understanding of themselves and of those with whom they were called to love and coexist.

We prayed that our God would take all he had taught us and fashion the information into a work capable of bringing new light to the dilemma of human relationships. We longed for tools to help the family find unity through compassionate acceptance, and we prayed for our Lord's hand to inspire our work as a healing touch for hopeless relationships and hurting hearts.

9

This book is the result of those prayers. Florence has once again written that which will change lives and bring new hope. Her style and sensitivity make the information both exciting and inspiring. Treat yourself now to the work of a master teacher, writer, and speaker and prepare for a whole new world of relationships.

Lana Bateman
Founder/Director
Philippian Ministries
Dallas, Texas

Introduction

My Dear Reader:

With lines forming outside the psychiatrist's office, Christian psychologists working into the night, and pastors adding counselors to their staffs, it is obvious there are many people who need help. This book is not meant to replace counselors or to refute their usefulness, but to give some simple insights that may arrest an irritation in its infancy before it grows into a situation that needs outside help. We'd like to take care of our own problems and live in harmony with our family and friends, but somehow we don't know where to start. We've been told Christians shouldn't have any problems and they should be prosperous, so our failure is often coupled with guilt.

Many of us have tried so hard to be all things to all people that we are not sure who we are. Is this the real me or what I've learned to be? Am I as an adult still struggling to become what mother had in mind for me? Have I blended so completely with my mate that I can't recognize an independent thought when I have one? Am I wearing a mask to hide the anger bubbling below the surface? Am I not clear as to what parts of my personality are genuine or what traits are responses to the adversities of life?

In the past twenty years of study, speaking and writing, I have attempted to discover who I really am and to share these insights with others. In addition I have set out to uncover the roots of my personality tree, to find out where my traits originated, and to observe where my own feelings were suppressed, repressed, or depressed.

In this book you will find out who you really are and begin to see why others function as they do. Those of you who have read *Personality Plus* or *How to Get Along with Difficult People* will find new, additional, and deeper information, and those of you for whom this concept is new will have an eye-opening experience which could change your self-image and your ability to get along with others.

Let's have an exciting adventure as we laugh, think, and occasionally cry together. Take my hand as I guide you along the path of personal wisdom and insight.

You will discover who you really are, uncover the roots of your Personality Tree, and recover the original spark and spirit that God intended you to have.

> With love and anticipation
> Florence Littauer

[Wisdom] is a tree of life to those who embrace her; those who lay hold of her will be blessed.
> —Proverbs 3:18, NIV

PART I

DISCOVER
THE REAL YOU
AND
AIM TO HEAL YOU

DISCOVER:

> *To obtain, for the first time,*
> *sight or knowledge of a thing*
> *existing already but not per-*
> *ceived or known.*

Our aim in this book is to examine ourselves in a new way, not just on the surface, not just as we appear to be to others, not just as mother wanted us to be. By looking at our inborn desires, our underlying needs, and our repressed emotions, our eyes will be opened and we will obtain, perhaps for the first time, some insight about who we really are. There is no magic wand to transform us into angels, but as we look at ourselves as God created us to be and come before him in honesty, he will touch us with his healing power.

> *"The fruit of the righteous is a tree of life."*
> —Proverbs 11:30, NIV

❧ 1 ❧

Were You
Born Like This?

The question "Who am I?" has been around since Adam wondered what dust he'd come from and the Serpent told Eve to eat the fruit of the tree of life so her eyes would be opened and she'd know who she really was.

Throughout the centuries people have been searching for a sense of identity and a feeling of worth. As a nation we went through the pangs of new birth and the struggle to come out an independent personality. With liberty and justice for all, we attracted people from around the globe to a land where they would live happily ever after; but somehow in our dream of fairy-tale endings, we lost the sense of who we were as individuals. As we grew up and began to look at ourselves, we didn't like the confusion we saw. The sixties brought an unpopular war and the beginnings of a national sense of self-examination. Who are we and how did we get ourselves into these problems?

Sociologists named the seventies the Decade of Depression, a discouraging and defeated time when the ME generation realized that in spite of their quest to find themselves, to do their own thing, and to search for their inner consciousness on a higher plane, they still didn't know who in the world they were. Months of mystical meditation didn't seem to stir up a life-changing thought, peace marches had not produced peace, and the flower children had lost their petals. President Carter, looking down-hearted himself, declared we were in a "national malaise" and that announcement depressed the rest of us.

As the eighties crept in we began to wonder if we ever would find ourselves and so we rushed out to sign up for courses in self-help, self-improvement, and self-actualization. We bought life-long memberships in health spas, held hands in sensitivity groups, and gyrated around gypsy gurus. Surely the ME generation who had dragged through the Decade of Depression deserved a break today; but in spite of exercise and bean sprouts, we kept getting older, the sensitivity sisters showed little sensitivity beyond themselves, and the gurus were packed up and deported. What if we never got a grip on ourselves? What if we couldn't create heaven on earth? Fear gripped us, phobias replaced depression as the nation's number one mental health problem, and the decade was dubbed the Age of Anxiety.

What about you and me? We may not have drowned in depression or worried through our weeks, yet we tend to pick up the malaise and insecurities of others. We may be certain of life everlasting, but do we know who we are today? As I have taught leadership classes, I have found that education, money, prestige or a big house do not insure a feeling of worth. Even though we may have memorized Law One, "God loves you and has a wonderful plan for your life,"[1] few of us seem to believe it.

Yet it is true: God does love us and he has created us for a purpose. As David wrote to God in Psalm 139, "When I was woven together in the depths of the earth, your eyes saw my unformed body. All the days ordained for me were written in your book before one of them came to be" (vv. 15–16, NIV).

Yes, God knows us and he wants us to understand ourselves— not to be worried, confused, or depressed. He has made each one of us as a unique individual, and he uses our talents, personalities and gifts for his good purpose.

In the Bible Joseph was intelligent, charming, well-dressed, and had a gift for interpreting dreams, yet his brothers were envious of his abilities and they sold him as a slave. Because Joseph believed that God had an ultimate plan for him, he was able to stay optimistic even in difficult times and people saw that "the Lord was with him and that the Lord gave him success in everything he did" (Gen. 39:3, NIV).

Even when falsely accused and put in jail, Joseph kept his faith and behaved in such a manner that he rose to the prison's top position and cheered up those who were depressed. Later, those same personality traits that had disturbed his brothers were what found favor with Pharoah, and his gift of interpreting dreams saved the land. When his brothers came before him he wept, forgave them, and relieved their fears. He told them not to feel guilty because what they had meant for evil, God had turned into good.

God took Joseph's inborn traits, his personality and talents, and used him to save an entire nation and his own family.

Esther was an exceptionally beautiful Jewish woman who was both exiled and orphaned. King Xerxes chose her to become his queen without knowing her heritage. Because of her godly behavior she became a virtuous example to the other women and was dearly loved by her husband. When an order went out to kill all the Jews, she was used by God to persuade the king to change his mind. Her Uncle Mordecai stated wisely, "Who knows but that you have come to royal position for such a time as this" (Esther 4:14, NIV).

God used Esther, when she was willing and obedient, to save the exiled Jewish race and her own family also.

In the days of the New Testament when God was ready to evangelize the world, he needed someone who was a Jewish Christian, who spoke and wrote Greek, and who understood Roman law. He chose Paul who, while he had never taken any charm courses or self-improvement seminars, fit the job description. He was raised in a Jewish home, was educated as a Hebrew scholar, and was both a Pharisee and a member of the Sanhedrin. He spoke and wrote Greek, understood the classical intellect and had studied philosophy. Because the people of Tarsus had been cooperative with the conquering Pompey, he had granted them Roman citizenship, thus making Paul a citizen with an understanding of Latin plus a comprehension of Roman law, its government, and the military. All God had left to do was knock Paul to the ground, bring him face to face with Jesus, and convert him to Christ.

Paul might not be acceptable in the Christian pastorate today, but God saw a man for all seasons and he had a plan for his life.

When Winston Churchill was called to be Prime Minister of England as the European continent was falling prey to Hitler's greed, he proclaimed, "My entire life has been but a preparation for this very hour."[2] On his eightieth birthday Churchill summed up his contribution to his country by saying, "It was the nation and the race dwelling all round the globe that had the lion's heart; I had the luck to be called upon to give the roar."[3]

How about you? What has God called upon you to do? Do you know that God wants to use your personality, your background, your abilities, your gifts for his glory? He created you for such a time as this, but he wants you to know who you really are so that you will be a genuine and sincere person, not one hiding behind a mask of confusion.

You may ask, "Do I have to sign up for some course or move to Jerusalem?" No, just read on and enjoy discovering your true self by uncovering the roots of your family's Personality Tree.

During the Decade of Depression and Age of Anxiety I have been teaching people how to find themselves by using the strengths and weaknesses of the four basic personality patterns. Many have asked, "Were we born this way?" This question has had sociologists working feverishly to ferret out the answers. They have tried to show us that environment is more important than heredity, that we are born as little blank pages for Fate to write upon. We've been told that if you change a person's dwelling place or standard of living, or put money in his pocket, you will change him. In spite of millions of dollars spent in moving people into new buildings, the experiment has failed. We are not all the same; God created each one of us as a unique individual, a blending from our parents whether we are observing hair and eye color or analyzing personality.

In 1979 Dr. Thomas J. Bouchard, Jr., started a study in Minnesota of "Twins Reared Apart." Since then researchers have examined thirty-eight identical and sixteen fraternal sets of twins reared apart. The tests measured the physical, psychological, and intellectual abilities. The results showed amazing similarities in choices of clothing, food, and names; not to mention parallels in medical, behavioral, and intelligence traits.[4]

Dr. David Lykken, a research team member observes:

Much of what we think of as human individuality—temperament and pace and all the idiosyncrasies that make you different from your friends—may relate a lot more to your particular genetic individuality than we thought. . . . The capacity for happiness seems to be more strongly genetically wired in than I had thought. . . .

Little Mary's sunny disposition may be part of her genetic makeup, enhanced by—but not the result of her adoring parents' care.[5]

The new thinking on old truths is that we are born as unique individuals. If we come prepackaged with certain blendings of our parents' personalities, isn't it our duty to the Lord to be as true to our basic traits as we possibly can? Shouldn't it be our goal to find out who we really are and take off any masks or pretenses that we may have put on for either self-preservation or a desire to be like someone else?

Think back to your childhood, to how you felt about your parents, to how you related with your siblings, to how you reacted from the heart before you built walls of protection from the hurts of the world. Remember, you were made for such a time as this.

Were you meant to be a Sanguine? Were you a cheerful, bubbling, happy-go-lucky child? Did you avoid chores and somehow manage to find friends who were willing to bail you out? Did you have little buddies who wouldn't go anywhere without you and who thought everything you said was funny? Did you have one parent who was always trying to get you down to serious business or one who couldn't understand why you wouldn't practice the violin? Did you get good marks in everything but conduct and penmanship? Then you are a Sanguine whose chief aim in life is to have FUN.

Were you created to be a Choleric? Were you in control of the family by the time you were three years old? Did you tell your mother what you would wear and refuse to put on what she had in mind? Were you able to observe from a young age that adults were bigger but not necessarily brighter? Did you get your school work done faster than the others and then wonder what was wrong with them? Did you become captain of the teams and president of the clubs? Then you are a Choleric whose compelling desire in life is to have CONTROL.

Were you designed to be a Melancholy? Were you sensitive to your surroundings and easily moved to tears? Did you line up your toys in rows and go around shutting drawers that no one else seemed to notice were open? Did you do your homework on time and even enjoy research projects? Did you practice your piano piece until it was perfect, but not want to play in the recital? Did you feel sorry for "poor children" and want to support the underdog in any situation? Did you get discouraged when things didn't work out the way you had in mind and no one else seemed to care? Then you are a Melancholy whose hope is to someday have PERFECTION even though that may be an impossible dream.

Were you born to be a Phlegmatic? Were you passive in your playpen and understanding if your bottle was overdue? Did your mother brag that you were a good baby and never gave her any trouble? Did you like naps? Did you do your school work on time but not look for extra projects? Did you get nominated for vice-president but not really care whether you were elected? Did you try to keep everyone happy and avoid getting into trouble? Then you are a Phlegmatic whose desire is to have PEACE at any cost.

The concept of the four basic temperaments is so easy to understand and quick to grasp that even a child can learn it. Bryan Taylor from Temple, Texas, was ten years old when he heard me speak on the temperaments. He brought his friends home to listen to my *Personality Plus* tapes, and later he did a school science project based on his personal analysis of his fellow students. For his project, this Melancholy child made a chart entitled "Questions Regarding Human Behavior." Each child in his class was asked to answer the following:

Suppose a play were to be done at Meridith School. How would you want to be involved?
1. I would like to work backstage._____Why?_____
2. I would like to be student director._____Why?_____
3. I would like to be cast in a leading role._____Why?_____
4. I would not want to participate._____Why?_____

The questionnaire he showed me had been filled out by a student who wanted the leading role because "It would be fun." From Bryan's tabulations there were eight Melancholies who wanted to work backstage, fifteen Cholerics who liked the idea of directing the others, ten Sanguines who all wanted to star, and three Phlegmatics who didn't care to get involved.

When I saw how simply Bryan had taken my hours of teaching and reduced them down to four simple questions any ten-year-old could answer, I was impressed. I then asked him if he had

PERSONALITY ROLES	
THE STAR	THE DIRECTOR
THE AUDIENCE	THE PRODUCER

won an award for his efforts and he replied sadly, "I would have but they ran out of ribbons."

Often we can tell a child's natural temperament pattern from an early age.

My two grandsons came equipped with the same parents, Lauren and Randy, but with very different personalities. From the beginning little Randy, Jr., was Melancholy with some Choleric: neat, organized, and in-charge. When I walk in the front door Randy says, "Sit here, Grammie," and I do. He then brings me his second-grade school papers and shows me 100 percent in spelling including the word *Hanukkah.* As we sit seriously together, four-year-old Jonathan, Sanguine with some Choleric, runs over the top of the coffee table in his Superman costume and is not content until he has disrupted our conversation on spelling and has managed to get Randy depressed.

Last Christmas Aunt Marita gave them a hamster named Ginger. Each boy was constantly opening the cage to see if Ginger was still alive, and often they would lose interest in her monotonous trip round and round on the exercise wheel and forget to shut the gate. Ginger, being bright, adventurous and always hungry would run away and look for food. One day Lauren opened the trash compactor to drop in an empty cereal box and screamed when she saw little beady eyes looking up from the darkness. It was Ginger happily munching on stale crackers and missing death by a moment. Had Lauren turned the key without looking, little Ginger would have been as flat as a fur mitten.

From then on each time Ginger was missing, the boys would go to the trash compactor and there she would be, bright-eyed and bingeing.

One night I called on the phone and Randy, Jr., said, "Have you heard the bad news? Ginger is dead." I could picture her flattened out among the boxes and cans, but Randy explained, "She died in her cage. I went to play with her and she was dead." He then delivered a fitting eulogy and gave me the details. In his Melancholy way he told me how he and his father had found a little box in the garage, lined it with paper towels, wrapped poor Ginger in tissue paper, taken the box to a far corner of the back yard and buried her. "We had a funeral," he explained. "We'll always remember poor dead Ginger."

I was close to tears over his mournful musings of the memory of the hamster. When little Jonathan got on the phone, I said, sadly, "I hear Ginger died."

He replied, "Yup, she's dead all right."

"Did you have a nice funeral for her?" I asked, giving him an opportunity to share his version of the tragedy.

"No, we didn't have any funeral; we just dumped her in an old box with clowns on it, stuck her in a hole in the ground, threw some dirt over her, and that's the end of Ginger."

"Will you get a new one?" I asked.

"Well, we might get another one, but if that one dies too then it's bye-bye hamsters!"

I had to laugh over his simple Sanguine dismissal of Ginger's death as just one more event in a busy day while his Melancholy brother was in mourning.

What fun it is to understand others and have an explanation for their behavior!

Our aim in studying the temperaments is to assess our basic strengths and realize that we are people of value and worth; to become aware of our weaknesses and set out to overcome them; to learn that just because other people are different doesn't make them wrong; and to accept the fact that since we can't change them, we might as well love them as they are.

What pressure it takes off of us when we realize that we are not responsible for the behavior of those other people. How liberating it is when we realize God created us as unique individuals and we don't have to conform to someone else's image.

As Pam Phillips wrote after listening to my tapes, "I have been amazed, thrilled and set free by your teaching."

The study of the temperaments is not a theology but a tool to understanding ourselves and learning to get along with others.

"If the Son sets you free, you will be free indeed" (John 8:36, NIV).

For Further Study, Thought, and Action

We are free indeed to examine ourselves and reach for our full potential. Some of us may have the heart of a lion while some are called upon to give the roar. As a first step, check off the traits on the Quick Quiz that sound the most like you. (See page 24.)

Remembering Bryan's simple questions, what were you like as a child?

Were you the Sanguine who wanted to be a star and entertain the troops?

Were you the Choleric who innately seized control of every cast with or without having read the script?

Were you the Melancholy who would rather stay in the wings of life than stand on center stage?

Were you the Phlegmatic who fled the smell of the grease paint and the roar of the crowd but enjoyed watching?

Throughout the book, to make the concept easier to grasp, I will use charts of the four kinds of personalities. In each case, the following letters representing the temperaments will be in the background.

S = Sanguine	C = Choleric
P = Phlegmatic	M = Melancholy

Occasionally I will use a combination of these letters after a name. For example, I will refer to someone as (S/C), meaning he is a combination Sanguine/Choleric or C/M, meaning he is a combination Choleric/Melancholy.

Now fill in the box on page 25 with your total from the Quick Quiz. Is there any inconsistency between what you remember being as a child and what you seem to be now?

QUICK QUIZ OF TEMPERAMENT TRAITS

SANGUINE PERSONALITY

The Talker _____
Fun-loving _____
Optimistic _____
Animated & Excited _____
Life-of-the-party _____
Undisciplined _____
Forgetful _____
Too talkative _____
Eager for credit _____

_____
Total

CHOLERIC POWER

The Worker _____
Controlling _____
Dynamic _____
Decisive _____
Goal-oriented _____
Outspoken _____
Bossy _____
Impatient _____
Domineering _____

_____
Total

PHLEGMATIC PEACE

The Mediator _____
Easy-going _____
Calm and relaxed _____
Patient & inoffensive _____
Quiet yet witty _____
Unmotivated _____
Unenthusiastic _____
Indecisive _____
Eager to rest _____

_____
Total

MELANCHOLY PERFECTION

The Thinker _____
Deep and purposeful _____
Sensitive to others _____
Talented & creative _____
Analytical & orderly _____
Moody & negative _____
Too introspective _____
Socially insecure _____
Easily depressed _____

_____
Total

PERSONAL COUNT	
SANGUINE _____	CHOLERIC _____
PHLEGMATIC _____	MELANCHOLY _____

To benefit the most from the growth of your Personality Tree, start a notebook in which you can begin to build a pattern of your personality from birth on to your childhood, educational years, career, and marriage up to the present. As you continue to read this book you will be led to review your parents and grandparents and how they may have influenced your personality for the better or forced you to play a role that was not your real self. By keeping notes on your answers and reactions, you will conclude with a broad view of yourself and your family. You will build a family tree based on each member's personality and see how they have affected each other and especially you. This would be a fascinating study to do either with your own family or with a group of friends. You may even want to add childhood pictures as you go along or include letters and stories from relatives which shed light on who you really are.

I have gathered childhood and ancestral pictures and have put together an album of my Personality Tree plus wedding invitations, birth certificates, baptismal records, and business cards of relatives. Also I've had slides made of many old family pictures for the entertainment and edification of my children and for use in teaching the Personality Tree to others. I have framed one picture of each ancestor and have them hanging on a family tree painted on a wall in my home. I hope these ideas stimulate you into examining your roots and creating your unique Personality Tree.

Ask yourself the following questions, plus any others you create, and write down your answers. If you do this chapter by chapter, you will produce an amazing record, perhaps an autobiography, for yourself and for your children.

What is your full name and where did it originate? from a grandmother? a TV star?

What was your mother's and father's initial reaction to your looks and sex at birth? Ask them or others who were around.

What did they call you as a baby?

Were you labeled as the smart one? The pretty one? The redhead? The dummy? The black sheep? List all the labels you can remember. Have any of these labels affected your opinion of yourself?

Describe any type of participation in some memorable production of your youth. I remember trying out for the Rose and being chosen to play the Cowslip.

Do you have pictures of you in costume?

PERSONALITY GOALS	
HAVE FUN	HAVE CONTROL
HAVE PEACE	HAVE PERFECTION

From what you've read so far do you think you were born to be . . .

A Sanguine who wants to have fun?

A Choleric who wants to be in control?

A Melancholy who wants everything to be perfect?

A Phlegmatic who wants to keep out of trouble and have peace?

If you are planning *Your Personality Tree* as a group study have each person bring a baby picture, his/her baby book, and any momentos of interest for your next meeting. Discuss the previous questions and ideas and find out who you were born to be. This is the beginning of an exciting adventure.

"Memory is the diary that we all carry about with us."[6]

❧ 2 ❧

What Is
Your Personality?

"You are just like Ruth," my mother would say to me in disgust. As a child I had no idea why I was like Ruth, my mother's younger sister who had been a talented violinist, had graduated from Boston University and then eloped with a mechanic from Canada and disappeared from family view. I'd never seen Aunt Ruth, but the mere mention of her name would bring my petite Phlegmatic grandmother to tears as others would shake their heads and mumble in unison, "After all we did for her."

Somehow Aunt Ruth hadn't lived up to the family's image of her potential, and I didn't see how I was like her. I was only a child and had no feel for the violin, even though my mother had patiently taught me where to put my fingers and how to move the bow. After two years of lessons I came across more as Jack Benny than Aunt Ruth. People laughed when I played and finally Mother said to my dad, "Give her elocution lessons for she has no talent."

How could I be like Ruth if I'd failed at violin, hadn't been to college, and had surely not eloped to Canada?

One day when I was visiting at my grandmother's house in Merrimac, Massachusetts, a big semi-truck stopped out front. It was so huge it filled the entire width of Orchard Street. We ran to the window at the sound of the motor and saw a lady jump down from the cab. "It's Ruth!" Grandma cried as she ran to the door.

"*The* Aunt Ruth?" I wondered. "Now I'll find out why I'm like her."

I saw her pick up little Grandma and swing her around. She laughed as she explained how she'd met this truck driver in Canada. He'd said he was driving to Massachusetts and she'd thrown a few things in a paper bag and hopped in with him.

"Oh, you shouldn't have taken such a chance," Grandma reprimanded.

"It was the only way I could afford to get home, nothing went wrong, and we had so much fun on the drive down." Aunt Ruth turned and waved goodbye to her new "best friend" as he labored to turn his rig around at the end of Orchard Street and get on the road again.

"He was such a nice man," she said with a feeling of nostalgia while Grandma muttered, "Well, I don't know about that. Who knows what could have happened to you?"

During the next few days I watched Aunt Ruth's every move and listened to what she said and what the others said when she left the room. I found her fascinating fun, but I could see how the family found her to be a rebel. Every time she went to the bathroom, cigarette smoke came wafting through the cracks and the key hole. No one ever faced her with this "sinful behavior," but whenever she'd head for the bathroom, the sisters would whisk Grandma out on the porch to look at the birds.

Aunt Ruth always seemed to "get by with things" as my mother put it, using one of the many clichés her family lived by. I observed how Aunt Ruth charmed people into going along with her ideas and how she could take mild criticism and turn it into humor. She made the very best of a not too positive situation, and I quietly admired her skill and personality. As I listened, I realized that Ruth had always been able to "get away with murder" and that the others had often been left "holding the bag" while Ruth would be sitting on her papa's lap telling him how much she loved him. My mother refreshed Ruth's memory. "You may not recall, Ruth, but I took many spankings from Papa just to 'save your neck.' " Instead of thanking mother for her sacrifice, Ruth put her head back and laughed heartily. "I sure did know how to handle Papa." Mother sighed. Aunt Ruth was fun, and I felt sad when the truck returned to pick her up and Grandma cried, "We'll probably never see her alive again."

From then on I took note of my comparisons with Ruth and saw that my mother would comment when I had "wormed my

way out of some trouble" or when someone would say I was a
"bundle of laughs." I remember years later when I was teaching
at Haverhill High School and my brother Ron "fixed me up"
with Phil the Canada Dry salesman. As I was trying to impress
him while placing an order for gingerale, I looked out the store
window and saw my new friend Dick who had just "returned
from the war." As he parked his restored Model T at the curb,
I excused myself and turned the order over to my mother while
I slipped out and led Dick across the street to Mrs. Bartlett's
front steps where we sat to chat. After a few minutes I ran back
to the store to get something to drink for Dick. While pouring
some Canada Dry I "took up with Phil where we'd left off" and
made a date for Friday. I brought the drink to Dick on the steps
and was back in time to say goodbye to Phil. As I poured some
gingerale for myself my mother sighed, "You're just like Ruth."

Now that I look back upon the Florence/Ruth comparison with
a knowledge of the different personalities, I see that my similarities had nothing to do with the violin or smoking but with the
emotional response I brought forth from my mother. She had
unconsciously resented Ruth's ability to charm others while she
was charmed herself into defending Ruth's actions. She had disliked Ruth's personality yet wished she were "more like Ruth."
She had been judging of Ruth's behavior but had covered for
her when "the chips were down."

Mother was primarily Phlegmatic like her mother—quiet, withdrawn, and unwilling to take chances. She was also Melancholy
with the musical talent and ability to play and teach both violin
and cello. She was always loyal to Ruth as a Melancholy is and
admired her charm, while the Phlegmatic part of her was unwilling to ever confront Ruth on what she didn't like. The two of
them had the typical differences of the Phlegmatic/Melancholy
being unhappy but not daring to discuss it with the Sanguine/
Choleric who enjoyed shocking the family and was insensitive
to their inner feelings.

Without knowing what I was doing as a child, I became "like
Ruth" because we happened to have the same personality.

I enjoyed "giving my mother fits" and constantly was telling
her to stop worrying and to have a good time. Once I asked her
why she never gave me compliments, a deep Sanguine need, and
she replied, "You never know when you'll have to eat your

words." How I wish now I had understood my mother's cautious clichés and realized her need to be respected as a person of value instead of my constantly seeking the praise she couldn't give me and trying to do dramatic things to make her "sit up and take notice."

People compare us with another member of our family tree not only because of our looks but because we somehow unwittingly elicit the same inner response of emotion. Our particular pattern of personality brings out in others the same feelings they have for relatives or friends who are similar.

According to Mother, my brother Ron (S/C) is just like my father. She often said, "He takes such good care of me and he's always fun, but if you cross him up, watch out."

My daughter Lauren (C) is just like Aunt Sadie. "She's talented and brilliant, but she controls the family and you'd better step to it when she says so."

My daughter Marita (S/C) is just like me and Aunt Ruth. "She's always rushing around trying to do too much but somehow it always comes out all right in the end."

My grandson Randy (M/C) is just like my husband Fred, and little Jonathan (S/C) looks like his father but is "just like Marita."

How my mother loved to sit back, quietly assess our family's aggressive behavior and sigh, "You're just like Ruth."

Although Mother came to our *Personality Plus* seminars, every time I'd try to get her to do her Personality Profile, she'd shake her head and say, "It just sounds too much like work."

How grateful I am to know that her response is not a condemnation of my teaching temperaments but a typical Phlegmatic reaction to an analysis that might suggest change and a fear of an unknown theory that might put her in a negative light. Well, Mother always said, "What you don't know won't hurt you."

One woman whose whole family was changed through an understanding of the different personalities wrote the following in a letter:

> Your *Personality Plus* revolutionized our lives, at the very least. Our family was loving but discordant until you made us realize what our different personalities meant. . . . I believe your temperament study may possibly be God's answer to the "horror-scope." When someone mentions his "sign," I explain the temperaments.

Thank you for this gentle witnessing tool. . . . In His love, Phyllis Beever, Pearsall, Texas.

In these days of soul searching what a blessing it is to understand our personality strengths and weaknesses and to trace them back to some of those other Aunt Ruths hanging on the family tree.

How about you? Are you just like your Aunt Ruth? Your Uncle Ethan? Or your grandpa?

Where can we find out who we really are? The philosophical Socrates said, "To know thyself is the beginning of wisdom." Aldous Huxley explained, "There's only one corner of the universe you can be certain of improving, and that's your ownself."

But how?

One summer when Fred and I were vacationing in Maine and chatting about nutrition while eating blueberry pancakes, a Sanguine man sitting nearby said, "My doctor diagnoses by computer."

"How does he do that?" I asked, surprised at this sudden interjection.

"He's made out a big questionnaire that took me over an hour to fill out. It asks things like, 'Are you overweight?—If yes, do you eat too much?—Do you enjoy Mars bars? chocolate malts? hot fudge sundaes?—Are you happy with how you look?—What have you done to remedy this problem?—What do you intend to do about it in the future?—' By the time I'd answered the questions, I'd solved my own problems."

As I thought about this method of medical self-analysis, I realized that many of us could solve our own problems if we had some suggested guidelines and if we'd take the time to think before we ran off to the doctor or counselor.

Aside from the administering of drugs, the doctor spends much of his time in listening to piecemeal problems and then making calculated prescriptions based on his intuition, education and experience.

If we withhold specific information, his assumption may be incorrect. One girl who has been in therapy for months told me, "I never tell the counselor how I *really* feel because I'm afraid she won't like me."

How can the counselor possibly give accurate advice when the subject gives a distorted view of her life?

How much better it would be if we who know ourselves well could search for truth in our innermost parts.

It was twenty years ago that my husband Fred and I began an informal study of the four basic temperaments. At first we looked at the concept lightly and initially used it almost as a parlor game by inviting friends into our home to "play personality." Fred made a quick chart for us all to check off, and we took his test together. We had such fun that everyone asked if we could do it again. The next week as we gathered, the conversation was high-pitched and excited. Quiet people were sharing how learning about themselves had opened up their eyes and how they were beginning to look at others in a new light. People who usually wanted to laugh and play could hardly wait to get down to business.

As we met that second time, Fred and I saw living proof that when people had some simple tool that explained their behavior, they could immediately put their new information into practice. We saw in one week's time a new understanding between husbands and wives, a release of tension and self-judgment, and a new freedom to be what God wanted each one to be.

Our parlor game turned into a time of mutual self-analysis, and as we began to find ourselves and accept those who were different, our group transformed from some people who saw each other in church on Sundays to a close Christian fellowship who loved each other and became emotionally supportive.

Since that first experience, Fred and I have taught the temperaments to thousands of people and have seen so many lives changed by a simple understanding of strengths and weaknesses brought before the Lord for his transforming power.

Although there are many other types of personality analysis, I have found that the basic theory came from Hippocrates two thousand years ago. His terms have been modified and relabeled many times, but their usefulness and validity remain the same today as they were in ancient Greece.

Temperament is a term from the Latin meaning "a mixing in due proportion." What they were mixing were fluids, or *humors,* from the Latin word for moisture. A person with a lot of red blood coursing through his veins was Sanguine: cheerful, outgoing and optimistic but not very serious or organized. The original Choleric had too much yellow bile making him "bilious," short-tempered and ill-natured, but giving him a dynamic desire for action. As his *chole,* Greek for "bile," was "mixed in due proportion," he charged into leadership positions. Too much *melas,* Greek for "black," and *chole* added up to Melancholy: deep, sad and depressive, but also a thoughtful, gifted and analytical genius. *Phlegm* was a cold, moist humor which caused people to be slow and sluggish but enabled them to stay calm, cool, and collected under pressure and heat.

According to Michael Gartner, writing about the original concept,

> If you had too much of any one humor you were considered unbalanced, a little odd or eccentric. Sometimes, normal folks would laugh at their friends with too much of a humor, and that's how the word *humor* got its present-day meaning of ludicrous, comical or absurd.[1]

When Mark Antony spoke of the murdered Julius Caesar he proclaimed his personality as a perfect blending.

> "His life was gentle, and the elements
> So mix'd in him that Nature might stand up
> And say to all the world, 'this was a man!' "[2]

How are the elements mixed in you?
Bishop Ernest A. Fitzgerald writes,

> Wise is the person who wrestles for self-understanding. Life can be wasted in anxiety over the lack of certain abilities or talents. The 'wishing well' syndrome is futile and destructive to our well-being. An intelligent analysis of self, however, and the determination to be the best we can be make for exciting and healthy living. There are really no inferior people. We all have our strengths and weaknesses. When we utilize our strengths our weaknesses are minimized.[3]

As we counsel using the temperament strengths to encourage and the weaknesses to point out areas for growth and improvement, we are still amazed at how quickly a person can see himself in the examples we use and choose to change. In Champaign,

Illinois, my husband Fred met with Terry Ridenour. Terry did not understand why he was having certain relationship problems; he was predominantly Choleric, strong and successful but typically unable to see any possible weaknesses. Terry had been seeking answers but until he saw his own problem areas, he couldn't imagine why his sincerity had not been enough.

Later Terry wrote us in gratitude for our introducing him to the basic temperaments of human nature.

> I now know that many of my frustrations and searchings over the past three years were perhaps of my own doing. . . . I needed to hear the things that Fred and I discussed Saturday morning. To hear those things and to realize that I was not the only one experiencing such frustration gave me extreme encouragement. However, true to a Choleric, now that I know what the problems are, I have set a goal and will be successful. . . . I pray that I can continue to improve my temperament weaknesses and that God will use the experiences in my life the last three years to help support others, . . . Your friendship will be a constant reminder to listen to the Lord and to let my weaknesses become strengths in the Lord.

In these times of global tension and inner turmoil, I find so many Christian people who are longing for some sense of identity and self-worth, some answers to their frustrations and searchings as Terry expressed. They study the Word; they know they are created in God's image and made slightly lower than the angels; they've been crucified in Christ and have taken off the old clothes and put on the new. They've gone to church, knelt at the altar on Sunday, and taught Bible studies. In spite of all these positive spiritual steps, they still need some simple solution to who they really are as individuals.

After these twenty years of studying and teaching the temperaments, I am still amazed at how God uses this tool to open people's eyes to themselves and their relationships with others.

A young lady wrote how my putting the temperaments into "real live people situations" was what changed her life.

> Thank you for being available and touchable. . . . We now have such insight in dealing with my Fred's wretched Melancholy father! Oh, what freedom for Fred at age 37 to realize he will *never* be

able to reach his dad's standards—for me to now understand why my precious Phlegmatic/Melancholy dad drank himself into an early grave at 66 after living with my Choleric mom all those years. We could go on for hours and still not be able to express to you and to your Fred our thanks for your countless hours of preparation, for your willingness to be used of God in such a mighty way.

Another girl came to our CLASS (Christian Leaders and Speakers Seminars) and just gave her name as Dee. When we asked what her last name was she said, "I don't have one because I don't know who I am."

Later after hearing our explanation of the personalities, she wrote that at first she had listened intellectually but now the information had gone from her head to her heart. "The Lord really impressed these truths upon me along with Romans 8: 1–2. I now feel 'no condemnation' and the 'law of the Spirit of life has set me free.' "

Among her other comments she explained, "Remember I told you I have *no* last name. That's because I've had four marriages, and my mother was married three times. I've had a total of seven last names. Who am I anyway? You should have seen the fiasco at my daughter's wedding when 'everyone' showed up! Thank you so much for all you've given me. 'It is more blessed to give than to receive.' Dee"

As I have taught the use of the temperaments to churches, medical conventions, leaders and speakers, couples and families, businesses and other groups, I have been frequently asked how the original terms compare with other personality tests or systems. In an attempt to answer questioning minds, I have read, gathered, and sometimes "taken" different forms of analyses.

It would fill a book to report on all the theories I've examined, so I have made a chart—yes I, a Sanguine/Choleric have made a Melancholy chart comparing the different terms used. The one overwhelming conclusion I've come to is that no matter what the traits are labeled, they all seem to spring from the same rootstock of Hippocrates' theory of the humors. Few of the new theory originators make this connection and in several articles about testing, the announcement is made about an exciting "new concept." While this "new concept" has been around for over two thousand years, it can always take on a fresh face with new labels and I'm sure many of the current testers may sincerely think they thought it all up. For more detail on other forms of temperament analysis, see the chart on page 235.

For Further Study, Thought, and Action

Oswald Chambers in *My Utmost for His Highest* says, "Personality is that peculiar incalculable thing that is meant when we speak of ourselves as distinct from every one else. Our personality is always too big for us to grasp."[4]

Because it is "too big for us to grasp," we need to break our personality into chunks we can ingest with ease. We have already taken the Quick Quiz; now let's examine ourselves more deeply. At the end of this book (page 220) is a Personality Profile for you to take. Check off one word on each line of the Personality Profile that is closest to you. To help make your decisions easier there is an explanation of the words. (See Personality Test Word Definitions, page 221). After marking the best choice for you, transfer your checks to the Personality Scoring Sheet (page 232) where the list is in order and add up your totals. If you chose *adventurous* on the profile, check it off on the score sheet and you will see your personality fall into line. As you add up your scores, you will observe your own personal blending of the "humors" mixed in a "due proportion" that is uniquely yours. No two of us are exactly alike and yet our similarities are what provide us with a framework by which we can measure our strengths and weaknesses.

PERSONALITY PROFILE COUNT	
SANGUINE ____	CHOLERIC ____
PHLEGMATIC ____	MELANCHOLY ____

Record your scores from the Personality Profile in the chart on the previous page, and compare them with those on the Quick Quiz. For further study, read the strengths and weaknesses listed on pages 233, 234 and compare them with your scores and your feelings about yourself.

Are you beginning to get a grasp of who you are?

As you prepare to trace the roots of your own Personality Tree, you will want to have an understanding first of your own "blending of the humors." By adding this knowledge to the perception your family already has of you, you will begin to piece together the puzzle of your personality.

If you are in a group study, go around the room and have each person share what he has learned about himself so far. Don't allow others, such as mates, to correct or second guess each person's opinions or this will stifle meaningful conversation. Each person must be free to express his feelings without fear of judgment. What a great way to get acquainted with others on an emotional as well as a social level.

Think about those people in your family who are alike. In your personality notebook list those that come to mind and then beside the names jot down the personality similarities, both strengths and weaknesses. Discuss these individuals with any family member available in order to garner information. As you plant these seeds of thought in your mind, you will begin to water your seedlings with additional material as you are alert to any reference made of your "Aunt Ruths."

If you are using *Your Personality Tree* as a group study, bring your list of comparisons and be ready to share your results. There's no way we can carry on positive tradition or eliminate repeated weaknesses until we bring them to light and take an objective look at them. You will be amazed at the information there is available when you begin to seek. Older family members are flattered when you ask them to fill in your memory blanks, and even family friends may have nostalgic stories they would love to tell.

In placing these personalities of the past think about how each individual approached projects. What was their way?

PERSONALITY DIRECTIONS	
THE HAPPY WAY S	MY WAY C
THE EASY WAY P	THE RIGHT WAY M

Commit your way to the Lord.
—Psalm 37:5, NIV

The Lord delights in the way of the man whose steps he has made firm.
—Psalm 37:23, NIV

❧ 3 ❧

What Are Your Desires and Underlying Needs?

Without an understanding of the basic temperaments and the desires and needs of each, we tend to spend much of our time trying to get from other people responses that they just can't give. Many marriages, for example, come to a grinding halt because neither partner knows what the other wants or needs. With no simple tool to use, success is an accident. Once we begin to understand the basic desire of each nature, however, the veil is lifted and we have the key to getting along with others.

WHAT ARE YOUR DESIRES?

The Sanguine from the beginning wants to have FUN. Accepting this fact will keep us from false expectations that some day he or she will grow up and get down to business.

My Phlegmatic mother, after spending a week with my brother Ron, top radio personality in Dallas, Texas, and proclaimed in the *Dallas Morning News* as the one who "owns the morning,"[1] said with a sigh, "I wonder if Ron will ever grow up and get a real job." She didn't understand that a Sanguine doesn't want to grow up, that his aim is to have fun, and that he is at the top of his profession.

The Choleric wants to have CONTROL and is only comfortable when he has choreographed the cast of his world and has it completely under his inspired direction. Knowing this fact will prevent us from staging a struggle for power which we would probably lose.

The Melancholy's desire is to have PERFECTION. To know what that is, we have to enter into his perfectly organized and categorized mind and see the situation with his eyes. When we realize he cannot relax until life is in order, we can make a conscious effort to meet his standards.

The Phlegmatic's aim in life is to stay out of trouble and keep PEACE. He will not become enthusiastic about anything or take chances, so don't push him and think you can alter his personality. All that badgering him will do is increase his resistance to change.

When we see and accept that each temperament has a different desire in life, we can function out of knowledge and not ignorance. "Be ye therefore wise as serpents, and harmless as doves" (Matt. 10:16, KJV).

SANGUINES: HAVE FUN

Heaviness in the heart of man maketh it stoop:
but a good word maketh it glad (Prov. 12:25, KJV).

When we realize the Sanguine's desire for fun, we can perhaps grasp why things that would embarrass others are positive experiences for the Sanguine. As I tell my story of losing my car in the seven-story parking garage, Melancholies and Cholerics shake their heads in disbelief. Phlegmatics somewhat understand the possibility and Sanguines get so excited they can hardly wait to rush up to me with tales of their own losses. Several ladies have detailed how they lost their cars at Disneyland and had to wait until midnight when the place emptied out to find them.

One Sanguine who went to the Cotton Bowl for the New Year's game wanted to make sure she wouldn't get lost. She wrote down "Bus #104" on the back of an envelope so she would know which bus was hers when she returned. What she had not anticipated was that there were hundreds of buses all lined up and she had no idea which one was #104. "I would have been there yet," she exclaimed in typical Sanguine exaggeration, "if a friend hadn't found me gasping from the exhaust fumes and led me to Bus #104."

An adorable Sanguine girl told me that her husband brought

home a client for dinner. As she was preparing the meal she
discovered she was missing a key ingredient. She didn't want
her Melancholy husband to know since he constantly criticized
her lack of organization, so she tiptoed to the front door. As
she looked out she saw the client's car was behind hers in the
driveway and she would have to go ask him to move it. But
wait! There were his keys on the table so why not quietly take
his car? She parked in the large lot outside the supermarket
and when she came out she not only didn't know where she'd
parked, she didn't have any idea what kind of a car it was. All
she could remember was that there was a letter on the front
seat and the only reason she recalled that was because she'd
read it! She pushed her cart up and down lanes peering into
each car looking for the letter which she ultimately found. She
got home safely and no one ever needed to know, but in typical
Sanguine fashion when there was a long pause in the business
conversation, she felt led to entertain the client with her escapade
of taking his car without permission and reading his letter. Much
to her surprise he didn't find it humorous, and her husband was
both humiliated and incensed. "Everyone else I told it to thought
it was hilarious. I don't know what's the matter with them!"

A Sanguine receptionist came out after work and her '67 Gold
Dodge was gone. She called the police, filled out all the forms
and asked the policeman to drive her home. When they pulled
into the driveway the man asked, "Do you have two '67 Gold
Dodges?"

"No, why?"

"Because there's one sitting here in front of us."

She looked up in wide-eyed surprise.

"Oh, I guess I forgot. My girlfriend drove me to work this
morning."

One lady told me she was hunting for her keys at the cleaners
and concluded, "I must have left them at the church."

The Phlegmatic cleaner said half under his breath, "If you
left them at the church how did you get the car here?"

A girl from Fairbanks, Alaska, sent me this story after I spoke
there in September of '85.

I went to [the supermarket] for a few quick items, but as I walked

the aisles I decided I might as well shop. By the time I wandered
the aisles (with payday's bulk in my purse), I had a cart chockful
of meals. I also had a 'reduced for winter' Boston fern drooping
atop the edibles!

Through the checkout stand, $158 later, I pushed my laden cart
into the parking lot. Adrenalin pumped as I went row by row, puzzling over *why* I couldn't remember where I'd parked. Still puzzled,
I pushed the cart (topped by my Boston fern) back towards the
store.

The outside of the store was being painted by a crew on a scaffold-
ing. As I dodged their equipment with my unwieldy cart, I saw
it—beneath their tarp sat my yellow 10-speed bike!

I had *biked* the five miles today! Now, as a newly single parent
whose ex-husband was out of town . . . who was in the 'proud' stage,
too proud to call on a friend . . . I began packing:

—groceries into boxes stacked on the back rack
—cord tying the Boston fern pot firmly atop the boxes
—four loaves of bread tied by their ends to the handle bars.

I rode all the way home on a bike that was ready to flip over at
every little bump! My daughters saw me come up . . . looking like
a gypsy caravan!

How did I feel? . . . How did they feel? Resourceful! Capable!
Independent!

My very favorite episode is the lady from Newport Beach who
went shopping at the vast South Coast Plaza. When she came
out of Bullock's her car was gone. After hunting around by herself, she called the security guard who drove her up and down
each row in the entire set of parking lots. There was no question;
they both agreed; the car had been stolen. She filled out the
forms and later filed an insurance claim. When she received the
money, she bought a bright new car and liked it even better
than the first one. Later she received a phone call from Sears,
"Hey lady, when are you going to come back and pick up your
car that you left here a month ago for us to rotate the tires? If
you don't come soon, we're going to charge you for storage!"

Many Sanguines have sent me "car stories," but just as many
Melancholies have mailed me detailed information for forgetful
Sanguines on where to buy a key ring that beeps when you clap
your hands or a Car Finder which costs only $99.95. These inven-
tions were surely made for Sanguines and, if they become popular,

could eliminate this Sanguine habit as surely as small pox was eradicated. One ad stated confidently:

Spot your parked car instantly!
Misplaced your car in a crowded parking lot? Touch the Car Finder, and your car will honk its horn and flash its lights so you can locate it at once.
Car Finder is a miniature transmitter that attaches to any key chain. When you push the button, your car answers up to 750 feet away.

I knew the gadget was for sociable Sanguines when the ad concluded "The Car Finder is a real friend with user-friendly instructions."

So that you Sanguine men won't think these stories leave you out, here's an episode from my favorite minister of music, Jim Lacy, after his move to Columbus, Ohio.

Sanguine Jim and Melancholy Sherri went to a church Christmas party. Since they were new in town and hadn't become acquainted, Sherri was a little nervous about making a good first impression. Jim had the map to the people's home on Angela Street and Sherri was comforted when a car with some friends she recognized honked as they drove by. Since Jim had a quick errand to run at the church, he dropped Sherri off at the curb where she joined some others who were heading into the party.

Being new to the church and trying to be as outgoing as possible, Sherri greeted the hostess at the door and drifted into the room full of chatting couples. She stood by herself and observed that the new guests were all bringing wedding presents. She wondered why they were bringing these to the church Christmas party, and when she asked, the hostess replied, "This is no church Christmas party. This is a wedding reception. Are you supposed to be here?"

Sherri was so embarrassed that she got her coat and left just as Jim was driving up oblivious to the fact he'd dumped her out at the wrong party. While Jim laughed Sherri went into a depression. When they got to the right house down the street, Sherri made Jim go in and make sure first. She begged him not to tell a soul, but in true Sanguine fashion, Jim made a comedy act of the whole episode. He wrote me, "I told everyone including my *Sanguine choir!* What fun!"

Yes, "what fun" when the Sanguine tells his own story of his own error depressing his own wife. The Sanguine's aim is to HAVE FUN.

CHOLERICS: HAVE CONTROL

Sink the heathen into the pit.
Catch their feet in thy net.
Execute proper judgment. (See Ps. 9:15–16.)

The Choleric's basic desire is to be in control. A Choleric woman told me about the battle she was having with her Choleric ten-year-old son. Every day after he goes to school, she goes in and moves the furniture in his room into the position where she and the decorator want it. The first thing he does when he comes home is change it all back to the way he likes it. She maintains it's her house and she has the right to put the furniture wherever she wants it. Besides, what if her friends came to visit, and the room wasn't in order! He, being a chip off the old block, claims his room as his territory where he has the right to arrange it whatever way he wants. Here are two Cholerics fighting so hard for control that they are playing Mayflower Movers every day. I shared with her how important it is for a Choleric child to be in control of something at home, for if he is thwarted there, he will likely go out and beat up his friends. With this new thought in mind, she went home to make peace.

A Choleric man who sold medical supplies to doctors told me how he hated his job. When I asked him why he continued, he said, "I make a lot of money, and I like what I'm doing."

"How can you hate it and like it?" I asked.

He thought for a minute and concluded, "I like the job, but I hate the fact that I'll never be the boss."

Here was a Choleric in a good position but chafing because he had to play second fiddle and couldn't see any possibility of being in charge.

Another Choleric salesman told me about his "stupid" Sanguine boss. "She never gets anything done right, and she spends most of her time on the phone. I tell her each day what she's doing wrong and how to improve, but she never gets any better."

I reviewed our lesson with him. "What does the Sanguine desire in life?"

"Fun."

"What does the Sanguine need more than anything else?"

"Attention and approval."

"Now that you know this, think about your situation. Let's pretend I'm your boss and everyone tells me I'm fun to be around. Each day they all compliment me, bring me little presents, and listen to my every word. You, however, try to straighten me out each day and criticize my time on the phone. I get a memo from above that instructs me to lay off one of my salesmen. How long is it going to take me to decide which one it should be?"

He got the point.

A Choleric lady remembers when as a child she "played war" with the neighborhood boys. "They wanted me to be the nurse since I was the only girl, but I said, 'No, I'll be the general.' And I was!"

A Choleric man told his Phlegmatic wife, "I hate hard-headed people."

She dared venture, "Sometimes you are hard-headed."

He snapped back, "Only when I'm right!"

Another Choleric man told me, "I may not always be right, but I'm never wrong."

Even the Choleric disciples were scrapping for control. "There was . . . strife among them, which of them should be accounted the greatest" (Luke 22:24, KJV).

A Choleric doctor took the Personality Profile, and I observed him checking off all the strengths and none of the weaknesses. I commented on this to him and he replied, "That's because I *have* all strengths and no weaknesses, but I'll be glad to check off a few weaknesses if it will make you happy." Oh, noble man!

Later he came up to me and said, "I thought it over, and I do have one weakness. I seem to always choose weak sniveling nurses. They seem normal to start with, but they get worse. Just this morning when I walked into the office they all flattened against the wall and began to cry. I asked them what was the matter and they said they were afraid of me. I let them know right off it was their own fault. If you'd do what I told you to do when I told you to do it, you'd have no reason to be afraid!"

What compassion and understanding!

The Cholerics not only want to be in control but, as you can see, they have little ability to catch even a glimpse of their weaknesses. They have the greatest bent for leadership, but a blind spot in seeing how they affect other people.

They agree with Robert Service:

> This is the Law of the Yukon
> That only the strong shall thrive
> That surely the weak shall perish
> And only the FIT survive![2]

The Choleric's aim is to HAVE CONTROL.

MELANCHOLIES: HAVE PERFECTION

> I am weary of groaning;
> I make my bed to swim;
> I water my couch with tears.
> I cry with grief. (See Ps. 6:6–7.)

How weary the Melancholy is from trying to get life in order, watering the couch with tears and crying with grief. From the time the Melancholy can stand up and move around he is trying to make the crooked paths straight. My Melancholy son Fred was tidying up the house as soon as he could get out of his playpen, and he started collecting and sorting laundry when he was two. He's been my "housekeeper" for years, and if I leave something out on the kitchen counter, he quickly puts it in the nearest drawer. Since I can't remember where I left it, this disappearance causes me quite a search as I tear through kitchen drawers looking for a lace slip he stuck in with the dish towels.

A Melancholy pastor told me how as a child he kept all of his games in order, numbered each box and had a master list posted in his closet. He never lost so much as a puzzle piece in his whole childhood. When he had his own children and gave them his well-preserved games to play with, "They had all the parts messed up within a week. How could I have kept them perfect for all those years and see them wreck the whole system in less than a week?"

A Sanguine girl told me her Melancholy husband has rebuilt

her closet three times in hopes he'll strike the right plan which will make her keep it neat. If only he knew the temperaments, he could save his time and money. No matter what plan he has, she'll still throw the shoes in a pile on the floor.

Another girl wrote, "My Melancholy husband keeps his side of the closet in perfect order with all of his pants folded exactly the same. You can imagine what my side looks like! He even gets bothered when I don't put the shampoo and creme rinse bottles back on the rack with the labels facing forward in perfect order! It took him six months to tell me this bothered him."

One Melancholy man kept a "mileage chart" on his shoes from the time he bought them until he gave them away to the Salvation Army. He found out when he divided the cost of the shoes by the number of days he wore them that the shoes had cost him nine cents a day. Only a Melancholy would care!

Another man dates every light bulb in his house at the time of purchase. This way he is able to keep a record of each bulb and know the exact length of service.

A girl at CLASS (Christian Leaders and Speakers Seminars) took her Personality Profile and divided it into percentages proving she was 82.5 percent Melancholy. Not that we needed proof!

One father kept a file box on all his son's dates with full family background and his candid opinion of each one. The girl that married him was not pleased when she found her report that said, "Surely, he won't marry this one!"

A girl in Florida sent me this account of the man next door.

The tire on one of their trash can carriers broke. The husband replaced it. However, he noticed that it didn't match the other trash can carrier tires. To him, that was unthinkable. So he immediately ran out and bought three new tires for the trash can carrier and replaced the non-matching but perfectly good tires. A few days later he noticed that the tires on the lawn mower didn't match the new trash can carrier tires, so he replaced those tires with new ones to match. There was another vehicle on the premises with non-matching tires, which he also replaced. To top it all off, this husband realized that if one of the new tires became defective and had to be replaced, he might not locate a matching tire which would necessitate starting all over again, so he bought a second set of tires for each machine and stored them in his impeccably neat garage. His wife said one broken tire cost them $250 because of her husband's concern for matching everything! Guess which type personality he is!

All Melancholies would agree with Ludwig van Beethoven.

> Then let us all do what is right,
> Strive with all our might toward the unattainable,
> Develop as full as we can the gifts God has
>   given us,
> And never stop learning.[3]

The Melancholy's aim is to HAVE PERFECTION.

PHLEGMATICS: HAVE PEACE

> Lay me down in peace to sleep
> Make me dwell in safety. (See Ps. 4:8.)

The Phlegmatic's desire is to lie in peace and dwell in safety. While the Sanguine has a compulsion to have fun, and the Choleric has a compulsion to control everything and everyone in life, and the Melancholy has an almost fanatical compulsion to get things in perfect order, the Phlegmatic has no compulsions. They will avoid problems whenever possible and quietly face those they can't get around.

When the Melancholy says I have to think about it, he really thinks about it, but the Phlegmatic uses this expression to postpone action. It isn't that he wants to think; it's that he doesn't want to act. One lady who was taking me out to dinner asked her Phlegmatic husband for his decision on where to go. "Are we still thinking about it or are we ready to do it?"

A Phlegmatic man told me, "I'm not lazy; I'm just conservative on my energy level."

A Phlegmatic woman shared, "I married a Phlegmatic and our baby was so Phlegmatic it was like she was born in a coma."

Making decisions is difficult for the Phlegmatic. I loved the paperweight on a Phlegmatic's desk that carries the message, "Maybe—and that's final." A greeting card showed a Phlegmatic tiger draped over an easy-chair. On the inside it said, "Get up before they make a rug out of you."

Because the Phlegmatics desire peace, they are easy to manipulate and frequently find themselves pushed around by Cholerics who need someone to control. Although they usually will take whatever's handed out, once in a while, to keep peace with themselves, they will refuse to conform and they will hold their ground.

The last Christmas we had with my little Phlegmatic mother was one to remember. Her Choleric sister Jean, my favorite aunt, came out to California bringing a special present for Mother from her friends at the church "gift shop." As Mother was carefully unwrapping the present in such a way as to preserve the paper for next year, Aunt Jean spoke up. "This is a very special present. Your friends made this by hand for you and you will love it." As Mother took a look Aunt Jean continued, "That is an apron, made of unbleached muslin and edged in red bias binding." Cholerics somehow feel Phlegmatics are not bright enough to know an apron when they see one, muslin from satin, or red from green. "Written all over the apron in liquid embroidery are all your friends' names. See them right there. They all sat down and signed the apron so that every time you wear it you will think of them."

Mother quietly stated, "I won't wear this apron; it's too good to use."

"What do you mean you won't wear this apron! Do you think I'm going back to 'gift shop' and tell them that after all their time and effort you wouldn't even wear the apron!"

Lauren on the other side of Mother said firmly, "You *will* wear this apron. In fact right after Christmas dinner you will put it on to do the dishes."

As Mother folded it back up, Aunt Jean added, "I didn't drag this apron all the way out here on the plane from Massachusetts to have you refuse to wear it!"

Lauren affirmed to Aunt Jean, "She *will* wear it. I'll see to it."

Mother put the cover on the box and said softly, "I will not wear this apron." Lauren and Aunt Jean, two Cholerics having trouble with their control, said in harmony, "You *will* wear that apron."

A month later when I was conducting a *Personality Plus* Conference in Dallas, Mother was sitting right in the front row. As I was speaking I wondered if I dared tell the story about Mother and the apron. I remember thinking, "Well, she's eighty-five.

She can't hate me for too long." I took the big chance and went through the whole scene ending with, "And Mother said, 'I won't wear that apron.' "

Much to my absolute amazement, Phlegmatic Mother stood up, turned to the crowd and stated clearly, "And I didn't!" They loved her and gave her a rousing ovation.

Later when I commended her performance I told her, "You ought to be the speaker. I spoke all day and you got an ovation on one line." She gave a little Phlegmatic shrug and I could tell, in her terms, that she was "pleased as punch."

Two months later as she had desired, she died *peacefully* in her sleep to join the Prince of Peace and Lord of Lords. She never did wear the apron.

The Phlegmatic's aim is to HAVE PEACE.

WHAT ARE YOUR UNDERLYING NEEDS?

As each one of us has certain aims and desires, so also do we have underlying needs that we don't always communicate clearly to others. We think if they really loved us, they would know what we needed, but unfortunately we tend to give what we want to receive and then wonder why we don't get it back.

Fred loves colognes so he is constantly buying me perfume to make me happy. I don't have as keen a sense of smell, I have more bottles than I could ever empty, and I keep forgetting to put the perfume on; therefore, when he gives me another new spray I don't get too excited. He takes that to mean I don't appreciate his thoughtfulness. Because he has such a collection of colognes, I never think of buying him more, but in his mind he could never have too many. In his romantic heart I am neither caring nor grateful, but I see my attitude as practical. I had no idea that fragrance was an issue until one night after I had ignored a new bottle, Fred stated clearly, "I will never buy you any perfume ever again. You don't even notice what I give you."

That caught my attention. As we discussed the situation and I apologized for my callousness, we agreed that he was attempting to meet a need I didn't have in hopes it would spur me into meeting his for him. He needed sentimental signs that I loved him, and I had figured there was no point in buying more of what he already had in abundance. We were at a perfume stalemate and didn't recognize our opposite needs.

To prevent this type of problem in your life or to heal some underlying wounds of which you may not be aware, sit down with your mate and ask, "What needs do you have that I'm not meeting?" Listen, take notes, and don't be defensive. Thank him, and if he shows interest, share one or two things that you would appreciate from him.

The Sanguine Needs Attention and Approval

By learning the underlying needs of each temperament you will have an advantage in your human relationships. While the Sanguines want to have fun in life and appear to have no serious requirements for happiness, underneath they have a craving for approval. They need to know they are acceptable in your sight. They feed on compliments and criticism wounds them deeply. Usually they are married to Melancholies who see no reason to give praise to something that's not done properly in the first place and who feel constant criticism will provide positive motivation. How pitiful it is to realize how many couples are sitting in this stalemate, neither one meeting the other's need.

The Sanguine needs approval and will wilt into uselessness under negative comments. Given praise and encouragement the Sanguine will go to extremes to please you, for they want to be loved.

When Marita and I come home from a trip, Fred asks, "How did it go?" We reply in unison, "They loved us." Only Sanguines would be this presumptuous even in humor. Once Fred questioned us, "Did the people say they loved you in so many words?"

"Well, no, we just know they did."

The Melancholy often won't believe compliments when they are verbalized, but the Sanguine will make positive assumptions even when no one said a word.

My little Sanguine grandson Jonathan stood on the edge of the pool and stated loudly, "My Mommy loves me! My Daddy loves me! Grammie loves me! Poppa loves me!" He added a few extra names, stretched out his arms and looked to the heavens proclaiming, "The whole world loves me!" Another type personality might take this statement as juvenile conceit, but at four years old he is expressing how he actually feels and demonstrating that Sanguine need for love.

In the *TIME* cover story on the Statue of Liberty Celebration, the question was headlined, "What Makes Reagan So Remarkably Popular As a President?" They then listed many Sanguine strengths: he has found the American sweet spot, he grins his boyish grin and bobs his head; he has a genius for American occasions; he is a magician, a master illusionist; he will hand out the sparklers; he has a genial, crinkly face that prompts a sense of wonder; he has the luck that comes to the optimist. His life is a sort of fairy tale of American power.

They then ask, "How does he do it? How does he always come out on top? Why is he called the 'Teflon President'?"

The answer they give is, "He enjoys an easy and sometimes mysterious communion with the American people. He has become a ceremonial presence."

As the interviewers listened to his humorous anecdotes, they asked why he was so successful and he answered simply, "I love people."[4] When you love people, they love you back, and oh how the Sanguine loves love.

Everyone likes attention and approval, but for the Sanguine it is an emotional need.

The Choleric Needs Achievement and Appreciation

Because the Choleric is a born leader, he has the need to see things accomplished and has a mental progress list stored in his brain. Where the Melancholy writes his agendas on paper, the Choleric plots his life out quickly in his head and gives instant commands to everyone in sight. He assumes others both need and want instruction and feels those who aren't marching to his drumbeat are lazy. A Choleric man wants to know what his wife did all day. One man told me if he didn't post a list of what needed to be done each day his wife wouldn't get out of the chair.

Choleric women keep the children moving, use all available manpower, and get frustrated when their husbands don't respond to their call to arms. Since they are usually married to Phlegmatics who look forward to the weekend's rest, their insatiable need for getting things done now is often thwarted. Once they've tried suggestions, lists, demands, and threats, they storm off in anger and the husband says, "I wonder what's wrong with her?" He may not care enough to get up and find out, but he does think about it during commercials.

Because the Choleric wife is now on the roof nailing down loose shingles, she is expecting some moderate praise for her noble efforts; however, the husband will choose not to mention the subject at all in hopes she won't remember he didn't do it. She waits for the appreciation she feels she deserves, and the more she hints for it the more determined he is not to give it. Unfortunately this cold war exists in many marriages and even in business situations where the Choleric will do extra work and then expect credit for his efforts. Since the others didn't want to do the job and he jumped into it on his own, no one sees a reason to praise him. What a cycle of misreading one another's needs.

The Choleric workaholic nature appears self-satisfied, but much of what he does is inwardly a cry for recognition. If he has not received praises as a child, he will work himself to death trying to stimulate his parents to enthusiastic comments. He wants to hear those words, "I don't know how you've ever accomplished this much!" When Cholerics don't receive credit or others don't thank them, they often say, "After all I've done for them."

Because of her need for achievement, a Choleric woman can't watch TV without something moving in her hands. She must knit, paint, or iron—anything rather than waste precious time. I even consider brushing my teeth a time-waster, and I often polish the mirror with my other hand while shutting a drawer with my foot. Sometimes I walk through the house picking things up while brushing, get a phone call, lay the brush down, and that night I have no idea where my toothbrush could be. Yes, Cholerics have a compulsion for constant achievement.

We all like to accomplish what we set out to do and we enjoy being appreciated, but for the Cholerics, these become emotional needs.

The Melancholy Needs Order and Sensitivity

The Melancholy is a perfectionist who must have his life in order and hopefully everyone else's as well. For some, this desire is restricted to the area of artistic expression while others need perfection in physical surroundings. A Melancholy with a Sanguine wife who is a poor housekeeper either takes over the duties, criticizes her mistakes, or gets depressed.

If the Melancholy leans toward the Choleric he will be much harder on himself than if he is part Phlegmatic, in which case he will occasionally give up and say in disgust, "Oh what's the use." The Melancholy also has a deep need to be understood and longs for others to respond with sensitivity to his inner struggles and to commiserate with him over flip comments made by shallow people attempting to be funny.

Because the Melancholy mind is a series of charts, you can be sure he knows when you have sent a gift and when you forgot. He will say, "It doesn't matter," but it does. Fred's grandfather, who always insisted that we not buy him any presents, was able each Christmas to keep a mental record of what each family member gave him. Even though there would be droves of great-grandchildren, he was able to check off each one without benefit of paper or pencil and announce at the end of the day, "I guess little Tommy doesn't love me any more. He didn't give me a thing."

Because the Melancholy is so unwilling to express his needs, he throws others into a constant guessing game. Each year I tell Fred everything I see that I would possibly want for Christmas—which is of course almost everything I see. Although I ask him often what he'd like, he never tells me. This year I asked him why he wouldn't give me gift suggestions when I am so helpful to him. He replied, "If you really loved me, you would be sensitive enough to my needs to figure it out. If I tell you, there's no joy of response." He then proceeded to gently reprimand me for my constant suggestions that I had considered a virtue. "When you point out everything you like, it leaves nothing to my imagination and there are no surprises."

Isn't it amazing how different we are? How what seems right to one is wrong for the other?

I now bite my tongue when I see a soft aqua robe that I would love to have, and I try to read Fred's mind before Christmas.

This intense need of the Melancholy for others to delve deeply into his subconscious and come up with his innermost thoughts puts a tremendous amount of pressure on any relationship, and because the Melancholy keeps score, this combination can terminate friendships.

One young couple with a Sanguine wife and a Melancholy husband rented a large cabin sailboat for a weekend. Another couple had expressed interest in going out with them sometime, so they invited them. The rental was several hundred dollars, and at the end of the three days, the other couple thanked them for the good time and left. The husband kept waiting for them to send him a check for their part of the bill.

When I asked, "Had you made this clear to them ahead of time?" He responded, "If they had any sense they would have known how much it cost and that they should pay half."

"They should have known" is a frequent statement of the Melancholy. Probably they should know, but what a shame that the hurt Melancholy refused to ever see this couple again.

We all appreciate order and hope for sensitivity, but for the Melancholy these traits become emotional needs.

The Phlegmatic Needs Respect and a Feeling of Worth

The Phlegmatic's goal in life is to keep the peace, and when this is not possible, the Phlegmatic sometimes withdraws and emotionally shuts down, often refusing any communication until some facsimile of peace is restored. Rather than face the enemy, the Phlegmatics retreat until one side wins the war, and then they join the victorious team.

Because the Phlegmatic's desire is to have peace, we might assume that a quiet room with a recliner chair would meet his needs, but underneath, like Rodney Dangerfield, he is longing for respect.

Because I am not Phlegmatic, it took an inspiration from the Lord for me to see this need for worth in my Phlegmatic mother. It is so easy for the other temperaments to ignore the Phlegmatics since they are not crying out for attention and after a while the Phlegmatic feels useless and of no value. Others seem to want to change the Phlegmatic to be what they are.

Sanguines assume no one could be happy if they are not jumping up and down with enthusiasm, so they feel called upon to elicit some cheer from the Phlegmatic. I would try to excite my mother with tales of grandeur, and she'd only respond, "That's nice." I felt I'd failed and so I'd get more dramatic. The harder I tried, the less she responded. I didn't realize that my adventures made her feel as if she didn't "amount to a row of pins." She needed me to settle down and give her credit for her peaceful accepting attitude about living in the retirement home.

Because Sanguines want approval, they try to make the Phlegmatics excited and fail to realize their need for respect.

The Choleric tries to make the Phlegmatic get moving. For the Choleric what they perceive as laziness is a sin unto death. How could anyone not want to produce? I asked a Phlegmatic friend to pass out some outlines at the beginning of a seminar. She dutifully agreed. Next to the morning pile of outlines was a stack clearly labeled "Afternoon Outlines." When the program started after lunch I noticed no one had outlines. As I went to get them and hand them to her, she said, "I didn't know I had to do it twice."

A Choleric cannot understand this passive thinking, or lack thereof, and the Choleric's innate reaction is one of disgust which signals to the Phlegmatic, who truly did not understand, that he is stupid and worthless.

The Melancholy tries to get the Phlegmatic interested in details and seeking perfection. The harder he pushes, the more the Phlegmatic pulls back and softly comments, "It doesn't make that much difference to me and who cares anyhow." The Melancholy cares and can't imagine how anyone with intelligence could possibly be indifferent to the complexities of life. The Melancholy ponders awhile and assumes he didn't make the point clear enough, so he tries an explanation of greater detail which so turns the Phlegmatic off that he just shrugs. This lack of zeal is taken by the Melancholy as rejection, and he becomes depressed. Isn't it amazing how we so badly misread others unless we understand their basic personalities and their underlying needs? The Phlegmatic does not want to be goaded on by the others to become something he really isn't; he just wants to be accepted as he is and be considered a person of value and worth. Where would we all be if we didn't have the peace-loving Phlegmatic to give us much needed balance and to tone down our compulsions? Thank your Phlegmatic mate, friend, or child for their easy-going nature. If they didn't have it, how would they put up with the rest of us?

We all want to feel that we are people of worth, but for the Phlegmatic, respect is an emotional need.

While I often get letters with fun examples I could use from Sanguines and straight suggestions from Cholerics and additional facts and details from Melancholies, I seldom hear from Phlegmatics. I assume their feeling of not being worthy prevents their writing me a letter, but when I do receive one like this I get excited.

Your seminar helped me so very much to understand who *I* am. . . . One of the things that has been so difficult for me to grasp is the fact that God accepts me just the way I am. My question has always been, "But who *am* I?" I am . . . always trying to figure out why I am so blaaaa. . . . Something must be wrong because I can't organize a good outline like another Sunday School teacher, or always have boundless bursts of energy, planning lots of things and staying up late, and making fun out of cleaning my house. You described me well, when you said if you gave a Phlegmatic two hours to do the job, they would take all of two hours, (with me it is usually more!) When I finally got ahold of the truth that it is OKAY for me to not have all those qualities that everyone else has, and that there was nothing wrong with *my own* character, I began to see myself for the person I really am. How freeing, and what hope! I am excited about me. I'm not dumb and stupid and non-interesting. My blankness that I sometimes feel is not because the Lord left something out of my brain. Just because I can't follow directions as well as I am expected to, doesn't mean that I "don't listen."

How refreshing it was to sit for three hours after I drove home from the retreat and to share with my husband these simple, and yet vital truths about our personalities. And he listened!

We hear so much about accepting . . . other[s] "just the way they are," but we really don't know who they are so that we can accept them.

May God bless you and your ministry in bringing people to a position of knowing themselves so that Christ can balance their lives to be a glory to Him!—Loretta McClure

One lady came to a *Personality Plus* seminar and later wrote, "Since I've started to grow up emotionally, I've stopped playing *What's My Line?* and I'm into *To Tell The Truth.*"

In the Shakespearian play *Hamlet,* the aging Polonius gives his young son some advice.

> This above all; to thine own self be true,
> And it must follow, as the night the day,
> Thou canst not then be false to any man.[5]

For Further Study, Thought, and Action

It's hard to be true to yourself until you know who you are. Is it possible to understand others when you are confused over your own identity?

According to what you've already learned—

What is your primary personality? _____

What is your basic temperament desire? _____

What are your general underlying needs? _____

If you are married, answer the following about your mate:

What is his/her primary personality? _____

What is his/her basic desire temperamentwise? _____

What are his/her general underlying needs? _____

Now that we have looked at the general underlying needs of each temperament, let's get more specific. One day I sat down and made a list of the three personal emotional needs I had as a child.

1. Because I lived in three tiny rooms behind my father's store and ate in front of the customers, I longed for a normal house with a dining room. Everyone else had at least a front door, and to go from *their* bedroom to *their* bathroom they didn't have to pass a cash register. I felt abnormal and deprived, and a simple house became an emotional need.

2. Each night when my father counted up the day's receipts there was anxiety over whether we could pay our bills. We always did manage to eat, but there was never anything left over and the total allowance for us three children was one cent's worth of candy a day. I can remember longing for enough money to have a banana split, and I went to work at fourteen, selling chocolates in Mitchell's Department Store so I could have some sense of security. For me, money became an emotional need.

3. Because there were no cosmetics or permanents when I was young, a girl was either a natural beauty or plain. I fell into the latter category. I envied Peggy who had thick blond braids, long eyelashes, and a turned up nose with freckles on it. Her

mother bought her dresses while mine were homemade, and Peggy was pretty. A longing for looks and clothes became an emotional need.

Before showing my list to Fred I asked him to think about his three emotional needs.

1. He immediately remembered how he never felt loved. Although he lived in a big house with a maid and nursemaid, he never felt his parents really cared. They both worked daily and while he was well provided for, he felt ignored. The lack of personal and physical love created a vacuum in his life and became an emotional need.

2. Because no one seemed to pay attention to what he was doing, Fred excelled in sports in the hopes of winning his parents' approval. The only time his father came to an event was at a track meet where his dad arrived after Fred had won the race. Even though he won letters and trophies, he never felt his parents took note of his achievements, and his desire for approval became an emotional need.

3. Fred remembers being lonely even when there were people around. Activities seemed to be planned by adults for adults, and in his Melancholy memory, homelife was not much fun. Although large parties took place on weekends, Fred felt he was on the fringes of the family fun. This lack of participation and excitement became depressing, and his desire for family fulfillment became an emotional need.

As Fred and I compared our childhood needs we saw that they were not at all alike. We then added a Sufficiencies column and were even more surprised.

FLORENCE		FRED	
NEEDS	SUFFICIENCIES	NEEDS	SUFFICIENCIES
House	Love	Love	House
Money	Approval	Approval	Money
Looks & Clothes	Family Fun	Family fun	Looks & Clothes

My needs were his sufficiencies and his sufficiencies were my needs. No wonder we had failed to communicate our opposite needs to each other. He had the big house, plenty of money, and was voted most handsome boy at Camp Agawan.

I was surrounded by love, people were applauding me as I recited my elocution pieces to an ever-changing audience in the store, and life was one comical Sanguine experience after another.

As you pause to analyze your needs and write them down in your personality notebook, first look at those that are general for your temperament pattern, and then list your personal child-hood needs and sufficiencies as Fred and I have done. Are they opposite or similar? Have you ever discussed your needs before? Can you accept that even if yours aren't anything alike or even if your mate's seem foolish to you, if that's how they feel, it is a genuine emotional need for them?

For a group study compare your needs and sufficiencies list with that of others noting similarities and differences. Be careful not to put down another person's feelings if you have a different point of view. Group fellowship takes place only in an accepting atmosphere.

If you have time, project the understanding of your needs into your relationships at business, in church, or in your family. Have each person share a marriage, business, or social problem that could have been avoided "if you'd only understood."

PERSONALITY NEEDS	
ATTENTION AND APPROVAL	ACHIEVEMENT AND APPRECIATION
RESPECT AND SELF-WORTH	ORDER AND SENSITIVITY

How much more appreciation we have for the game of life when we hold the scorecard and understand the personalities, aims, and needs of the players. One morning on the "Today" show Norman Vincent Peale explained why he and his wife Ruth have had such a successful marriage.

We each do what we do best, and we respect the other's differences. [6]

❦ 4 ❧

What Leads You into Temptation?

From the time we were children, many of us have been able to recite the Lord's Prayer at least in a group situation, and we know the line, "Lead us not into temptation, but deliver us from evil." However, few of us ever thought the verse applied to us, as we are "good people" not given to plucking forbidden fruit. We were brought up on Bible stories and know that if we ever ran into Evil in an alley he would be properly dressed in a red costume, would carry a pitchfork and would look like the Devil. In my childhood church we worshiped the god of good works and were taught the Five Commandments essential for eternal security: Don't drink, don't smoke, don't fool around, don't play cards, and don't sew on Sunday. I knew how to not smoke or drink, but I wasn't too clear on what it meant to not fool around although I didn't think I was doing it. In college I went through a rebellious period where I learned to play bridge, and once when visiting my virtuous grandmother, I sewed on Sunday and stitched my thumb into the seam. Grandmother looked first to the heavens and then down at me as she intoned, "God is punishing you for your sin," a condemnation I would still hear today if I should sew on a quick button before leaving for church.

When I wrote *After Every Wedding Comes a Marriage* in 1981, I inserted the chapter on "The Other Woman" with some apprehension. Was I bringing up a subject the Christian world didn't want to handle? Was I answering a question no one was asking? Was I five years ahead of my time? In retrospect the topic of infidelity in the church was brought up none too soon and the

"Other Woman" chapter has been the most popular. The list of *do*s and *don't*s for those women who find themselves with an unfaithful husband has brought forth repeated comments such as: "I wish I'd read this a year ago. I did all the *don't*s and none of the *do*s."

As I speak on this subject I take the assumption that no one in the audience has an adulterous mate, but "If your husband was looking for another woman, what would she be like?" We then go over a chart where each woman fills in what her husband would want. Perhaps the most provocative question is, "If your husband were looking for a place to have an affair this afternoon would he choose your bedroom the way you left it this morning?"

This thought produces gasps, screams, and occasional laughter from the ladies as the image of their bedroom flashes before their eyes in living color. Many have whispered to me on the way out, "I'm going home to clean the bedroom," and some have written later to tell of redecorating in the hopes of restoring romance to a boring relationship.

We ought to spend some creative time in analyzing our partner's obvious desires and underlying needs. While a messy bedroom and a dead philodendron on the windowsill probably won't send a man off to search out a new mate, these conditions do indicate a lack of concern for the other person. A man who says he'll be home for dinner each night at six and repeatedly returns hours later with no call of explanation may not be "fooling around" but he surely communicates to his wife that her time is of no value and that she is not worth much more.

As Christians we should be examples to our children and our community of what a loving marriage is like and of how it is still possible to have a positive relationship in an increasingly negative world. Yet as I listen to stories of rejection and rebellion among Christian couples, I know we all need help.

If I had a magic formula for a happy marriage, I could make a fortune, but I can at least share that when we start understanding and then meeting our partner's needs, we do reduce the risk of their looking somewhere else for fulfillment. Isn't it worth a try?

We often read in magazines and self-help journals about "meeting needs," but seldom are we told how to do it. We don't know what other peoples' needs are, we don't think to ask, and if we do, they give us the wrong answers. It's difficult to put your finger on an emotional need. We can look around our home and notice we need new carpeting; we can look in our closet and see we need new clothes; we can look in our refrigerator and see we need new supplies; but we don't know how to look into our hearts, or harder yet into the hearts of others, and see what's needed.

Now that we understand the four basic temperaments, we have a most practical tool for sensing inner hurts and needs. We are no longer grappling in the dark. We have just seen in the last chapter that each personality has its own needs. The Sanguine needs approval, the Choleric appreciation, the Melancholy sensitivity, and the Phlegmatic self-worth.

THE SANGUINE LONGS FOR ATTENTION
AND APPROVAL

The Sanguine who appears on the surface to be happy in any situation is, underneath, longing for attention, acceptance, and approval. Sanguines need to know they are loved and that you accept them just as they are. They want an audience who applauds and they wilt under criticism and poor reviews. Now that we know these needs, let's carry this information one step further.

What happens when the Sanguine does not get his needs met? As a child, he will do whatever it takes to get attention, often becoming too loud, too annoying, and too much of a show-off. The worst punishment for a Sanguine child is being put in a room alone with no phone or TV. In school the Sanguine child will usurp the teacher's attention and chatter constantly with others. This child is craving attention, and he will get it in either positive or, if necessary, negative ways.

When the Sanguine grows up, he marries with the idea that he will finally have someone who will have to pay attention to him. He buys himself an approving audience.

Since we tend to marry opposites whose needs are totally different from ours, the mate doesn't have the same point of view. While the Melancholy may have applauded the Sanguine's humor before marriage, it soon wears thin and after a while the Melancholy won't even sit in the audience, let alone clap enthusiastically.

Because the Sanguine can always charm someone into being his friend, he begins to wonder why the only person who doesn't think he's cute is his mate. The combination of an outgoing personality and the need for attention makes the Sanguine the most vulnerable for temptation from the opposite sex.

A Sanguine flight attendant named Tricia told me her story. I had noticed her friendly, bubbly personality and started to talk with her. When she found I was a speaker and often spoke on marriage she sighed, "Well, maybe you can help me with mine."

Tricia had married a Melancholy businessman who had been attracted by her zest for life. In typical fashion, he wanted her joy, and she was impressed by his stability and success. On their honeymoon, he got upset over her dropping her clothes wherever she stepped out of them and hanging her wet bathing suit on a doorknob instead of rolling it up in a towel and twisting it dry as he did. He picked up after her and pointed out the error of her ways. Tricia assumed he'd stop all this correction when they got home and he was busy, but she didn't understand the Melancholy nature.

She was stunned when he made her place a large towel on the floor each time she sprayed her hair so that the "residual chemicals would not ruin the carpet" and when he gave her a polishing cloth to use in shining the bathroom mirrors immediately following her hair sprayings or tooth brushings. Because she resisted his best-laid plans, he continued to criticize her casual behavior.

He hoped his withdrawal of approval would encourage her to change, but he didn't understand the Sanguine. He stopped complimenting her on her looks and personality that he had worshiped before marriage, and he shook his head when she told him exaggerated stories from her latest trip—the kind of stories that had formerly amused him.

Soon they were both discouraged with each other and they didn't know why. They each felt they had somehow made a terrible mistake in selecting their mates.

Tricia didn't set out to be unfaithful, but because of her need for approval and acceptance which was not being met or even understood by her husband who was trying to make her "toe the line," she was vulnerable. By the time she told me this story she had already been out for dinner a few times with a handsome pilot "Who thinks I'm just adorable." You don't have to be a marriage counselor to see what will happen to this couple as each one heads off in opposite directions seeking someone who will say, "I understand."

So many feel that sex is the initial attraction between those who ultimately become unfaithful, and while that may often be the case, I find that the underlying cause is that they are seeking fulfillment of unmet and unexpressed needs.

While just knowing this principle may not change a marriage, if both partners are aware of the other's needs and try to meet them, the understanding alone will make a difference. As one lady said, "Just knowing he knows gives me hope."

THE MELANCHOLY SEEKS A SENSITIVE SPIRIT

The Melancholy above all others craves a mate who will be sensitive to his deepest inner needs, and yet he tends to marry a Sanguine who doesn't even think of digging below the surface. As the Melancholy gets depressed, the Sanguine turns to happy people plunging the Melancholy deeper into the pit where he awaits someone with sensitivity to rescue him.

The Melancholy doesn't set out to be unfaithful, but some are led into temptation because their own marriages are not filling their needs. Many years ago Fred and I were in a church where the Melancholy pastor felt unloved and misunderstood. While he was telling Fred his part of the story in the church office, his Sanguine wife was crying to me in the foyer. The "other woman" had walked through the hall, and the wife had fallen apart at the sight of her. The "other woman" was plain at best, while the wife was stylish and attractive. Surely he had not been drawn to this woman by her looks, but somehow she had been meeting his needs to have someone who was sensitive, thoughtful, and caring—attributes that were not natural in his wife.

This woman had been "volunteering" to help in the church office and had a knack for anticipating the pastor's needs. She came in each day, straightened up his office and served him coffee.

When he finished a long day of counseling, she'd drop by and listen attentively to the depressing problems which he couldn't share with his chatty wife who didn't like to listen, who would have spread the case histories as gossip, and who didn't like sad stories anyway.

Here was a man who hadn't meant to stray and who knew better, but who was vulnerable. Gratefully, the eruption took place when Fred and I were there, and when he saw what he was heading into, the pastor was willing to keep the woman out of his office and cease the relationship; his wife became willing to discuss his needs, which she had never even noticed before, and to curb her tongue which had gotten them both into trouble in the past. What a difference it can make when we start meeting each other's needs at home.

THE CHOLERIC WANTS TO BE APPRECIATED

Because the Choleric appears to have life under control, his mate, usually Phlegmatic, doesn't sense he's craving appreciation for "all he's done."

One lady said of her husband, "I just thought he loved to work—it never occurred to me to make a big deal of each project." A man stated, "She knows she can run circles around everyone else. If I tell her she's great, she'll get a swelled head." In today's world where any man can find someone to smile at him, or any woman can find a listening ear, how important it is for all of us to understand each other's needs, talk about them, and try to fill them before it's too late.

A doctor's wife told me, "He thinks he's God. The nurses bow when he enters and the patients' very lives depend upon him. When he comes home, I bring him down to size." That's exactly what this Phlegmatic lady was doing, and he didn't appreciate her deflating and sarcastic comments.

Since Cholerics only want to play games they can win, they will avoid any place where they are looked at as losers. This Choleric doctor had ceased coming home until late at night when his wife was already asleep. In the morning for punishment she'd not talk to him, and she'd purposely neglect to pick up his shirts at the cleaners until he ran out, at which point he'd yell at her. She then blamed his terrible temper and unreasonable nature for their marriage problems.

Neither one was meeting the other's needs, and they had declared war. He was already spending his evenings with an assortment of nurses, and she was taking a course at church on raising her self-image. Once she understood that he needed to come home to a positive personality and be praised for how hard he worked and how well he provided for the family, she was willing to make these changes. Once she saw that his apparent conceit was increased by her lack of affirmation and that he wasn't out to get her, she stopped her quiet war to scuttle his ship of state.

THE PHLEGMATIC JUST WANTS RESPECT

Because the Phlegmatic is a low-key person, the mate often takes him or her for granted. As one wife said of her Phlegmatic husband, "I hardly notice he's there, for he and the couch have become one." A busy Choleric wife tends to pass the Phlegmatic husband by in a hurry and think, because he's quiet and undemanding, he has no needs. It is true that the Phlegmatic can become content in whatsoever state he's in, but after a while he wonders if he matters at all. One Phlegmatic man stated about his wife and family, "It's like they are on some great team and I'm in the last row of the grandstand."

A Phlegmatic wife said, "Our family is an army battalion. He's the general and I'm on K.P."

While the Phlegmatic with his cool relaxed nature doesn't set out to have an affair, it is easy to see that when someone makes him feel important, he perks up. A Phlegmatic lady came to me at a conference after I'd spoken on adultery to tell me of her relationship with the church choir director. "My husband hasn't even noticed me for years. No matter what I wear or do, he doesn't see it. He hasn't given me any presents, and he just takes me for granted."

In contrast, the choir director complimented her on everything she wore and gave her solo parts because he loved her voice. He had sent roses to the hotel that day and had called her three times while her husband hadn't phoned once. As she stated, "I haven't done anything wrong yet, but it's the first time I've felt worth anything in years."

If only her husband knew that inside that quiet, unassuming woman was a heart crying out for some feeling of significance, some sign that he cared.

If only each married person could meet the other's needs, we could cut down the rising number of divorces in the church. Without any "how-to's" we tend to bumble along, but from here on as we function with knowledge, we can redeem our marriages before it's too late. Remember:

Sanguines need attention and approval; they wilt under criticism.

Melancholies need order and sensitivity; they become depressed in chaos.

Cholerics need appreciation for all they've done; they stay away from ungrateful people.

Phlegmatics need respect and a feeling of worth; they withdraw when they are ignored.

Don't let your partner be led into temptation.

For Further Study, Thought, and Action

Remembering what I wrote about "The Other Woman" or could have written about "The Other Man," state your partner's desires and underlying needs as you now understand them.

Ask yourself:

If my partner were vulnerable to temptation, what would the other person look like?

What needs would he/she fill that I don't fill?

In what kind of a setting would they choose to meet?

What would they talk about?

What can I do to prevent another person from coming on the scene?

Am I willing to do that?

Write down your answers.

Sit down with your mate when the two of you are alone and ask these same questions. Do you both agree?

In a group, draw up a profile of a typical person of each temperament and what each would be most easily tempted by. Then personalize this list with group members. Discuss one underlying need that each person has that is not being met and what can be done about this.

For those who are single, divorced or widowed, review past relationships, see where mistakes were made, and prepare for prevention of these problems in the future.

Study Philippians 4:8 and apply it to mates or friends.

What about this person is . . .
True and honest?

Noble and worthy?

Right and orderly?

Pure and blameless?

Lovely and attractive?

Admirable and appealing?

If anything is excellent or virtuous or praiseworthy, think on these things!

PERSONALITIES LED INTO TEMPTATION	
When mate doesn't give compliments or laugh at his humor.	When mate doesn't get things done and doesn't appreciate his achievements.
When mate takes him for granted and he feels worthless.	When mate lacks sensitivity to his needs and life is no longer in order.

Now that you know this truth how happy you will be if you put it into practice.

—John 13:17, TEV

❧ 5 ❧

What Gets You Depressed?

Life's but a walking shadow, a poor player that struts and frets his hour upon the stage and then is heard no more.[1]

There is a national depression today similar to this statement by Macbeth. We're all playing our parts, doing what's expected, but for what? Where are we going anyway? What's the use? Soon we'll be gone, heard from no more.

In the past twenty years I have observed increasingly more depressed people than I ever thought possible. Every one who has a problem is depressed to some degree. People with marriage conflicts are depressed; parents with rebellious teens are depressed; patients with incurable diseases are depressed.

The word *depressed* literally means "pressed down" or as my mother would say, "just not up to snuff." Picture a foam rubber pillow and then push your fist into the center. The pillow is depressed; it's not up to its usual bounce. Pull your hand out and the pillow pops up. This is a simple example of a mild depression, that pervasive feeling that we're somehow not functioning at our usual capacity.

There's not one of us that's not pressed down occasionally as we strut and fret our hour upon the stage, and some of us may sense that someone is standing on our pillow and trampling us underfoot. As depression overtakes us, we begin to have feelings of helplessness followed by hopelessness. If I can't help myself, then there's no hope.

In my book *Blow Away the Black Clouds* I give the symptoms

of depression and some solutions both self-directed and spiritual. This has been my best selling book and I have just revised it to add an analysis of teen depression and suicide, some suggestions for the healing of pains of the past, and a chapter on Christmas depression. The one area I have not covered is the different causes of depression according to a person's temperament pattern.

Since we now understand the desires and underlying needs of each personality, we can see how these traits relate to depression, that feeling of inner loss. As we view the Sanguines' desire for fun and need for attention and approval, we can easily guess at what depresses them. Even though they are optimistic people with an above average ability to bounce back from adverse circumstances, if they find themselves in a position where life is no longer fun and where no one is giving them attention or approval, they will become depressed.

As the Cholerics innately seek control and need appreciation for their achievements, they drop into depression when they find life out of control with no one applauding their good deeds.

The Phlegmatics just want peace and need to feel that someone considers them worthwhile, so when they are dropped into a cauldron of constant contention and controversy and can't face the conflict, they drown in depression.

Because the Melancholies have the deepest natures to begin with and want the most out of life, they are the most easily disappointed. Because they are aiming for perfection in both themselves and others and because they expect those others to be sensitive to their inner feelings, they are laid open for frequent bouts of depression. When perfection is the goal, disappointment is often the result.

Since the Sanguine and Melancholy usually marry each other, they are doomed for depression if they don't understand each other's personalities. The Sanguine needs praise, and the Melancholy won't give it until the Sanguine is perfect. The Sanguine isn't ever going to get perfect so he doesn't get the compliments he desires and he quits trying. When the Sanguine performs more poorly than usual, the Melancholy gets depressed and the Sanguine goes out to find someone who will appreciate him.

When these two can see each other's weaknesses as part of their opposite natures and accept them, this frees the offending person to put his strength into improvement and not use it all up on defense and depression.

SANGUINE DEPRESSION

A Sanguine deprived of fun and attention may become depressed.

After speaking at a luncheon and explaining the underlying needs of each personality, I was surrounded by people who suddenly realized why they were depressed. One Sanguine lady told me of her husband, the leader of a large Christian organization. She explained he had married her for her bright personality and sense of humor and then had worked to eliminate all her creativity and zest for life. He told her she was trivial, superficial, and self-centered while he was deep, intellectual, and concerned for others. With his superior abilities, he had worked his way up Jacob's ladder to the top of his denomination, priding himself on his spirituality while totally ignoring her personal needs.

As she told me her story, I could see before me a typical depressed Sanguine, one whose greatest abilities were considered as faults, whose joy of life had been stamped out, who received no praise from her husband. She was pretty but overweight, another sign of Sanguine depression; when life is no longer fun, cheer yourself up with hot fudge sundaes.

She realized as she poured out her heart to me that the reason she worked full-time was twofold: (1) She had to get out and find people who would praise her, (2) She had to earn money to be able to buy the things that would pull her up from her Sanguine depression.

If only I could have talked with her husband and explained her innate needs—so simple to fill—shown him she was normal to crave praise and dislike constant criticism, and taught him that the root of her depression was not a spiritual problem, but the fact that he, a well-known Christian leader, wasn't willing to meet his wife's emotional needs or even consider she had any.

Another Sanguine lady sought relief from her headaches and after much questioning by different doctors was shown that these pains appeared only on days when her husband took her car to work and she was left without easy transportation. She was wide-eyed as she told me that her pains were produced by the depressing realization that she couldn't go anywhere for the whole day and by the unacknowledged anger she had for her husband's leaving her wheelless. Once she found the source of her problem, she was able to laugh about it and share her recovery with me. She explained, "It wasn't that I needed to go anywhere every day, but just the thought that I couldn't get out if I wanted to had me close to sick." When she stopped complaining about headaches, her husband became willing to carpool and leave her the car.

Anyone that's not Sanguine would find this case to be ridiculous, but those who are can relate to that need for the easy accessibility of fun and for the constancy of an applauding audience.

As I talk with Sanguine women, I find that their most consistent cure for depression is to go shopping. The basic negative to this program is that the Sanguine is usually married to a Melancholy who can count and when the bills come in, *he* gets depressed.

Marita and I both love to take an hour here and there across the country and go shopping. Even when we need absolutely nothing, we love to look. Cholerics consider this shopping without goals to be a waste of time, Melancholies feel these forays are without purpose, and Phlegmatics find these wanderings to be too much like work. But for the typical Sanguine woman, "just looking, thank you" can be the upper in a down day.

One rationalized it this way, "Even if I do buy something to cheer me up, it's cheaper than a psychiatrist."

In *USA Today* an article, "The Lure of the Store," examined the attitudes of different celebrities about shopping.

Singer Jennifer Holliday said, "I love shopping for shoes with a passion. I feel that shopping has numerous psychological benefits in that it can provide consolation in times of depression, and on the other hand it can provide ultimate reward in time of success. Everyone should go shopping!"[2]

Well, maybe not everyone, but for Sanguines just knowing they can get to a sale provides "consolation in time of depression."

When Sanguine men get depressed because work is no fun, or the wife doesn't laugh at their jokes, or a check just bounced, contrary to logic, they go out and treat everyone in sight. They

must be accepted by their friends and buying their way to popularity is one method of cheering themselves up while denying
there is any problem.

Melancholy wives find it hard to imagine that their Sanguine
husbands can so easily transfer negatives into "out of sight out
of mind," that they can sign up for a lifetime membership in
Jack LaLanne when the Cadillac is about to be repossessed, that
they can go off on an important business trip when they have
no business.

One frustrated wife told me of her Sanguine/Phlegmatic husband who was a builder. The new homes hadn't sold and the
bank kept calling and insisting he get down there immediately.
She was deeply depressed over the embarrassing situation, for
as a Melancholy she could see that nothing was going right. As
she went into his office to beg him to go to the bank she found
him happily typing. When she asked, "What are you doing typing
at a time like this?" he replied, "I'm writing a novel."

In just telling me the story she burst into tears. She had been
in a long-range depression of humiliation as the bank foreclosed
on the houses, and he had been discouraged for a while but had
abandoned his literary career for a new venture manufacturing
air-conditioned dog houses. The thought of another financial risk
had her distraught, but he was happy because he'd managed to
get financing from a rich man he'd met while playing golf.

Besides buying things, treating everyone in sight, and starting
new ventures, another way the Sanguine handles depression is
to overeat. Somehow the pleasure of pasta and petits fours picks
up their spirits. Unfortunately this momentary lift doesn't last,
for the Sanguine loves clothes and gets additionally depressed
when nothing seems to fit right any more. To solve this a new
wardrobe is needed giving reason for more shopping. One Sanguine I met has three separate wardrobes hanging in her closet:
one in size 8, one in 10–12, and one in 14. As she ate chocolate
donuts while telling me this story, she laughed and said, "The
size 8 is pure history."

Sanguines are very circumstantial people and while they may
drop into a depression when the fun slows down and they are
no longer the center of attention, a change of scene or outlook
will help them bounce back again. While growing up and becom-

ing responsible would be a better choice, it is unlikely without a clear revelation from the Lord.

Remember, a Sanguine without a spotlight may become lonely and depressed.

CHOLERIC DEPRESSION

A Choleric without control becomes depressed. This concept has opened the eyes of many women as to why their out-going optimistic, goal-oriented husbands have totally changed their personalities. A fifty-year-old woman came up after a seminar to tell me about her husband, a Choleric with some Melancholy, the director of an engineering unit. He had always been a healthy, dynamic man until he went for a routine physical and found he had a degenerative eye problem. Even though his vision had not bothered him to that point, he instantly changed and began saying things such as: "What good will I be with no sight? An engineer who can't see might as well be dead. They'll fire me any day now. I might as well quit and die."

His wife was so stunned by this "crybaby" attitude that she didn't know what to do. "He sits around at home and drinks and he's started to smoke. These are two habits that the doctor told him would make his eyesight worse, and yet when I tell him that, he gets mad at me." She explained how angry she was at him and how she'd pulled away from him emotionally. These moves have obviously affirmed to him that she doesn't love him in his time of need.

When she heard me say a Choleric who is physically disabled often gets depressed, she brightened up and exclaimed, "Now I see the problem. He's got both of the Choleric causes for depression, a disease that will destroy his eyesight and the fear that he will lose his job. He sees a future where he will have no control. Now that I understand what's wrong with him I can be more compassionate and encouraging."

Another lady who was standing in line waiting to see me spoke up and said, "I can't believe this coincidence; my husband has got eye problems also, and he's in a depression. He got fired from his executive position while he was in the hospital having eye surgery. He was so upset that his blood pressure went up complicating his recovery. Since he's come home he's become addicted to Pepsi Cola and he eats Oreos by the bag. If I hide them, he goes to the store and buys more. He's gained weight and looks awful; he's developed a speech impediment, and he's no longer even polite to waitresses."

Here was a typical description of a depressed Choleric man, both physically disabled and unemployed.

Many healthy men also get discouraged at the mere thought that they might not be eternally invincible. They see no realistic challenges, and they're afraid they're going downhill. I feel that many mid-life crises are caused by men who sense they may be losing their grip, their hair, their shape, their macho image, or their sex appeal. To overcome this fear they tighten the reins at home, start rubbing Miracle-Gro into their scalps, join a health spa and buy jogging suits, lease a Mercedes and take the secretary out to lunch. What they're saying is, "I've got to do everything I can to make sure life doesn't slip out of my control. I've got to prove to myself that I'm a man."

How many Christian homes I've seen destroyed by a Choleric man who feels no one at home appreciates all he has done for them and who reaches out for something to restore his slipping self-confidence. In strutting his stuff, he finds a friend who makes him feel like a man again, and he walks away from his family.

An understanding of the personalities is so important in a marriage, for without it both partners may be depressed and not understand why they tend to think the marriage is failing and a new mate might make a difference. Without any new concept of their temperaments, changing partners just moves the actors to a new stage but the plot remains the same. A California marriage therapist warns, "Remarrying on the rebound is self-defeating. Unless one takes the time to learn something from the collapse of the first marriage that will make the second stronger, he or she is likely to repeat the destructive behavior, or pick another unsuitable partner."[3]

Choleric women tend to marry Phlegmatic men and unconsciously take control of them and the children. As long as everyone has an obedient attitude, the mother stays happy; but when anyone of the group rebels, she may become depressed. Without a knowledge of her temperament, she won't understand what's wrong. One lady handed me a note ripped out of a spiral binder, "Today you gave me the answer I have searched for, for years! I am terribly depressed. I can't remember when I haven't been. It's been so long. I now see it's my eighteen-year-old son that I have held down for years and tried to make into a different personality from what he was meant to be. He hasn't turned out right and now I see why. I didn't know about these personalities, and I've been pushing him in the wrong direction. I couldn't understand why he was so different, and he's had me depressed for years. Now I see that it's because I couldn't get him under control. I didn't think I needed this seminar, but I was wrong. I pray I can use this information correctly. Thank you so much!"

Dale and Sherry came to me with their problems after one of our CLASSes. They had each done their Personality Profiles; he came out Phlegmatic with some Sanguine and she, Choleric with some Melancholy. Dale was handsome, charming, and laid back as he sprawled in the most comfortable chair. Sherry was sitting straight, almost rigid, and she looked angry. Even if they had not shown me their scores I would have known what their personalities were. The question they came to ask was whether or not he should give up his job and go into full-time Christian service.

I started with him by asking an appropriate question for a Phlegmatic/Sanguine man. "Do you have any problems with handling money?" Before he could take a breath, she answered his question, "He's impossible with money, and I can make more money in a day than he can make in a week!" Just this one outburst gave me a quick view of their marriage: an easygoing friendly man who was viewed as incompetent by his Choleric wife.

When she finished her statement Dale asked me, "Why did you start with a money question? How'd you know?"

"Because Phlegmatic/Sanguine men frequently have money problems."

As I heard their story, I heard nothing new. Dale had shifted jobs at least twice a year in the eight years they'd been married. He got bored easily and several of the jobs were just "too much like work." Because of his cool charm, he could always get a new one and he lived on dreams of what might be.

Sherry jumped in, "He had one decent job and while he had

that we got out of debt for the one and only time in our marriage!"

"But it was so boring. It was a government job where you just did the same thing day after day. It was no fun."

"Does everything have to be fun to you? Don't you ever think of us? Don't you feel any obligation to support your family?"

With this outburst Sherry banged her fist on the table and Dale turned to me, "Do you see what it's like to live with her? It's impossible."

"I might not be so impossible if I could pay the bills. Tell her what you're doing now." The "her" was me and I then listened while he explained that he was in sales, but he didn't realize before he took the job that there was no draw and he wouldn't receive any money until he sold a whole roomful of office furniture. Since he hadn't sold so much as a desk in three months, there had been no income. Sherry jumped in, "Didn't you even ask them before you took the job?"

"I just assumed."

"You always just assume."

So far I had done nothing but ask the opening question on money and they had produced a soap opera.

"The worst thing is he thought he was going to make a lot of money and we bought a new house on his anticipated income. Now we have high payments and no money."

"If you didn't charge so much we might be able to make it."

"I only charge to show you what a mess you've put us in. If it weren't for the three kids, I'd go to work and show you up— and I wouldn't just *assume* I'd get paid."

At this point I decided to step in for a commercial.

Here were two Christian people who were both depressed and who couldn't carry on a civil conversation in front of an audience of one.

Sherry, the Choleric, was desperate because life was out of control and Dale, the Phlegmatic/Sanguine, was sick of constant conflict. Sherry had come from an affluent family, and she wanted Dale to be like her successful father. She had goaded him on and was partly responsible for his changing jobs so often. She had also been the one who wanted the new house and had encouraged him to buy at a point when he had no fixed income. She constantly berated him and reminded him of how much she could make if he hadn't stuck her with these three children. Can you imagine how the children felt?

Dale was tired of being badgered and admitted he only came home to see the children. He had a poor grasp of money and didn't care if he ever "got rich." There was no chance of his getting rich with his low income and her high style.

As I showed them what typical problems they had and did a little arithmetic with them, they began to see their mutual responsibilities for the depression they were in and the destruction they were bringing to their home. I learned that she was an excellent typist, but she had refused to do any work "because I didn't want to make it easy for him." And she hadn't.

He agreed to get a job with a steady income, at least until they caught up, even if it was boring. She then became willing to do some typing in her home office to help make the payments on the big house she felt she needed. They saw that they had been on opposing teams, and they determined to stop undermining each other and get on the same side. Sherry understood that in her mind her depression came from his lack of achievement and his inability to give her what she wanted, but that underneath she was angry because she couldn't control him and his jobs. Because her underlying need to be appreciated for all she'd done for him had not been met, she had quit helping him at all.

With no help or encouragement he had been unable to achieve and was facing daily conflict that he didn't know how to handle. His underlying need, to be considered a person of worth, had not even been considered, and she took pleasure in putting him down.

After laying out a realistic plan for them, I complimented them both on their acceptance of this new solution and then prayed with them before leaving. On the way out I said to Sherry, "Dale's so adorable if you don't watch out he'll find some woman who will be glad to support him."

He replied, "If I weren't a Christian, I'd have already left."

Too many have already left, often because they don't understand either themselves or their partners; they're depressed and don't know why, and they've grown up in a society that's said, "If it doesn't work, throw it away."

A few months later I received a letter from Sherry telling me how they'd pulled their marriage together through mutual understanding and support. At the end she said, "I realized later that you never answered our original question about whether we should go into full-time Christian service. In looking back I can see why. We didn't have our own life in order; how did we think we could shape up others? I see now that Dale wanted an escape into ministry and I wanted a Christian excuse for why we were losing our house. I hope God has a sense of humor."

Remember, a Choleric out of control, unappreciated, or sick may become depressed.

PHLEGMATIC DEPRESSION

As we have seen with Sherry and Dale, Cholerics get depressed when they don't have control or don't receive appreciation for the good works they've done. The Phlegmatic sinks into despair when he faces daily conflict or contention and concludes he is not worth, as my Phlegmatic mother often said, "a pinch of snuff, a row of pins, a tinker's dam, or the powder to blow him to thunder."

Because the Phlegmatic is a low-key person who is not pushy or pretentious, others often overlook him and don't bother to pull him into the conversation. Although the Phlegmatic doesn't appear to mind being ignored, there comes that day when he asks himself, "What am I doing here? If no one seems to need me, why don't I find someone who will really care?"

Where the Choleric male in mid-life goes into a crisis when he feels he may be losing his grip, the Phlegmatic is groping for some significance. By mid-life, he looks around at his children who only speak to him when they want money and his wife who is busy running whatever she can get a hold of, including him, and he suddenly wants out. He wants out of crises into coasting, out of insignificance into somebody, out of subordination into some kind of control.

The Phlegmatic control is a different breed from the Choleric's in that he doesn't want to climb mountains or join a wrestling team, he just wants to feel that he could do something his way once in a while. This mid-life shift of attitude, or display of a suppressed attitude, may take the Phlegmatic's wife by surprise, as he's never appeared to even care before; however, if she does not see these symptoms of depression as significant and help him to feel he's a substantial member of the family, he may find someone who will.

Do you remember the Peter Principle that says we all tend to rise to our own level of incompetence? For the Phlegmatic this applies when he rises from a peaceful position where he performed well to a place of perpetual problems. Although a Phlegmatic stays content in almost any state, when put in a spot where he has to face controversy each day and has to fire an occasional orphan, he may sink into a depression which even he doesn't admit or understand.

Strangely, the Phlegmatic can handle conflict if he is not personally threatened, and he makes the best mediator or arbiter between factious Cholerics. He is an excellent counselor giving objective views to other people's problems, but he doesn't want to be the center of the controversy or be told by someone else to change his ways.

A Phlegmatic mother is the very best at adaptability and in keeping her head when all about are losing theirs; however, she is easily threatened by a Choleric child who finds sport in controlling mother. Usually the husband is a Choleric whose very word causes the child to shape up and the mother to feel helpless. She wonders, "What is wrong with me? Why can't I handle this child? Why is he out to get me? Oh, woe is me!"

If the Choleric partner understands the Phlegmatic's problem with control and conflict and wishes to be of help, he will provide his discipline in cooperation with the mother and not in contrast, but left to his own, the Choleric will take charge of the child, exclude the mate, and make both her and her offspring see her as incompetent. Piecing this puzzle together, it's easy to see why the Phlegmatic parent often feels betrayed by the Choleric mate and overwhelmed by the children. This combination of conflict and insignificance leads the Phlegmatic into depression.

One couple that came to Fred and me following a marriage seminar were both depressed. She was Choleric and he was Phlegmatic/Melancholy and the understanding of their differences started them on the road to a healed and happy marriage. Ginny started the action and Wally responded. She wrote:

I guess I so desperately want this marriage to be great because it's my first and only marriage and it is Wally's third. Both his other wives left him, and although I can see why, those things would *never* prompt me to divorce. (Murder maybe.)

You really opened my eyes in your seminar. I had always deep inside wanted to know why his other marriages failed (hoping to prevent the same tragedy in ours).

I've tried to chart out his two other wives and they were both Choleric and could not take the slow moving pace of a Phlegmatic who seemed to never get ahead. They both left for other good-looking men and more money. (Wally's so kind and Phlegmatic he never would tell me really why.) He used to always say he never understood why they left. During each marriage he gained up to nearly 300 pounds.

Well, here he's married another Choleric, me. I don't see his past as the tragedy he does. I say, move on, forget it. The Lord put me in your life. His income has doubled in four years and we've started an additional business, and he's seemed happier than ever in his life.

But these old destructive traits keep cropping up on him. He's just recently become vice-president of a huge management company, but has put on seventy-one pounds since we married. Of course the obesity affects every area of our life.

Sometimes I feel I need some kind of a chart to have Wally live by. He's a little Melancholy but he's too Phlegmatic to fill in the chart!!

I see that I won't always be able to have my way, but at least I'll still have Wally. He's so good to me, so patient, all those wonderful things Phlegmatics are, but because he does not see results from his efforts, he feels a failure. I know he doesn't need another Choleric wife to drive him into the ground and then walk off in disgust. We love each other so much and with the knowledge of our different personalities I know we'll make it!

Even though Fred and I put our marriage back together through the understanding of the different personalities, we are still amazed and thrilled when others let us know what has happened to them. One woman who had been to our *Personality Plus* several years ago came again and heard what I had added about depression. She then wrote:

As outstanding as the material was for me before, it is even more beneficial now.

Three weeks ago my husband was dismissed unexpectedly from his job of 24 years. With my Choleric personality I want to get right in with investigating all possible careers and franchises and then move into a decision. But my Phlegmatic husband, so afraid of change and the unknown, keeps dragging his heels.

Understanding temperaments is helping me to sit on myself and choose to trust God with my husband and our future, rather than pushing on him to do things "my way." I know that once he makes a decision it will be a good one, and he will do well in it. But it is hard watching him move at his pace rather than in mine. He's a wonderful balance for me with my eager, let's-get-it-moving attitude, and understanding this has kept me from getting depressed.

Remember, a Phlegmatic facing conflict and feeling insignificant may become depressed.

MELANCHOLY DEPRESSION

The reason I have left the Melancholy depression to the last is because it is the classic case of what we all think of as depression. It's not so circumstantial as the Sanguine's or Phlegmatic's and it's opposite from the Choleric's. The Choleric hates sickness and will work to his dying day while the Melancholy is apt to gather up ailments during depression and in extreme cases simply takes to the bed in a bid for sympathy and sensitivity.

A lady came up to me recently and explained, "My mother is Melancholy and depressed. She doesn't work anymore and she seems to go from one ailment to another. She has had blood tests, liver tests, and x-rays of all her parts. Is she really sick?" What a question for me who has never seen the sick lady and who is not a doctor! However, a calculated guess would be that she is depressed and has focused her attention on her health, hoping someone will care enough about her to listen to her symptoms and be sensitive to her needs.

The Melancholies are depressed more frequently than other types because their deep desire is to get everything and everybody in perfect order. Since this nirvana never comes, the Melancholy either has to lower his expectations and accept life as it is or sink into despair. How many of us have ever had our house perfectly decorated, our tulips in bloom and all our buttons sewed on at the same time?

The Melancholy depression is harder to pinpoint because it is a generalized feeling not caused ostensibly by any particular event or deprivation. Things just aren't right—and don't look as if they ever will be. Because the Melancholy is innately sensitive and is easily hurt, he has no trouble remembering the negatives which when filed in the mind become heavy and depressing.

A Choleric woman wrote to tell me about administering our Personality Profile to her family.

> What a time we had with your test! My Choleric father loved it and told my mother that she was Phlegmatic. She believed him because it was easier than doing the test and what does it matter anyway? My Melancholy sister-in-law opened up to us for the first time in seven years. She said it was the only time she'd ever felt we cared about her feelings or thought we'd listen. We apologized, which is not easy for Cholerics. Two weeks later my husband's family came and we had to break up fights over the test. The Cholerics started telling the Melancholies what was wrong with them and they took it all to heart and got upset with each other. My husband's mother and aunt got depressed and went to bed crying, but the next day they all made up and could see how the different personalities had all behaved in typical fashion. Amazing, isn't it!

The Melancholies are so sensitive and have such a need for order that it is easy to see how they get so quickly depressed. A Melancholy pastor's wife received my *Personality Plus* tapes from a friend who in turn sent me a copy of the thank-you note.

> Dear Suzie, You will never know how much the tapes by Florence Littauer meant to us. They came at a very crucial time when I as a Melancholy had given up on ever understanding my Sanguine husband. I was sick of doing all his behind the scenes work and having everyone tell me how lucky I was to have a husband with such personality. The whole situation was depressing.
>
> He seemed to be sensitive to everyone but me, and I was left to be the disciplinarian of the family. As I listened to the tapes, I found why I was so easily slighted and realized that my husband wasn't out to ignore me, he just went where the audience applauded him. I analyzed the family and found I have one child of each kind. No wonder I'm depressed. I've been trying to make them all perfect

and alike. What a lot of wasted effort I've spent trying to turn Sanguines, Cholerics, and Phlegmatics into Melancholies.

Your gift may have saved our home! The tapes have meant so much to us that we are circulating them in our church. Everyone is excited as they find out who they are. It's really been life-changing!

Remember, a Melancholy facing an imperfect life with insensitive people may become depressed.

For Further Study, Thought, and Action

We know it is not God's will that we be depressed. "A merry heart doeth good like a medicine" (Prov. 17:22, KJV).

Do you have a "merry heart" today? If not can you pinpoint the reason?

Are you a Sanguine who is in a situation that's no longer fun? Where no one pays any attention to you? Where you're not getting any compliments? Are there people who don't think you're funny any more?

Are you a Choleric who is somehow out of control? Not full of your usual energy? Unemployed? Sick? Are there people who don't appreciate *all* you've done for them?

Are you a Phlegmatic who is facing conflict? Who is sick of trying to mediate everyone's problems? Who's tired of being ignored or made fun of? Are there some people who make you feel you're not worth a nickel?

Are you a Melancholy who knows nothing is ever going to get straightened out right? Who hasn't asked for more than perfection? Who doesn't feel anyone loves you? Who can't find a doctor who can help you?

Are there some insensitive people who just don't seem to understand your needs?

After thinking on these questions about yourself, project them onto your mate and other members of your family. Are there times when you can see you didn't understand each other's needs and you both became depressed?

If doing this as a group study, you may want to read *Blow Away the Black Clouds* for a more thorough study of depression. In your discussion time let each one share what really gets him depressed and what others could do to help him. Most people would be understanding if they were only told the situation and what they could do to be of service. Hiding your problems and then being depressed when no one seems to care only isolates you from any solution.

PERSONALITY DEPRESSION	
When life's no fun and there's too much criticism.	When life's out of control and there's no appreciation.
When life's full of problems and there's no peace.	When life's a mess and there's no hope.

Review some basic steps in overcoming depression.
Analyze your temperament needs.
Admit you have a problem.
Consider what you can do about it personally.
Discuss your differences with your mate, children or friend.
Devise an appropriate plan of action.
Write down your true feelings as David did in the Psalms.
Pray to forgive those that you perceive have hurt you.
Commit to changing what you do that bothers others.
Ask the Lord for Joy.

Hitherto have ye asked nothing in my name: ask, and ye shall receive, that your joy may be full.
—John 16:24, KJV

❧ 6 ❧

Are You
Wearing a Mask?

When I first started CLASS (Christian Leaders and Speakers Seminars) in the fall of 1980, I intended to teach Christian speakers how to "Say it with CLASS," but as I worked closely with the men and women who attended, I became increasingly aware of their emotional needs. As I began a study of the four personalities on a deeper level than I had ever done before, I looked beyond the obvious behavior characteristics of each temperament type and into the hurts of the hearts. I found Sanguines who were depressed, Cholerics who were out of control, Melancholies who had given up on life and Phlegmatics who were overwhelmed by adverse circumstances. I saw women who were repeating their mother's mistakes and men who refused to be introspective or enlightened any more than their fathers had been.

Marriages of Christian leaders were falling apart and no one seemed to be doing much about it. Currently, we find that anywhere from one-third to one-half of those attending CLASS are already divorced. As I teach about the personalities, the different desires and underlying emotional needs, lights go on and people begin to find themselves and understand why they are in their present dilemma.

As Lana Bateman came on our CLASS staff, she began an indepth study of what she perceived to be the masks people wear to cover up their birth personality. In both our CLASS counseling and her own Philippian Ministries, Lana took note of the different types of masks, when and why people wore them, and how they

87

could be removed. Eventually we both started teaching Lana's concept and recording the reactions and results.

As I researched the personalities of both my family and Fred's, I saw repeated patterns of behavior and areas where some of us had unconsciously stifled our natural traits in a vain effort to please a parent or partner. Some had played a part foreign to their own inborn personality and in the process had lost any sense of who they really were and any sight of who they might become. Some had put on the mask of comedy or tragedy to get applause from the crowd and some had changed costumes so many times that they had forgotten their original identity.

One day I traced our family's personality tree on the board at CLASS and showed how many of us strong Cholerics had put on Phlegmatic masks when repressed by other Cholerics. Immediately people came up to confess that they had been wearing masks and hadn't realized what they were doing.

NATURAL PERSONALITY TRAITS

Some people couldn't "find themselves" because their true God-given nature had been trampled under, had died for lack of attention, or had been masked by rejection or guilt. I began to see how childhood abuses of any kind from emotional neglect to physical mistreatment could warp a little one's feelings about himself and make him unable as an adult to know who in the world he really was.

Some women I talk with don't have any grasp of which traits are real and which are learned. What I'm now observing in the above-average men and women we train at CLASS is that a totally subconscious manipulation has changed them from what they were meant to be to the insecure questioning people they are today. These are adults who have dedicated their lives to the Lord and thought they had taken off the old clothes and put on the new. Somehow new clothes haven't been enough, but as we help them examine their personalities by looking back to what they were meant to be, the blinders fall away and they begin to see with a new light.

The Bible tells us that Jesus is the vine and we are the

branches, yet some of us are not connected with what we were originally intended to be. Because of adverse circumstances, lack of love, sibling rivalry, or the desire to please demanding parents, we unconsciously changed our birth personality to fit our situation. Fun-loving children were forced to get serious and keep quiet, while introverts were told to put on a happy face to be popular. Born leaders were disciplined into an unnatural submission and those who would rather watch were pushed into leadership.

Some who stayed true to their birth personalities through childhood put on accommodating masks after marriage in order to please a mate.

Let's look first at the natural traits of each temperament and how uncomfortable we feel when we try to be like someone else.

Personality

When we think of someone who has "personality" we are usually referring to a Sanguine even though we may not know the term. If we enroll in image improvement lessons, we want to learn how to lose our self-consciousness, be confident before groups, be the life-of-the-party, and ingest an instant sense of humor. There is nothing wrong with these goals, but we must realize that unless we are Sanguine to start with, these traits may come across as unnatural. A Melancholy may try to repeat a story he heard a Sanguine tell and wonder why no one seems to respond. A Choleric may try to make jest over a person's pratfalls and appear critical. The Phlegmatic, even with his natural dry wit, may twist his tongue and easily become sarcastic.

Enjoy the Sanguine personality, but don't be envious, for with their charm comes a lack of discipline and they seldom reach their full potential even after receiving the ribbon "Most Likely to Succeed!"

I once took a charm course from a teacher who was naturally charming. She sat with her hands delicately posed and her legs crossed neatly at the ankles. While this looked fine for her, it didn't do the same for the rest of us. As I glanced around the room it was laughable to see all of us sitting in identical positions trying to be clones of our teacher. We should look, sit, and walk

our best, but it should be "our best" not a replica of someone else.

Be yourself; for a phony personality is never attractive.

Power

In an age where we are all stimulated to become supermen
and superwomen, we are often jealous of those who seem to have
it all together. Why can't we be in charge? Why don't we seem
to have the power of persuasion?

As a member of the National Speakers Association I have the
opportunity to spend time with some of the top motivational
speakers, and I have learned that most seminars are conceived
by Cholerics, written by Cholerics, taught by Cholerics, and only
the Cholerics can catch the vision. The Cholerics in the audience
can relate to the speaker, charge forth, follow the grail, and meet
the challenge. The Sanguine girl who attends means well and
wants to get her act together, but she can't even lift the syllabus.
If she doesn't lose it on the way home, she'll put it away to
look at another day and when she can't remember where she's
put it, she'll take this as a sign from the Lord that she's good
enough as she is and doesn't need the book anyway. The Melancholy at a seminar comes prepared with his own notebook, as-
sorted pens and 3 x 5 cards. He can follow the details and sense
the direction of the speaker's "Seven Steps to Success," but he
becomes overwhelmed with the vitality of the visionary waving
his arms wildly as he yells "terrific" and "tremendous." *No one
is really that terrific or tremendous,* he muses. Once the Melancholy senses the speaker is insincere and shallow, he loses interest
in the program.

The Phlegmatic didn't want to go to the seminar in the first
place, and he has no intention of changing his way of life. He
measures all activity by how much energy it will take to succeed,
and this all looks too much like work. People who are flambouyant
and frequently shout "fabulous" strike fear in the heart of the
Phlegmatic. He can't believe they are for real and he plans to
leave at the next coffee break.

Enjoy the dynamic delivery and powerful confidence that is
natural in the Choleric and learn what you can from his presenta-

tion, but don't get depressed if you don't desire to go out jogging at 5:30 each morning or meet Zig Ziglar at the top. Cholerics are sensational at seminars, but they aren't always a big hit at home.

While speaking to a group of motivational speakers I inserted a line that I had no intention of saying. "You may be terrific and tremendous and fabulous and fantastic on stage, but you may have a sad wife at home who, if she hears one of those words again, is going to throw up."

I bit my tongue as I heard those words slip out, but when I finished, a nationally known motivator came up with an uncharacteristically humble expression. "Just this week my wife said, 'You may be a hot shot on the stage but you're a zero at home, and if you say "fantastic" one more time, I'm going to throw up.'"

The Choleric has power in his presentation but he needs to get off his pedestal and look into the hearts of the people.

Be yourself; and don't envy those leaders who seem to have it all together.

Perfection

"Can't you ever do anything right?" How many of us heard that as we were growing up? For the Melancholy there is no other way. As a man said to me, "Why would anyone want to do less than his best?" And he is right. Certainly we would not aim to fail or want to do a shoddy job, but only the Melancholy has the innate drive for perfection. The Melancholy male must have his shoes polished, his mirror spotless, and his toothpaste tube without wrinkle. He can't possibly understand how his Sanguine wife could lose her shoes, keep open jars of make-up all over the counter and twist the tacky toothpaste tube beyond recognition. He is constantly picking up behind her, shutting doors she's left open, and putting the cap on the catsup.

Fred is so neat that he has been known to fold up his clothes before putting them in the hamper. One day I took his pile of laundry to the foyer and placed it on the table while I went into the kitchen to collect the dish towels. Within a minute I came out and the laundry was gone. I assumed he had taken it to the washer, but there was no pile there. When I found him and asked what he'd done with the laundry, he replied, "I thought it was clean and I've put it away."

The Melancholy mind is constantly tying up the loose ends of life and they wonder, since they are right, why the rest of us don't see it their way. The Choleric is more interested in getting things done quickly than perfectly. The Sanguines don't realize they haven't done it right and the Phlegmatics just don't care that much. The world needs the Melancholy to keep the rest of us on track, but sometimes the standards are set so high that no one can achieve them and then we all get depressed.

Be yourself; life is never going to be perfect.

Peace

While the Sanguine is running around spreading joy unto the maximum, and the Choleric is trying to get things under control, and the Melancholy is dusting off the details, the Phlegmatic is trying to keep peace among us all. Lana says her husband calls her a natural tranquilizer. When his Choleric energy bursts in the door at night, he takes one look at her calm, cool, and collected expression and begins to come down to earth. The heart of the Phlegmatic is peaceful and he will do anything, including compromising his principles, if he can avoid a potential problem.

From the time the Phlegmatics were children, they had a calming influence on others, and while they may enjoy some sports, especially those on television, they do not have the competitive spirit of the Choleric.

Other temperaments admire the Phlegmatics' ability to keep their heads when all around are losing theirs.

Be yourself; and don't obliterate your personality to keep peace.

As you begin to understand the truth of your personality, the Lord will show you who you were born to be and remove any mask you might be wearing. He wants you to be yourself for he has created you for such a time as this.

CLUES TO MASKING

One of the first clues that you might not be functioning in total honesty with what you were born to be is when your Personality Profile comes out with relatively even splits between Sanguine (outgoing-optimistic) and Melancholy (introverted-pessimistic) or when you are half Choleric (aggressive-active) with half Phlegmatic (passive-peaceful). Since these are diametrically opposed sets of traits, these combinations indicate there may be a masking. God didn't create us with antagonistic personalities in one body. "A double-minded man is unstable in all his ways" (James 1:8, KJV).

As Lana began a study of all those she counseled who had these splits, she found that the individuals with opposite scores were somehow masking their true identity. They weren't phonies in that they had determined to be something artificial, but they had unconsciously adjusted to some set of circumstances where a change was necessary for acceptance or survival. Based on Lana's discovery, our staff began to counsel with a new set of tools and we immediately saw results. Take, for example, the following letter I received from a woman who spent a day in counseling and prayer with George Ann Dennis, our CLASS principal.

So much has happened to me since I last saw you at CLASS. I kept my appointment with George Ann Dennis on October 31. That was seven weeks ago, and I think I've started another life at a different level. I talked fast enough in those eight hours with George Ann to find forty-one areas to pray about. I finally found out I am a Sanguine/Choleric. What a shock to me as I had always seemed to be so Melancholy. George Ann laughed when I asked her what she saw. It seems my whole foundation is Choleric. God has been showing me glimpses of my childhood as this Choleric kid. I never knew I was. I'm so excited, I'm having fun getting to know the real me. She said I never really had a childhood and I was dealt double whammies ever since I was born. Now Jesus is between me and all those negative memories. Praise God. I'm not out looking for someone to like me like the lost little child I was before, as I know I'm loved!

Because of the difficult and repressive circumstances of this woman's childhood, she had grown up thinking she was Melancholy and yet not comfortable about it. When she saw herself as she was meant to be, a Sanguine/Choleric, she was free to be herself and get out from under the pressures of the past.

The person who functions as a Sanguine/Melancholy split has

happy highs alternating with deep periods of depression. The Choleric/Phlegmatic, on the other hand, swings in and out of controlling and submissive responses. Although many studies of the four basic temperaments, no matter what labels are used, show the Sanguine/Melancholy and Choleric/Phlegmatic combinations to be normal blends of people who have fluctuating extremes in their natures, we have found these conflicting traits to represent an adaptation to adverse circumstances of the past.

We feel that a God who created man to live in peace of mind would not have built opposite traits into one person causing him lifelong inner turmoil. As we sought answers to this apparent contradiction, we asked individuals with conflicting traits to review their childhood and their parents' personalities. And we soon found that one of the opposite temperaments is a mask, an unnatural veiling of the original personality.

A Greek sage once said, "I take the world to be but as a stage whence net-masked men do play their personage."[1]

I've found that many honest Christian people are playing roles they never auditioned for, on stages they didn't design, while glued to masks they don't know how to remove.

How many bewildered individuals we see who say, "I just don't know who I am." We are never truly content when our inner feelings and our outer personality don't match up.

When do these masks first appear? Usually we find that a child who lives in a stressful environment where his natural personality is not acceptable for one of many reasons will try to adapt to what is expected of him. He may have pain he cannot express, trauma that shocks him out of his true nature, molestation that floods him with guilt, an oppressive parent that grinds down his personality, a well-meaning but dictatorial parent who plans out his life, a favored sibling he is encouraged to emulate, unrealistic goals not suited to his abilities, or crisis situations where he has to adapt to survive.

At the time he is faced with odds he can't hope to beat, he may put on an appropriate mask and play a role for which God was not the casting director.

Nathaniel Hawthorne said in *The Scarlet Letter,* "No man, for any considerable period can wear one face to himself and another to the multitude without finally getting bewildered as to which may be the true."

Maxine Bynum grew up wearing a mask of Phlegmatic submission and wondered why she never felt right about herself. After coming to both *Personality Plus* and *Lives on the Mend* conferences and spending some counseling time with me she wrote:

> I was very interested in your "family tree" concept with the temperaments. I've been looking back and thinking about how my grandmother influenced my temperament and actions as I was growing up, and even after my marriage when I was nineteen. My mother died three days after I was born and my father couldn't deal with her death or with me, so he gave me to my mother's mother when I was three weeks old, rejecting me, and was never a part of my life when I was growing up.
>
> My grandmother was a strong Choleric and I became Phlegmatic to make sure I did just what she wanted, so as to win her approval and love. I couldn't stand another rejection. My grandfather died when I was six years old, so I really don't remember much about him, but he was probably Phlegmatic. The only times I could really be in control were the two summers while a college student at S.M.U., when I was a camp counselor and away from home for three months each summer. It was then that the Choleric part of my temperament surfaced and I could be in charge of a girls' cabin and tell them what to do. And I did! Except for these two summers, I've worn a Phlegmatic mask.

I'm so grateful that God has used me to help Maxine remove a Phlegmatic mask that was hiding a repressed Choleric nature. Now she is free to be herself without feeling she must apologize for her actions.

Another lady who has been wearing the Phlegmatic mask of peace wrote, "I feel like a chameleon, taking on the color of each situation, trying to be all things to all people, never saying how I really feel about anything. Now I'm so mixed up I have no idea who I really am."

A man stated, "I had to play one part to please my mother and a different one to humor my father. I don't know which one—if either—is the real me."

Lana tells of a woman who came to her for counsel:

> Joy showed me her temperament test revealing her personality to be Melancholy/Sanguine. She was convinced that this was a true

evaluation so we did not pursue any other possibility until after she had spent a day with me in a time of emotional healing and prayer.

During our counseling time together, we found that she had experienced a very painful childhood under the oppressive hand of a powerfully manipulating and controlling Melancholy/Choleric mother and a sadly passive Phlegmatic father. The mental abuse was agonizing and left that little one totally incapable of expressing her true self. A well of pain and repression filled her heart, and a broken spirit rather than a broken will resulted.

After that pain was released in tears and prayer, a whole new flower blossomed. Joy's friends found a Choleric/Sanguine with a heavy emphasis on the Choleric, a major change from what she had originally seemed to be.

What an amazing thing it is to see the real creature after the environmentally imposed facades have been stripped away. Joy is but one of many examples of those who thought they had two incompatible temperaments as the major components of their personality. Words cannot properly express the peace that comes from discovering one's true identity.

Yes, what a freeing experience it is to finally know who you really are. One day after a seminar where I had put the Littauer Family Personality Tree on the board and had explained how the Cholerics in Fred's family had been forced by the preceding generation to play Phlegmatic, a lady wrote me this letter.

> Thank you so very, very much. I feel so free. . . . [What] you shared about parental influence masking traits that show up later was such a key for me. I have yet to take the personality inventory over again with this new information in mind, but know when I do it will be much more accurate. . . .

How free the butterfly feels when it first flies out of the cocoon!

Dr. James Carr, a management consultant, writes, "We cultivate illusions of competency—masks—which help us to camouflage our anxieties. And the precious drive we have within us . . . becomes obscured in compromise, complacency and concern for immediate, rather than long-range goals. . . . What are the masks behind which so many hide?"[2] What are masks that a person puts on "because he doubts his ability to handle some area of human relationships?"[3]

THE SANGUINE/MELANCHOLY SPLIT

So many of us don a false front when we meet up with circumstances we can't control or relationships we can't handle. We wear masks that so gradually become a part of us that we no longer know where the mask ends and we begin. If your Personality Profile shows an unusual split, if you feel uncomfortable about your identity or if you sense your offspring are confused, begin to question these conflicting patterns.

"Why is my teen-age son Melancholy at home and Sanguine outside?" a mother asked me after I spoke on the personalities. "His friends say he's the life-of-the-party, but he has nothing very bright to say to me." As we conversed I quickly learned that the father was Melancholy/Choleric and the mother Melancholy/Phlegmatic. Neither one put much value on humor and without realizing what they were doing, they had let the boy know his light-hearted Sanguine nature was trivial and without any serious purpose.

When we review the Sanguine desire to have fun and his underlying need to feel approval and want attention, we can see that this boy received neither. Brought up in a wealthy home with achieving parents and goal-oriented siblings, he just didn't fit the mold. When he found his funny stories received no applause at home, he gave up trying. Why not save your good lines for those who are appreciative of wit? Don't waste your best stuff on an empty house.

This boy is not a Melancholy/Sanguine split but a Sanguine who feels depressed at home. He wears a Melancholy mask caused by parents who didn't accept him as he was. He becomes his true self when in the presence of his friends who find him funny.

To remedy this situation both the mother and father would have to understand what they had done to show this boy he wasn't acceptable and begin a conscious course of affirmation and approval.

THE CHOLERIC/PHLEGMATIC SPLIT

A pastor's wife told me of her daughter-in-law who seemed to be a Choleric/Phlegmatic split. Before marriage she had seemed good-natured and willing to go along with any family plans. After marriage she took over strongly and now does not want her in-laws to even visit or see their grandson. In tracing the girl's family background, we found a Choleric mother with a Phlegmatic father. The mother had disliked her in-laws and wouldn't allow them to be part of the family. The daughter had played Phlegmatic at home, but upon marriage she took over her Phlegmatic husband and reenacted her mother's role even though she didn't personally approve of her mother's domineering personality. She was subconsciously perpetuating her mother's sin and was excluding her in-laws without a valid reason.

Since it was the outcast mother-in-law who came to me, a solution was not easy. She had already sat down with her daughter-in-law and asked if she had in any way offended her. The answer had been, "No, but this is just the way it's going to be." The daughter-in-law herself didn't even understand why she was laying down these rules or see that she was patterning her marriage after the poor one her mother had produced.

Her Phlegmatic husband doesn't dare to cross her, and so he secretly brings the little boy to visit his mother while lying to his wife about the trip.

Here is a repressed Choleric who wore a Phlegmatic mask at home to keep peace with her mother, married a Phlegmatic, took over with a vengeance and is now taking out her hostilities on her in-laws. This girl has to be unhappy and confused, but she doesn't see what she's doing and is not looking for any answers.

She is not only destroying the in-law relationships which she doesn't seem to care about, but she is emotionally destroying her husband and turning him into an unwilling liar. Ultimately, her child will suffer as he lives under the overbearing dominance of his mother and the frightened submission of his father.

Possible Homosexuality

Unfortunately, this parental combination is one which fits the pattern of potential homosexuality: a strong mother who emasculates a weak father who in turn provides no "normal" role model for the boy. Other combinations are a weak possessive mother who binds the boy to her weeping side while the father has either left completely or is the workaholic who has no time for the family. In either case, the boy is in an emotional search for a loving father figure and is therefore vulnerable for the inordinate affections of an older male who presents himself as a genuinely caring friend.

The gays I have talked to, including seven young men in one seminary who were all training to be youth pastors, were all led into their current "life-style" by Christian leaders—scout masters, choir directors, youth pastors—who originally filled the void of a missing or emotionally bankrupt father.

A well-meaning Christian father told me he had been so concerned about the possibility of his ten-year-old son becoming gay that he had stopped hugging or kissing him and had pulled away from any physical contact with him. After hearing me speak on the pattern of potential homosexuality, he realized his withdrawal of affection was exactly the opposite of what he should be doing, for when a boy gets no healthy love from his father, he is open to receive it from someone whose motives may be unhealthy for the normal growth of the child.

Because this subject is so seldom dealt with in the Christian community, we don't understand the enormity of this pervasive problem. As the divorce rate has risen, removing the "real father" from the home, so has the increase of homosexuality followed closely behind.

A nurse told me of her conversation with a handsome young man in the hospital awaiting a sex-change operation. She asked him openly how he got to this point. He explained that his father had left when he was a baby and all he knew for a role model was his mother. He played with her clothes and make-up and loved feminine things. When he was in his pre-teens, a scout master took an interest in him, and he now sees how he attached himself to this man as a father image. The man told him, "You're too pretty to be a boy. You should be a girl." Later this affectionate man led him into a homosexual experience. "Once you've done that you know you're not normal and you don't feel right about yourself. I'm having this operation so I'll be on the outside what I feel on the inside." This was his way of trying to become real.

As I talked with one divorced lady, raising two boys alone after her husband had left her for another woman, I asked her what the church could do to help her. She immediately answered, "What my boys need is for some normal Christian man to take them out occasionally to a ball game or some activity where they can see a positive male role model to make up for the rejection they feel from their father."

What a service that could be for the men of your church and how many potentially distorted lives might be spared.

We first put on masks as some form of protection, and the young person who turns to homosexuality is often trying to put on a happy face over the rejection he feels from the same sex parent or the absence of any emotional attachment to that parent. He tries to hide his hurt and find a live substitute for the father God intended him to have. As he gets involved, he then tries to hide his activity from his mother, leading him into guilt-producing deceptions.

As we have seen, there are all kinds of masks put on initially for some kind of protection or self-preservation, masks to hide guilt, abuse, rejection, perversion, and poor parenting. In order that we can most easily examine what masks we are wearing or, equally important, what masks we have forced our children to wear, let's use our tool of the temperaments and divide the possibilities into four types.

SANGUINE MASK

This fellow's wise enough to play the fool,
And to do that well craves a kind of wit.[4]

The person who puts on the Sanguine *mask of personality* is usually one who learned early in life that his parents valued a happy face beyond any other attribute and that being "on stage" brought approval and applause. A child does not need to know his own name before he can sense what brings affirmation from his parents. When parents, one or both, need an adorable child to bolster their own self-worth, they communicate this to the little one. I often see Sanguine masks worn by Melancholy musicians who are part of a performing family of gospel singers. Usually one of the parents is Sanguine and is the crowd pleaser while the other Melancholy partner arranges the music and is the pianist. As the children come along they must all duplicate the Osmonds and sparkle out front. The Sanguines fall into this easily and are the favorites of the "stage-mother," but the others have to put on Sanguine masks or be considered rebels or at least poor sports. I counseled one Choleric girl who had refused to sing along and had been left home with grandparents. By refusing to wear the Sanguine happy face and bang a tambourine, she had been, in effect, dismissed from the troupe who went bubbling on without her. By the time I talked with her she was so angry at what she perceived as rejection that she had developed stomach ulcers in her teens. One of the Melancholy sisters who had been a forced Sanguine for years had gone on drugs, but the parents refused to see her problem and kept marching onward as Christian soldiers.

What a shame it is to see Christian entertainers who are more interested in what's up front than what's inside.

Not all Sanguine masks are on performers. Many are put on unconsciously to keep someone happy. One girl with a many-times married mother told me that she learned to be cute to keep her mother's varied spouses from "getting mad" at her. She was Choleric underneath but learned how to be coy and adorable. By the time she was a teen, this appeal she had developed led her into being molested by one of the "fathers" and telling me, "I'll never be charming again. Who needs it?"

The difference between a born Sanguine and one masquerading is how natural the personality is. Anyone can learn to say cute lines and memorize jokes, but any astute person can tell when it's strained. The real Sanguine has a sense of humor that bubbles out easily, and he can take any ordinary event of life and turn it into a hilarious story. The one wearing a Sanguine mask, on the other hand, doesn't have the innate sense of timing and can fail to be funny when repeating a story exactly as he heard it.

When Fred first came to visit me in our store, he saw what a comedy routine my brothers and I kept alive and tried to fit in and be like us. I'll never forget the long joke he told that seemed to go on forever. As my brothers were looking at me sideways, Fred stopped and said, "I've forgotten the punch line." And indeed he had if there had ever been one.

Now as we have learned to accept each other as we are, he is happy for me to be funny and for him to provide the depth and stability so natural for the Melancholy.

In taking the Personality Profile, the person with the Sanguine mask checks off the strengths that he has worked so hard to possess, not realizing they are acquired. If you suspect you have been forcing your fun, ask yourself how you really feel about these traits versus how you think you ought to feel. Many a mask has been thrown away by the mere asking of this question.

A young journalism major listened to my tapes and realized she was wearing a Sanguine mask. Her mother wrote to tell me of the relief Lynn felt when she found she could relax and be herself.

> Lynn has had her life changed from your insights. She now realizes that her Melancholy traits are part of her natural makeup . . . like her dad. But, she can now see her weaknesses and strengths and better understand how to make changes. Prior to this, she said that she thought there must be something wrong with her because she didn't feel comfortable being the cheerleader-type, and was more content to listen to others in a quieter way. Now, she feels free to just be herself.

Lana Bateman puts it this way:

> The Sanguine mask is a clown's mask demanding that its possessor be cute, funny, and constantly striving for center stage. It doesn't matter that he may not be innately humorous or sociable. This mask may take a normally quiet, sensitive person and thrust him into a very uncomfortable role of constant chatter and force him to try to become the life-of-the-party when in truth, he may have been terrified to even appear at the door.
>
> I first saw the Sanguine mask in a young woman who was thirty-two years old. Leann had grown up in a home with a sister who was almost entirely Sanguine. It was obvious that Leann's older sister Suzanne was her father's delight. Leann, however, was a more sensitive and quiet child. She felt deeply and therefore seemed to have more struggles as a little girl.
>
> Every time Leann had a problem or hurt, she would run to her dad, as most girls long to do. Her father would listen to her and answer, "Oh, Leann, why can't you be like your sister? Why do you let things bother you? Just watch Suzanne. She knows how to handle these situations. You need to learn to laugh and be fun like her. That will take care of all of these problems, and you'll find you have more friends than you know what to do with!"
>
> Leann lived on a steady diet of this response from her well-meaning father. This little one was soon engulfed by a Sanguine mask. She tried to be cute and funny. She memorized things her sister

said, jokes she heard and any attention-getters she noticed. In spite of the fact that she tried as hard as she could to be another Suzanne for her father, she never found his words to be true.

The friends he had promised never came and while she was laughing and joking on the outside, she never stopped crying on the inside. As a Melancholy child she was never encouraged toward the strong points of her true temperament. She was covered by her Sanguine mask and by her late twenties she began to cry out, "Who am I?"

After I led her through some emotional healing, she found out who the real Leann was. It was not until then that she could accept herself and begin to function as the person God made her to be.

The Sanguine mask is indeed a tragedy for it produces not joy and laughter but pretense and loneliness. The people responding to such a mask are repelled. They hear the funny clever words, but somehow sense the inconsistency between what is said and the person saying it. It is not surprising that the wearer of this mask experiences a great deal of rejection. Perhaps we need to look a little more closely at our Sanguine friends for some are not truly Sanguines at all. Not all talkers are Sanguine; some are masquerading under a torrent of nervous chatter. Understanding this mask will better equip us to minister to that hurting heart and will keep us from pulling away when our friend genuinely needs love and wise counsel.

The mask of the clown never quite seems true even though a casual observer will not understand why he senses this person to be phony. It takes an effort to play a role God never intended us to fill.

Jane came to CLASS elegantly dressed and meticulously groomed. When any funny line was given she would respond loudly and clap her hands. As I observed her I sensed her enthusiasm was forced and there was probably some masking of her real personality. During a break time I asked to see her Personality Profile which was scored half Melancholy and half Sanguine. I said nothing about the totals but asked her about her childhood relationships. She explained that her mother was Melancholy and frequently depressed. The continual gloom weighed heavily upon Jane and when her mother cried she would cry also. She was so frightened that her mother might get upset again that she made a pledge, "I will never do anything that will make my mother cry."

Her Sanguine father would often send her to her mother's

room to cheer her up. "See if you can say anything that will make your mother smile. If you succeed, I'll give you a dollar." Jane, in trying to please her father and cheer up her mother, developed funny things to do and say. She tried to do only what would make her mother happy, and she never dared express how she really felt.

As Jane told this story, I could see that she was innately Melancholy like her mother and felt deeply for her mother's moods even though as a child she was frightened by the crying. Because of her circumstances, Jane put on a Sanguine mask and tried her best to make her mother smile, encouraged by dollar bills from her father.

As an adult her personality shifted in different situations. She was ill at ease with people and frequently depressed when alone. Whenever anyone was sick or discouraged she would don the mask of the clown and endeavor to cheer them up. She was married to a Sanguine like her father who fled when she was depressed and told her to "cut it out" when she tried to be funny and failed. Her daughter was the one bright light of her erratic life, and she suddenly saw she was producing a confused replica of herself in her child, calling her in when she needed a lift out of her own depression as her mother had done to her.

Because Jane was intelligent and wanted God's will for her life, she was able to work on her personality without further counsel. She began to emphasize her Melancholy strengths and stopped her unnatural bursts of phony entertainment. Even more important was the freedom she gave her daughter to be herself and stop having to be her mother's dose of "happiness pills" as she had been for her mother.

What a blessing it is when we are able to see ourselves as we were meant to be and are willing to break the cycle of artificial habits. As with any problem in life, we have to see what we're doing that's unnatural before we can make constructive changes.

William Thackeray tells of the depressed patient whose theatrical profession made him wear the mask of the clown covering his true feelings.

Harlequin without his mask is known to present a very sober countenance, and was himself, the story goes, the melancholy patient whom the Doctor advised to go and see Harlequin.[5]

MELANCHOLY MASK

The world's "a stage, where every man must play a part; and mine a sad one."[6]

The Melancholy mask is one of *attempted perfection and frequent pain.* When I was first married and Fred announced he was going to put me on a training program, I was stunned. The Sanguine part of me saw this would be no fun and the Choleric part didn't want to be made over; however, for self-preservation I put on a Melancholy mask of attempted perfection and tried to act out the role Fred wanted me to pursue. I played a part and it was a sad one.

I knew nothing of the four temperaments in those days, and I accepted this unnatural role as the price of being a wife, part of growing up. What a relief it was when I found my first description of a Sanguine and realized my basic personality was acceptable. I didn't have to be serious and sober to be an adult.

Now as I look back on it, I functioned for those first fifteen years of marriage as a split personality. At home I alternated the Melancholy mask with the Phlegmatic pseudosubmission of "Yes, Fred dear," while in public I was myself: directing plays, teaching speech, and being president of women's groups. As soon as I'd walk in the door, the mask would go back on and I'd hide my frivolity until I ventured out again. I was afraid if I looked too happy, Fred might think I was "up to something." I love this little verse that sums me up in my early years of marriage.

> I'll make my Joy a secret thing,
> My face shall wear a mask of care;
> And those who hurt a joy to death,
> Shall never know what sport is there![7]

Those who put the Melancholy mask on as children were often ones with parents who demanded perfection either because they were Melancholy and knew no other way or because their status couldn't accommodate a frisky child. I find this latter masking frequently among pastors' children whose fathers feel their whole ministry depends upon the proper behavior of their children.

One Choleric man told me how his pastor father had insisted

he be a model child, but set the Choleric mother on the task of enforcing the rules. He said, "I always felt like a whipped dog with my tail between my legs. My spirit was broken early, but my repressed anger was boiling beneath the surface. I played the perfect role, and my mother praised me in public but disciplined me harshly at home. I grew up feeling I had no personality, but now I see it was because I was playing a role foreign to my nature. I did things to scuttle my mother's plans, and as an adult, I've had to work at even liking her. When she died suddenly, I was left with a terrible guilt because I never made peace with her."

This dear man is now in therapy trying to resolve the pains of his past and the guilt of his present, neither of which was necessary had his parents had any realization of what changing his nature was going to do to his life.

The Personality Profile of one pastor who came to CLASS came out Melancholy/Phlegmatic. But the twinkle in his eye and the bounce in his step told me he was a Sanguine. As I sat down to talk with him, he asked me about his score and I began to question his childhood behavior. His father was the pastor and his mother the organist. They made him sit in the front row and not wiggle and they both kept a watchful eye during what he remembers as endless church services. The one statement he heard over and over again was, "Don't you dare cause any trouble." Once his father had pinned him up against a flimsy wall in the church men's room and said, "Here's what I'll do to you if you ever cause any trouble." He then smashed his fist into the wall going right through to the ladies' room. "I knew right then I had better not cause trouble."

As he told me this story his eyes got big, his voice gained volume, and he literally bounced up and down in the church pew where we were sitting. Here was a Sanguine man who had been scared out of his wits as a child by a Choleric father who had to appear in perfect control to his parishioners. He had played Melancholy, tried to be perfect, and wondered why he'd never felt comfortable with himself. When I asked him to think of Sanguine-type actions of his childhood, he answered, "I used to go out in the fields and preach to the trees. Would that be Sanguine?"

As we reviewed his life together and saw repeated Sanguine

incidents, he began to cry. "Why did it take me this long to find out who I really am?" Before he left CLASS two days later he thanked me and said, "This freedom I feel is worth a thousand dollars."

Later he told me how his sermons had changed since he found out it was "okay to be funny" and how his people had noticed a big improvement in his preaching.

We will never reach the potential that is within us until we pull off the mask and become the real person God intended us to be.

A Sanguine tour guide from England told me a familiar story. She had married a Melancholy professor who had made her over until she was wearing a Melancholy mask every minute that she wasn't describing the architecture of St. Paul's Cathedral to an appreciative audience. One day he came home and out of the blue stated that she wasn't the fun she used to be. Ultimately he divorced her and even had the nerve to tell her that the new woman had a great sense of humor "like you used to have when I married you."

How often I've heard the pitiful story of a person who puts on an obliging mask for his or her mate only to be cast aside for a copy of the original model.

Divorce frequently changes a person's apparent temperament. If a woman has been held under in marriage, having to wear a false front for survival, divorce often frees her to become herself. If she has been her normal self in marriage and has been cast aside for another woman, she often puts on a Sanguine mask to hide the pain and tries to become a new person who hopefully will be more successful than the last one.

Besides the Melancholy *mask of perfection,* there is the very common Melancholy *mask of pain.* When the Personality Profile comes out with Sanguine strengths and Melancholy weaknesses this is a clue that the person is either a Melancholy wearing a Sanguine mask or a Sanguine that has somewhere along the line put on a mask of pain and become depressed. Phlegmatics and Cholerics may also wear this mask of pain if they have met with severely traumatic situations or have lived in homes where very little love was ever expressed. When a child does not experience love by being held or touched during the formative years of birth to eight, there can be an inner unexplained feeling of rejection even though both parents may be in the home, and this can damage his natural personality for life.

When a child is abused or molested, the victim usually puts on the mask of pain unless he is Choleric enough to push away the pain, deny reality, and forge ahead to become an achiever. The victim usually loses his own feelings and drowns in depression and guilt.

As adults, victims assume they have put these problems behind them and can't understand why the black cloud is always with them.

They are often negative, resentful, and complaining. No matter what people do for them, it is somehow not enough. They frequently have unexplainable physical symptoms such as headaches, body pain, asthma, and allergies. Sometimes in extreme sexual abuse cases they have blocked out the original attack and can't understand why they always feel guilty for something.

Whether the cause was trauma or lack of love, the person wearing the mask of pain needs help in releasing these past problems. For some, sitting down with a patient and compassionate friend who will listen may be enough to peel away the mask. Some may need a pastor or counselor who will work with them over many months. We have seen miraculous results when Lana, or any of her Philippian Ministries counselors, spends a day in searching the memories, praying intensively over the past pains, and healing the hurts through God's almighty power.

Lana tells her own story:

My life is an excellent example of the Melancholy mask. I grew up in a home where well-meaning parents did not know how to express physical affection and were not able to effectively communicate with children. While there was no abuse of any kind, I was left with a deep longing for love, and that need, eventually distorted, drove me to emotional bankruptcy. It turned me into a totally negative child and adult. Those who knew me would have declared me 100 percent Melancholy, at least where all of the weaknesses were concerned. That is a key for discerning the Melancholy mask which expresses itself through the Melancholy weaknesses rather than strengths.

The longing for love which produces the Melancholy facade cannot be overstated for it crushes many of our children and leaves them "licking their wounds" rather than leading productive lives. One who unknowingly wears the Melancholy mask will often show an expression of deep pain, hurt, or deadness in the eyes.

When I was speaking in California, I met a young man who responded to my description of a Melancholy mask. He came to me after I had spoken that evening and described the feeling he had experienced while I was speaking.

He said, "I've had everything a man could ever want in life. I graduated from a large university as an All-American football player. I was the athlete of the decade in that university. I married a Miss Universe. I own my own bank and trust company and am a prosperous man, but I have never been happy.

"When you were sharing your childhood and the Melancholy mask you wore, I found myself five years old again. My dad had lost his temper with me and told me to go out into the woods. He said, 'Don't you ever come back!'

"I was terrified out there alone. I cried and cried. The sun went down and it got very dark, and still no one came. I can't tell you the terror I felt as such a little boy. I knew I'd never see home again.

"At last, late into the night, someone came to rescue me. I guess I'll never forget that night. When you started talking about your childhood, I found myself wandering in those woods again, lost and afraid. I think I've been there all of my life and I wonder if I'll ever come out."

This was a gentleman who wore the Melancholy mask. His life was permeated by the pain of his childhood and the pain was produced by far more than one frightening incident in the woods. Until this man could work through that deep hurt and fear, releasing the accompanying emotion—the world would see him as a Melancholy rather than the Choleric/Sanguine he truly was. And not until then would he be able to leave the prison of his mind and rest in the productive and humorous person God created him to be. What a glorious transformation comes when one can cease striving and find freedom in God's original design for life.

CHOLERIC MASK

"Boldness is a mask for fear however great."[8]

In our modern American society power denotes success. We see magazine articles giving us the secrets to happiness and health, prosperity and wealth. Everybody wants to be somebody and the somebodies all seem to be Choleric. These powerful people are earning their livings by showing people with no power how to get it. The diploma from success courses could well be a Choleric *mask of power*. Unfortunately for many who get caught up in the "Ten Easy Steps from Wimp to Wonderful," a mask is all they have. They don't suddenly acquire a longing for the eighteen-hour work day, and the simple stairway to the stars seems to have no end.

I often talk to Phlegmatic men who have had Choleric masks of power put on them by eager mothers or aggressive wives whose own self-worth will rise proportionately with their husband's income. The man feels he's on a treadmill to nowhere and when he adds up the Personality Profile he is half Choleric and half Phlegmatic and frequently depressed. A Phlegmatic with a Choleric mask and a lack of understanding of the temperaments is a very discouraged person. He's trying to be dynamic without the drive, he's trying to be aggressive when his nature is passive, and he doesn't have a clue as to why he's killing himself and not becoming president. What relief comes over the Phlegmatic when he finds out he doesn't have to be a Choleric. He can drop the phony back-slapping personality that has turned people off and become the pleasant, agreeable, and witty peacemaker he was designed to be.

Bill came to CLASS as an aggressive Choleric who was depressed. In counseling we found he was a Sanguine who had been told by his father that real men were serious and high achievers. He tried to become what he thought he ought to be, and even though he was popular in the family business, he knew he wasn't what his father wanted. After listening to our teaching on the temperaments, he suddenly saw he was a depressed Sanguine struggling to keep on a Choleric *mask of power*.

Alicia came thinking she was Choleric but not showing any of the true signs of overt leadership. In talking with her we found a Melancholy girl whose Phlegmatic mother had been sickly and whose Sanguine father had taken off with a healthier model. Alicia called him her "runaway" father and branded him irresponsible. Because there was no one in charge at home, she had to take control and hold things together for her mother and younger sister. By practicing the actions of a nature not her own, she became an obsessively controlling adult and had a constant fear of losing the control she'd worked to develop.

Alicia married a Sanguine/Choleric man, the opposite of her true temperament and they battled for control. She was not about to give up until she got her first glimpse of the four personalities at CLASS and began to see the Choleric mask she had been wearing. Once she realized where her unnatural Choleric had come from and why she didn't need to fight for control any more, she was able to relax and slowly become the easy-going person God had intended her to be.

Besides the *mask of power* that makes any temperament appear to be an ill-at-ease Choleric, there is the related *mask of anger*. Any person who represses anger over a long period of time can appear to be Choleric when the cork blows and a temper tantrum surprises those in view. Often a Phlegmatic who keeps all his feelings under wraps will put on a Choleric *mask of anger* when he sits behind the wheel of a car. He can vent his anger on other drivers and shake his fist at traffic lights. When he gets to work, he often puts the mask away with his coat and doesn't put it on again until he hits the freeway at night.

Often we spot a Choleric mask when a person has Choleric weaknesses and strengths of another type, indicating valid strengths paired with controlled anger. This person may be working under extreme stress where he is helpless to do anything about it or he may have had a repressive childhood causing him to fight for survival. As he grew up the anger produced impatience, bossiness, and an argumentative nature that so overshadowed his strengths that he appeared to be Choleric. Extreme cases like this would be the person who handles his emotions at work and then one day murders his wife. Everyone is in shock as he seemed like such a nice man. Rapists and molesters are often low-key people who are carrying inside them the residue of an abusive childhood that comes out in violent acts.

Lana tells of a charming performer who came to CLASS.

Brian had taken the Personality Profile and scored about 80 percent Choleric and 20 percent Sanguine. We found he did not know his real father but his mother had remarried when he was five years old. His stepfather was mentally ill and would sometimes threaten to kill the boy's mother, occasionally even getting a gun and aiming it at her.

The little boy's response was to pick up a stick or rock or gun in order to protect his mother. He was drawn into the adult world of emotions and responsibilities through the sick relationship of his parents, yet he derived none of the benefits of that world, for when he would try to protect his mother, the stepfather would beat him unmercifully.

The product of such a distorted childhood is not hard to imagine. As Brian became a teenager, he had to find a place to express this terrible churning inside of him, this repressed rage and sense of injustice. He found release on the athletic field where his aggressiveness knew no limit, causing him to get his letter in virtually every sport the school offered.

It was not until this man faced himself honestly and released this inner rage through counseling and prayer, that he was able to rest in his real and God-given personality. Once the pain was poured off, a new temperament was discovered. This man was 80 percent Sanguine and only 20 percent Choleric. What freedom came when he understood what God had created him to be! His response? "I can't tell you how many questions this answers for me. I feel a peace I can't begin to describe."

Because Brian is now a friend of our CLASS family, I can joyfully attest to the changes in him which have also produced a restoration of a shaky marriage. Now, both his career and his ministry for the Lord are on the rise.

Many times we have found pastors who had repressed anger because they had been pushed into being pastors by their families and had not known how to say no. They were all godly men, but were in the wrong calling. One explained to me, "My mother told me from the time I was little, 'We've had six generations of preachers in this family and you are it.'" She nicknamed him "Rev" as a child, and he seemed to have no options in life.

Two of the pastors, when they realized why they had physical manifestations of their controlled anger, decided to leave the clergy for more appropriate careers. Another, after freeing himself from having to be a pastor, decided, now that he had a choice, that's really what he wanted to be. In all three cases the pent-up anger has been relieved, and the men feel at ease with themselves and are in better health.

PHLEGMATIC MASK

The words of his mouth were smoother than butter, but war was in his heart: his words were softer than oil, yet were they drawn swords (Ps. 55:21, KJV).

The Phlegmatic mask is often the result of someone who gives up on life and becomes apathetic, deciding it's easier to mouth agreeable words than to fight for what's right. Cholerics who can't win in a given situation may put on a Phlegmatic *mask of peace* and pretend they don't care. Sanguines who marry mates who no longer think they're cute may turn Phlegmatic at home and save their humor for social occasions. Melancholies who sense no one cares just won't bother to even communicate any more.

A Choleric girl told me she had two Choleric parents who so overwhelmed her as she was growing up that she realizes now she played Phlegmatic "just to stay alive." She remembers "There were no additional opinions needed, and I was raised by the saying children are to be seen and not heard. I didn't know I had anything to say until I went away to college." Even though she had no understanding of the temperaments, she married a Phlegmatic, the opposite of her natural Choleric, and soon found herself having to make decisions for both of them. After hearing me speak, she suddenly saw her personality pattern and later wrote me, "Now that I'm working on removing my mask I shift back and forth. When my Phlegmatic husband wants to stay home my Choleric says 'I'll go anyway,' but then I sink back to Phlegmatic and mutter 'What's the use and who cares anyway.'"

A teenager whose mother told me he was Phlegmatic, asked if I'd do the Personality Profile with him when I was visiting in his home. The more we conversed the more Sanguine he became. I asked him why his mother felt he was Phlegmatic, and he replied, "My whole family is Sanguine/Choleric, and they are all talking at the same time and bossing each other around. It's a lot easier to keep quiet, play Phlegmatic, and stay out of trouble."

A Melancholy doctor explained, "By the time I get home at night I have no heart to buck my Sanguine wife's ideas, ridiculous though most of them are, so I keep my mouth shut, nod often, and say 'yes dear' once an hour whether I agree or not. I guess you'd call that playing Phlegmatic."

One evening I went out to dinner with a family who seated me next to their twenty-five-year-old son who had moved home after a divorce. "We can't get a thing out of him. Maybe he'll talk to you." Once they'd given me my assignment, they all started talking at their end of the table. I asked the young man how he felt about himself. For over an hour he told me his life story. His parents were both professionals, one Choleric/Sanguine, one Choleric/Melancholy, and as long as he could remember they'd always worked. "They always gave me everything I needed, but they never had time to listen. Now that they're trying to pump me for information, I'm not going to tell them anything."

Later his mother asked, "What did you ever do to make him talk so much? We can't get a thing out of him?" As I opened my mouth to answer her question, she changed the subject, and I could see why this sensitive Melancholy boy had not bothered to share his feelings.

Who really cared?

Often when children grow up with scrapping parents, they take on the role of peacemaker or mediator no matter what their own personality was meant to be.

Lana tells of a girl she counseled with this type of background.

Sherry came to me several months after taking the Personality Profile and she was very confused. The only temperament she thought might adequately describe her was the Phlegmatic, and yet she had many checks in the other columns as well.

I couldn't come up with a logical answer until a year later when she had thought her life over and she realized that she had indeed taken on the false responsibility for not only her parents' happiness but also for keeping peace in the home. This need had permeated every area of her life and had masked her true temperament which was Sanguine/Choleric. Once she was able to reject that unnatural sense of false responsibility and stop being all things to all people, Sherry's real personality began to clearly emerge. The fun-loving Sanguine part of her expressed itself more freely and the Choleric became obvious as she began to verbalize her need for order and for quick responsiveness to her leadership.

Once more we see the results of finding one's true self and removing undesired pretenses. Free to be what God created her to be,

Sherry is now a joy and delight. Her spiritual and emotional growth is marked by a new reality of her true strengths and weaknesses as the distortions have been properly put away.

There is a fine line between the Phlegmatic *mask of peace* and the one of *apathy* when the person gives up on life and just doesn't care any more. Carried to an extreme this person could become catatonic, unable to express himself at all.

One young girl who had developed severe emotional problems told me that she was two different personalities. Because her home life with an abusive stepfather and weeping mother was so traumatic, she had learned to literally tune out and shut down any feelings or emotion. This repression had caused her headaches, and she only felt good when she was away from home. In going over her Personality Profile with her, I found she was a Choleric who had put on the Phlegmatic *mask of apathy* and was out of touch with reality.

Her comment on our meeting was, "As you talked I realized all these years I had been covering my true God-given personality with a Phlegmatic mask. That's the reason I was struggling with two people. Now that I know this, I have taken home the real me, I'm claiming my true personality and celebrating the freedom. My family won't know how to deal with me, they haven't seen me for so long, but as I explain the change, I hope they'll learn to love and accept me."

Since Lana first started teaching the masking concept at CLASS, we have had hundreds of people who have found out why they didn't know who they were. What a joy it is to take off the mask and find the real you underneath. How exciting it is to me when I receive a letter like this one that says, "You've just saved a life—mine."

Two months have passed since you presented CLASS here in the Seattle area. Little did I realize how transforming that experience would be. My parting comment to you that snowy day was "You've just saved a life. Mine." And those words are a living testimony daily. How desperate I was—in need of unlocking the prison of myself hidden behind a concrete mask that covered me from head to toe. Your material on temperaments revealed gaping discrepancies. Once shattered by truth, the REAL ME GOD CREATED is slowly emerg-

ing. . . . A miracle continues to unfold bringing healing and whole-
ness. . . .   God Bless, MarVel Berglund

For Further Study, Thought, and Action

In Psalm 51:6 David states, "You desire truth in the inner
parts" (NIV), and in Psalm 19:12 he asks, "Who can discern his
errors? Cleanse thou me from secret faults" (KJV).

As we meditate over these verses, let's realize that God does
want us to know who we really are. He wants us to discern that
original child within us and get rid of any masks or pretenses
we may have been hiding behind.

In reading this chapter, has the Lord shown you any masks
you've been wearing? What are they? When did you first adopt
a behavior pattern that was not how you really felt inside? Can
you see how this mask warped your original personality? Do
you or any family members wear the

Sanguine mask of Personality?
Sanguine mask of the Clown?
Melancholy mask of Perfection?
Melancholy mask of Pain?
Choleric mask of Power?
Choleric mask of Anger?
Phlegmatic mask of Peace?
Phlegmatic mask of Apathy?

If you are doing a group study, review these different masks
noting that the second of each type is the more serious. The
Sanguine mask of personality—a phony charm—is insincere but
carried to an extreme the individual trying to play the fool becomes ludicrous. The Melancholy mask of perfection may start
as the only way to get along with a demanding parent or mate,
but eventually the person is so full of pain and rejection that
he no longer can see himself objectively at all. The Choleric power
may be a learned response to situations that demanded decisions,
but the mask of anger is like a cork pushed down into a bottle:
under heat it may explode. The Phlegmatic mask of peace never
seems to bother others, but if it becomes a lifelong cover up, it
will lead to feelings of apathy where real emotion is totally suppressed. An example of this anesthesia over feelings comes from
a girl who had a nervous breakdown, was put in a mental hospital,

and played the game she called "I'm ok" just to get out. She wrote, "When I started coming apart at the seams, I put on a mask. In counseling I couldn't open up, share, or be honest. I've done this so long I pretend with everybody. I've developed the attitude, 'I don't care whether you understand me any more.' I have no feelings at all."

How about you? Do you have feelings you can't express? Start sharing with someone today. Pull off your mask and find out who you really are.

PERSONALITY MASKS	
Personality Clown	Power Anger
Peace Apathy	Perfection Pain

Oh what a tangled web we weave,
When first we practice to deceive. [9]

PART II

UNCOVER YOUR ROOT AND PROTECT YOUR FRUIT

UNCOVER:

To expose to view by removing some form of covering.

As you look at your family history to see what personality traits you have inherited, you will uncover your roots and expose to view some of the positive qualities that have been passed down to you and some of the manipulations and controls that have shaped your Personality Tree. By taking off the masks that you may have developed for self-preservation throughout the years, you will see yourself as God originally intended you to be, you can lay down the burdens of the past, you can throw off the covers that have hindered your progress, and you can be free to spread out your roots.

. . . be as a tree planted by the waters . . . that spreadeth out her roots by the river.

—Jeremiah 17:8, KJV

❦ 7 ❦

What Is a
Personality Tree?

*The trees in the street are old trees
used to living with people,
Family-trees that remember
your grandfather's name.* [1]

Throughout the Bible the Hebrew people show a continuing interest in genealogy, family ancestry and history. The pattern of their past played an important part in their present. They referred to themselves as from the tribe of Judah or Reuben or one of the other twelve tribes of Israel. The apostle Paul often mentioned his rootstock from Benjamin. The New Testament opens with the genealogy of Christ, and in the back of study Bibles, we find family trees of some of the greats of the faith.

When I got married in 1953, my generation, having come out of the Depression, worked hard at forgetting our past. We were sick of old furniture, and we wanted to put the pangs of poverty behind us. The word *ethnic* had not come into vogue, and people with obviously "foreign" names were changing them to Smith and Johnson. We wanted to send our European stock away and become affluent Americans. My mother and I threw out several sets of washbowls and pitchers that reminded us of pre-plumbing days and I'll never forget the look of unbelief that came over her as we saw a similar set on sale in an antique shop for over one hundred dollars.

In the last few years there has been a renewed interest in discovering our roots. The ME generation decided *me* wasn't

enough and turned to *them. Roots* became a bestseller and served
as a catalyst for research of relatives. Genealogists sprouted up
and family trees began to flourish.

Ethnic neighborhoods dared to label themselves. And dressing
as if you had the lead in a Russian folk opera became chic. Conti-
nental cuisine was chopped up in chunks, and one buffet could
easily include Turkish melon, Swedish meatballs, Armenian
crackers, French bread, Belgian endive, Mexican frijoles, Irish
potatoes, Spanish paella, and Hungarian goulash followed by Ital-
ian *gelati,* English trifle, Danish pastries, and oriental fortune
cookies whose hidden message might well say, "Eating this dinner
may prove to be a big mistake."

Cajun food is the current rage, giving casual cooks a new line
of excuses for errors. The next time you forget the poor poultry
until the oven is in flames, serve it proudly as Blackened Chicken,
and you'll have a hit on your hands.

With all this interest in our roots, you may have already done
a family tree for yourself or perhaps you hired some certified
genealogist to do "tomb rubbings" of your royal ancestors. For
the last twenty years I have had a family tree painted on a wall
of my home. I gathered pictures of each family member and
hung them on the branches framed in gold. An ancestor fitly
framed is like an apple of gold.

I remember at first that Fred's mother didn't have time to
hunt up pictures of any of the dead relatives, so I proceeded
with the artwork and created a heavily lopsided tree in the foyer
full of Chapmans and MacDougalls. At the first sight of this
tree with bare branches on Fred's side, Mother Littauer gasped,
"You didn't tell me what you were doing was going to amount
to something!"

Within days she had collected up a veritable heritage including
Ludwig and Louisa *von Littauer,* meaning "from Lithuania."
These new ancestors balanced out the tree which I still have
in my current home. My children have grown up knowing where
they came from and what each ancestor looked like.

What is the difference between a family tree and a personality
tree? The first has pictures and biographical research while the
latter adds the temperament traits to the best of your ability
and assumptions.

I first thought up this idea when Fred's Choleric mother took the Personality Profile and came out Phlegmatic. How could a dynamic, controlling woman who was constantly seeking affirmation of how much she had done for you, possibly see herself as Phlegmatic? I was confused. How could a competent Choleric, a superachiever who graduated from Cornell University at nineteen, a businesswoman whose walk and talk exhibit confidence and strength possibly come out Phlegmatic?

Several times she has come to hear Fred and me teach *Personality Plus* and each time she scores Phlegmatic. Once when we divided the audience in four sections, she chose the Phlegmatic group. Fred went over and said, "Mother, you are Choleric. You don't belong in this group." She slammed her fist on the back of the pew in front of her and vehemently replied, "I'm here because I'm Phlegmatic, and this is where I'm going to stay, and you aren't going to move me!" Does that sound like a Phlegmatic?

I remember saying to Fred, "Your mother has less idea of who she really is than anyone I've ever met."

Once she left my home to go to a grandchild's graduation where the parents were divorced. The two parents had predetermined there would be no controversy, but they were concerned that Mother would "stir something up." She attended with the conviction that she was needed as a peacemaker "in case there's any trouble."

How could a Choleric, who would by her mere entry into a room of relaxed people bring them to their feet, possibly think she was a peacemaker?

This contrast in her behavior and her perception of herself led me to think back to when I first met her. I remember standing in the Littauer library wearing my purple knit dress with matching shoes, purple paper violets behind one ear, and a gray kidskin cape I had bought in Filene's basement for ninety-nine dollars. By Haverhill's standards I was put together, but I faded back a step when Mrs. Littauer came sweeping in the front door wearing a full-length mink coat. Do you know what happens to a gray kidskin cape when it stands next to a full-length mink? It turns into what it really is: dead goats. I stood there trying to look chic and realizing I had, as my mother would say, "more than met my match."

From this moment on, I could see this elegant lady was firmly in control of every situation. Fred's Phlegmatic father had died a few years before, and she ran the household with authority and style. Her sons stood up when she entered the room, held her chair as she was seated, and ate only after she had lifted her fork. She kept everyone motivated to good deeds. She plumped pillows the moment your seat left the sofa, and she gave instructions to everyone as if we were all in first grade.

On one of my visits I was to spend the day alone at Orienta Beach Club while everyone else went to work. I had been there several times before and knew the way. "To make sure"—one of her Choleric expressions—Mrs. Littauer drew me a map and explained in detail what color building was on the corner at each turn and taught me the difference between North and South. I listened patiently while wondering how dumb she thought I was. As I was leaving, she called out, "Remember to turn left on the Post Road, not right or you'll overshoot the club." Then she added, as I soon learned she always did, "I've put my phone number on the bottom of the map for when you get lost."

When any one of her sons would be driving to New York City, she would tell them how to go, over and over again, even though they had been doing it since they were sixteen. One day Fred and I were taking Grandpa to the city and Mother Littauer made it very clear we should "take the Cross County, not Hutchison River." Since Fred is also part Choleric, he decided to go down the Hutchison River Parkway in spite of what she'd said. As we drove defiantly along, a patrolman pulled us over for speeding, and we were taken to the police station where Grandpa paid for the ticket. When we returned that night, Grandpa told Fred's mother about our troubles on the Hutchison River Parkway. She immediately looked at Fred and said, "What were you doing on the Hutchison River? I told you to take the Cross Country. If you'd gone where I told you to go, this wouldn't have happened."

Even though I didn't know about the different personalities then, I learned that if Fred's mother said, "turn left," I turned left. Cholerics constantly give instructions to "the dummies," and they are usually right.

After Fred and I were married and Mother Littauer would come to visit, I was shocked and hurt that she would dive into cleaning my house with a vengeance. Once she spent a full day on the stove, scrubbing each rod on the oven racks with Brillo. One February when she had cleaned everything imaginable, I came home to find she had brought in all the deflated pool rafts that had been folded up on the patio for the winter and laid them out on the kitchen counters where she was hard at work scrubbing them.

I used to get so crushed at her cleaning campaigns that I would polish for weeks ahead of her arrival so there would be nothing she could find to do. She didn't seem to notice and as she repolished shining shower doors, I would withdraw insulted. Once I began to understand the different personalities after fifteen years of marriage, I saw Mother Littauer in a new light: a Choleric person whose self-worth was wrapped up in accomplishing tasks and who couldn't relax. As I realized that, for her, work was fun and that doing nothing was a horrible waste of available manpower, I could accept her constant cleaning as her way of being a positive house guest and not as a criticism of my housekeeping. I stopped dreading her arrival and left the kitchen floor in need of a powerful waxing.

The last time she cleaned the stove I rewarded her by opening the top oven doors which automatically put on the light showing up the gleaming oven racks and I placed a potted philodendron on the top shelf to draw attention to the cleanest stove in town.

What a difference it makes in our attitude when we understand the other person's personality and know why they behave as they do.

Now I can see how Mother could go into Howard Johnson's on a rainy day and bring the whole restaurant to attention. My shy, Phlegmatic/Melancholy sister-in-law Nancy recalls how they entered the restaurant together. Mother saw there were two empty seats at the counter, one at one end and one at the other. Without a moment's hesitation, she picked up a knife from a man who was already eating and clicked loudly on his glass. As all eyes turned in astonishment, Mother Littauer announced, "My daughter-in-law is a little weak and she needs me to stay beside her. Would all of you please stand up and move yourselves down one seat so we can sit together at this end of the counter?"

Nancy watched in humiliation as each patron dutifully arose; shifted plates, silver, and glasses down one spot; gathered rain coats and umbrellas; and relocated without objection.

As Nancy collapsed in the newly vacated seat, Mother clapped her on the back and said proudly, "I did it for you, dearie."

As I thought over this Choleric woman, I truly wondered what ever gave her the idea that she was a peacemaker!

This question led me to a new study of the four personalities taking our ancestors into consideration. What are we really like? Are some of us playing a role written early in life by other authors?

Have some of us been wearing a mask for so long we think that's who we really are? What about you?

Do you have an underlying doubt as to who you are? Does your mother have a confused self-concept? Is your mate in an identity crisis? Start answering these questions by tracing your family back and seeing at what point your natural personality was turned in a different direction.

THE LITTAUER PERSONALITY TREE

As I reflected on Fred's grandparents and gathered information on them, I came up with a fascinating profile. Richard Oelkers was a self-made Melancholy/Choleric. His parents immigrated from Germany to New York, and his tailor father died when young Dick was fourteen. As the oldest of the family, he went to work to support the others. By long hours and extreme diligence, he fulfilled the American dream of rags to riches and never ceased to preach the work ethic. He married Maria Louisa Schissel and together they built a successful chain of millinery stores in New York. Maria Louisa was Sanguine/Choleric—she wanted everything done her way, but she wanted to have fun doing it. Grandpa wanted everything done his way, but it should be serious, purposeful, and not taken lightly.

I have learned that when two Cholerics are married, they do one of two things: either one puts on a Phlegmatic mask and plays a submissive role or they choose to fight. Grandpa and Grandma chose to fight. They scrapped for control constantly but seemed to thrive on controversy as is so typical of Cholerics.

Grandpa would today be called a workaholic and Grandma was a forerunner of women's lib. She "went to business" each day and had little interest in domesticity. A family joke was that Grandma's most complicated culinary achievement was three-layered Jello. Grandma's flair for glamor led her to change her name to fit the Hollywood image of the time. She went from German Maria Louisa to a French version, Marie Louise and later hyphenated it to Mari-Luise.

Fred's mother was born into this feisty family and was called Pearl Louise, a compromise name that neither one of the parents really liked. Shortly thereafter Grandpa won some money on a horse named Marita and he had the birth certificate changed to reflect his good fortune. Grandma liked the name better, but couldn't let anyone think she had given in to Grandpa so she always claimed she had found "Marita" in a romantic novel she had been reading.

Later when Fred's mother Marita gave birth to her first son, she named him Frederick Jerome Littauer, Jr., after her husband. The grandparents went into a Choleric tear and insisted the name be changed to Richard Oelkers Littauer after Grandpa. Threatened by disinheritance the new parents hastily made the change, and it wasn't until the second son, my husband, that the Phlegmatic father was allowed to name one after himself.

From the time Fred's mother was eleven, she ran the household. Her innate Choleric nature gave her the ability to take charge and raise her young brother, but when she was in her parents' presence, she played a submissive role. It was either fight or switch. Their word was law and they became as close to royalty as I've ever seen.

When I first met the Littauer-Oelkers family, I was amazed at the regal control which the grandparents had over everyone. We would all be sitting in the parlor and Mother would look up to see Grandma making a dramatic appearance down the circular staircase. Mother would rise to her feet, gesture toward the stairs, and sing out, "The Queen is here!" We would all stand and applaud as she made her entrance. Even her daytime dresses were dotted with sequins or beads, her neckline pulled low by a heavy diamond brooch and her fingers so bejeweled she could hardly lift them for her grand gestures.

What made Grandma's theatrics acceptable was her Sanguine wit and an occasional wink that let us see even *she* knew she was an act—but wasn't it fun! As Grandma stood centerstage, Grandpa lined up the grandchildren and with a brief clear message on the value of money, he would hand out quarters to each child who would kiss him. No kissey—no money. When my Lauren was little she refused to kiss Grandpa because "his face is prickly." He not only refused to give her a quarter, but he went into a sulking depression for the rest of the day.

I thought back over what Mother Littauer's childhood must have been like. Grandma saying, "You will do it my way and you will enjoy it." Grandpa saying, "You will do it my way and you will not laugh about it."

She had to work hard and be quietly obedient, she had to be the buffer between their Choleric tempers, she had to be serious and deep for Grandpa and yet imitate the Sanguine humor to keep her mother happy.

I can remember a visit to the Oelkers' apartment when they were both over ninety. Grandma sat at the head of the table waving hands heaped with diamonds at Mother who quickly responded in a servant's attitude. Grandma, just a touch senile, kept sending for the mythical chauffeur to take her to the ball. Grandpa, disgusted with her histrionics, tried to quiet her down, an effort which only made her more anxious to leave for the ball.

My husband, assuming a French accent, started charming Grandma by pretending to be the chauffeur. He kissed Grandma's hand and on up her arm while saying sweet nothings in pseudo French. Grandma giggled like a school girl and quickly fell in love with the "French chauffeur."

Grandma's memory at that point in her nineties lasted about two minutes, and she constantly asked us who we were. Because of this inability to know her own children, Grandma surprised us all when Fred walked in the next morning for breakfast and Grandma looked up with a radiant smile of recognition and exclaimed, "The French chauffeur is back!"

While Grandma was ever dramatic and the queen in her self-constructed castle to the very end, Grandpa was the hard pragmatist constantly commanding the real people around him. One day when Fred's mother was seventy-two she asked Grandpa if it would be all right if she went to the bank. He said, "No, you stay right here."

She replied, "Certainly, Daddy dear," and did not leave.

Now let's analyze this family situation. We have a Choleric daughter born of two Choleric parents. What options do two or more Cholerics have? Fight or submit. Grandpa and Grandma fought; their daughter gave in and played Phlegmatic. She became all things to both people: Grandma's happy servant, Grandpa's serious business partner and a buffer between the two of them as they fluctuated between romance and reality.

No wonder when she analyzed herself she came out Phlegmatic. She was the peacemaker, the mediator, the administrator. She had to be patient, keep her true feelings hidden, and be an all-purpose person. When she took the Personality Profile, she perceived herself as she was trained to be as a child. She looked at the words and resumed the daughter role she played in her parents' lives until they died at ninety-seven apiece.

What happens to a Choleric child who has to suppress her true feelings? What type of a mate does she choose? Does her Phlegmatic role make her marry a Choleric?

As Lana Bateman and I have observed, we have found that people usually seek out the opposite of their true temperament even if it has been successfully masked for years. If the individual is a "closet Choleric" he will probably marry a gentle Phlegmatic and then take over with a vengeance. The wedding ceremony is like taking the cork out of a bottle. Out shoots the natural personality which takes over in the extreme to make up for all those unnatural years under pressure.

Fred's mother married a quiet, easy-going Phlegmatic, the son of a wealthy silk-merchant. Before long he was brought into the Oelkers' business, Bargain Bazaar, where he served dutifully under the three Cholerics. Fred remembers little of his father except that he hardly ever spoke up and didn't attend the athletic events in which Fred participated.

Fred's natural temperament is Melancholy/Choleric like his grandfather and the sensitive part of him was frequently hurt because as the middle child of five, he was too young to get the privileges and too old to get the attention. Childhood movies show him crying frequently, and he was called "Lala" for his many tears.

Every time his Choleric part would try to win, he would either be ignored and thus become depressed, or thwarted and become angry. Since his family was deeply involved in a cult that worships happiness, both depression and anger were totally unacceptable emotions in his childhood.

Frequently he and his mother disagreed and she always won. Her parents had always been victorious over her. Wasn't it her turn now?

She once told me Fred was her worst child. "He always bucked everything I told him to do."

Fred tried to be himself but that didn't work, so he put on a Sanguine mask as a teenager. He became the loudest boy in every group and tried on dirty jokes for size, an effort rewarded by the nickname of Filthy Fred. He practiced fancy dives so that each time he went out on the board everyone would look up and watch him plunge into the pool.

What happens when someone tries to be something he isn't? When a serious Melancholy tries to be the life-of-the-party, people look up and say, "Who does he think he is?" The answer is, "He has no idea!" How many confused teens I talk to today who have no idea who they are, who have tried to be what their parents wanted when even their parents couldn't agree on a mutual goal.

How helpful it is to understand these basic personalities and know who we are. Only then is there any hope we can help our children in their insecurities.

Because Fred felt emotionally neglected at home, although he was physically well-provided for, he was constantly seeking attention and reading any rebuff as a rejection. He tried tears, athletic prowess, and a Sanguine mask, but none brought him the love and sense of approval he longed for. When I asked why he put his Sanguine mask away, he thought back for a moment and then replied, "When I realized it wasn't going over well."

In his relations with his mother, nothing went over well but dutiful obedience. Since he loved her dearly and wanted to please her, he learned in his late teens to agree with her and keep his opinions to himself. He put away his Choleric desire for control and played Phlegmatic with his mother who responded well to his new submissive spirit.

While Fred was attending the University of Miami, his father died and Fred was the son available to return and take over the male responsibilities of the home.

In order to show compassion for his mother and avoid conflict, he continued in a peace-keeping role through college and a brief stint in the army. When I appeared on the scene just before Fred was discharged, I saw him as the strong, silent type. He was extremely respectful to his mother, always calling her "Mother-dear," and I was impressed with how he put her needs before his own.

I remember the weekend I went down to visit and we had planned to go into New York City. At breakfast Mother announced, "Fred, today you will cane two chairs." I had no idea what caning a chair meant, but I learned as I sat all day watching Fred pull cords through chair seats. Fred's mother's wish seemed to be his command.

I expected this dutiful spirit would carry over into marriage. Had I understood the four basic temperaments then I would have assumed Fred to be Phlegmatic (agreeable peacemaker) and Melancholy (deep, thoughtful, and introspective) and myself to be Sanguine (life-of-the-party) and Choleric (let's get this show on the road.)

Surely a marriage made in heaven!

For Further Study, Thought, and Action

On the next page is the Littauer half of our family tree. As you record the husband's half of your tree, first write their names under each leaf and then insert the personality combination in each leaf. If you don't know what each ancestor was, ask questions.

Was he optimistic or pessimistic?

Was he controlling or passive?

Was he fun-loving or serious?

When looking at any given project did he want to talk about it? get to work on it? think about it? observe others doing it?

By asking questions such as these, you will be able to at least guess at what each person's personality was meant to be. Copy this tree into the notebook you've been keeping.

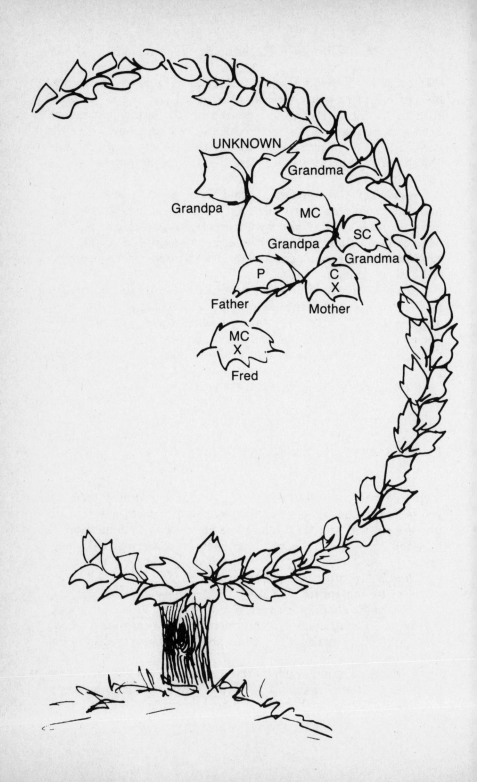

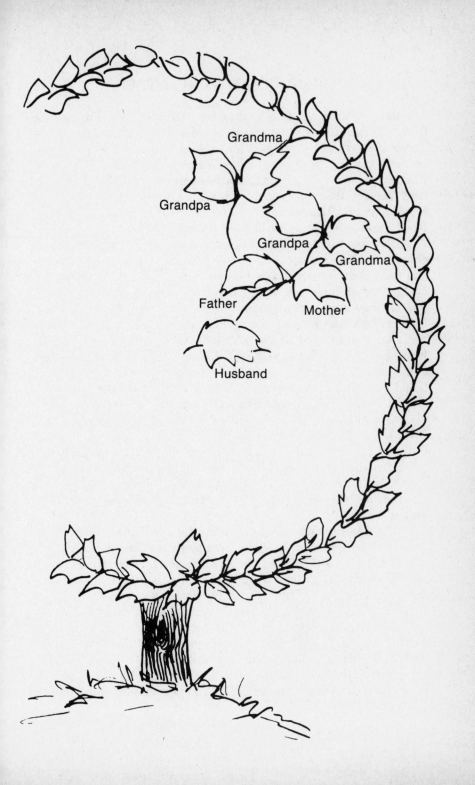

THE CHAPMAN FAMILY TREE

Today we often hear the expression "Here's where I'm coming from." Taken literally, we will all be able to understand ourselves better if we take the time to go back and find out where we're actually coming from. My father Walter Chapman was born in England, son of Thomas, the harness-maker, and Mariah, who died when Walter was fourteen and his brother Arthur was still a small child. Thomas moved the remaining family to Exter, New Hampshire, and my father became mother to his brother. His Sanguine/Choleric temperament gave him the ability to take charge and the humor to make the best of difficult situations. His formal education stopped when he was sixteen, but his love of the English language and history and his keen sense of politics and oratory kept him a student of the mind forever.

I remember as a child sitting next to the arch-shaped Zenith radio with my father as we both listened to Winston Churchill, Franklin Delano Roosevelt, Alf Landon, Wendell Wilkie and James Michael Curley (mayor of Boston who was convicted of fraud, ran for governor from jail, won the election and pardoned himself). Although Curley's honesty was frequently in question, he was a master orator who freely quoted Shakespeare and the Bible with equal ease. At the conclusion of each Curley broadcast Father would say, "Always listen to him, but never vote for him."

On my maternal side I remember my grandmother Florence Ann Conrad, a Phlegmatic/Melancholy milliner who sighed a lot. She had married James Ellis MacDougall, a Choleric carriage-maker.

Katie Florence MacDougall, my mother and their third child was born in Dartmouth, Nova Scotia, prematurely, with teeth and no fingernails, and was kept alive on the oven door which served as an incubator. When she was a few months old, the family moved to the States and continued to grow until there was Annie, Sadie, Katie, Willie, Ruthie, Jeanie, and Donnie.

While Grandma baked bread, preserved pickles, sewed all the clothes by hand, and made Easter bonnets, Papa kept a tight control on his brood of children, similar to the lead in the play *Life with Father*. When the five o'clock whistle blew on the roof of Judson's Carriage Factory in Merrimac, Massachusetts, the

MacDougall children ran from all over town to get home before Papa did or get a licking.

Music was the central core of family interest. Annie wrote poetry which Sadie, the pianist and organist, set to music. Katie played both violin and cello, Willie the cornet, Ruthie and Jeanie violin, and Donnie sang "Asleep in the Deep" and "The Lost Chord." They had their own chamber music ensemble. Sadie and Katie took advanced studies in Boston and later opened a studio together where they taught music. Their recitals included an orchestra of pupils with my mother, Katie, as the conductor.

Annie, Sadie, and Katie all married men about twenty years older than they were—father images, men who were about the same age as the girls' diminutive mother.

Katie was often sickly and was so frail and consumptive at the time of her wedding that the honeymoon was scheduled for the White Mountains where she could breathe cool, clear air. Walter, who had been a controlling adult since he was fourteen, became her new father and enjoyed protecting his delicate Phlegmatic/Melancholy bride.

By the time I was four and my brother James was a baby, the Depression had set in and money was scarce. Four years later when Ron arrived, I overheard Mother ask, "Will there be enough money to feed him?"

Each night when my father counted up the cash from the day's sales in our little Riverside Variety Store, my mother would sigh and worry.

Each morning at breakfast she would start with "Another day, another dollar." There was always another dollar when it was needed, but I grew up with the underlying fear that there might not be any money next week.

Another concern I had was my mother's health. When she had to go to the doctor's, I would accompany her on the bus. My father's last words would be, "You take care of your mother. Do you hear?" I heard what he said and what the doctor said as he gave me the instructions. "She needs to drink a half pint of heavy cream each day to put some meat on her bones. See that she takes three of these pills a day for her nerves. You make sure that she does it. Do you hear?"

Mother gagged on the heavy cream so I whipped it up and

put it on top of everything imaginable. I kept a mental record of when she took her pills and how often she ate as I felt responsible for her health.

I doted on my little brothers, protected them, helped with their homework, and represented my mother at P.T.A. In high school, I got on the high honor roll and desperately wanted to go to college, but there was no money, and my father felt what little might be found should be used for my brother James. "Boys need education more than girls." I persuaded him I had to go; I would get a scholarship, I would work to support myself, and I would put James through afterwards. The Choleric part of me loved goals and challenges and the Sanguine bounce kept me from seeing this project of putting myself and my brother through college as overwhelming. I would make it. I would have fun doing it. And I did!

I carried enough credits to graduate with three full majors and a minor. Not only that, but I stayed on the dean's list and received honors in speech. At the same time I performed in or directed many plays and musicals, was on the debate team, and orated myself into becoming the "Best Female Speaker in New England Colleges" in 1948.

My British father who had sent me to fifty-cent-an-hour elocution lessons from fourth grade on and who had taught me to recite poetry for minstrel shows was thrilled that I excelled in the one area where he had the greatest interest. Months before I got my degree, Dad dropped dead of a heart attack and my cheering section was gone. This encouraging, uplifting man with his English sense of humor, this store keeper whose personal charisma had caused customers to continue buying throughout the Depression, this father who would pat me on the back and say, "You can make it," was gone. Suddenly there was no one to play to; my grandstand was empty.

I had planned to teach as far away from Haverhill as possible, but now my mother needed me at home. If my father was light to me, he was life to her. For months she languished while a family friend ran the store, and in June, I moved back to those three little rooms behind the store. At twenty-one I took on a mantle of responsibility for my mother and two brothers. On thirty-three dollars a week I helped James through college and became mother-sister-friend-guardian-mentor-teacher to Ron.

With my mother's permission, I took control of the family and because my brothers are both Sanguine, I had fun doing it.

Mother slowly recovered, in spite of the harsh realities of her life. She continued to run the little store while Ron and I went off to Haverhill High School together each day.

When I met Fred I was attracted to his all-American good looks and to his deep and sensitive nature. He saw me as a ray of sunshine adding sparkle to his serious style. Although we knew nothing about personalities at that time, we were attracted to our opposite strengths; we innately looked for those positive qualities we lacked in ourselves.

Fred described us to his mother as "two irregular gears which, when turning towards each other, mesh perfectly." It sounded almost poetic.

Had we understood the four basic temperaments at that point, this is what we would have seen on the Chapman Personality Tree. (See p. 138.)

For Further Study, Thought, and Action

Following the instructions from the Littauer half, fill in the female half of your Personality Tree. Copy this into your notebook and add pictures.

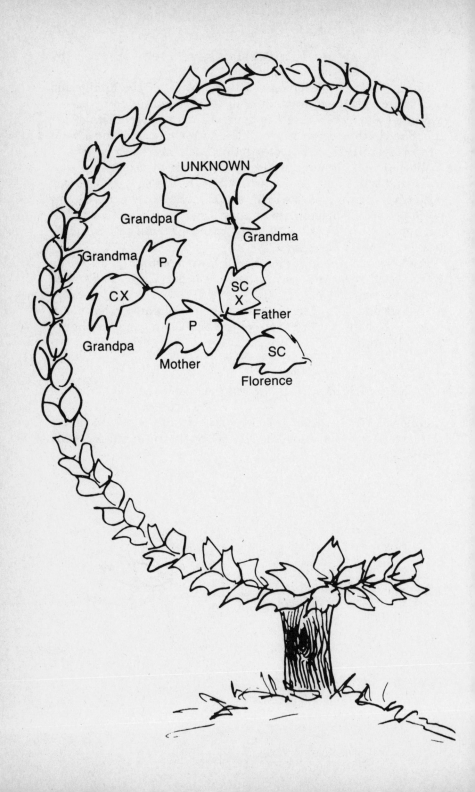

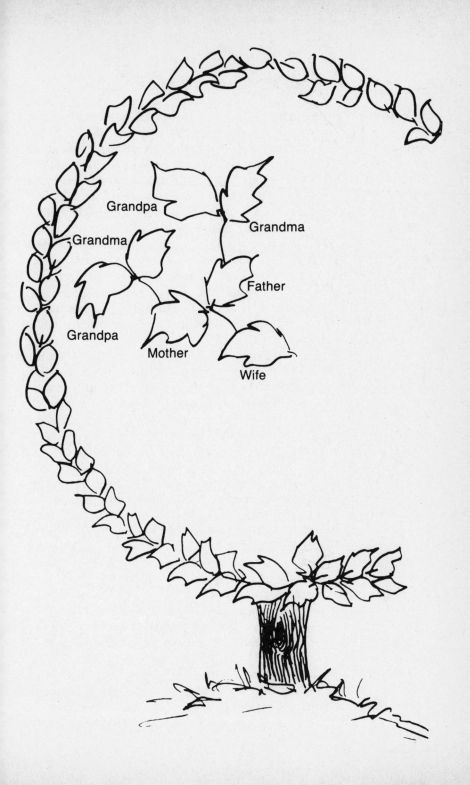

OUR PERSONALITY TREE

On the Oelkers branch we trace back to two Choleric grandparents who were attracted by each other's Sanguine/Melancholy opposites and who enjoyed scrapping throughout their seventy-five married years. Since each one ran into resistance in attempts to remake the other, they unconsciously threw their Choleric control and power onto their Choleric child. With such overwhelming pressure, she was forced to put on a Phlegmatic mask and become, against her own nature, a low-key mediator and the household manager at an early age. She sought permission for each step of life when in their presence, always nodded with "Yes, Daddy dear," and was still seeking to please her perfectionist father up until the moment he died at ninety-seven. For social occasions her mother insisted she be a charming hostess, and so she developed a Sanguine mask to put on for company and to satisfy her mother.

This Sanguine mask was an asset in their church, the Cult of the Perpetual Smile, as everyone was expected to be universally happy. They all smiled the same and talked cheerfully about the weather. It never rained on their parades. On Sundays they would put on a happy face, turn on their "infinite minds," and eliminate sin and mortal error from the earth. Their theme song was "Pack up your troubles in an old kit bag and smile, smile, smile."

Here was a lady with a confusing identity, to herself and to others, a natural Choleric who had to suppress her desire to control and put on a Phlegmatic mask of obedience alternated with a Sanguine mask of almost boisterous cheerfulness. What happens to a "closet Choleric" when this person marries a Phlegmatic? She takes over with a vengeance and so Fred's mother did. Possibly, had she really been able to "leave and cleave," she might have "come into her own" and been able to establish her inborn personality, but because her parents stayed strongly influential and they all worked together, she remained a mixed bag of tricks, shifting roles readily while in the middle of a sentence.

Her repressed Choleric would surge out in her raising of five children, instructing the maids before going off to business, and in dealing with people on a level below her brilliant abilities.

Fred's Melancholy caused him to pull back from her power and when he dared put forth a Choleric thought of his own, it caused conflict. His Melancholy tendency toward depression caused him to don a Sanguine mask during teen years in his quest for popularity and later a Phlegmatic mask to get along with his mother.

Again, what happens to a "closet Choleric" when he gets married? He takes over with a vengeance, and so Fred did. I'd been steeped in Sanguine fun and games and my Choleric had been in high gear from shepherding my mother, to supporting my brothers, to stimulating my students. I gave no thought to the realities of marriage as I expected to live happily ever after, so I was in for a shock when Fred announced he was putting me on a training program. It was a simple "shape up or ship out" approach and I became instantly submissive on the surface while chafing underneath.

Fred took off his Phlegmatic mask at the wedding (although he kept it in a drawer for when his mother came for a visit), and his strong Choleric control came out to join his perfectionistic Melancholy. He became a tempermental duplicate of his grandpa and forced me into a "yes, Fred dear" approach. I put on a Phlegmatic mask for the first time in my life. My Sanguine sense of humor was no longer found funny and any sign of Choleric decision-making was considered bucking for control.

As our children were born, Fred took over the complete direction. Nothing was left to chance. Before our first arrived, Fred wrote pages of sample names, assessing their value as to how each one would look on a high school diploma. Lauren Luise Littauer won. By the time of her birth, Fred had become somewhat discouraged with his training of me. My Phlegmatic mask often slipped revealing a rebellious spirit that Fred found frustrating.

Lauren represented a blank page, a new life untainted by the past, his chance to create a perfect child. His dedication to her training made my contributions superfluous, and I often felt like the proverbial fifth wheel. As the two of them became increasingly devoted to each other, I sometimes felt in the way, and when Fred and I would go into our bedroom, Lauren would sit sadly at the door awaiting Fred's return. In retrospect, I was somewhat the "other woman."

Both Lauren and I played Phlegmatic for Fred. When I left the house I became myself and achieved the presidency of each organization I touched. When Lauren got with her peers she became bossy and tried to run the nursery school. When Cholerics are held down at home, they will, without even knowing what they're doing, find something or someone to control. They may wear a Phlegmatic mask at home, but there's a Choleric will lurking underneath waiting for any chance to take over.

When Marita was born, four-year-old Lauren, looking for a project, took her on. Lauren was a mature and competent child and always assumed responsibility beyond her years. Lauren had learned that conscientious "good works" impressed her father and freed me up to have fun, so she became a junior mother.

Marita was bubbling and happy right from the beginning and she became my toy, my baby "Bundle." Now we each had a child who served our needs even though neither one of us would have admitted this division had it been pointed out to us at that time.

The next few years threw us all into a most unnatural situation as I gave birth, one after another, to two sons who were both fatally brain-damaged.

Lauren dedicated her little self to being their mother-nurse, and she was broken-hearted when the first one died and the second went to a children's hospital never to return. In those days no one talked about depression, there were no books or seminars on handling grief, and we were of the school "the less said the better," added to my mother's favorite cliché, "Never air your dirty wash in public."

Fred's Melancholy could not allow him to think that he could be responsible for two imperfect sons. His Choleric said, "Put it behind you and get on with life," and his religion taught, "Deny any sin, disease, or death and smile, smile, smile."

As Fred expanded his business and came home less, Lauren was deprived of her father's attention and her brothers' presence. My response to depression was to run away from it to theatrical productions where I could create fairy tales on a stage where they all lived happily ever after.

Neither Fred nor I spent time in self-analysis, counseling was unheard of unless you were crazy, and we both tried to make the best of two excruciatingly painful losses. In our quest for activities to keep us from crying round the clock, we didn't realize that Lauren's heart was breaking. We neither discussed the babies' incurable problems or explained where each one had gone. "She's just a child. She'll get over it."

She never really "got over it" and she has written an impressive chapter, "The Forgotten Griever," in her helpful book *What You Can Say When You Don't Know What To Say*.

During that period of mourning we were all depressed in different ways. The Sanguine in me could see no hope for fun at home any more so I went to seek diversions. The Melancholy in Fred could see no hope in a family that would never be perfect so he stayed at business where he could direct the details. The Choleric in Lauren had learned that no matter how hard her young self tried, she had no control over her circumstances. She had nowhere to go, and she wore a dutiful Phlegmatic mask. Marita was too young to be involved in the tragic circumstances so she remained happily above it all and became our dose of much needed sunshine.

Lauren grew up seriously, obediently without rebellion. She was always mature beyond her years, stayed close to her father in business, and was the family's rock of dependability. What happens to a "closet Choleric" when she gets married? She chooses a Phlegmatic and takes over quickly.

Because Lauren and her delightfully easy-going husband Randy had studied the different personalities before marriage and knew what they could expect from each other in both strengths and weaknesses, they have been able to accept each other realistically as they are and not try to transform each other.

They now have two boys, Randy, Jr., a Melancholy/Choleric, and Jonathan, a Sanguine/Choleric personality duplicate of his Aunt Marita and perhaps a little like me! With a newly added Bryan Frederick, what a challenge Lauren and Randy have to raise these three as they were created to be and not try to mold them into the "perfect" children they might want. It's time to break the cycle of Cholerics being forced to wear Phlegmatic masks and to train up these children in the way each one should go.

Tracing My Roots

While I was writing this book, Fred and I went back to my home area in Massachusetts. Our first stop on our roots trip was the MacDougall home in Merrimac where my mother was brought when she was less than a year old. Even though some new rooms had been added on the back, the frame of the house was just as it was when I got married from it in 1953. As Fred took pictures, standing at the foot of the cracked cement front walk, I wandered around the side to the grape arbor where I had picked Blue Concords as a child. The present owners, the Lavelles, who had purchased the house from my mother in 1959, were at home and warmly invited us in.

Upstairs I stood in the front bedroom where Grandma Mac had given birth to her last four babies. I pictured each one in the handcarved cradle Grandpa Mac had created that sits in my living room today. As I descended the narrow stairs to the front hall, I saw the sparkle of the square window full of colored glass where I as a child had sat on the steps with my little brothers trying to catch rays of color in our hands.

A lump came into my throat as the setting sun danced rainbows of memories into my life.

We moved into the parlor where my mother had been married by the bay window and where I had played the wedding march on the piano while my mother accompanied on the violin when Aunt Sadie Beatrice MacDougall, in her fifties, had wed Charlie Porter the upholsterer.

Mrs. Lavalle reminded me that Grandma Mac had been "laid out" in front of that same bay window where the sisters had said their vows before the soft syllables of Reverend Loud.

As I looked around this room, where as children we could only enter if we were good, it seemed strangely empty without the huge portrait of Queen Victoria that had stared sternly down upon us.

The dining room was just the same except that Aunt Sadie's piano, where she'd taught me and many other little ones their scales, was missing. I could easily remember those Christmases around what could have been the same table, especially after Aunt Sadie married Charlie and he brought his sister Carrie Bacon for the holidays. She was both a foot doctor and hairdresser and I can still hear my father say, "She tries to make both ends meet."

As I looked at the table, I remembered how upset my mother got when Dad encouraged Carrie to do her infamous imitation of a sea gull during Christmas dinner, causing little brother Ron to laugh so hard he spit his milk out on the table.

Oh, what memories flood back when we stand in the traces of former times.

A visit to the Locust Grove Cemetery was a personal parade into the past. Grandma and Grandpa MacDougall, the founders of our clan, their names chiseled on the same stone with Aunt Sadie's. Behind them lay Aunt Annie with her husband Benjamin Franklin Sargent and their son James who'd been killed in the Battle of the Bulge when I was in high school. Across the way was Uncle Willie and his infant son William, Jr., and a marker for Uncle Donald's baby grandson. I told Fred what I could remember of each person, and he got to know those in my family he'd never met.

An added note of sadness struck both of us as we knelt by the stone of my father "Walter Chapman, 1878–1948," and the fresh markings of "Katie F. Chapman, 1898–1984."

That same day we went back to Mitchell's Department Store where I had my first job selling chocolates, to the defense factory where I worked one summer in a noble effort to help win the war, to Haverhill High School where I attended and taught so many years ago, and to the Riverside Variety Store, now turned into apartments. As we drove away from Haverhill Fred said, "This has been one of the most beautiful days we've ever spent together."

Littauer Family Personality Tree

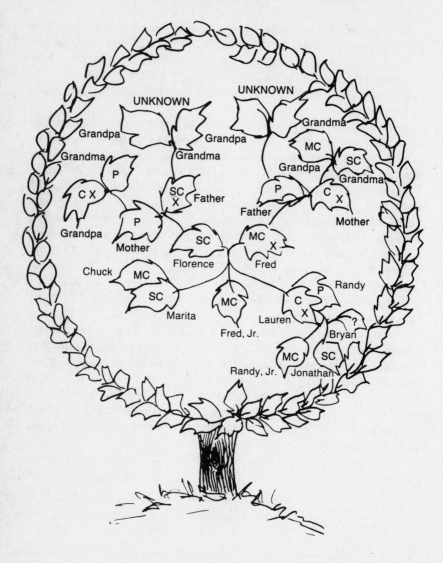

YOUR PERSONALITY TREE

So often as young couples marry, they assume that because they are in love and are Christians all will be well with their souls. They quote, "Love covers a multitude of sins," (1 Pet. 4:8 RSV) and "Perfect love casts out fear" (1 John 4:18, RSV).

The maiden marries a robust acorn and expects him to grow into a mighty oak. She'll fertilize him into strength and prune him into shape. She forgets that as the twig is bent so will it grow. She assumes that once she transplants him into her yard, the fresh air will do him good and he will leave behind the aroma of the little bushes he buddied up with on the old plantation.

She doesn't realize that when she pots up this one sapling to take him home to her garden, she's buying a whole forest of family—parents, siblings, aunts, uncles, grandparents. He may renounce them or refuse to see them, but he can't remove their influence for they all came out of the same package of seeds. Some may be bigger, better, or brighter, but they've got the same rootstock underneath.

Since you, at your best, cannot weed out the whole heritage, even though you can clearly see the crabgrass in the other family, you would do better to research their history, write down what you find, and recognize the repeated traits. You will then find the reasons for reactions your mate has that have nothing to do with your behavior.

I used to think that if Fred had married anyone but me, he could have been happy. But as I traced back his family, I found that before he even met me, he had a Melancholy personality that was predetermined to persist until he produced a perfect wife no matter who she started out to be. If Fred had married the Proverbs 31 woman, he would have made her get up earlier than dawn, polish the gates where he sat, and stop wearing purple. I used to encourage our children to rise up and call me blessed but only so we would present a unified front of insurrection as we mutinied against our master.

Now that I've spent time perusing Fred's predecessors and see him as a duplicate of his grandfather, I can accept that he came to me prepackaged as a pure progeny of his past and that I'm not his problem. What a relief!

As I've learned that "closet Cholerics," those made to play a

Phlegmatic role in the past, take over their mates with a passion for producing perfection, I can see why he put me on a training program. I can let him alphabetize the spices and not take it as a weakness in me that I had basil behind salt.

As Fred has examined my background of taking charge of everybody from the time I was a child, he now can accept a directive statement from me without expecting me to wrest control of his life away from him. Now that he understands how my mother unintentionally planted seeds of poverty in my mind, he can see why I seem to be preoccupied with ready cash.

There are two major reasons for taking the time to plot out your Personality Trees: You'll see where you've all come from and why you are the way you are; then you'll be aware of what you are passing on to your children when you have no understanding of their individual needs or personality profiles.

In the process of researching these forebears, you may get acquainted with some fascinating faces of the past who step into the reality of the present.

As you look at our completed tree do you see how Grandma and Grandpa Oelkers were the same personality pattern as Fred and me? How Fred's mother, Fred, and Lauren had the same traits and as Cholerics were forced into unnatural submissive roles? Do you see how the three of them before marriage, and me after marriage, had to wear Phlegmatic masks for survival? Do you see how easily we fall into raising our children as we want them to be, according to our personalities instead of helping them develop their own unique God-given abilities?

Fred's mother didn't have a chance to be herself. She was a natural Choleric with a touch of Melancholy depth, forced to wear a Phlegmatic mask for her father and a Sanguine one for her mother. I had personally felt there was little hope of ever understanding her, but that was before two things happened. Fred and I committed our lives to the Lord Jesus, and we plunged into a personality study of ourselves, trying to restore our lost years that the locusts had eaten.

We stopped attending the "Cult of the Perpetual Smile" where the whole church was a grand masquerade. We'd been so disillusioned when our sons had not been healed by their religious practices and I'd been told it was all my fault. "These babies are perfectly healthy and the error is in your mind. When you can see them as whole, they will be whole."

It had been hard to pretend that my convulsive babies were normal and to force a smile on Sundays, so I was relieved to attend a church where I didn't have to play charades and where God's Word was preached clearly.

One Sunday evening when Fred's mother was visiting, the pastor gave an altar call, and our family was stunned as Mother pushed past us in the pew, walked up the aisle and committed her life to the Lord Jesus. As the Lord began to work in her heart, she needed her masks less and less and she allowed herself to reveal the realities she'd hidden even from herself.

I found we had something sincere to talk about, and as we both changed for the better, we were drawn together in a mutual "open-heart operation."

What a blessed opportunity you have right now to examine your family background for a cushion of knowledge and then prayerfully seek God's wisdom. Open your eyes and view the vision that he has in mind for your children so that you won't be guilty of changing his plans.

What happens when we try to change other people? Even if we're successful and get a Choleric so under control, he appears Phlegmatic, or a Melancholy forcing big smiles to appear Sanguine, or a Phlegmatic exhausting himself trying to run up mountains, or a Sanguine following charts so closely he's no fun any more—what if we are successful? What do we have on our hands? A person who has no idea who he really is.

It's like crossing a Poodle with a Schnauzer. The puppy's cute, but what is it?

For Further Study, Thought, and Action

God created each one of us as individuals with different personalities, strengths, and weaknesses. If he'd wanted us to be alike, he could have created us that way. Since he didn't, our job is (1) to find out what our natural personality is and who we really are so we can function at our maximum ability and (2) to make sure we're not changing our children into confused mongrels.

Before reading further, stop and think about your family background. Join your two halves together and fill out Your Personality Tree. How I wish I'd done this years ago before my father and Fred's father were gone, taking with them the knowledge of their parents. You will be amazed as you question grandparents and older aunts and uncles at how much you can learn about family personalities and how much they will love you for caring enough to ask.

As you're filling in the different temperament combinations, your eyes may be opened as to why your mate is one way with you and a different personality with his mother; or one way at home and one way at work. You may see repetitions in succeeding generations and become aware of masks that some have worn based on parents' personalities or extraneous circumstances. Try to find your original God-given temperament pattern, for we can only function in our fullest capacity when we know who we really are.

Put your complete tree in your personality notebook.

In the process of digging up information for your Personality Tree, you may want to take a trip back to your hometowns, as Fred and I did while I was writing this book. Take pictures of significant landmarks and include these in your notebook for the enjoyment of your family. You may even want to organize a family reunion. Be creative. My sister-in-law Katie designed T-shirts for her Tharp Family Reunion. On the front of each shirt she put the individual's name, and on the back she put a silkscreen of the entire family tree. On the first night of the reunion she gave each member of the family his or her own personalized family tree T-shirt.

Each one of us has a fascinating background, a cast of characters that would defy fiction. How often we let it all slip by without sharing it with our partners or our progeny. How much we could learn about each other's personality if we'd take the time to find out where we've really come from.

I heard Alex Haley on a TV talk show and the host asked, "Where did you get your material and your storytelling ability for *Roots?*"

Alex replied, "From sitting around the cracker barrel with my father listening to all the men tell stories of how life used to be." He told of this rich tradition where the men passed down the family tales to the boys at the general store and the women did the same for their girls in rocking chairs on the front porch.

What a shame it is that so many of us today watch television versions of other people's lives instead of passing on our own heritage while rocking on the front porch.

Start today to make a Personality Tree of your background. Whenever you find an ancestor whom you don't know, ask some relative about him, settle down by the cracker barrel and be prepared to hear a story that may defy the "soaps."

Never be afraid when God brings back the past. Let memory have its way. It is a minister of God . . . who will turn the 'might have been' into a wonderful culture for the future. [2]

Your Family Personality Tree

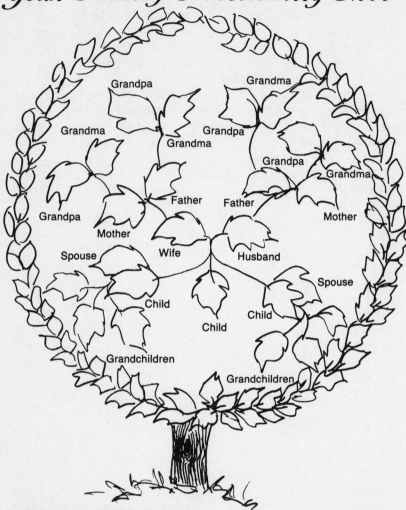

GENERAL INSTRUCTIONS

1. With help of spouse, complete your "Family Personality Tree" in pencil.
2. Starting with yourselves, mark in each leaf, the primary and secondary personality traits of each person. (i.e., "SC" = Sanguine/Choleric)
3. Put an "X" in the leaf of the <u>one</u> partner of each couple on the tree whom you perceive to be the dominant personality.
4. Now fill in the personality traits of all other persons as indicated.
5. Consider which ones may be wearing, or have worn a mask.

Fred and Florence Littauer • 1814-E Commercenter West • San Bernardino, CA 92408 • (714)888-8665
Tree designed by Gretchen Jackson

❧ 8 ❧

What Are Your Children's Personalities?

*Tis education forms the common mind
Just as the twig is bent the tree's inclined*[1]

As I have taught *Personality Plus* over the years, some of the most gratifying results have come when parents suddenly realize why they haven't been able to understand a certain child. One couple came up to me and said, "You have just saved our child's life." The father, a Choleric, then explained his problem with what was obviously a Phlegmatic boy. "I just can't get him moving. No matter how I bribe him or threaten him, he just won't jump! This morning on the way to the seminar I said to my wife, 'That kid has got to shape up or I'm going to kill him.' I've always had pep and ambition and this kid is never going to make it."

The Melancholy mother added, "He's really a sweet boy; he never gives us a moment's trouble and everyone loves him but us. Now that I see he is Phlegmatic and that we've been trying to make him Choleric like his father and that's not going to work, I feel so guilty."

The father added, "I really thought there was something wrong with him, but now I see he's just different from me and that's okay. You've saved the boy's life."

How many fathers are there like this man who assumed his son would be like him and when he didn't perform, let him know how disappointed he was. Without an understanding of the temperaments we assume everyone ought to function as we do, and when they don't, we abandon them emotionally and give our attention to the one who fulfills our image of what a child should be.

Another couple came up to me to discuss their twelve-year-old twin sons. One was Melancholy and one Sanguine. They had shared the same bedroom since they were born and had been in the same school class each year. The Melancholy boy was serious, a good student, well-behaved, and kept his half of the room neat. His parents both complimented him in front of the brother, and then they would admonish the Sanguine by saying, "Why aren't you like your brother?" The boy got the same comments from the teachers as he seldom did his homework on time and talked when he was supposed to be quiet. His parents looked at his popularity as a negative since he tied up the phone, and the teachers didn't find his spontaneous humor to be funny but a class distraction. Because no one understood the boy's temperament, he was constantly the bad guy, and one day he came home from school and went berserk. He pulled the sheets off the brother's bed, emptied all the drawers onto the floor and pulled the drapes, fixtures, and all off the walls. When his mother yelled at him to stop wrecking the room, he lunged at her and pushed her to the floor. He ran wildly through the house as she called the police who came and strapped his hands behind his back and took him off to the mental ward.

As the mother told me this sad story, the boy was still in the hospital where he was being tranquilized and counseled by a Melancholy therapist who was trying to make him perfect like his brother. The mother cried as she realized what they had all done to this Sanguine child who just wanted to have fun and instead was laden with guilt that he was never going to be good enough for his parents' approval.

Unfortunately, this boy is not an isolated case. According to the data compiled by the House Select Committee on Children, Youth, and Families, admissions to inpatient psychiatric services of children under eighteen more than doubled between 1970 and 1980. Between 1980 and 1984 adolescent admissions to private psychiatric hospitals increased more than 350 percent.[2]

The use of drugs at a young age and early sexual promiscuity account for many of the teen problems and are situations which were not heard of twenty years ago, but the majority of the young patients are under treatment for general depression. Ralph Alsopp, an Atlanta psychologist reports that the teenagers he sees "feel helpless, not in control of their lives. Their support structures are falling away."[3]

As I have talked with depressed teens, some who have attempted suicide, they all indicate a vague feeling of not knowing really what's wrong with them, and they seem to have no sense of who they are.

While I am not so naive as to think a knowledge of the temperaments would solve the problems of troubled youth today, I do know from my own family experience and the hundreds of other families I've counseled over the years that when they will take the time to sit down as a family and check off the profile together there will be a positive result. Possibly if we sat down and played a national game of Monopoly, family life would also improve, but I know if we were able to discuss in a nonjudgmental manner the strengths and weaknesses of each family member and let them see their uniqueness, we would not have so many young people wandering around wondering who they are and trying to find themselves.

Why don't we Christian families make it a point to develop each child according to his talents and temperament? Doesn't Proverbs 22:6 tell us to "Train up a child in the way *he* should go" (italics mine) not in the way *we* dreamed up? What guidelines do we have available by which to measure their abilities? Do we have to take them to a psychiatrist?

Dr. Judith Wallerstein, speaking about adolescent insecurities on the "Good Morning America" television show said, "They are in so many changes, physically and emotionally, that they desperately need coherent rules and family stability."[4]

As Fred and I ask our children what was meaningful to them in our bringing them up, they mention the family meetings where we set the rules of operation for the family. They will admit they were a little apprehensive about what new standards would be set each time, but there was a feeling of security in knowing there were some accepted standards. Understanding their personal abilities and temperaments was the other major plus they remember.

I had always assumed that since education was such a high priority for Fred and me that my children would all go to college.

Since I worked literally night and day to get myself through college when there was no money available, I knew my children, without this struggle, would be excited to go. Lauren followed what I felt was a normal program. She got excellent grades in high school and majored in business and psychology at Cal State, San Bernardino. She married a brilliant numismatist and is raising three boys, the three little Briggs. Her Choleric nature with a secondary in Melancholy has made her both capable and sensitive to others. She helps her husband with his stamp and coin gallery, has been on the stage since I put her in a Christmas play at the age of four, and is both a speaker and author of a most helpful book, *What You Can Say When You Don't Know What To Say*.

Had I stopped with Lauren I might have been a little smug about my motherhood abilities; having Sanguine/Choleric Marita who was going to do things her way right from the beginning showed me differently. While Lauren wanted me to be room mother, Marita tried to keep me away from school. Mischievous would have been a mild term for Marita.

One night when I was prepared to go to PTA in her junior year of high school, she suggested I stay home as I looked so tired and needed rest. Since she was right, I almost fell for her ruse, but a flood of good sense came over me and I pulled myself together and went. When I arrived in Algebra, the teacher said she did all right when she came but somehow his class frequently interfered with her lunch at McDonalds. The typing teacher suggested she drop the course and the French teacher said she couldn't keep her quiet. Only in scuba diving where she was the only girl in a class of boys was the male teacher enthusiastic; however, I wasn't sure she was good enough to make a living scuba diving.

Had I not known her temperament pattern and been assured of her basic intelligence, I would have been a wreck trying to get her through school, but since I knew she could achieve anything she wanted to do and could charm her way through the rest, I didn't waste much time in worry. I was amazed when the guidance counselor phoned me in Marita's senior year of high school. I assumed Marita was going to be reprimanded for cutting too many classes, but instead the counselor said Marita was so far ahead of the others that they were going to graduate her early. Right then I knew the whole educational system was in trouble.

Instead of going to Vassar or Radcliffe or Westmont or Biola, Marita went to the local junior college, started her own business at eighteen, traveled with me learning to be a speaker and now is a full-time Christian speaker and on our CLASS staff. I am so grateful that I did not try to push her into a "perfect child" mold. Instead, I encouraged the talents she had in verbal skills and didn't worry about college degrees.

Young Fred never liked school and even though he went away to college for one year, he left to come back and take over his father's car business. He likes cars and cares little for books. He is a deeply sensitive Melancholy and has never moved as fast as Fred and I would have liked, but we have accepted his choices, encouraged his strengths, and praised his sweet spirit.

Two years ago when I went on a speaking tour through Europe I took young Fred along. There was a girl who followed me around taking my picture whenever I was in a somewhat ungainly position. One day she said to me, "Your son sure loves you a lot." She then told me that the day before on the bus I had fallen asleep with my head against the window. She had thought a picture in this position would be humorous so she had focused on me from across the aisle. As she was peering through the lens a dark shadow filled the square and she looked up to see young Fred leaning across in front of me. He asked, "What are you planning to do?"

She replied, "I'm going to take a picture of your mother asleep."

He stated, "No you're not. You will *never* take a picture of my mother without asking her permission first."

The girl had been stopped in her little tracks, and Fred didn't move until she had put the camera away. He never mentioned what he'd done, but she didn't take any more pictures of me without asking me first.

There may be some mothers with sons who have gone to Harvard or Stanford or Yale, but I doubt they have ever been touched so deeply by the loving protection of their young man as I was by Fred's.

We have learned in our family to train up our children in

the way each one of them should go according to their abilities
and temperament even if it was not always what we originally
had in our minds.

How many young people I talk to who have been pushed into
schools or careers where they didn't want to be, have socialized
with the right people at the right club, even married the catch
of the town and yet have never had an independent thought of
their own and are miserable.

In the other direction, how many parents have let their young
men and women do their own thing with so little guidance or
encouragement that they are still wandering aimlessly in life
not having quite settled on anything?

We are to train them up—guide them, love them, discipline
them—but in the way *they* should go, according to their own
personality traits. We will never regret the time we spend with
each child showing him his unique strengths that may be nothing
like those of his brother and making him aware of his weaknesses
so he will know what he needs to overcome to be his own brand
of success in life.

Lana Bateman remembers the first time she heard Haddon
Robinson, Dean of Homiletics at Dallas Theological Seminary,
explain this verse.

> He said that the original Hebrew was more literally translated,
> "Train up a child according to his way. . . ." It wasn't until I un-
> derstood the temperaments that I began to realize what this
> verse really meant. Did every child have a particular way to be
> raised? Did that mean that all children should not be treated the
> same way?
>
> Within the confines of my childhood family, there was a certain
> pride taken in the fact that all three children were treated and
> raised the same way. I'm afraid that most parents feel this attitude
> is the fair and correct one for raising more than one child. What
> a tragedy, for if the words of this proverb are true, then each child
> has a certain bend which makes him/her different from every other
> child in the family. This unique being would require a special under-
> standing in order to draw each one to his/her greatest potential
> for living a wise and full life. We as parents have an obligation
> and duty before God to discern the way of each child and endeavor
> to maximize strengths and diminish weaknesses in the most loving
> way possible. With an understanding of the temperaments, we have
> tools readily available.

Cathye Stout of Austin, Texas, wrote me the following after hearing me teach about the temperaments.

> . . . each of my three teenagers and husband (only one of him!) evaluated themselves and then each other.
> This was used as a great tool for family discussion (the TV actually went off before 10:30) as we looked at our strengths *and* weaknesses.
> It led into our nightly family devotions and prayer. Out of our strengths, we were able to praise and thank the Lord for the gifts and abilities He created us with. We reaffirmed our commitment to give back to Him what He's given us, for *His* honor and glory and His use.
> And out of our weaknesses we could see where improvement was needed in each of us. . . .

Debby Laurie of El Toro, California, wrote me the results of her teaching her two children, eleven and fourteen, to understand the temperaments.

> They never cease to be a daily help. One day our kids figured out the 'First Family.' Eve was a definite Sanguine. She'd talk to anyone, even a snake. Adam was Phlegmatic. When it came time to make the important decision whether to eat or not to eat he let Eve influence him. She was much better at decisions anyway. Abel was Melancholy. He made the perfect sacrifices, and that garden was so tidy and precise. Cain, the Choleric, got so mad at his brother he decided to take matters into his own hands. He felt the end justified the means. And there we have it: the birth of the four personality types!

Who knows what kind of a discussion your family may have, but it will surely be better than TV!

YOUR CHILD'S TEMPERAMENT

Although you probably understand the basics of the temperaments by now, let's apply the principles as they relate to children and see what we can learn about training our children in the way they should go. We must realize first that young children grasp love in two ways. One is physical touching, hugging, kissing, and affirming; and the other is verbal communication given by parents who take the time to get to know their children and listen to what they're saying. I remember when Marita was first reading books and she would want to tell me the story. She would follow me all over the house and the book review was longer than it took to read the book. When I would stop, sit down and listen, the review would be much shorter, but as long as I kept moving the review kept going. She could make the *Cat in the Hat* sound like *Gone with the Wind!*

A child who does not have the warm physical touch of a loving parent and the open communication that child desires will grow up with a deep unfulfilled longing for love and may end up "looking for love in all the wrong places."

Beyond this universal need for love in each child, there is a personality need. Understanding the temperaments gives us a special grasp of the particular "way" or need of each child.

As the twig is bent, the tree will grow. Is it true? Let's take a look at some twig-benders and let you decide for yourself.

SANGUINE

Your lively, bright-eyed Sanguine child is full of curiosity and laughter. He may not always have an audience, but that never seems to stop the constant chatter which is the first step toward that center stage personality. This child is full of wonderful creative ideas but is often defeated in carrying them out by a short attention span which keeps this child from doing as well as others academically. He will, however, excitedly strive to be in any production the class has to offer, from singing to playing the bird-whistle in the rhythm band. Education takes a back seat to more important pursuits such as cheerleading, drama class, student council, dancing lessons, or anything else that will provide an escape from the books.

Look for this child to come up with endless excuses when facing confrontation, not because of a need for peace which is the Phlegmatic's reason for avoiding conflict, but because of his deep need to be accepted. Your disappointment or anger spells rejection to this temperament and is to be avoided no matter how many excuses the child makes.

Popularity is an overwhelming need for this boy or girl. The lack of it can cause a great deal of pain and frustration for there is no other temperament that needs social acceptance as badly as this one. Because of this need, the Sanguine child is the most likely to "go along with the crowd" or be drawn into an unwise situation. If he is a Sanguine/Choleric he will be more bossy and organized; if he is Sanguine/Phlegmatic, he'll have fun but never get his act together and not even care.

Tools to Help[5]

1. Have the child tested at a children's learning center or with a child psychologist to determine the area of creativity and aptitude.

2. Encourage this child in the areas of performance singing, dancing, acting, speaking, art, design, sports, scouts, or group play. This child is very active and needs something exciting going on every minute. Because of a short attention span, this child will have some difficulty with those pursuits such as piano that require practice and will need an adult to sit with him on the bench in order to give constant encouragement and approval. Unfortunately he will only do well if the duty can be made into a game, for only with a prize ahead will the Sanguine child keep pressing toward the goal. In some cases, simple peer approval will suffice, but if the parent desires a final accomplishment, he will probably need to hang in there with the child to produce results.

3. The parent of a Sanguine child must carefully weigh the wisdom of allowing each activity, keeping in mind this child's deep need for acceptance and knowing they always want to do what "everybody" is doing. You can be encouraged by knowing if you don't let them go to some event, they will soon forget and not hold grudges or sulk long.

4. This child has a greater need for physical affection than any of the other temperaments so parents need to do a lot of hugging, holding, and touching.

5. Start early to teach this child the discipline of a clean room and the importance of handling money wisely. Understand that you will have to stay right with this offspring to guarantee any kind of results. Without such a commitment from parents, this child can easily slip into irresponsibility and never quite grow up.

6. Understand that when your Sanguine child tells a fib, it is out of a deep need for approval. Find other healthy ways to give that approval as you deal with this problem and praise them for telling the truth. Some of their colorful stories get such attention that they begin to believe what they're saying.

7. Find at least one thing your Sanguine child can do well and then encourage, encourage, encourage. Sanguines have the greatest potential, but often fall far short of the mark when parents don't understand their needs.

8. Remember that a Sanguine child will do more through one word of encouragement than he will ever accomplish through your yelling, criticizing, or constant spanking.

9. Don't foster negative behavior by telling everyone how cute she was when she did it. Marita used to take money from my purse and then go down the hill behind our house and buy me a plant from the florist. She was so adorable bringing me presents that I would praise her for thinking of me. Suddenly I realized I was promoting stealing as long as she spent the money on me.

Remember

Virtually every move this child makes is based upon a desire to have FUN and a driving need for APPROVAL with a deep sensitivity to even the slightest possibility of rejection. The Sanguine child must be a part of the gang, whoever the gang is today.

MELANCHOLY

Your Melancholy baby came into the world with intensity written all over his face. When we adopted Fred the case worker said, "He lies quietly in the crib analyzing everyone who goes by. This is that special infant of whom everyone says, 'Doesn't he look intelligent? Are you sure he's not a big person in a little person's body?' "

Intensity is a word that cannot be overworked for this little one feels, thinks, reacts, responds, and reflects everything deeply. In *Parade Magazine* there was an article "When Your Baby Seems Depressed." The author, Susan Lapinski, described a perfect Melancholy baby and pointed out how parents with what appears to be a depressed baby feel they must have done something wrong. They assume the baby doesn't like them, and they don't know what to do. "The goal of the therapists is to help parents avoid a build-up of problems that can send a whole family into worry and despair. These problems usually spring from an inability to understand and cope with a baby's puzzling temperament."[6]

Throughout the article health professionals describe the Melancholy baby, but without ever using the term or explaining why some children are so different. They suggest that parents not blame themselves but "concentrate on respecting the baby's individual personality and on reacting appropriately to the baby's responses."[7] Even though the depressed babies they describe are not compared with the Sanguine (bubbly), Choleric (demanding), or Phlegmatic (passive), Dr. T. Berry Brazelton of Children's Hospital, Boston, does conclude, "Babies are competent little numbers. They can tell you a lot. And when you can spot the differences in your baby and value them, being a parent becomes a lot more rewarding and a lot more fun."[8] He's right and that's why it's so important that we know all the types so we won't think we've got the only unusual baby in town.

Of all the temperaments, the Melancholy is the most deeply creative and genius-prone. Some parents may actually feel threatened by the innate mental capacities of such a child. Sadly, the Melancholy child cannot grasp why no one else seems to experience such depth of emotion and understanding, why no one else seems to care.

In early childhood, your Melancholy boy or girl will cling most closely to you and will have the greatest need to have parents physically present. This temperament can be damaged by neglect or abuse during childhood more than any other personality due to his deep sensitivity and propensity to withdraw when he really wants to reach out.

Through Lana Bateman's counseling in Philippian Ministries, she notes that many alcoholics, drug addicts, and homosexuals appear to be of the Melancholy temperament. It isn't difficult to understand why when we think of how easy it is to wound or scar such gentle, sensitive children and how their insecurities make them vulnerable to outside substances which offer to give them confidence or relieve their depression.

The intelligent Melancholy offspring will seldom need prodding, for he will be a good student with very high standards. If your child is heavily Melancholy, you will find he has a deep need for perfection in many areas of his life. If he is Melancholy with Choleric he will be meticulous about his desk and paper work and be more outgoing and bold than a straight Melancholy. One four-year-old Melancholy/Choleric girl was driving her mother crazy, and the mother said in exasperation, "Don't be such a perfectionist!"

The child responded quickly, "I'm not a perfectionist. I just want things done right."

If he is Melancholy/Phlegmatic he will not care quite so much whether things are in order and will be less compulsive about getting life pulled together perfectly.

One of the great struggles for this child will come in the area of negative thought patterns and refusal to communicate needs before his feelings are hurt. This lack of communication causes the Melancholy child to internalize his deep need for approval rather than openly seeking that approval in the manner of the Sanguine child. He feels if you really loved him, you would be sensitive to his needs and he wouldn't have to tell you.

Tools to Help

1. Check your child's school to see if testing is available to determine your son's or daughter's educational and creative bent. If it is not available, go through a local children's hospital or psychologist. Look for ways to affirm and encourage your child in those areas of his/her own personal expertise, knowing that he probably has some special talent waiting to be discovered. Some children may be gifted in the area of music, the arts, design, or may show an intense interest in a chosen hobby such as photography or model building.

2. Protect your child from too much involvement in sad books, music, or television programs. Because this child has such a vivid visual memory and tendancy toward intense reaction, keep him away from disturbing entertainment such as horror movies or films depicting violence or macabre behavior. They're not good for any child, but the Melancholy may be seriously affected by trauma dramas.

3. Starting early in childhood, focus the Melancholy minds on what they have to be thankful for. Spend some time at least once or twice a week having these boys or girls list all the good things God has done for them or given them. It is important to constantly direct their thoughts to the positive rather than the negative. One mother actually has her Melancholy son verbalize a praise list every morning with her before she takes him to school, and she has been very pleased with the results.

4. One of the most important things you can do for this temperament is to teach him to communicate his needs and feelings without your having to play twenty questions each time he gets moody. Use every tool you can muster to draw out the thoughts and emotions of this child. Remember, he will be quick to withdraw without ever verbalizing what caused the pain, so be quick to help this child find words to express what he is feeling.

Example: "Honey, I know there are times when others do or say things that really hurt your feelings. Try to help me understand when I do that to you. If you will stop the moment you feel that pain and just say, 'Mom, you probably didn't mean to, but you hurt my feelings when you said or did that.' It is so much better when we can talk about hurt feelings. Then we don't have to hold that pain inside because we can love away the hurt with a special, 'I'm sorry,' and a big hug. I want to understand when you are hurt because I love you and I know that talking about these things can keep them from taking away your happiness."

6. It is important to begin early to teach the Melancholy child that both success and failure are a part of what our Lord allows in each life in order to make us ready for heaven. This child is terrified of failure and has a difficult time trying anything unless success is guaranteed. He will often spend excess time on preparation to perform a doubtful project. Explain to him that each setback in life gives us compassion for others who are hurting. How could we ever know how *they* feel if we have never known failure ourselves.

Remember

This Melancholy child is driven not only by a need for perfection but also by a desire for you to sense and respond to his needs and feelings without their ever having been verbalized. Teaching this child to communicate needs and feelings is a powerful key to short-circuiting chronic unhappiness and may be the salvation of a future marriage.

CHOLERIC

Your Choleric child is the original strong-willed child, full of energy, adventure, and impatience. This toothless wonder is born to lead. Hard to believe, isn't it? Leadership begins with demanding to eat and to sleep only when he chooses and moves on to exercising control through temper tantrums. One lady told me her Choleric child's first sentence was a loud, "Eat now!"

These anger displays seem to express themselves in one of two ways, depending on the temperament combination. The Choleric/Sanguines tend to have both verbal and physical temper tantrums, the Choleric anger and the Sanguine performance which may include kicking, screaming, and pounding the floor, wall, or whatever is near. Breaking a dish or two is a dramatic addition.

The Choleric/Melancholy, however, tends toward a more dignified tantrum. Not wanting to call undue attention to himself, the Choleric/Melancholy child is more likely to hold his breath until turning blue and then quietly passing out on the floor. This apparent swoon is a quiet attention-getter and tells mother not to let this happen again.

Control is the key Choleric word here, and it follows this child to the grave. Whether it is through leadership or anger, the Choleric must be in control. A tantrum gives this child just that!

How excited I was when I opened a December *USA Today* and saw a full-page headline "Temperament, Not Poor Training, Ignites Tantrums." It told about little Jillian who cried all night, threw tantrums daily, and wouldn't eat. Her father, a child psychiatrist, couldn't believe he was involved in a power struggle with a two-year-old. The more he fought the worse it got, but Dr. Stanley Turecki did what any psychiatrist in his position would do; he wrote a book about Jillian and others like her. The book is called *The Difficult Child.* In it he says, "These children aren't spoiled brates. They have difficult traits, but their behavior is a result of their temperament which they can't help. These children aren't out to get their parents."[9]

Dr. Saul Brown of Cedars-Sinai in Los Angeles warns parents not to make a scapegoat out of this child; doing so could lead to possible child abuse. He also tells them to only fight battles that they need to win, not to make a scene out of everything, and not to look for a source to blame for the difficult child's behavior. "Some people are just born with different personalities."[10]

This little Choleric powerhouse is very productive, is able to make quick and competent decisions, and often can outsmart his parents. He is full of confidence and pride and is often bossy and tactless.

Tools to Help

1. You have on your hands the greatest potential for future leadership positive or negative. Marita's teacher once said, "I hope Marita never goes wrong because she would lead the whole school over the cliff with her." Remember that this adventuresome child needs challenge and change. Because of an innate logic, this child will thrive on educational toys, puzzles and play times that allow for expression of leadership.

2. It is important to stand "toe to toe" with this strong-willed child in order to break the will and not the spirit. Phlegmatic Lana Bateman says, "When my Choleric son reached eighteen months, we squared off for control of the home. For three months, we battled. I never let him win, not even the battle over bedtime. Because I hung in there, the victory was won, and we never contended over leadership again. Be willing to stand against the will of this child no matter what the cost. You won't be sorry. The rewards are great!" If you don't persist and if you aren't consistent with your discipline and follow through, he will soon be in charge of you.

3. Keep this child busy and give him responsibilities, for this temperament has a deep need to be productive. If he is not in control of something, his room, the dog, the back yard, he will take it out on his friends at school. Cholerics often have poor peer relationships.

4. Be sure to reason sensibly with your Choleric child for he will tend to rebel when discipline or demands lack a logical explanation. He will want to know why before doing what he's told.

5. Respect this child's innate need for fairness and justice and be open and honest with him or he will catch you up on your inconsistencies.

6. Use those situations when your Choleric child is hurt or disappointed to point out that our Lord will sometimes allow us to experience these struggles in order to give us a compassionate heart toward hurting people who may come into our lives. Since the Choleric child is short on mercy and tenderness, it is important to utilize each of their struggles as a teaching tool for these very areas. Don't let them develop the "look down on the dummies" attitude. Show them that while goals are good, occasional failure is part of life and doesn't mean the person who didn't make it is stupid.

Remember

The Choleric child's greatest need is to be in control. With that need comes impatience-based anger when things are not going his way. Because the Choleric is thinking way ahead of his parents, plotting for control, he will sense when you are most vulnerable and attack. When you have ladies in the living room, he will feel free to eat a dozen cookies, a chance he would not take if you were alone. A young woman came up to me after I spoke on children. "I think my three-year-old is in control of me." She then told me how the child kept taking cookies while she was visiting a friend. She told the child quietly not to take another one, but she did. After several gentle warnings to no avail she said sternly, "If you take one more cookie, I'll spank you when we get home." The child looked her in the eye and took one.

I asked, "What did you do?"

She replied, "Well, I couldn't do anything there in front of my friends."

"What did you do when you got home? Did you spank her?"

"I forgot."

This little imp has got her mother under firm control. She

knows the first rule of battle. Attack when the enemy is weak. Don't let this happen to you. On the first disobedience drag the child off to the bathroom and explain you mean business. If she reaches for one more cookie, remove her again and spank her. Do not worry about your friends' reaction. They are probably delighted to see that you're as strong as the child and that you may have a fighting chance at keeping her from being the child that no one wants to come to their house.

It is most important that a Choleric's parent provide healthy areas where the child can exercise control while at the same time standing firm and immovable when that need for control supersedes the limits of balance for that child's life and relationships. For instance, the Choleric child might be allowed to construct a circus in the back yard and invite friends to come be involved in the performance. He could be encouraged to direct the activities and delegate jobs to the children who want to participate. This would be an opportunity to monitor such things as bossiness or a domineering attitude and at the same time teach your child to be a wise leader. A Choleric child may want to start a children's neighborhood newsletter with tidbits of information about each child living nearby. These are constructive activities that allow the child some healthy control and expression of leadership; however, when that need for control extends itself to defiance, such as refusing to come home when told or refusing to adhere to an appointed bedtime, then the parent must consistently stand firm. Inconsistency can be fatal with this particular temperament as he's out to win and will take great pride in outsmarting you.

Years ago when Lauren was in high school, a church friend of mine came to visit and brought her four-year-old son. When it was time to leave she called Bobby out of the pool. He pretended not to hear her and continued splashing around. She sighed and said, "He never does a thing I tell him."

After a few more feeble attempts that failed, she settled down and stated, "I'll just have to sit here until he decides to get out of the pool."

That comment was all Lauren had to hear. She marched over to the edge of the pool and yelled, "Bobby, get out of this pool and do it now!" Instantly Bobby swam to the steps and climbed out. As Lauren wrapped a towel around him, his mother said, "I just can't believe it. He'd never do that for me."

He would if he knew she meant business, but this Choleric child already had his mother under firm control. Imagine what this undisciplined boy will be like by the time he's fourteen!

PHLEGMATIC

Your easy-going Phlegmatic child with simple goals of sleeping and eating is seldom a problem. Phlegmatics seem to entertain themselves so easily, it takes little to make them happy and they seem to require minimal care and attention. They are permanent press children. Of all infants, this one is the most calm, agreeable, and undemanding.

As your Phlegmatic child begins to grow, you may notice that he seems to be watching the world go by. That's because watching requires far less energy than getting involved. Because virtually every Phlegmatic action is subconsciously evaluated in terms of how much energy it will require, this child finds few activities worth the effort. Television was no doubt invented by a Phlegmatic who remembered his childhood longing for a movie he wouldn't have to walk down the street to view. What greater gift could mankind provide than a box which would be entertaining and would allow one to lie down and do nothing but watch! That is Phlegmatic heaven but also a breeding ground for laziness.

The Phlegmatic child is not an openly rebellious one but is known to possess a quiet will of iron. This child may smile and agree to do whatever you ask while inside he knows he has no intention of complying with your request. He may even lie to avoid any form of conflict or contention. He doesn't set out to be dishonest, but if shifting blame will eliminate responsibility, he's willing to take a chance.

While your Phlegmatic child is a good listener and peacemaker, his indecisiveness and lack of motivation can paralyze him with procrastination and inactivity. A Choleric parent cannot understand why this child has no ambition and doesn't want to get on with life.

Tools to Help

1. This temperament has the greatest need to be tested in order to discern areas of interest, creativity, or motivation. This is by far the most difficult child to direct toward a lifetime work for there is little the Phlegmatic can get excited about enough to persist to a positive conclusion. Check for a local child learning center or children's hospital for a testing referral and don't give up until you have a clear picture of your child's special strengths both educationally and creatively.

2. This child, of all the temperaments, has the least natural imagination so begin early in childhood to read to him and to stimulate creativity through games of make-believe and mental challenge.

3. Seek to involve this child in sports, tumbling, or dancing in order to encourage physical activity. He may not do well in team sports as he doesn't have much drive, and he may upset the other children when he's dreaming in left field.

4. When the parents of a Phlegmatic child seek to eliminate the problem of lying, they must deal first with the root problem which is not the lie itself but the fear of conflict. Because of this paralyzing fear, the child will say anything the parent wants to hear to avoid anger or punishment and that isn't always the truth. Conflict robs the Phlegmatic of peace, so the parent should first control his own anger and then face the child with quiet reason. Once the Phlegmatic is taught to deal with conflict in a healthy way, and he is assured you won't yell at him, the need for lying disappears. You need a heavy hand to control the Choleric and sometimes the Sanguine, but the same strong language will depress the Melancholy and overwhelm the Phlegmatic.

5. Begin at a very early age to present simple choices to the Phlegmatic child. Help him to make decisions on his own and praise him warmly for each one even if it wouldn't have been your selection. Remember that the Phlegmatic's problem with procrastination is based not just on inactivity but indecisiveness as well. He literally does not know which way to turn. The decision-making process is in very low gear in this temperament and must be taught simply, lovingly, and patiently with much

affirmation along the way. Let him choose the dinner menu once a week or select the cookies before his Choleric sister has grabbed the Oreos.

6. Your Phlegmatic child is the most underdeveloped in the area of expressing anger. Because anger must find some form of expression, it bubbles up as sarcasm in this personality. Sarcasm always hurts some vulnerable victim. The Phlegmatic child may exercise a twisted type of control over others through his use of sarcastic humor and has the ability to make another seem very foolish in the process. Begin at a very early age to explain the link between sarcasm and anger and how this type of humor can destroy friendships and alienate others. Help this child to find a creative outlet for his repressed anger through "talking out" his responses to conflict in an unthreatening environment. Never tell him, "Don't cry; that's for sissies; grow up and be a man!" This repression of his inner feelings will accentuate the negative, and if stored up, these hurts will later lash out on to others.

Remember

Your Phlegmatic child is driven by a need for peace and can become physically ill in the face of conflict or contention. When forced to deal with another's anger, the Phlegmatic actually loses all thought processes and goes mentally blank. This child has a deep need to feel special to someone so don't ignore him just because he's not demanding. Value your Phlegmatic child and say so!

We've talked about the most basic love needs of each child and we've looked at the temperaments as they relate to childhood personalities. We've even discussed the need to understand each one of our children and the particular strengths and weaknesses that cause him or her to require unique care and nurturing. Scripture has shown us that child-rearing using the group technique of treating everyone the same will not meet our children's needs if we are to raise a child up in the way he should go.

For Further Study, Thought, and Action

Spend some family time in teaching your children about the different personalities. Help them find who they really are and don't tell them they are wrong. Any negatives will cut off communications and turn what should be fun into a parental lecture, the dread of all children.

Add your children's personality types to your family tree and show them what relatives they resemble temperamentwise. Let them choose a picture of themselves to add to your personality notebook.

Restudy this chapter and mark any suggestions that fit a certain child with his initials. Check back often to see how you are doing in training up each child in the way he should go.

In a group study share what you have done with this information in your home. Take a quick survey of the personality types for the group's collective children. Those who find they have children that are alike will be able to share helpful tools with each other in the future.

The time you spend in thoughtful and prayerful training of your children today may well keep them from being rebellious teens. The understanding of who they really are based on the temperament tools will give them something to share with their friends who are floundering for some sense of identity.

In this day when permissiveness often leads to confusion, don't be afraid to teach, train, and discipline your children.

The rod of correction imparts wisdom, but a child left to itself disgraces his mother.
—Proverbs 29:15, NIV

❧ 9 ❧

How Can You
Bend the Twigs
As They Should Go?

No one sets out to be a bad parent; no one desires to fail. In that case, how do so many of us end up feeling that we've blown it—that there's no hope?

As we grew up we could so easily see where our parents went wrong. One was too easy, one too hard. One was fun; one was serious. In our childish wisdom we vowed we would never be like them; we would never make their mistakes. And yet, here we are doing exactly what they did. Even though we didn't mean to, we subconsciously picked up their method of reacting in stressful situations. I was in one home where the young father grabbed the noisy Sanguine child by the ear and pulled him screaming from the room. When I dared ask about this off-beat manner of discipline, he replied, "Well, that's what my father did to me."

"Did you like it?" I ventured.

"No, I hated it, but you're not supposed to like discipline."

This young man had not given any rational thought or fervent prayer over proper methods of discipline. He reacted out of his past and did just what his father had done.

Dr. Harold Bloomfield, author of *Making Peace with Your Parents* writes, "The relationship of our parents, because it is so fundamental, affects virtually all relationships, including those with our children. Parents often repeat the same objectionable behavior they resented as children."[1]

Statistics prove that a large majority of those who were beaten as children, much as they hated it, do the same thing to their children. Marilyn Murray, CLASS staff and abuse therapist, says of the young rapists she works with in the prisons, "Almost all of them were abused in some physical way as children, and they are subconsciously lashing back at their parents by molesting or attacking others."

Dr. Bloomfield also says that 90 percent of the people he counsels have an "incomplete relationship with at least one of their parents."[2]

Considering that the odds aren't with us that we will be inspired parents properly blending love and discipline, shouldn't we grasp for any help we can find? There are no simple answers or Paul would have written more specifics than "Fathers, do not exasperate your children; instead, bring them up in the training and instruction of the Lord" (Eph. 6:4, NIV). While these are surely words of wisdom you may need more specific advice.

As we look at the different personalities relating them to parenting, you will have to fit together the blend you and your mate have as they are probably not the same. Since the Bible aim is for unity of spirit, you can easily grasp that with two parents who see things from a totally different point of view, harmony is far from automatic. A child does not need to have studied the temperaments to know how to play one parent against the other. He has an inbred sense that says:

"Go to Sanguine Mother when you want fun, but don't be surprised when she forgets to pick you up at school."

"Melancholy Father will be on time, but he'll make you feel guilty for needing a ride."

"Don't try to pull anything on Choleric Mother or she'll let you have it. Test out her mood before you ask for anything."

"Try to ask Phlegmatic Dad first as he'll let you do anything as long as it's quiet and out of sight."

Are these not similar to thoughts your children may have? In order to be "of one mind" the parents must first understand who they are separately and then discuss their blending as to how it affects the training of children. The thought of making a job out of raising children sounds "too much like work" to most parents. It's much easier to deal with each emergency as it comes along. That may be true, but think of the confusing signals you are sending your children. There's no consistency and you encourage them to pit you both against each other, turning family life into a sporting event with opposing teams.

Please take the time to examine your temperaments as they relate to parenting for if you make major mistakes of neglect, indulgence, or abuse, you are affecting other lives and not just your own.

SANGUINE PARENTS

Sanguine parents are obviously the most fun. The Sanguine loves the storytelling, wrestling-on-the-floor years of a child's life and of all parents is the most free to play with the children. Sanguine parents elicit laughter and squeals of delight as they read or tell childhood stories and often act them out. I memorized *Green Eggs and Ham,* then taught it to the children so we could perform it in choral speaking at the drop of a "Cat in the Hat." It is no surprise that this parent is best liked by the children's peers. What other parent can turn a house into a circus and a disaster into a hilarious story?

Paula Lively of Dallas is the most perfect Sanguine I have ever met. She is adorable, has huge expressive eyes, and captures that youthful innocent look that is ageless in Sanguines. Her husband Fred is a classic Choleric/Melancholy who by living with her has developed a reflective sense of humor. She wrote to tell me how understanding the temperaments had helped her as both wife and mother:

> By the time Monday afternoon had come I was so tired of washing 16 loads of clothes (not really—only 4). Fred had a meeting and wouldn't be home for dinner so I didn't want to cook. Carrie and Jim were begging me to make pizza so I decided the quickest way to get out of this work was to make them do it. (My children even at age 10 are totally self-sufficient; do their own beds, can wash their own clothes, prepare recipes, on and on). Realizing they would be much more willing to make pizza themselves if it were fun, I decided to have a pizza-making contest!!! The winner (most creative AND best clean-up [who cares what it tasted like]) wins a $2.50 shopping spree at the 5 and 10 store. (There still are some bargains at M. E. Moses!) Jim, my precious and thoughtful Melancholy/Choleric son made a pepperoni with perfect rows, I mean PERFECT, of mushrooms, carefully arranged with all the stems turned in towards the center so as to achieve that sun-burst effect!!! Are you ready for

this one? Our Sanguine/Choleric daughter, Carrie, topped the pepperoni pizza by making a sausage pizza with the head of a mallard duck in the center. We collect mallards so she knew that would sway the judge! She chopped up a green pepper and somehow very creatively filled in the sausage-duck with bell pepper for color. The beak was made of crushed Doritos and the breast feathers were strips of bacon. When I came into the kitchen for the judging I immediately became hysterical at my own textbook case of a Sanguine turning work into fun and my children's textbook cases of being so classic, practically right off the pages of *Personality Plus*. We invited the Japanese neighbors from across the street and the Orthodox Jewish neighbors from next door (they didn't eat but enjoyed the company). Fred came home and was so upset 'cause he'd missed the party that he went into a depression! Not really. Oh, what fun!

Don't you wish Paula had been your mother?

There are, however, problem areas of parenting even for the "Santa Claus" personality.

Because it isn't fun to be consistent, the Sanguine is often a permissive parent. Setting standards for behavior and enforcing them is not something the Sanguine mom or dad does easily, and equally painful is the prospect of facing rejection from the offspring. Yes, the Sanguines even need to be accepted by their children, and let's face it, structuring healthy behavior and discipline in one's children doesn't put a parent in a popular position.

When the children become teens, the Sanguine parent may look for ways to escape the increased demands and responsibility. Sports, social functions, the country club, even a fun job can become excuses for not spending time at home. When the fun-loving, disorganized Sanguine can't be bothered by the details of keeping up with appointments or getting the children where they need to be on time, the more responsible parent, usually a Melancholy, has to be the family manager, sighing with martyrdom while doing it, "Your mother would lose her head if it weren't attached" or "Your father never knows which end is up!" This struggle may not be quite so radical if the Sanguine's secondary temperament is Choleric, bringing a more responsible and organized balance to the personality.

It is truly amazing how quickly the Sanguine parent disappears when the children become demanding or aren't fun anymore.

This retreat can cause a spouse to feel like he or she is raising a single-parent family with the questionable help of a drop-in playmate now and then to provide entertainment.

One area that is troublesome for the child of a Sanguine is that of competition where friends are involved. Often there is some jealousy when the child's friends seem drawn to the Sanguine parent more than they enjoy spending time with the child they came to visit. This type of personality competition can become more severe as the years pass and dates arrive at the front door to be charmed away by a Sanguine mother.

The combination Choleric/Sanguine seems to be the parent most enjoyed and accepted by children growing up for they have the Sanguine magnetism and yet know how to lead effectively and accomplish something when properly motivated by potential praise.

Often the Sanguine/Choleric mother who has trouble getting a simple dinner on the table at a consistent time can produce instant banquets for crowds of cheering teen-agers. While this excited mother is accepting the accolades of the youth, her Melancholy husband comes home to find a circus with his wife as the cooking ringmaster. Instead of joining in the fun with her, he tends to take her talents as a personal affront wondering why she can't get this enthusiastic over cooking for him, not understanding that if he gave her a standing ovation for each steak, she might grill one more often. He can't tolerate the noise of the crowd, so he withdraws to his room waiting for her to come and soothe his hurt feelings. Since she's insensitive to his needs and wouldn't leave the party anyway, she shrugs and asks, "I wonder what's wrong with your father tonight?" Waiting alone for sympathy that doesn't arrive shows the husband that his evaluation was right. "She doesn't really love me—in fact, she cares more for that bunch of strangers than for her own husband." He sinks into a deep depression, doesn't speak to her for two weeks, and she has no idea why.

What a lot of hassle we can be spared when we understand why we behave as we do. The father in this case can save himself heartbreak if he knows her cooking for the crowd has no bearing on her love for him. Even if he told her how hurt he was, she would not have the sensitivity to understand and would call the whole idea ridiculous. He should join in with the gang and force himself to have a good time or greet everyone and retreat with a positive attitude.

If the Melancholy does not have the authority to handle this situation, we could hope the Sanguine wife could develop an awareness of his needs and lovingly take a tray of food to his room. An improvement on either side would make a difference in the harmony of the home.

Because Sanguine/Cholerics are able to combine goals with fun, they make excellent youth leaders and can influence questioning teens in a positive and godly direction.

I was in one church where the youth pastor was a straight Sanguine, charm without discipline. He had taken fifty youth for a hike in the mountains to return at 5:30 P.M. at the church. Parents were sitting in cars waiting and no one came. The pastor was called and two hours later the police. At 8:00 P.M. the group arrived happy and singing. They'd had a great time, and no one, including the youth pastor, had any idea what time it was!

MELANCHOLY PARENTS

The Melancholy is a dutiful, responsible parent who will often try to expose the children to piano, trumpet, dancing, art, or other cultural pursuits. Because Melancholies set such high standards, they usually press for intellectual achievement as well and long for a child to appreciate the deeper things of life. They read them poetry, listen to classical music, and get them to their lessons on time.

Fred and I were recently the guests of Dr. and Mrs. Hans Diehl. Mrs. Diehl holds a doctorate in musical arts and is an accomplished concert pianist who performs all over the country, and Hans is both a doctor and lecturer on nutrition. The grand piano filled a large section of their living room and next to it under a spotlight were two chairs each with a violin leaning against them. Mrs. Diehl explained that the instruments were left out at all times to encourage their two children Byron (age ten) and Carmen (age eight) to play their violins whenever they wanted to. "Their violins should be their friends."

After dinner we found out these two precocious, talented children were dear friends with the violins as they gave us an astonishing concert. Byron also played duets with his mother on the piano, not little plodding numbers like "Row, Row, Row Your Boat," but sonatas by Schubert and Mozart.

I was so overwhelmed with the depth of talent and the obvious loving care that the parents had given these two brilliant children that suddenly I felt like a laggard. My mother had been a violin and cello teacher. Where had I gone wrong? I remember my mother trying to teach ten-year-old Marita the violin. Somehow just seeing her hold the instrument in her hand was hilarious. Each time she picked it up to practice we all laughed so hard we cried. She was somewhat a child's version of Jack Benny.

As I listened to Byron and Carmen performing so effortlessly, I wondered would Marita have been a violinist today if I'd been a Melancholy mother?

Unfortunately, the Melancholy's child may be overwhelmed and discouraged if the parent sets the standards too high and consistently puts those goals beyond the child's reach. Such a child would feel as if he could never do enough to please the Melancholy parent, for indeed, nothing is quite good enough. It is of paramount importance that the Melancholy parent learn to set those standards at a reachable level for the child to experience feelings of accomplishment and to realize that unless the child is also a Melancholy, he may not be able to achieve what the parent desires. This understanding alone can be such a healing instrument in those parent-child relationships.

Some parents with this Melancholy temperament will subconsciously choose an opposite sex child to be a special companion. Generally, the Melancholy has become badly disenchanted by inability to conform his spouse to the image he has of a perfect wife and will then move on to the more flexible material of a child. This parent will tend to draw that little one out of a child's world and into an early adult one by sharing everything from emotional struggles or discouragements to business problems or failures. Without realizing what is happening, the parent robs the child of a childhood and draws him into an adult world of problems, pressures, and emotions. The parent feels he's giving this child special attention and can't possibly see that what he's doing is causing future emotional problems.

Eventually the child reaches adulthood but not without an illusive root of bitterness and anger due to that lost childhood.

Eventually those feelings will surface in a negative or resentful way, and the parent will place the blame on the child. "I can't imagine why she turned against me after all the love I've given her." Lana Bateman tells of one such situation that was presented to her for prayer counseling.

A lovely Choleric/Melancholy lady named Terry came to see me complaining of marriage problems. She didn't believe that her husband loved her, but when I asked her to explain his actions toward her, she told a different story. He sounded like a gentle, caring husband who longed for his wife to be herself and not to put unhealthy worth in him.

As we talked, I found that this young woman grew up with a Melancholy father, who made her his companion from her first breath. He told her of his hopes, dreams, inventions, disappointments, and struggles. He drew her into his world of business and emotions. She lost her real identity and became the extension of a great man. She also lost her childhood as he opened his world with all of its stresses to her.

Because this father didn't know how to give healthy love, Terry had to redefine love in terms of what he *was* able to give. Love became an aspiration to carry on his greatness. Love became being that extension of a man who would constantly push you on to bigger and better achievements.

It is no surprise that this young woman couldn't accept healthy love from her husband. He just wanted her to be herself and not an extension of her father. She had never experienced such a strange attitude. He must not love her! Her idea of what love really was had been so distorted by the Melancholy parent who made her a substitute wife, that she couldn't perceive genuine love when it was presented to her. This distortion almost destroyed her marriage and took several years to successfully grow beyond.

While this relationship problem certainly doesn't exist for all Melancholies, it does occur with some frequency among those who may have experienced painful childhoods. This is an area for preventative prayer if a parent with this temperament finds himself seriously favoring and spending time with one particular child.

The Melancholy mother with Sanguine children has difficulty realizing the value of laughter for these little ones. They will work to "make mother happy" and if mother responds they will be overjoyed. I can remember how my father, two brothers, and

I would do everything we could to amuse my Phelgmatic/Melancholy mother who would just sigh and say to my father, "If you don't stop teaching them all these tom-fool things they will never amount to a row of pins." Every once in a while we'd get to Mother and she'd really laugh. These were high points in our childhood. So Melancholy mothers realize, life may be difficult but a laugh here and there may help.

A woman from Texas wrote me this following letter.

> I have just finished reading your book, *Personality Plus*, and wanted to tell you how very much I enjoyed it and how helpful I found it to be. It met the *true* test of "enjoyable," as my mainly Melancholy temperament (with much Phlegmatic) rarely is moved to LAUGH OUT LOUD! Your delightful illustrations were so *true* to life . . . that I repeatedly found myself laughing with deep "ha, ha, ha's." My precious, Sanguine four-year-old daughter had no idea what I was laughing at, but, delighted for the chance to laugh and have some fun, would laugh in high-volume unison. And once she even brought me the book, saying, "Here Mommy . . . let's read your book and laugh together."
>
> But the laughter was a "fringe" benefit . . . the main thing I thank you for is the understanding this book has given me. My husband has always believed . . . that "everything would be all right if she'd just loosen up," while I, on the other hand, have had trouble even *believing* that someone would hang a picture without "measuring the wall."
>
> Reading to my daughter yesterday, P. D. Eastman's *The Best Nest*, a delightful children's book, I found myself chuckling to discover why Mr. and Mrs. Bird kept relocating their nest . . . poor Mr. Bird—Phlegmatic, contented—prodded on by his Choleric Mrs. Bird. Even the illustrations prove the theory: she *looks* bossy!
> Linda Klatt

Some Melancholies are hampered during the parenting years by constant bouts with depression while others battle the syndrome of martyrdom. While it is true that any temperament could fall prey to the beast of martyrdom, the Melancholy is by far the most susceptible. This forces us to take a closer look at the most self-sacrificing temperament for an understanding of its vulnerability. The Melancholy may suffer from one of two different types of "martyrmania."

The first is called *the overt martyr*. This type of martyr is constantly verbalizing all he has done for the children. The overt martyr might sound something like this, "Don't you care how hard I have to work to give you what you have?" or "I never get any time to myself. All I ever do is work my fingers to the bone, and this is the thanks I get." Obviously this type of emotional unloading produces a burden of guilt in the child.

The second type of Melancholy martyr is called *the subtle martyr.* The subtle martyr seldom if ever verbalizes his or her self-sacrifice, but simply pours out a life on the altar of the children's needs. The subtle martyr's children may spend a lifetime watching the parent pick up after them, clean their rooms, and in some extreme cases even do their homework.

This type of martyr will give all to the child even when it is extremely unwise to do so. Such a parent will often sacrifice his own needs to buy for the child without ever verbalizing the personal cost.

The child of the subtle martyr will feel tremendous guilt but the guilt will be on a subconscious level. Just as the martyrdom of the parent is subtle or hidden from open understanding, so is the guilt of the child hidden away in the subconscious mind. The only touch such a child might have with that illusive pressure might be a sense of needing to spend a lifetime repaying the parent for that which no one can explain. The child might verbalize it this way, "I'll never be able to do enough to pay my mom or dad back for all they've done. I try so hard and it never seems to be enough. Why do I always feel guilty?"

We're beginning to see that while the Melancholy is a dependable, concerned parent, there are definitely trouble areas in the parent-child relationship.

The Melancholy is one of two controlling personalities, second only to the Choleric. Perhaps in a quiet way the Melancholy is the most controlling of all. This temperament can do more damage with eye-rolling, looks of disappointment, and deep sighs than all of the other temperaments can do with a thousand words. This is a powerful and subtle control and makes the child feel guilty, inadequate, and smothered all at the same time.

When the Melancholy lets these tendencies get out of hand, a child will pull hard and fast to get away from home and in adulthood many will effectively distance themselves from Melancholy parents who will weep to their friends in self pity.

CHOLERIC PARENTS

The Choleric parent is dutiful and responsible and will virtually never forget where the child needs to be or when he needs to be there. A Choleric exerts sound leadership in the home and invariably has the right answer for every question a child might ask.

Not only does the Choleric establish goals for his children but has no trouble moving the whole family to action. The Choleric can be counted on to organize and perform what is necessary to meet the needs of his children in almost every area except that of emotions. Since the Choleric looks upon people who cry as weak, he transmits to his children that they should not let their feelings show.

Like the Melancholy, the Choleric must maintain absolute control of his children. While the Melancholy controls emotionally, the Choleric controls openly and is known as the aggressive temperament. His children learn there is only one way to behave and many put on Phlegmatic masks of submission hiding their real personality even from themselves.

Another area of struggle for the Choleric parent-child relationship is that of quality time spent together. The Choleric is often a workaholic and assumes if he makes a good living that's all that should be expected of him. When the Choleric *is* home, he demands constant productivity from children and gives them little time to relax. One lady told me she had been raised on a farm and once a week they all went to town to a drive-in movie. Her Choleric mother could not let them waste time, and so the children would all sit in the back of the pick-up truck and husk corn, string beans, or shell peas while watching *Snow White*. The Choleric's motto is "Never let them rest." Productivity is next to godliness. Sadly, the Choleric would rather do a task himself than put up with what is conceived as a poor performance by a child. Unfortunately, there is no other way but the Choleric's way and this can wipe out a child who needs so badly to learn from an open and patient teacher and be allowed to make mistakes.

Often the Choleric parent will grab the project out of the child's hand and say, "I knew I should have done this myself." A comment such as this devastates the child and signals to him he is incompetent. Later when this parent says, "What's the matter with you stupid?" the child confirms in his mind that he is worthless.

This type of parental behavior is so frequent with Cholerics that I often see very successful men whose children have all turned out to be failures. They can't understand how this happened when they gave them every opportunity in the world to succeed.

A millionaire who came to a *Personality Plus* seminar took me afterwards to see his new private airplane. When we were alone he told me a typical story of his son. The young man had been given every advantage imaginable and had doors opened to him that the average person could never hope to enter. He'd done poorly in school and seemed inept in the family business. "Have you sent him out on his own?" I asked.

"Oh yes and that was a fiasco. He ruined both a family and a business while he was gone, and I had no choice but to bring him back home and support him. He wants to be rich, but he has no idea of how to work." Then the man dropped his head and calmed his anger. "After listening to you today, I can see I'm a Choleric, and I guess I did all the wrong things as a parent."

It is so hard, close to impossible, for a Choleric to see that his drive and supposed inspiration make a child feel worthless. "What's the use? I'll never make it anyhow." Sometimes a Choleric child will determine to show his father up, but in his angry pursuit, he overshoots the mark and fails. He may come home subdued like the prodigal son or sink into a way of life that brings shame onto his parents. This negative life-style seems to be the only way he can exert control and win. He's no longer in competition and he's caused his father to have a heart attack.

Teens who have lived under a strong Choleric parent and who know they can never be what Superdad or Supermom want them to be tend to become depressed. Parents are always stunned when smart children from good homes suddenly commit suicide "for no good reason."

If you are a Choleric parent be brave enough to sit down with your children and ask them if you are somewhat like these parents I've described. Watch their body language as well as their words as they may be too afraid to tell the truth.

The Choleric parent quickly becomes impatient with a child's immature decision-making abilities so he makes all the child's decisions. This problem area coupled with a demanding, unemotional, domineering personality can crush and wound a young child's sensitive spirit and produce rebellion in an older youth making them unable to decide on anything in life.

Lana Bateman tells of an experience with her son.

> Our Phlegmatic son, Rob, was in from college. He had done something that was thoughtless, and his dad responded out of Choleric impatience with volatile anger. This resulted in Rob's being embarrassed in front of a friend who was present. After the natural instincts of that Choleric had been communicated, God began to press Marc's heart and show him that while he had stated a valuable principle to his son, the message would be lost amidst the embarrassment of calling him down in anger before his friend. God showed Marc that while his words were wisdom, his manner of expressing them destroyed their influence.
>
> Marc got up out of bed that night, got dressed and went upstairs to apologize to Rob in the presence of his friend. What a beautiful illustration of what God can do to overcome our natural temperament weaknesses if we will just be open to him and desire to please him in our parenting. God longs to deal with the destructive parts of our personalities, and for the Choleric, rash anger is often at the top of the list.

One memory a child has difficulty releasing is the sensation of a parent's anger which seems to have a profound and lasting effect on a young mind.

If you are a Choleric parent do not give up in disgust and brand yourself a failure. You have probably not done many of these things yourself, but the tendency is surely there, and you must take caution not to wipe out the needed ego-strength of your child. You have a strength other parents covet—you can get more accomplished in a shorter time than anyone else, but relax, take the pressure off the home front, and let them see the charm you exhibit when out in the world. If your son never wins a game pitching for Little League, it won't matter if you let him know you love him as he is—with or without winning games. But if he wins nine out of ten and you ask why he didn't win the tenth, his whole season will become a wipe-out.

Motivate, encourage, and inspire, but don't dominate and put the family on an endless treadmill experience.

PHLEGMATIC PARENT

The Phlegmatic's peaceful personality has a way of stabilizing children. Little ones have a need for routine in their lives, and the Phlegmatic is a person who will thrive on that very thing, for they don't like change and don't feel a need to be unnecessarily creative. That easy-going quality of this temperament makes them calm, accepting parents who don't get upset easily and always seem to have time for the children. The Phlegmatic mother will put playing with the children ahead of cleaning the house. There are, however, certain drawbacks for the Phlegmatic parent just as there are with the other three temperaments we've already discussed.

The Phlegmatic tends to be a permissive parent in order to avoid conflict. Duty and responsibility are not words in the Phlegmatic vocabulary, and he or she often takes the easy road. Since the Phlegmatic does not like to be told what to do because of the underlying stubborn streak, the pressures of responsibility are most easily left to the Choleric whom the Phlegmatic usually marries.

Children of a Phlegmatic often see this parent as lazy and weak and feel he or she is unwilling to defend himself in time of conflict. It is important that this attitude be faced if the Phlegmatic is confronted by a child approaching adulthood.

One Choleric young man went to his mother and complained bitterly that she was weak and let "Dad" run over her. It was obvious that this boy was taking up the offense for his mother, but, unfortunately for him, he had not properly perceived the relationship between his parents. This was his mother's response.

> You don't seem to understand, son. When an issue truly matters to me, I will work it through with your dad. Most things just don't matter that much. Why should I have it my way when the outcome means so little to me—and why shouldn't we do it his way, when it means so much to him?

This young man finally began to realize a temperament truth where his mother was concerned. She really *didn't care!* He was wasting his frustration on a situation that didn't really exist. He was able, at last, to lay down the emotional responsibility of protecting his mom. She may have appeared to be vulnerable, but she wasn't quite as helpless as he had thought.

Another type of family struggle may occur because of the Phlegmatic parent's tendency toward being somewhat slow or lazy. Children may witness parental conflict over lack of organization in caring for both home and children. A Phlegmatic father might neglect to get the bills paid or necessary house repairs accomplished. A Phlegmatic mother may not get the Christmas decorations put away until Easter looms on the horizon. Although the Phlegmatic has the ability to accomplish these tasks, we must remember that this personality evaluates almost everything in subconscious terms of how much energy it will take, up to and including the raising of children. Unfortunately this parent can often be found in front of the television set doing what comes most naturally, watching!

While the Phlegmatic parent is the most easy-going and unpressured, he must make the major effort to get what needs to be done finished on time and to get out of the chair and discipline the children.

For Further Study, Thought, and Action

Because parenting is such a serious subject, you should take time to sit down with your mate and list your individual strengths and weaknesses as parents. Look at the different approaches you have to discipline because of your temperaments. See where your conflicts are. Do your children pit one of you against the other? Does one of you always give in? Is one of you the easy mark?

As Fred and I were raising our children, we had a simple rule: Whichever one of us was asked first gave the answer and that was it. There was no running to the other parent for a second opinion. This eliminated bartering and established unity.

As you list your differences as parents in your personality notebook, discuss each one and begin to make some basic rules for each one of you to follow. To win as parents you both must be on the same team, not on opposing sides. You must be playing the same game with the same set of instructions. Even young children know when there is no unity between the parents, and they begin early to work the moods of their mother and avoid the anger of their father.

In your group study, bring in articles and case histories about teen depression and suicide. Notice what characteristics these disheartened teens have in common. Read my chapters on teen depression, one in *Lives on the Mend* and one in *Blow Away the Black Clouds* (revised edition). Discuss the causes of teen depression listed in these sources and consider those which might apply to any of your children. Has there been divorce or death in the family giving them a feeling of rejection? Have there been frequent moves causing instability? Have there been illnesses, deprivation, or traumas leading to fears?

Have your children watched frightening or explicit TV? Do they play Dungeons and Dragons? Do they have friends who take drugs? As you go over these and other questions in your study group, make some basic policies of parenting that you all agree on. Make this a beginning for your whole church to take a new interest in raising up their children under godly and practical principles.

Parents are desperate for help today. Why not be the catalyst for a unified approach to childraising in your church and community? If you are a single parent, it is even more important that you initiate a group with similar problems that may work together for positive solutions.

Fathers, do not exasperate your children; instead, bring them up in the training and instruction of the Lord.
                                              —Ephesians 6:4, NIV

PART III

RECOVER THE PAST WITH A FUTURE THAT WILL LAST

RECOVER:

To restore to its original form

Now that you have looked deeply into your life, taken off the masks that had hidden the real you, and begun to understand those other people in a new light, it is time to recover the original spirit that God had in mind for you and to restore your emotional health and inner peace. If in examining your roots you find some repeated negative traits or actions, determine to halt them now before you pass on to your children what may have been transmitted to you. Be an encourager to others and help them become what God has in mind for them. He created each one for such a time as this.

For the Lord is always good. He is always loving and kind, and his faithfulness goes on and on to each succeeding generation.
—Psalm 100:5, TLB

❧ 10 ❧

What about
the Bruised Fruit?

As we aim to RECOVER from the mistakes or maskings of the past, we want to restore ourselves and our children to our "original form." What were we intended to be like?

The birth of each new child brings with it an exciting opportunity for creative growth. Grandparents instantly spot physical features like someone on their side of the family. Mothers hope she'll be pretty and fathers wonder what he'll be like when he grows up. The range of potential for each new life is limitless, and yet not all of us achieve the abundant life God offers.

In the parable of the Sower in Luke 8, Jesus tells of four types of growth. Using the seed as the word of God, he shows how seed develops differently according to where it is planted and how it is nurtured. Let's apply these same truths to our seed, our children, or to ourselves.

"Some fell along the path. It was trampled on, and the birds of the air ate it up" (Luke 8:5, NIV).

Some of us grew up as seed scattered on the path. We had life in us, but somehow it got trampled down; people walked over us and some kicked us. Birds flew over head and some pecked at us and made fun of us. After a while on the dry road of life, we withdrew, built a wall of protection around us and said, "I'm not going to let anyone hurt me ever again."

"Some fell on rock, and when it came up, the plants withered because they had no moisture" (Luke 8:6, NIV).

Some of us grew up on the rocks with no moisture to maintain us, no nurturing to let us know we were of value. We didn't have the encouragement we needed; we wondered who we really were. When we cried out for attention, we were told to be quiet like our sister or sit still like our brother. We were trained up to be good, but not to be anyone in particular. We tried shifting our personalities to be what others wanted us to be, and we grew up confused with roots that never quite took hold. We thirsted for love from parents who had hardened hearts and who had lived on the rocks themselves. They did the best they knew how, but it wasn't enough for us, and we withered and dried up emotionally.

"Other seed fell among thorns, which grew up with it and choked the plants" (Luke 8:7, NIV).

Some of us grew up among the thorns, choked by the worries of the world; we had parents who were fearful or who always thought the worst of us. Some told us what was wrong with us, but seldom what was right. Some of them sought riches and some the pursuits of pleasure, and we seemed somehow to be in the way. Some left us completely and our little hearts were broken as we wandered in the weeds of the world hiding our feelings and smiling at grief. We felt we must be to blame for each one of their failures, and we tried to free them from their briar patch without getting caught up ourselves.

Some of us had siblings who were our thorns, who mocked us, who were considered better than us, who may have even abused us—thorns who grew up with us and choked out our emotional growth.

"Still other seed fell on good soil. It came up and yielded a crop, a hundred times more than was sown" (Luke 8:8, NIV).

Some fortunate ones of us grew up in good soil with parents who were emotionally mature and stable themselves, who gave us healthy unselfish love, and who treated each one of us as a precious gift from God. These parents knew Proverbs 22:6 not only as a verse but as a clear directive. They sought to understand each child's individual temperament, creative talents, and spiritual gifts and to train us up as we should go so that when we grew up, we would know who we were and wouldn't have to be on an endless search to find ourselves.

How rewarding it is to a parent to look at his crop and see it has matured beyond expectation. Each child has grown to his own potential. The rose hasn't been painted to look like a zinnia;

the smile hasn't been wiped off the daisy's face; the bluebell hasn't been told not to ring.

In God's Garden there are many people who are blossoming for his glory, but what about the bruised fruit: those who have grown up in soil that was far from ideal, those who have had to struggle to stay alive, those whose roots aren't deep enough to keep their tree upright, those who have fallen off and been hurt when hit by winds of adversity? What about the bruised fruit?

If you have read through each chapter in this book, have thought introspectively about your life and still have some unanswered questions about your identity, perhaps you have grown from seed that was trampled on, that had no watering or fertilizing, that was choked out by the demands of others. Think back on your childhood and ask the Lord to reveal any traumas you may have stuffed away in the cracks of your life, any hurts or bitter weeds that you have not pulled up and dealt with realistically and spiritually. We first have to see the wound before we can repair the damages. Counselors usually agree that it is difficult to help a person with a problem who is in firm denial of its existence.

As I have been teaching seminars based on my book, *Lives on the Mend,* I have increasingly encountered women who have suppressed the hurts of the past and who have denied that childhood deprivations or abuse have anything to do with their chronic headaches or eating disorders.

Often after listening to me review the symptoms of a victim, a woman will come and say quietly, "I've never told this to anyone in my life before." I then take the person aside and listen to the hurts and heartaches of a lifetime. We know today that abuse of all types—physical, sexual, and emotional—is rampant in the world, but few of us realize that there are victims with repressed pains of the past sitting in our congregations, victims who have never dared to tell the pastor or the other apparently perfect parishoners of their problems.

Some who do confess their hurts are told by well-meaning Christians to pray about it, think positive thoughts, or forgive the perpetrator—all good ideas; however, some have sincerely followed all these suggestions and are still in emotional pain.

Much as we would wish to ignore the facts, incest and abuse

are alive in our churches, and we are just becoming aware of the devastating and long-range effects. Aside from the abuse itself, the great tragedy is that these children grow up emotionally crippled. As adults they are still suffering from the pains of their past, and often they have submerged their bruised feelings so deeply that they have gaps in their memories, often an indicator of severe childhood trauma.

Do all victims respond the same way to childhood trauma? Obviously not, as there are so many variables, such as intensity and frequency of the attack, the relationship of the victim to the perpetrator, and the basic temperament pattern before the fruit was bruised. Although this chapter is not intended to be a psychological treatise, I have found that when I show a generalized picture of the responses according to personality types, it helps people examine themselves, their hurting friends, and even their own children.

When a child is abused—physically, sexually, or emotionally— he or she is initially in a state of shock. Even though the attack or the emotional abuse is not the child's fault, the victim feels guilty and somehow to blame. Way inside, the child feels dirty and of little value. Whatever the child's basic temperament, the inner child accepts the verdict, "I'm guilty." However, the reaction to the abuse varies according to the innate personality.

To give us a tool, a simple set of guidelines, let's divide ourselves into two categories: the combination of (1) Melancholy/ Phlegmatic—introverted, guilt-absorbing, easily depressed, and passive—and (2) Sanguine/Choleric—outgoing, optimistic, achieving, and resilient. How would each set probably respond to trauma?

The symptoms of the Melancholy/Phlegmatic start with an acceptance of themselves as unworthy of love and unable to amount to much in life. From normal children they become pessimistic, unenthusiastic, guilt-ridden, and often withdrawn after being abused or emotionally deprived. They often have early depression, seldom seem truly happy, and may suffer from phobias. Some develop a dependency on other people, and later on alcohol or drugs to keep them going or to make them feel of worth. As they grow up, some develop eating or digestive disorders and signs of emotional problems. Because of the guilt they assume from their past victimization, some may develop deep inferiority complexes or associate with people of a lower class to lift their self-image.

Sending them for assertiveness training or even to seminary may do nothing more than pull them up a few notches, unless the underlying root cause is exposed and dealt with.

They see others succeeding while everything they touch seems to turn to ashes. Even their achievements appear to them as failures. As women, they often seek counsel from each visiting speaker or evangelist but never seem to profit from logical advice. They keep hoping the next counselor will give them a formula for success, but all too frequently the counselors never even asked about the possibility of childhood molestation or deprivation. Until the abuse victim with this type of personality gets loving counsel that deals with her deep-seated guilt, she will continue to be depressed and not really understand why.

The Sanguine/Choleric victim who is of a stronger personality feels the guilt but refuses to give in to it. She determines not to let this trauma or series of events ruin her life. She wants to achieve, no matter what; she has a compulsive need to prove to herself, God, and others that she is all right. She covers up her abuse, puts a big Band-Aid over her hurts, and gets on with life. In school she is hard-driving, active, and often over-achieving. She becomes a caretaker for those with problems, is usually an aggressive leader, and often dates older and successful men. As an adult she may become a perfectionistic workaholic. Often these victims go into full-time Christian service or become social workers where they seem to live sacrificial lives. They may exhibit obsessive, even neutrotic, drives which cover the deep hurts hidden inside and the physical problems which they don't let anyone know about, such as allergies, migraines, ulcers, colitis, and unexplained aches and pains.

While the symptoms of the passive victims show as emotional problems to those who are at all observant, the aggressive victim fools most people and even is praised in church for her all-consuming dedication to God and charitable works.

The Sanguine/Choleric victim-achiever many times feels proud of how she has handled past abuses and, without realizing the differences in personalities, looks down on those who can't hold it all together. They are usually the ones who speak out against counseling or any outside help because they've been able to control themselves in spite of problems. "If I can make it, what's the matter with you?" They often have little compassion for the "weak links" and add guilt to them by saying, "If you were really a Christian you would have gotten over this by now." While I'm sure they mean well and may help some hypochondriacs, their confidence and authority may be the proverbial straw that broke the camel's back, the word that says, "I'm okay but you are pitiful and surely not spiritual." We must all be so very careful to avoid heaping guilt on people who can't cope with life as we are able to do. How helpful it is when we realize the different personalities and their reactions to adverse circumstances so we can handle others with wisdom and not ignorance.

In CLASS we find many Sanguine/Choleric victims who have stayed on top of their emotions appearing to be confidently in control until they hit forty. Why that is the turning point we don't know, but suddenly this over-achiever begins to fall apart. She apologizes for crying and hates herself for being weak. Some have been taking medication for pain that suddenly does no good, and they are driven into a depression they have always been able to control in the past. Pain is a great leveler of all personalities and often forces the strongest of us to seek help.

No matter which personality combination a person is, the first step in overcoming the pains of the past is to admit there is a problem and be willing to deal with it. Denial only deepens the depression.

For Further Study, Thought and Action

Read the parable of the Sower in Luke 8 about the different types of seeds and soils. Does any one of these situations ring any familiar bells from your past? As a child did you feel pushed around? stepped on? walked over? Were you ever abused? Was your childhood spent on the rocks with no attention or nuturing? Did you seldom receive selfless love? Were you fighting your way through the weeds feeling rejected, lonely, or guilty?

Or were you the child of loving, emotionally stable parents who treated you with respect and trained you according to your own personality and talents?

Start by asking a friend to listen to your life story and see if he or she discerns any inconsistencies. If you are doing this study in a group, don't turn it into a mass confession time which will embarrass some of the members. Instead, pair up for this part of the analysis and have each person sensitively share with one other person what he or she remembers of childhood pains. Often the verbal expression of past hurts will initiate a healing process. Encourage the individual who has never shared this with anyone before and insure confidentiality. Some will be helped by talking with the pastor, although often women tell me they are afraid if the pastor "knew all" he wouldn't like them. Victims of sexual abuse frequently cannot relate to a counselor of the same sex as the perpetrator.

Read the "Incest" chapter (10) in *Lives on the Mend,* and review the ten steps to recovery plus the chapter on "Emotional Pains of the Past" (15) which includes the process for inner healing. Many have also found that writing down their thoughts and feelings in a journal can be very helpful.

Do a study on the available counselors and support groups in your area. Find out what assistance your church has and then inquire about others. Sometimes one church in an area will have a staff person who specializes in incest cases while another church may deny they have any victims. It takes people who care for others to spend the time necessary to provide a list of sources for those in need.

Trees whose fruit withereth, without fruit, twice dead, plucked up by the roots.

—Jude 12, KJV

❧ 11 ❧

How Can You Dig Up
the Old Roots?

Because they had no root, they withered away.
—Matthew 13:6, KJV

As you have thought over your past and researched your ancestors, you may have found more than positive personality traits;
you may have unearthed some patterns of abuse or some repeated
diseases. Statistics prove that those who were abused often become abusers, that those who had parents who were fearful often
become phobic, that over half of those who had an alcoholic parent marry or become alcoholics.[1]

A girl we shall call Jan did a study to see the effects of alcohol-
ism on her family. She researched her own background and with
her brother and husband interviewed many relatives, all of whom
were delighted to add their opinions and anecdotes. As I recount
what she wrote to me, perhaps these summaries will encourage
you to ferret out some of your family stories and trace repetitive
problems.

Jan's grandfather on her father's side was an extremely abusive alcoholic who deserted his family, refused to support them,
yet dropped by often enough to get his wife pregnant and produce
nine children whom he beat up whenever he came home. With
this background of a pathetically poor childhood and a loathing
for their father, nine out of nine became alcoholics, one of them
Jan's father. He had nine auto accidents in ten years, ran over
a child while drunk, and was once pronounced dead and on his
way to the morgue before he revived.

Jan's mother came from a family full of emotional, physical, and sexual abuse. She was one of six children, two of whom died in infancy and one in a hunting accident. In her anguish Jan's grandmother made a commitment not to love any of her other children so she wouldn't be hurt when God took them away. Jan's mother, one of the remaining three children, felt rejected and eventually married to get away from home and find some one who would really love her.

Wed to an alcoholic, she became a foodaholic and together they produced five children who grew up in this sick setting. Jan describes and labels each one as the cast in an alcoholic drama.

Oldest brother—SUPER HERO—Choleric.

He is both a workaholic and an alcoholic, is verbally abusive to his wife and neglects his children who feel unloved. He totally denies he has a problem, he is filled with hidden hostilities and repressed rage, and he feels because he keeps a job that he is not an alcoholic.

Oldest sister—BORN LOSER—Phlegmatic.

At thirty-nine this sister cannot function without the help of her mother who cooks for her and stuffs the four children who range from fourteen to newborn. She has been married twice to "losers" and is both physically and verbally abusive to her children. There is little hope for any of them as she is emotionally incapable of any healthy relationships.

Me—GOOD GIRL—Choleric

By God's grace I could see early in life that I didn't want to be like the others. I determined not to marry a loser or jump into a marriage to get away from the home problems. I was the good girl who went to church and did her homework. God's love helped me deal with the family neglect and abuse on a level I could bear. I married a pastor whose unconditional love has given me a feeling of worth and his fathering of our children has given me a model of God's love for us.

Younger brother—SCAPEGOAT—Melancholy.

He was the black sheep of a dark family, a whiney sensitive little boy raised by women (mother, grandmother, and sisters). He had a dependency personality and went into drugs and sex in high school. By a miracle of the Lord he has been redeemed and is in training to be a pastor.

Younger sister—PET—Sanguine

She was the last, became the family pet, and is both spoiled and dependent. She is divorced and is emotionally, verbally, and physically abusive to her children often kicking and slapping them. She is still seeking someone to take care of her and is pursuing a lifestyle which will lead to no good end.

From Jan's summary of her family history, we can see how amazing it is that she extricated herself from the repeat patterns and became proof that with God all things are possible.

On a trip from Cleveland to Chicago I was placed next to an off-duty male flight attendant. As he poured out his life story to me, he told how his father was an alcoholic and never came to any of his school functions. "All I wanted was a normal father who would show up sober." By questioning I found that the grandfather was also an alcoholic. When I explained to him how important it was that he break this chain of addictive weaknesses, he told me, "My friends tease me because I'm too straight and won't do the things they do, but I'm not taking any chances."

Alcoholic problems are not the only ones passed down from generation to generation.

One woman who came to CLASS later wrote me that she had done a study on her family and found that in five generations the first child born was conceived out of wedlock. Another person told of how she couldn't understand why she felt a strong compulsion to beat up her child. As she controlled her urges and prayed fervently for deliverance, she remembered how her mother had beaten her. By asking an uncle, she learned that her mother had been abused by both of her parents.

A friend's father after watching *The Burning Bed* on TV became irate at the abusing husband and later disclosed how his father had beaten up his mother. He had never told anyone in the family how he as a six-year-old had grabbed a broom and hit his father with it in an attempt to protect his mother. The father had kicked him across the room, and the son had kept a burning anger within him since that time. This revelation explained why he had seldom wanted to spend time with his father and the discussion brought out hidden feelings he had never disclosed. As the family talked with him, he remembered his father's hatred of his own father and began to wonder if he had been abused also.

A counselor told me how frequently she finds divorce repeats itself in succeeding generations, often with the same excuses given as to why they could no longer stay together.

Migraine headaches, allergies, and other stress-related problems seem to wind a repetitive thread through families.

Even the manipulation of the Cholerics—the remaking of succeeding generations into submissive children no matter what the original temperament—forms a pattern that needs to be broken. People with high IQs who never seem to reach their potential are often similar to a parent and have an underlying fear of their inability to handle success.

Physical problems repeat themselves. In my family, diabetes and hypoglycemia have appeared many times in each generation as far back as we can trace. The reason doctors take down family histories is to help them spot potential problems and hopefully halt them in early stages.

As you look through your family's background, be alert to signs of negative patterns that need to be changed so that the REAL YOU can stand up.

One of the comments we get about our CLASS staff is that we are so real, so open, so honest. As people observe us for three full days, they can see that it is possible for people to be genuine. How sad that this Christian reality is also considered a novelty. What they see in us is not a lack of problems or stress, but the fact that we have dealt with the pains of our past. We have searched our backgrounds for repeated sins, and we have consciously brought these before the Lord. Each one of us has been through a day or two of counseling and prayer with Lana Bateman, and we have forgiven those who have wronged us. Some of us have spent time with Marilyn Murray at her Restoration Therapy Center and have received grace for a healing journey.

A girl from Ohio wrote on her CLASS evaluation:

> I praise God for calling me here (which he very clearly did). I have been so longing to share Jesus with my world yet not feeling confident. I discovered I had many pains passed down in my family that I hadn't dealt with, and I now realize I don't have a message of healing for the world until I first am healed myself.

During these three days God released me of masks I didn't know
I had because of the genuineness of the staff and the open acceptance
of the women in my small group. I know I will be healed by the
great physician so one day I too will have a message to share.

In an article, "Eliminate Your Pain by Knowing Its Cause,"
Dr. Katherine La Guardia challenges women to take responsibility for learning about their bodies and how they function.

Pain, especially chronic pain, is a combination not only of the
physical symptoms but also of historical biases, social factors, and
the environment.[2]

Do you have some pain that needs to be healed? Do you have
some heavy chains that need to be broken? Do you have some
roots that need to be dug up?
John said, "Produce fruit in keeping with repentance. . . .
The axe is already at the root of the trees, and every tree that
does not produce good fruit will be cut down and thrown into
the fire" (Matt. 3:8,10, NIV).
Throughout the Bible God blesses those who obey and punishes
those who are rebellious. He warns the people over and over.

You shall walk in all the way which the Lord your God has com-
manded you, that you may live, and that it may be well with you,
and that you may prolong your days in the land which you shall
possess (Deut. 5:33, NASB).

God not only wants life "to be well with you" but also with
your children.

So you shall keep His statutes and His commandments which I
am giving you today, that it may go well with you and with your
children after you, and that you may live long on the land which
the Lord your God is giving you for all time (Deut. 4:40, NASB).
Know therefore that the Lord your God, He is God, the faithful
God, who keeps His covenant and His lovingkindness to a thou-
sandth generation with those who love Him and keep His commandments (Deut. 7:9, NASB).

Because God loves his children, he grieves when we disobey and must be punished just as we are saddened when we must discipline our children.

If only you had paid attention to My commandments then your well-being would have been like a river, and your righteousness like the waves of the sea. Your descendants would have been like the sand, and your offspring like its grains; their name would never be cut off or destroyed from My presence (Isa. 48:18, NASB).

As we have thought over our families and analyzed their personalities, we may have come up with some distorted roots that need the axe. God is patient, he has great mercy, and he forgives our transgressions; but his Word tells us that the sins of the fathers are visited upon the third and fourth generation.[3]

For Further Study, Thought, and Action

Follow these steps individually and share the scripture and the lessons learned with your group. If you have gone through this book alone, start a support group for people who want to understand themselves and learn to get along better with others.

Trace your roots: Spend some time with the group in tracing any repeated traits rooted in your family tree. List these in your personality notebook and write a paragraph on each member of the cast as Jan did with her family. What sins have been visited upon your succeeding generations? Could you perhaps write a book? Copy each prayer into your notebook adding your personalized lists and petitions.

Dear Jesus, here are some of the problems and sins of our past generations. I repent for them and ask your forgiveness and cleansing power to break the hold these sins have on our family.

Pull up the weeds: As you observe the sins of the past, you may find some weeds in the present. What do you see in your life that needs to be uprooted now? Jesus says, "Every plant which My heavenly Father did not plant shall be rooted up"

(Matt. 15:13, NASB). He wants us to pull up anything that is not pleasing to him, any weeds sprouting up in his garden.

In Hebrews we read, "See to it that no one misses the grace of God and that no bitter root grows up to cause trouble" (Heb. 12:15, NIV). As you jot down the list of weeds that are tripping you up, remember what you are to do with them. "Throw off everything that hinders and the sin that so easily entangles, and let us run with perseverance the race marked out for us" (Heb. 12:1, NIV).

> Lord Jesus, I have found this list of weeds that are entangling my progress and keeping me from that harvest of righteousness you have prepared for me. I confess these failures in my life and ask you to forgive me and make clear my path before me.

Burn the dead branches: The Lord Jesus tells us that he is the vine and we are his branches. "If anyone does not remain in me, he is like a branch that is thrown away and withers; such branches are picked up, thrown into the fire and burned" (John 15:6, NIV). What dead branches have you been saving from the fire? What temperament weaknesses have you held on to and pretended that they were strengths?

List five behavioral weaknesses that the Lord has shown you while reading this book. Lay these on the altar of God's grace and burn the dead branches of your life. "The Lord called thy name, A green olive tree, fair, and of goodly fruit: with the noise of a great tumult he hath kindled fire upon it, and the branches of it are broken" (Jer. 11:16, KJV).

> Dear Jesus, I want to be a branch that bears fruit, but here is a list of weaknesses that I've been saving even though they are withered and dried up. I place them on your altar that you might kindle fire upon them and remove them from my sight.

Repair the wastelands: As you review your life and that of the preceding generations you may see some deserts without living water, some relatives who never knew the Lord. You may become aware of some years in your life that were wastelands that need to be repaired. "And they shall build the old wastes, they shall raise up the former desolations, and they shall repair the waste cities, the desolations of many generations" (Isa. 61:4, KJV).

God wants to rebuild your life and repair the desolations of many generations. Write down the periods of waste, the days in the desert. Remember that God often gets our attention by sending us to a desert. What did you learn from your wilderness experience?

> Dear Jesus, I reminisce with you about those days in the desert with no living water. Please restore unto me "the years that the locusts hath eaten" (Joel 2:25, KJV).
>
> Show me how to rebuild my wastelands, how to repair the damages I've done to my family. Refresh me with your living water and remind me again of the lessons you've wanted me to learn. Bring me out of my darkness into your light that I might praise your name forever. For we are "a chosen generation, a royal priesthood, an holy nation, a peculiar people; that ye should show forth the praises of him who hath called you out of darkness into his marvelous light" (1 Pet. 2:9, KJV).

Produce fruit that endures: In this day of teen depression and suicide, of child abuse and incest, of physical and emotional deprivation we must be aware of the special needs of our children. We must remember that money never makes up for mother; television and video games when watched alone don't equal a Big Mac with father. In an era when *things* have replaced *time,* we must stem the tide. We don't want to lose our children before their maturity; we want to produce fruit that endures. Write down some changes you must make as a parent.

> Dear Jesus, I have not been the parent I know you want me to be. I've tried to bend the twigs my way without any thought of what you had in mind. I've trained them up in the way I wanted them to go and sometimes not trained them at all. Please forgive me for bruising the fruit, forgive me for what I've done to _____, _____, and _____. Break the chains of defeat that my family has been tethered by and release my offspring to be free. "All who see them will recognize them Because they are the offspring whom the Lord has blessed" (Isa. 61:9, NASB).

Love and obey your God: Even though the Bible tells us that the sins of the father are visited upon the children to the third and fourth generation and that we do in fact reproduce after our own kind, God gives us a way out. As he carries on the results of sin to four generations, he shows mercy and love to a thousand generations of those who love him and keep his commandments. (See Exod. 20:6).

Oh that they had such a heart in them, that they would fear Me and keep all My commandments always, that it may be well with them and with their sons forever! (Deut. 5:29, NASB).

How gracious of our God to show mercy to those who love and obey him for thousands of generations, in fact forever. When we consider the influence our present actions and attitudes can have upon our succeeding generations, can we do less than love and obey our God? Write down whatever "commandments" of God that you have had trouble keeping. Why have you disobeyed? Is it rebellion toward your parents? Some church rules with which you disagree? A lack of belief that God either knows or cares? A determination not to give in to God?

After David had disobeyed three of the Ten Commandments he taught to others, coveting his neighbor's wife, committing adultery, and instigating murder, he cried out to God in Psalm 51. "I know my transgressions and my sin is always before me" (v. 3, NIV).

Dear Jesus, here are my transgressions:

——————————————————————————————————,
——————————————————————————————————,
——————————————————————————————————.

You desire truth in the inner parts.

Jesus, I've hid these thoughts and actions from others, from myself, and I thought from you, but you know the truth. Grant me a willing spirit to sustain me.

Until now I've not been willing to change, but I see what the past generations have done to me and what I may be doing to my children. Grant me Lord, a willing spirit that I may want to change. Open my lips and my mouth will declare your praise.

Yes Lord, let me sing a new song of praise to your power and glory. Let me love you with all my heart.

David had so much money, so many possessions, so many animals to sacrifice, but that's not what you want, dear Lord. You want a broken and a contrite heart. Lord, I give up my rebellious spirit, my wanting to do things my way, my lack of real concern for others. I pray to the God who saves me and loves me that I may be willing to obey what is your good will for my life.

Lord Jesus, I call upon your sacrificial blood to cleanse me from my secret and open faults. I call upon your Holy Spirit to empower me to necessary change and I call upon you to bind Satan and any dominion he may have on me and upon my children to the third and fourth generations. Get thee behind me, Satan, and away from each member of my family. I call upon you, Jesus, the name that is above all names, knowing that "Everyone who calls on the name of the Lord will be saved." (Rom. 10:13, NIV). Jesus save me and my family—forever.

In your precious name I pray, Amen.

❧ 12 ❧

Have You
a Song to Sing
in the Spring?

Come before his presence with singing.—Psalm 100:2, KJV

What lessons have you learned from tracing your personality tree? Have you found out who you really are? Have you accepted God's direction? Do you know you are created for such a time as this? Have you seen how parents, siblings, or mates may have warped your original personality to make you what was acceptable for them? Have you viewed, perhaps for the first time, what influence you have over your own children in training them up in the way you want them to go?

God created each one of us, and each one of our children, to be unique creations, special blendings of the four basic humors—Sanguine, Choleric, Melancholy, and Phlegmatic. As we have used these terms from Hippocrates as tools in following God's command that we examine ourselves and as we've seen how people have tampered with God's original plan for our life, each of us should now have a better understanding of our personality and the traits of those other members of our family tree.

In this closing chapter let me share two stories from our two families—the first about my father and the second about Fred's mother.

When I was a senior in college, I came home for Christmas vacation and anticipated a fun-filled fortnight with my two brothers. We were so excited to be together we volunteered to watch the store so that my mother and father could take their first day off in years. The day before my parents went to Boston, my father took me quietly aside to the little den behind the store. The room was so small that it held only a piano and a hide-a-bed couch. In fact, when you pulled the bed out it filled the room and you could sit on the foot of it and play the piano. Father reached behind the old upright and pulled out a cigar box. He opened it and showed me a little pile of newspaper articles. I had read so many Nancy Drew detective stories that I was excited and wide-eyed over the hidden box of clippings.

"What are they?" I asked.

Father replied seriously, "These are articles I've written and some letters to the editor that have been published."

As I began to read, I saw at the bottom of each neatly clipped article the name Walter Chapman, Esq. "Why didn't you tell me you'd done this?" I asked.

"Because I didn't want your mother to know. She's always told me that since I didn't have much education I shouldn't try to write. I wanted to run for some political office also, but she told me I shouldn't try. I guess she was afraid she'd be embarrassed if I lost. I just wanted to try for the fun of it. I figured I could write without her knowing it, and so I did. When each item would be printed, I'd cut it out and hide it in this box. I knew someday I'd show the box to someone, and it's you."

He watched me as I read over a few of the articles and when I looked up, his big blue eyes were moist. "I guess I tried for something too big this last time," he added.

"Did you write something else?"

"Yes, I sent into our denominational magazine to give some suggestions on how the national nominating committee could be selected more fairly. It's been three months since I sent it in. I guess I tried for something too big."

This was such a new side to my fun-loving father that I didn't quite know what to say, so I tried, "Maybe it'll still come."

"Maybe, but don't hold your breath." Father gave me a little smile and a wink and then closed the cigar box and tucked it into the space behind the piano.

The next morning our parents left on the bus to the Haverhill Depot where they took a train to Boston. Jim, Ron, and I ran the store, and I thought about the box. I'd never known my father liked to write. I didn't tell my brothers; it was a secret between Father and me. The Mystery of the Hidden Box.

Early that evening I looked out the store window and saw my mother get off the bus—alone. She crossed the Square and walked briskly through the store.

"Where's Dad?" we asked together.

"Your father's dead," she said without a tear.

In disbelief we followed her to the kitchen where she told us they had been walking through the Park Street Subway Station in the midst of crowds of people when Father had fallen to the floor. A nurse bent over him, looked up at Mother and said simply, "He's dead."

Mother had stood by him stunned, not knowing what to do as people tripped over him in their rush in the subway. A priest said, "I'll call the police," and disappeared. Mother straddled Dad's body for about an hour. Finally an ambulance came and took them both to the city morgue where Mother had to go through his pockets and remove his watch. She'd come back on the train alone and then home on the local bus. Mother told us the shocking tale without shedding a tear. Not showing emotion had always been a matter of discipline and pride for her. We didn't cry either and we took turns waiting on the customers.

One steady patron asked, "Where's the old man tonight?"

"He's dead," I replied.

"Oh, too bad," and he left.

I'd not thought of him as the old man, and I was hurt at the question, but he was seventy-three and Mother was only fifty-three. He'd always been healthy and happy and he'd cared for frail mother without complaint, but now he was gone. No more whistling, no more singing hymns while stocking shelves; the Old Man was gone.

On the morning of the funeral, I sat at the table in the store opening sympathy cards and pasting them in a scrapbook when I noticed the church magazine in the pile. Normally I would never have opened what I viewed as a dull religious publication, but just maybe that secret article might be there—and it was.

I took the magazine to the little den, shut the door, and burst into tears. I'd been brave, but seeing Dad's bold recommendations to the national convention in print was more than I could bear. I read and cried and then I read again. I pulled out the box from behind the piano and under the clippings I found a two-page letter to my father from Henry Cabot Lodge, Sr., thanking him for his campaign suggestions.

I didn't tell anyone about my box; it remained a secret until we closed the store two years later and moved in with Grandma leaving the piano behind. I gave my last look to the empty kitchen with the old black stove standing staunchly alone while the bottle of kerosene gurgled loudly in the corner. I went quietly to the den, and as if in some religious rite, I reached behind the old piano where I'd practiced lessons and played hymns on Sunday evenings and pulled out *the box*.

Father left me no money, but he left me the box. He had little education and no degrees, but he gave me and my brothers a love for the English language, a thirst for politics, and an ability to write. Who knows what Father could have done with just a little encouragement?

Today as I stand in my study and look at Dad's article there on the wall matted in blue next to his picture smiling down at me and reread the letter from Lodge framed with his picture just below Father's, I realize how close I came to knowing none of this. How grateful I am that Father chose that day to reach behind the piano and pull out the box.

I'll never know what Walter Chapman, Esquire, could have been. Was there a great American novel inside him or at least a weekly column for the *Haverhill Gazette?* Could his charm and sense of humor have brought him political acclaim?—or could he at least have been the mayor of Haverhill?

How many of us as wives hold down our husband's aspirations, stifle a little bud of genius that's longing to burst forth? Why? Because we're afraid if he fails, we'll be embarrassed. How many are daunted by lack of degrees and don't dare to have their reach exceed their grasp?

Oh God, let us encourage one another unto good works (Heb. 10:24–25).

In one rare evening of genuine disclosure Fred's mother told me of her disappointments. "I never could please my father no matter how hard I tried, and I did my best to make my mother the queen she really wanted to be." I encouraged her to tell me how she really felt, and she shared one heart-breaking story.

She was in love with a young man while at Cornell and they had talked of marriage. Her mother disapproved because she felt he did not come from an important or wealthy enough family. After college they went in separate directions for the summer, and he was to call her in the fall. She never heard from him again.

At the mention of this fact, this beautiful woman burst into tears, and I thought the sad story was over. I'd never seen her let down her guard before, and I felt so sorry for how this rejection still bothered her. As I sat quietly, wondering what I should say, she looked up and continued. "That's not the end of it. I went to a party just a few years ago and there he was. I found out he was a successful lawyer, and then I asked that question, 'Why didn't you ever call me?' 'Oh, I called all right,' he replied. 'I talked to your mother on the telephone, and she told me that you were engaged to another man, that you didn't love me, and that you'd asked her to tell me never to call again.' "

Mother's ample frame shook as she sobbed out these last words. I knelt beside her and felt a warmth and compassion for her I'd never known before. How seldom we sense what's stored up inside a person just waiting for a quiet moment, a nonthreatening situation to be set free. My heart was broken with hers as she confessed, "I never felt right about Mother, but I didn't know why. I felt guilty because I couldn't love her enough, so I waited on her like a slave to ease my conscience. I tried to become what she wanted me to be, and I'll never know what I might have been."

"Was there anything you really wanted to be?" I asked.

"An opera singer," she answered quickly. "I wanted to study music, but my parents felt that was a waste of time, that I'd make more money in the millinery business. But I was in one show in college, and I had the lead."

She got up quickly, went to a closet and pulled out a box of old pictures. She showed me a large photo of a stage setting with the cast posed for review. "There I am." She pointed proudly to a confident and beautiful young girl seated on an ornate chair, center stage, the obvious star of the show.

I'd not known of her operatic ambitions before, and I shared how I loved the theatre and had wanted to be an actress until my drama teacher told me I was much better at directing others. At the end of this memorable and meaningful evening, Mother gave me the picture of her on stage in her one starring role, and I treasure this memory of what might have been.

We'll never know what this talented, creative woman could have become had she been allowed to pursue her natural aims and abilities instead of being brought up to play the role of "perfect daughter." Suppressed ambitions never die; they wait inside for some moment of possible expression in the future.

Mother Littauer is now eighty-five years old, and her conscious mind is no longer functioning correctly. When Fred and I visited recently she had a peaceful expression on her face although she didn't seem to know who we were. When I talked with the nurse who cares for her, she said, "It's the strangest thing. She can't talk at all, but she sings opera each day and practices her scales."

As I told this story of Mother's broken dreams to an informal group of only twenty people, several responded with similar experiences. One pretty girl with sad eyes said, "I always wanted to be a dancer. My parents let me take lessons, but when I wanted to make dancing a career, they scoffed at the thought. 'You're not *that* good, and you'll never make it.'" Tears came to her eyes as she continued. "They may have been right, but I wanted to give it a try while I was young. Now I'll never know what I might have been."

A middle-aged lady stated clearly, "You've made me realize I gave up too quickly. I'm going to start back with my violin and get a chamber music quartet together again."

An elderly lady surprised me with, "I wanted to be an explorer, but my father wouldn't let me leave town. Every time I wanted to go out and seek adventure, he'd tell me about those 'other kinds of people' lurking out there ready to pounce on me. All my life I've had an adventurous spirit, but because of the few of those 'other kinds of people' I've never had an adventure."

This fascinating response to the operatic hopes of my mother-in-law led me to wonder how many others have had their dreams thwarted by well-meaning parents who, by insisting their offspring play it safe, destroyed a dream of the future.

How many of us have a suppressed opera, an imagined painting, a possible poem, the plot for a novel, the potential for a political career, or a thwarted adventure locked inside of us waiting for that magic key to set us free. Are you ready to sing a song in the spring? Perhaps like the Song of Solomon?

> *Arise, my darling,*
> *my beautiful one, and come with me.*
> *See! The winter is past;*
> *the rains are over and gone.*
> *Flowers appear on the earth;*
> *the season of singing has come.*
> —Song of Songs 2:10–12, NIV

You were made for such a time as this.

NOTES

Chapter 1.   WERE YOU BORN LIKE THIS?

1. Dr. William R. Bright, "Have You Heard of the Four Spiritual Laws?" Campus Crusade for Christ, Arrowhead Springs, CA.
2. Winston Churchill, tape purchased in London, recorded live.
3. William Manchester, *The Last Lion*, Little Brown, 1983, p. 7.
4. Alice Vollmar, "Together Again," *Friendly Exchange*, 1985, p. 28.
5. Ibid.
6. Oscar Wilde, *The Importance of Being Earnest*, Act I.

Chapter 2.   WHAT IS YOUR PERSONALITY?
1. Michael Gartner, "About Words," *Austin American-Statesman*, January 7, 1985.
2. William Shakespeare, *Julius Caesar*, Act V, Scene 5.
3. Bishop Ernest A. Fitzgerald, "It's All Right to Worry," *Piedmont Airlines*, July 1985.
4. Oswald Chambers, *My Utmost for His Highest* (New York: Dodd, Mead & Company, 1963), p. 347.

Chapter 3.   WHAT ARE YOUR DESIRES AND UNDERLYING NEEDS?
1. M. I. Blackwell, *The Dallas Morning News*, May 4, 1986.
2. Robert William Service, *The Law of the Yukon*.

3. Ludwig van Beethoven, as cited in *Forbes*, January 30, 1984.
4. *Time,* July 7, 1986, pp. 12, 16.
5. William Shakespeare, *Hamlet,* Act I, Scene 3.
6. Norman Vincent Peale, "Today," NBC Television program, February 14, 1985.

Chapter 5.   WHAT GETS YOU DEPRESSED?
1. William Shakespeare, *Macbeth,* Act V, Scene 5.
2. *USA Today,* "The Lure of the Store: It's OK If Shopping Buys You a Thrill," Nanci Hellmich, February 4, 1986.
3. Norman M. Lobsenz, "How to Make a Second Marriage Work," *Parade Magazine,* September 1, 1985.

Chapter 6.   ARE YOU WEARING A MASK?
1. Guillaume de Salluste Seigneur du Bartas, *Dialogue between Heraclitus and Democritus.*
2. "Illusions of Competency," *Piedmont Airlines,* July 1985.
3. Ibid.
4. William Shakespeare, *The Twelfth Night,* Act II, Scene 5.
5. William Makepeace Thackeray, *The English Humorists.*
6. William Shakespeare, *Merchant of Venice,* Act I, Scene 1, line 77.
7. William Henry Davies, *Hunting Joy.*
8. Lucan, *The Civil War,* Book IV.
9. Sir Walter Scott, *Marmion.*

Chapter 7.   WHAT IS A PERSONALITY TREE?
1. Stephen Vincent Benét, *John Brown's Body.*
2. Oswald Chambers, *My Utmost for His Highest* (New York: Dodd, Mead & Company, 1963), p. 94.

Chapter 8.   WHAT ARE YOUR CHILDREN'S
             PERSONALITIES?
1. Alexander Pope, *Moral Essays,* Epistle 1.
2. "Treating Teens in Trouble," *Newsweek,* January 20, 1986.
3. Ibid.
4. Dr. Judith Wallerstein, "Good Morning America," ABC Television program, January 16, 1986.
5. The sections in this chapter labeled "Tools to Help" are

based on material from Lana Bateman, *Personality Patterns,* Philippian Ministries, Dallas, Texas, copyright, 1985.

6. Susan Lapinski, "When Your Baby Seems Depressed," *Parade Magazine,* February 14, 1985.

7. Ibid.

8. Ibid.

9. Sally Ann Stewart, "Temperament, Not Poor Training, Ignites Tantrums," *USA Today*, December 11, 1985.

10. Ibid.

Chapter 9.   HOW CAN YOU BEND THE TWIGS AS THEY SHOULD GO?

1. Harold Bloomfield, *Making Peace with Your Parents,* (New York: Random House, 1983), as cited in *U.S. News and World Report* (Book Review), May 21, 1984.

2. Ibid.

Chapter 11.   HOW CAN YOU DIG UP THE OLD ROOTS?

1. Dr. Ron Daugherty, lecture at Pennsylvania Medical Society, April 30, 1986.

2. Carol Towarnicky, "Eliminate Your Aches and Pains by Learning about Their Causes," *The Dallas Morning News,* April 7, 1986.

3. Exodus 20:5, 34:7, Numbers 14:18.

PERSONALITY PROFILE

DIRECTIONS—In each of the following rows of four words across, place an X in front of the one word that most often applies to you. If there are two words that both clearly describe you, then mark them both, but select no more than two. If you reach a row of words that does not seem to apply to you at all, then skip that row.

Continue through all forty lines. Be sure to read the definition of each word on the following pages before you make your choices.

STRENGTHS

1	___ Animated	___ Adventurous	_✓_ Analytical	___ Adaptable
2	___ Persistent	___ Playful	___ Persuasive	___ Peaceful
3	_✓_ Submissive	___ Self-sacrificing	_✓_ Sociable	___ Strong-willed
4	_✓_ Considerate	___ Controlled	___ Competitive	___ Convincing
5	___ Refreshing	___ Respectful	___ Reserved	___ Resourceful
6	___ Satisfied	_✓_ Sensitive	___ Self-reliant	___ Spirited
7	___ Planner	___ Patient	___ Positive	___ Promoter
8	___ Sure	___ Spontaneous	___ Scheduled	___ Shy
9	___ Orderly	___ Obliging	___ Outspoken	___ Optimistic
10	___ Friendly	___ Faithful	___ Funny	___ Forceful
11	___ Daring	___ Delightful	___ Diplomatic	___ Detailed
12	___ Cheerful	___ Consistent	___ Cultured	___ Confident
13	___ Idealistic	___ Independent	___ Inoffensive	___ Inspiring
14	___ Demonstrative	___ Decisive	___ Dry humor	___ Deep
15	___ Mediator	___ Musical	___ Mover	___ Mixes easily
16	_✓_ Thoughtful	___ Tenacious	___ Talker	_✓_ Tolerant
17	_✓_ Listener	_✓_ Loyal	___ Leader	___ Lively
18	___ Contented	___ Chief	___ Chartmaker	___ Cute
19	___ Perfectionist	___ Permissive	___ Productive	___ Popular
20	___ Bouncy	___ Bold	___ Behaved	___ Balanced

WEAKNESSES

21	___ Brassy	___ Bossy	___ Bashful	___ Blank
22	_✓_ Undisciplined	___ Unsympathetic	___ Unenthusiastic	___ Unforgiving
23	___ Reticent	___ Resentful	___ Resistant	___ Repetitious
24	___ Fussy	_✓_ Fearful	___ Forgetful	___ Frank
25	___ Impatient	___ Insecure	_✓_ Indecisive	___ Interrupts
26	___ Unpopular	___ Uninvolved	___ Unpredictable	_✓_ Unaffectionate
27	___ Headstrong	___ Haphazard	___ Hard to please	___ Hesitant
28	___ Plain	___ Pessimistic	___ Proud	___ Permissive
29	___ Angered easily	___ Aimless	___ Argumentative	___ Alienated
30	___ Naive	___ Negative attitude	___ Nervy	___ Nonchalant
31	_✓_ Worrier	___ Withdrawn	___ Workaholic	___ Wants credit
32	___ Too sensitive	___ Tactless	___ Timid	___ Talkative
33	___ Doubtful	___ Disorganized	___ Domineering	___ Depressed
34	___ Inconsistent	___ Introvert	___ Intolerant	___ Indifferent
35	___ Messy	___ Moody	___ Mumbles	___ Manipulative
36	___ Slow	___ Stubborn	___ Show-off	___ Skeptical
37	___ Loner	___ Lord over	___ Lazy	___ Loud
38	___ Sluggish	___ Suspicious	___ Short-tempered	___ Scatterbrained
39	___ Revengeful	___ Restless	___ Reluctant	___ Rash
40	___ Compromising	___ Critical	___ Crafty	___ Changeable

**NOW TRANSFER ALL YOUR X's TO THE PERSONALITY SCORING SHEET ON P. 232
AND ADD UP YOUR TOTALS**

Personality Profile from PERSONALITY PLUS by Florence Littauer, © 1983 by Florence Littauer, used by permission of Fleming H. Revell Company.

PERSONALITY TEST WORD DEFINITIONS

Reprinted with permission from
Personality Patterns
by Lana Bateman

STRENGTHS

1.

ANIMATED	—Full of life, lively use of hand, arm, and face gestures.
ADVENTUROUS	—One who will take on new and daring enterprises with a need to master them.
ANALYTICAL	—One who is constantly in the process of analyzing people, places, or things.
ADAPTABLE	—One who easily adapts to any situation.

2.

PERSISTENT	—Refusing to let go, insistently repetitive or continuous, can't drop it.
PLAYFUL	—Full of fun and good humor.
PERSUASIVE	—One who persuades through logic and fact rather than charm.
PEACEFUL	—One who seems undisturbed and tranquil and who retreats from any form of strife.

3.

SUBMISSIVE	—One who easily submits to any other's point of view or desire. This person has little need to assert his own view or opinion.
SELF-SACRIFICING	—One who constantly sacrifices his/her own personal well being for the sake of or to meet the needs of others.
SOCIABLE	—This sociable refers to one who sees being with others as an opportunity to be cute and entertaining. If you are one who enjoys social gatherings as a chal-

221

lenge or business opportunity then do not check this word.

STRONG-
WILLED   —One who is determined to have his/her own way.

4.

CONSIDERATE   —Having regard for the needs and feelings of others.

CONTROLLED   —One who has emotional feelings but doesn't display them.

COMPETITIVE   —One who turns every situation, happening, or game into an arena for competition. This person always plays to win!

CONVINCING   —This person can convince you of anything through the sheer charm of his/her personality. Facts are unimportant.

5.

REFRESHING   —One who renews and stimulates or pleasantly lifts spirits.

RESPECTFUL   —One who treats others with deference, honor, and esteem.

RESERVED   —Self restraint in expression of emotion or enthusiasm.

RESOURCEFUL   —One who is able to act quickly and effectively in virtually all situations.

6.

SATISFIED   —A person who easily accepts any circumstance or situation.

SENSITIVE   —This person is intensively sensitive to self and others.

SELF-RELIANT   —An independent person who can fully rely on his/her own capabilities, judgment, and resources.

SPIRITED   —One who is full of life and excitement.

7.

PLANNER   —One who prefers to work out a detailed arrangement beforehand, for the accomplishment of project or goal. This person much prefers involvement with the planning stages and the finished product rather than the carrying out of the task.

PATIENT   —One who is unmoved by delay—calm and tolerant.

POSITIVE   —Characterized by certainty and assurance.

PROMOTER   —One who can compel others to go along, join, or invest through the sheer charm of his/her own personality.

8.

SURE	—One who is confident, not hesitating or wavering.
SPONTANEOUS	—One who prefers all of life to be impulsive, unpremeditated activity. This person feels restricted by plans.
SCHEDULED	—This person is controlled by his/her schedule and gets very upset if that schedule is interrupted. There is another type of person who uses a schedule to stay organized, but is not controlled by the schedule. If the second description is you, do not check this word.
SHY	—Quiet, doesn't easily instigate a conversation.

9.

ORDERLY	—A person who has a methodical, systematic arrangement of things. Can be obsessively tidy.
OBLIGING	—Accommodating. One who is quick to do it another's way.
OUTSPOKEN	—One who speaks frankly and without reserve.
OPTIMISTIC	—This optimist is an almost childlike, dreamer type of optimist.

10.

FRIENDLY	—This person is a responder to friendliness rather than an initiator. While he/she seldom starts a conversation, he/she responds with great warmth and enjoys the exchange.
FAITHFUL	—Consistently reliable. Steadfast, loyal, and devoted sometimes beyond reason.
FUNNY	—This person has an innate humor that can make virtually any story a funny one and is a remarkable joketeller. If you have a dry humor, do not check this word.
FORCEFUL	—A commanding personality. One would hesitate to take a stand against this person.

11.

DARING	—One who is willing to take risks; fearless, bold.
DELIGHTFUL	—A person who is greatly pleasing, fun to be with.
DIPLOMATIC	—One who deals with people both tactfully and sensitively.
DETAILED	—A person who prefers working with the minute or fields that require detail work such as math, research, accounting, carving, art, graphics, etc.

12.

CHEERFUL	—Consistently being in good spirits and promoting cheer.
CONSISTENT	—A person who is agreeable, compatible, not contradictory.

CULTURED —One whose interests involve both intellectual and artistic pursuits, such as theatre, symphony, ballet, etc.

CONFIDENT —One who is self-assured and/or certain of success.

13.

IDEALISTIC —One who visualizes things in an ideal or perfect form, and has a need to measure up to that standard.

INDEPENDENT —One who is self-sufficient, self-supporting, self-confident and seems to have little need of help.

INOFFENSIVE —A person who never causes offense, pleasant, unobjectionable, harmless.

INSPIRING —One who encourages others to work, join, or be involved. There is another personality that is deeply inspirational and has a need to bring life-changing inspiration. If you are the latter, do not check this word.

14.

DEMONSTRATIVE —One who openly expresses emotion, especially affection. This person doesn't hesitate to touch others while speaking to them.

DECISIVE —A person with quick, conclusive, decision-making ability.

DRY HUMOR —One who exhibits dry wit, usually one-liners which can be sarcastic in nature, but very humorous.

DEEP —A person who is intense and often introspective with a distaste for surface conversation and pursuits.

15.

MEDIATOR —A person who consistently finds him/herself in the role of reconciling differences in order to avoid conflict.

MUSICAL —One who either participates in or has an intense appreciation for music. This type of musical would not include those who find it fun to sing or play. The latter would be a different personality that enjoys being an entertainer rather than one who is deeply committed to music as an artform.

MOVER —One who is so driven by a need to be productive, that he/she finds it difficult to sit still.

MIXES EASILY —One who loves a party and can't wait to meet everyone in the room, never meets a stranger.

16.

THOUGHTFUL —A considerate person who remembers special occasions and is quick to make a kind gesture.

TENACIOUS —One who holds on firmly, stubbornly, and won't let go till the goal is accomplished.

TALKER	—A person who is constantly talking, generally telling funny stories and entertaining everyone around him/her. There is another compulsive talker who is a nervous talker and feels the need to fill the silence in order to make others comfortable. This is not the entertaining talker we are describing here.
TOLERANT	—One who easily accepts the thoughts and ways of others without the need to disagree with or change them.

17.

LISTENER	—One who always seems willing to listen.
LOYAL	—Faithful to a person, ideal, or job. This person is sometimes loyal beyond reason and to his/her own detriment.
LEADER	—A person who is a born leader. This is not one who rises to the occasion because they *can* lead, but one who is driven to lead and finds it very difficult to believe anyone else can do the job.
LIVELY	—Full of life, vigorous, energetic.

18.

CONTENTED	—One who is easily satisfied with what he/she has.
CHIEF	—A person who commands leadership.
CHARTMAKER	—One who enjoys either graphs, charts, or lists.
CUTE	—Bubbly-beauty, cutie, precious, diminutive.

19.

PERFECTIONIST	—One who desires perfection but not necessarily in every area of life.
PERMISSIVE	—This person is permissive with employees, friends, and children in order to avoid conflict.
PRODUCTIVE	—One who must constantly be working and/or producing. This person finds it very difficult to rest.
POPULAR	—One who is the life of the party and therefore is much desired as a party guest.

20.

BOUNCY	—A bubbly, lively personality.
BOLD	—Fearless, daring, forward.
BEHAVED	—One who consistently desires to conduct him/herself within the realm of what is proper.
BALANCED	—Stable, middle of the road personality, without extremes.

WEAKNESSES

21.

BRASSY —One who is showy, flashy, comes on strong.

BOSSY —Commanding, domineering, overbearing. (Do not relate this to the raising of children. All mothers seem bossy and domineering.) Think only of adult relationships.

BASHFUL —One who shrinks from notice, resulting from self-consciousness.

BLANK —A person who shows little facial expression or emotion.

22.

UNDISCIPLINED —A person whose lack of discipline permeates virtually every area of his/her life.

UNSYMPATHETIC —One who finds it difficult to relate to the problems or hurts of others.

UN-
  ENTHUSIASTIC —A person who finds it hard to get excited or feel enthusiasm.

UNFORGIVING —One who has difficulty forgiving or forgetting a hurt or injustice done to them. This individual may find it hard to release a grudge.

23.

RETICENT —One who is unwilling or struggles against getting involved.

RESENTFUL —This person easily feels resentment as a result of real or imagined offenses.

RESISTANT —One who strives, works against, or resists accepting any other way but his/her own.

REPETITIOUS —This person retells stories and incidents to entertain you without realizing he/she has already told the story several times before. This is not a question so much of forgetfulness, as it is of constantly needing something to say.

24.

FUSSY —One who is insistent over petty matters or details, calling for great attention to trivial details.

FEARFUL —One who often experiences feelings of fear, apprehension or anxiousness.

FORGETFUL —This person is forgetful because it isn't fun to remember. His/her forgetfulness is tied to a lack of discipline. There is another personality that is more like the absent-minded professor. This person tends to be off in another world and only remembers what he/she chooses to remember. If you are the latter, do not check this word.

FRANK —One who is straightforward, outspoken, and doesn't mind telling you exactly what he/she thinks.

25.

IMPATIENT —A person who finds it difficult to endure irritation or wait patiently.

INSECURE —One who is apprehensive or lacks confidence.

INDECISIVE —This person finds it difficult to make a decision at all. There is another personality that labors long over each decision in order to make the perfect one. If you are the latter, do not check this word.

INTERRUPTS —This person interrupts because he/she is afraid of forgetting the wonderful thing they have to say if another is allowed to finish. This person is more of a talker than a listener.

26.

UNPOPULAR —A person whose intensity and demand for perfection can push others away.

UNINVOLVED —One who has no desire to become involved in clubs, groups, or people activities.

UN-
 PREDICTABLE —This person may be ecstatic one moment and blue the next, willing to help and then disappear, promising to come and then forgetting to show up.

UN-
 AFFECTIONATE —One who finds it difficult to verbally or physically demonstrate affection openly.

27.

HEADSTRONG —One who insists on having his/her own way.

HAPHAZARD —One who has no consistent way of doing things.

HARD TO
 PLEASE —A person whose standards are set so high that it is difficult to ever please them.

HESITANT —This person is slow to get moving and hard to get involved.

28.

PLAIN —A middle-of-the-road personality without highs or lows and showing little if any emotion.

PESSIMISTIC —This person, while hoping for the best, generally sees the down side of a situation first.

PROUD —One with great self-esteem who sees him/herself as always right and the best person for the job.

PERMISSIVE —This personality allows others (including children) to do as they please in order to keep from being disliked.

29.

ANGERED EASILY —One who has a childlike flash-in-the-pan temper that expresses itself in a child's tantrum style. It is over and forgotten almost instantly.

AIMLESS —A person who is not a goal-setter and has little desire to be one.

ARGUMENTATIVE —One who incites arguments generally because he/she is determined to be right no matter what the situation may be.

ALIENATED —A person who easily feels estranged from others often because of insecurity or fear that others don't really enjoy his/her company.

30.

NAIVE —A simple and childlike perspective, lacking sophistication or worldliness. This is not to be confused with uninformed. There is another personality that is so consumed with his/her own particular field of interest that he/she simply could not care less what is going on outside of that sphere. If you are the latter, do not check this word.

NEGATIVE —One whose attitude is seldom positive and is often able to see only the down or dark side of each situation.

NERVY —Full of confidence, fortitude, and sheer guts.

NONCHALANT —Easy-going, unconcerned, indifferent.

31.

WORRIER —One who consistently feels uncertain or troubled.

WITHDRAWN —A person who pulls back to him/herself and needs a great deal of alone or isolation time.

WORKAHOLIC —This is one of two workaholic personalities. This particular one is an aggressive goal-setter who must be constantly productive and feels very guilty when resting. This workaholic is not driven by a need for perfection or completion but by a need for accomplishment and reward.

WANTS CREDIT —One who is almost dysfunctional without the credit or approval of others. As an entertainer this person feeds on the applause, laughter, and/or acceptance of an audience.

32.
TOO

SENSITIVE —One who is overly sensitive and introspective.

TACTLESS —A person who can sometimes express him/herself in a somewhat offensive and inconsiderate way.

TIMID —One who shrinks from difficult situations.

TALKATIVE —A compulsive talker who finds it difficult to listen. Again, this is an entertaining talker and not a nervous talker.

33.

DOUBTFUL —A person who is full of doubts, uncertain.

DISORGANIZED —One whose lack of organizational ability touches virtually every area of life.

DOMINEERING —One who compulsively takes control of situations and/or people. Do not consider the mothering role. All mothers are somewhat domineering.

DEPRESSED —A person who struggles with bouts of depression on a fairly consistent basis.

34.

INCONSISTENT —Erratic, contradictory, illogical.

INTROVERT —A person whose thoughts and interest are directed inward. One who lives within him/herself.

INTOLERANT —One who appears unable to withstand or accept another's attitudes, point of view or way of doing things.

INDIFFERENT —A person to whom most things don't matter one way or the other.

35.

MESSY —This person is messy because it isn't fun to discipline him/herself to clean. The mess is hardly noticed. There is another personality that gets messy when depressed, and yet another that is messy because it takes too much energy to do the cleaning. Be sure you are the first one mentioned if you check this word.

MOODY —One who easily slips into moods. This person doesn't get very high emotionally, but does experience very low lows.

MUMBLES —This person may mumble quietly under the breath when pushed. This is a passive display of anger.

MANIPULATIVE —One who influences or manages shrewdly or deviously for one's own advantage. One who *will* find a way to get his/her own way.

36.

SLOW — One who is slow-moving, easy-going.

STUBBORN — A person who is determined to exert his/her own will. Not easily persuaded; obstinate.

SHOW-OFF — One who needs to be the center of attention.

SKEPTICAL — Disbelieving, questioning the motive behind the words.

37.

LONER — One who requires a lot of alone time and tends to avoid other people.

LORD OVER — A person who doesn't hestitate to let you know that he/she is right or has won.

LAZY — One who evaluates work or activity in terms of how much energy it will take.

LOUD — A person whose laugh or voice can be heard above others in the room.

38.

SLUGGISH — Slow to get started.

SUSPICIOUS — One who tends to suspect or distrust.

SHORT-
  TEMPERED — One who has a demanding impatience-based anger and a very short fuse. This type of anger is expressed when others are not moving fast enough or have not completed what they have been asked to do.

SCATTER-
  BRAINED — A person lacking the power of concentration, or attention. Flighty.

39.

REVENGEFUL — One who knowingly or otherwise holds a grudge and punishes the offender, often by subtly withholding friendship or affection.

RESTLESS — A person who likes constant new activity because it isn't fun to do the same things all the time.

RELUCTANT — One who is unwilling or struggles against getting involved.

RASH — One who may act hastily, without thinking things through, generally because of impatience.

40.

COMPROMISING — A person who will often compromise, even when he/she is right, in order to avoid conflict.

CRITICAL — One who constantly evaluates and makes judgments. Example: One who is critical might see someone coming down the street and within seconds might try to evaluate their cleanliness, look of intelligence or lack of it, style of clothing or lack of it, physical attractiveness or lack of it, and the list goes on. This person constantly analyzes and critiques, sometimes without realizing he/she is doing so.

CRAFTY   —Shrewd, one who can always find a way to get to the desired end.

CHANGEABLE   —A person with a childlike short attention span that needs a lot of change and variety to keep from getting bored.

PERSONALITY SCORING SHEET

STRENGTHS

SANGUINE	CHOLERIC	MELANCHOLY	PHLEGMATIC
1 ___ Animated	___ Adventurous	✓ Analytical	___ Adaptable
2 ✓ Playful	___ Persuasive	___ Persistent	___ Peaceful
3 ✓ Sociable	___ Strong-willed	___ Self-sacrificing	___ Submissive
4 ___ Convincing	___ Competitive	✓ Considerate	___ Controlled
5 ___ Refreshing	___ Resourceful	___ Respectful	___ Reserved
6 ___ Spirited	___ Self-reliant	✓ Sensitive	___ Satisfied
7 ___ Promoter	___ Positive	___ Planner	___ Patient
8 ___ Spontaneous	___ Sure	___ Scheduled	___ Shy
9 ___ Optimistic	___ Outspoken	___ Orderly	___ Obliging
10 ___ Funny	___ Forceful	___ Faithful	___ Friendly
11 ___ Delightful	___ Daring	___ Detailed	___ Diplomatic
12 ___ Cheerful	___ Confident	___ Cultured	___ Consistent
13 ___ Inspiring	___ Independent	___ Idealistic	___ Inoffensive
14 ___ Demonstrative	___ Decisive	___ Deep	___ Dry Humor
15 ___ Mixes easily	___ Mover	___ Musical	___ Mediator
16 ___ Talker	___ Tenacious	___ Thoughtful	✓ Tolerant
17 ___ Lively	___ Leader	✓ Loyal	✓ Listener
18 ___ Cute	___ Chief	___ Chartmaker	___ Contented
19 ___ Popular	___ Productive	___ Perfectionist	___ Permissive
20 ___ Bouncy	___ Bold	___ Behaved	___ Balanced
TOTALS ___	___	___	___

WEAKNESSES

SANGUINE	CHOLERIC	MELANCHOLY	PHLEGMATIC
21 ___ Brassy	___ Bossy	___ Bashful	___ Blank
22 ✓ Undisciplined	___ Unsympathetic	___ Unforgiving	___ Unenthusiastic
23 ___ Repetitious	___ Resistant	___ Resentful	✓ Reticent
24 ___ Forgetful	___ Frank	___ Fussy	___ Fearful
25 ___ Interrupts	___ Impatient	___ Insecure	✓ Indecisive
26 ___ Unpredictable	✓ Unaffectionate	___ Unpopular	___ Uninvolved
27 ___ Haphazard	___ Headstrong	___ Hard-to-please	___ Hesitant
28 ___ Permissive	___ Proud	___ Pessimistic	___ Plain
29 ___ Angered easily	___ Argumentative	___ Alienated	___ Aimless
30 ___ Naive	___ Nervy	___ Negative attitude	___ Nonchalant
31 ___ Wants credit	___ Workaholic	___ Withdrawn	✓ Worrier
32 ___ Talkative	___ Tactless	___ Too sensitive	___ Timid
33 ___ Disorganized	___ Domineering	___ Depressed	___ Doubtful
34 ___ Inconsistent	___ Intolerant	___ Introvert	___ Indifferent
35 ___ Messy	___ Manipulative	___ Moody	___ Mumbles
36 ___ Show-off	___ Stubborn	___ Skeptical	___ Slow
37 ___ Loud	___ Lord-over-others	___ Loner	___ Lazy
38 ___ Scatter-brained	___ Short-tempered	___ Suspicious	___ Sluggish
39 ___ Restless	___ Rash	___ Revengeful	___ Reluctant
40 ___ Changeable	___ Crafty	___ Critical	___ Compromising
TOTALS ___	___	___	___
COMBINED TOTALS ___	___	___	___

PERSONALITY STRENGTHS AND WEAKNESSES

STRENGTHS

	THE TALKER — SANGUINE	THE WORKER — CHOLERIC	THE THINKER — MELANCHOLY	THE WATCHER — PHLEGMATIC
EMOTIONS	Appealing personality Talkative, storyteller Life-of-the-party Good sense of humor Memory for color Physically holds onto listener Emotional and demonstrative Enthusiastic and expressive Cheerful and bubbling over Curious Good on stage Wide-eyed and innocent Lives in the present Changeable disposition Sincere at heart Always a child	Born leader Dynamic and active Compulsive need for change Must correct wrongs Strong-willed and decisive Unemotional Not easily discouraged Independent and self-sufficient Exudes confidence Can run anything	Deep and thoughtful Analytical Serious and purposeful Talented and creative Artistic or musical Philosophical and poetic Appreciative of beauty Sensitive to others Self-sacrificing Conscientious Idealistic	Low-key personality Easygoing and relaxed Calm, cool, and collected Patient, well-balanced Consistent life Quiet, but witty Sympathetic and kind Keeps emotions hidden Happily reconciled to life All-purpose person
WORK	Volunteers for jobs Thinks up new activities Looks great on the surface Creative and colorful Has energy and enthusiasm Starts in a flashy way Inspires others to join Charms others to work	Goal-oriented Sees the whole picture Organizes well Seeks practical solutions Moves quickly to action Delegates work Insists on production Makes the goal Stimulates activity Thrives on opposition	Schedule-oriented Perfectionist, high standards Detail-conscious Persistent and thorough Orderly and organized Neat and tidy Economical Sees the problems Finds creative solutions Needs to finish what he starts Likes charts, graphs, figures, lists	Competent and steady Peaceful and agreeable Has administrative ability Mediates problems Avoids conflicts Good under pressure Finds the easy way
FRIENDS	Makes friends easily Loves people Thrives on compliments Seems exciting Envied by others Doesn't hold grudges Apologizes quickly Prevents dull moments Likes spontaneous activities	Has little need for friends Will work for group activity Will lead and organize Is usually right Excels in emergencies	Makes friends cautiously Content to stay in background Avoids causing attention Faithful and devoted Will listen to complaints Can solve others' problems Deep concern for other people Moved to tears with compassion Seeks ideal mate	Easy to get along with Pleasant and enjoyable Inoffensive Good listener Dry sense of humor Enjoys watching people Has many friends Has compassion and concern

WEAKNESSES

	SANGUINE	CHOLERIC	MELANCHOLY	PHLEGMATIC
EMOTIONS	Compulsive talker Exaggerates and elaborates Dwells on trivia Can't remember names Scares others off Too happy for some Has restless energy Egotistical Blusters and complains Naive, gets taken in Has loud voice and laugh Controlled by circumstances Gets angry easily Seems phony to some Never grows up	Bossy Impatient Quick-tempered Can't relax Too impetuous Enjoys controversy & arguments Won't give up when losing Comes on too strong Inflexible Is not complimentary Dislikes tears and emotions Is unsympathetic	Remembers the negatives Moody and depressed Enjoys being hurt Has false humility Off in another world Low self-image Has selective hearing Self-centered Too introspective Guilt feelings Persecution complex Tends to hypochondria	Unenthusiastic Fearful and worried Indecisive Avoids responsibility Quiet will of iron Selfish Too shy and reticent Too compromising Self-righteous
WORK	Would rather talk Forgets obligations Doesn't follow through Confidence fades fast Undisciplined Priorities out of order Decides by feelings Easily distracted Wastes time talking	Little tolerance for mistakes Doesn't analyze details Bored by trivia May make rash decisions May be rude or tactless Manipulates people Demanding of others End justifies the means Work may become his god Demands loyalty in the ranks	Not people-oriented Depressed over imperfections Chooses difficult work Hesitant to start projects Spends too much time planning Prefers analysis to work Self-deprecating Hard to please Standards often too high Deep need for approval	Not goal-oriented Lacks self-motivation Hard to get moving Resents being pushed Lazy and careless Discourages others Would rather watch
FRIENDS	Hates to be alone Needs to be center stage Wants to be popular Looks for credit Dominates conversations Interrupts and doesn't listen Answers for others Fickle and forgetful Makes excuses Repeats stories	Tends to use people Dominates others Decides for others Knows everything Can do everything better Is too independent Possessive of friends and mate Can't say, "I'm sorry" May be right, but unpopular	Lives through others Insecure socially Withdrawn and remote Critical of others Holds back affection Dislikes those in opposition Suspicious of people Antagonistic and vengeful Unforgiving Full of contradictions Skeptical of compliments	Dampens enthusiasm Stays uninvolved Is not exciting Indifferent to plans Judges others Sarcastic and teasing Resists change

PERSONALITY COMPARISON CHART

These comparisons are made for your enjoyment and are based on my personal study of these various systems.

Hippocrates	Sanguine	Choleric	Melancholy	Phlegmatic
[1] Merrill-Reid Social Styles	Expressive	Driving	Analytical	Amiable
[2] Fr. Werling	Butterfly	Elephant	Frog	Turtle
[3] Jack Williams Car Customers	Talkative	Impulsive	Deliberative	Timid
[4] Herbo-Psychiatrists	Pepper	Garlic	Ginger	Parsley
[5] Senn-Delaney	Promoters	Controllers	Analyzers	Supporters
[6] Leigh-Newcomb Business Personalities	Fast Track	People Catalyst	Hard Changer	Power Broker
[7] Friedman-Rosenman Cardiologists		Type A		Type B
[8] Furukawa Blood-types	Type B	Type A	Type O	Type A-B
[9] Peter Kostis Golf Personalities	Fuzzy Zoeller	Tom Kite	David Graham	Ben Crenshaw
[10] Dr. James Carr	Professional Good Guy	Fire-Eater	Resident Genius	Supreme Democrat
[11] Dr. Dennis Hensley Seminar Attenders	Late Arriver	Big Mouth	Would-Be Expert	Whisperer
[12] Billie Frazier Givers	Impromptu Givers	Strings Attached	Record Keeper	Hesitant Givers
[13] DISC Systems Performax	I = Influence	D = Dominance	C = Compliance	S = Supportive
[14] Activity Vector Analysis	Friendly	Aggressive	Prudent	Reserved
[15] Robert Bramson	Exploders	Sherman Tanks	Snipers	Indecisive Stallers
[16] Robert Lefton Effective Motivation	Dominant-Warm	Dominant-Hostile	Submissive-Hostile	Submissive-Warm
[17] Bernice McCarthy 4-Mat System	Colleague	Manager	Analyzer	Watcher
[18] Personal Dynamics	Expressive	Self-Reliant	Factual	Loyal
[19] Alessandra & Cathcart	Socializer	Director	Thinker	Relater
[20] Roger Hargreaves	Miss Sunshine	Miss Helpful	Miss Neat	Miss Shy
[21] Merrill Douglass	Talkers	Achievers	Thinkers	Affiliators
[22] Lawrence Crabb	Emotional	Volitional	Rational	Personal

PERSONALITY COMPARISON CHART

SOURCES

1. Susan Fletcher, "How Do They Manage?" *American Way,* October 1982, pp. 192–194.

2. Father Norman Werling, Ph.D., Master Graphoanalyst, Grapho Dynamics, Bergen Hall, Paramus, NJ 07652.

3. Jack Williams, "Selling to Customers' Dominant Characteristics," Jack Williams Chevrolet, Fort Worth, TX, 1976.

4. Jackie Richard, "Are You a Pepper, a Garlic, or a Parsley?" *The Sun,* San Bernardino, CA.

5. Beth Ann Krier, "Engineers Work on Developing the 'Fun Sides' of Their Brains," *The Los Angeles Times,* Los Angeles, CA.

6. Jason Leigh, "Executives & the Personality Factor," *Sky,* May 1985, pp. 34–38.

7. Jane E. Brody, "Slowing Down 'Type A' People," *The Dallas Morning News,* January 7, 1985, Section C, pp. 1–2.

8. "Japanese Resurrect Behavioral Theory Connected to Blood Types," *Austin American-Statesman,* May 24, 1984, p. D3.

9. Peter Kostis, "Analytical . . . Driver . . . Amiable . . . Expressive . . . Which One Is the Real YOU?" *Golf Digest,* September 1983, pp. 53–57.

10. Dr. James G. Carr, "Illusions of Competency," *Piedmont Airlines,* July 1985, pp. 20–2116.

11. Dr. Dennis E. Hensley, "Holding Successful Seminars," *Piedmont Airlines,* July 1985, pp. 66–68.

12. Dan Sperling, "The Presents We Give Unwrap Our Hidden Personality Traits," *USA TODAY,* December 18, 1984.

13. Judith D. Schwartz, "The Psychology of a Winning Team," *SUCCESS,* December 1985.

14. Kevin Shyne, "Personality Tests Get Down to Business," *SUCCESS,* August 1984.

15. Robert M. Bramson, Ph.D., *Coping with Difficult People,* (New York: Anchor Press/Doubleday, 1981.).

16. Robert Lefton, Effective Motivation.

17. Bernice McCarthy, 4-Mat System, 1980.

18. Personal Dynamics, 1983.

19. Alessandro and Cathcart, *Relationship Strategies and Personal Profile System.*

20. Roger Hargreaves, 2 series of children's books, Little Miss Books and Mr. Men Books, Price/Stern/Sloan, Los Angeles, 1981.

21. Merrill E. Douglass, The Douglass Companies, P.O. Box 5, Grandville, MI, 1984.

22. Lawrence J. Crabb, Jr., Ph.D., *The Training Manual,* Institute of Biblical Counseling, 1978.

KENTUCKY RICH

Also by Fern Michaels . . .

KENTUCKY RICH
CHARMING LILY
WHAT YOU WISH FOR
THE GUEST LIST
LISTEN TO YOUR HEART
CELEBRATION
YESTERDAY
FINDERS KEEPERS
ANNIE'S RAINBOW
SARA'S SONG
VEGAS SUNRISE
VEGAS HEAT
VEGAS RICH
WHITEFIRE
WISH LIST
DEAR EMILY

TEXAS SUNRISE
TEXAS FURY
TEXAS HEAT
TEXAS RICH

FERN
MICHAELS

KENTUCKY
RICH

KENSINGTON BOOKS
http://www.kensingtonbooks.com

While much research went into this book, it is still a work of fiction. In the interests of entertainment, I have taken the liberty of stretching the boundaries of the Thoroughbred breeding and racing world to allow my characters the freedom to break some of the "rules" and "traditions" that govern the industry.

KENSINGTON BOOKS are published by

Kensington Publishing Corp.
850 Third Avenue
New York, NY 10022

All Kensington titles, imprints and distributed lines are available at special quantity discounts for bulk purchases for sales promotion, premiums, fund-raising, educational or institutional use.

Special book excerpts or customized printings can also be created to fit specific needs. For details, write or phone the office of the Kensington Special Sales Manager: Kensington Publishing Corp., 850 Third Avenue, New York, NY 10022. Attn. Special Sales Department. Phone: 1-800-221-2647.

Kensington and the K logo Reg. U.S. Pat. & TM Off.

Library of Congress Card Catalogue Number: 2001086911
ISBN 1-57566-761-4

First Printing: October 2001
10 9 8 7 6 5 4 3 2 1

Printed in the United States of America

I'd like to dedicate this book to two wonderful people, Helen and Bob Kraushaar.

Prologue

∽

Thirty Years Later

The two brothers watched from the window as a black limousine crunched to a stop in the middle of the gravel driveway. In silence, they watched a uniformed driver step out and open the rear passenger door. Their jaws dropped when they saw a slender, long-legged woman dressed in brown-leather boots, well-cut jeans, and white shirt emerge and look around. A sun-darkened hand reached up to adjust tinted glasses before she tipped the brim of her pearly white Stetson to reveal a mane of thick sable brown hair.

"Who the hell is *that?*" Rhy Coleman demanded of his brother.

"How the hell should I know?" Pyne said. "Whoever she is, she's coming up to the porch. I think you should open the door."

When his older brother made no move to greet their guest, Pyne started toward the door, but it opened before he could reach it. The strange woman blew in like a gust of wind. Without a glance in the brothers' direction, she headed straight for the stairway leading to the second floor.

"Hey! Just a damn minute!" Rhy shouted. "Who the hell are you to walk in here like you own the place?"

She turned to face them and smiled as she lowered her dark glasses. "I do own it, Rhy, at least a third of it. Don't you recognize me, big brother?"

Rhy's eyes widened with shock.

Pyne walked toward her. "Nealy! Is it really you?"

"In the flesh," she said, thinking it funny that neither one of them had recognized her. She'd known them the moment she'd seen them, not by the family resemblance but by the slump of their shoulders. Her smile vanished as she glanced back at the stairs. "Where is he?"

Pyne's head jerked upward.

Nealy nodded. "You two stay here," she ordered. "This is between me and him. I have something I want to say to him, and I don't want either of you interfering. Do you understand? This is my business, not yours." When there was no response, she repeated her question. The brothers nodded reluctantly.

Nealy stared at the two men. They were strangers to her; she felt absolutely no emotion for them—not love, not hate, not even curiosity. They were just two men standing side by side in the hallway.

It had been over thirty years since she'd seen her brothers. Over thirty years since she'd left this house with Emmie in her arms. Over thirty years since she'd set foot on Coleman land. And now, after all this time, here she was, back in Virginia.

Home.

The word made her shudder. She turned her back on her brothers and gazed at the staircase that led to the second floor. As a child, she'd climbed those stairs hundreds of times, maybe thousands. Usually to run and hide so she could whimper in safety.

Shoulders stiff, back straight, she mounted each step with the same mix of confidence and caution she used when mounting her horses. At the top, she stopped and looked down at her brothers, who appeared to be debating whether or not to follow her. "Go about your own business while I take care of mine." She hurled the words at them in a cold, tight voice to ward them off. Nealy remembered another day, long ago, when they'd stood in the same spot watching her. She glared at them now as she had then and waited until they walked away before making her way down the hall.

Nealy hesitated only a moment outside of her father's bedroom, then opened the door and walked in. The room was just as she remembered it, gray and dim with ineffective lighting, a few pieces of battered pine furniture and worn-out, roll-down shades covering the two windows.

Her nose wrinkled at the smell of dust, mold, and medication. Hearing a groan, she turned her gaze toward the bed and saw a mound of quilts . . . her father, the man who had sent her fleeing from this very house over thirty years ago. How old was he? She knew he was over a hundred, had read about his getting a card from Bill Clinton when he turned one hundred, but gave up because she simply didn't care.

As she walked toward the bed, she sensed rather than heard someone follow her inside the room. One of her brothers, no doubt. Damn, didn't they know an order when they heard one? Of course they knew, she reminded herself. If there was one thing Pa was good at, it was giving orders.

A frail voice demanded to know who was there. Nealy stepped up closer to the bed and heard a footfall behind her. Rhy or Pyne? she wondered. More than likely Pyne. In his youth, Pyne had been the one to show concern about things and people. Rhy, on the other hand, had taken after their father, not giving a tinker's damn about anything or anybody.

"It's Nealy, Pa."

The voice was stronger when he spoke a second time. "There ain't nothin' here for you, girl. Go back where you came from. You don't belong here."

"I don't want anything, Pa," Nealy said, looking down at the load of quilts on the bed. They looked dirty, or maybe it was just the lighting. Clean, dirty . . . what did she care? She pushed the Stetson farther back on her head so she could get a better look at the dying man without any shadows over her eyes.

"Then what are you here for?"

Nealy felt a hand on her shoulder and glanced back to see Pyne. The hand was to tell her to take it easy.

Like hell she would. Her father had never taken it easy on her. Not even when she was so sick she couldn't stand on her own two feet. She removed Pyne's hand with her own and gave him a warning look. More than thirty years she'd waited for this moment, and neither Pyne nor Rhy was going to take it away from her.

"I came here to watch you die, old man," she said, looking her father straight in the eyes. "And I'm not leaving until I hear you draw your last breath. I want to see them dump you in the ground and cover you up. I want to make sure you're gone forever. Only after I've danced on your grave will I leave. Do you hear me, old man?" She glared at him, her eyes burning with hate.

The old man's face became a glowering mask of rage. "Get out of my house!"

"Still ordering people around, are you? Well guess what? I don't have to take your orders anymore. I repeat; I came here to see you die, and I'm not leaving until you go to hell. That's where you're going, Pa. Hell!" There, she'd said what she'd come to say. Why didn't she feel a bigger sense of satisfaction? Why did she feel this strange emptiness?

"Pyne! Take this devil child away from me. Do you hear me?" the old man gasped as he struggled to raise himself up on his elbow.

"I'd like to see him try," Nealy said bitterly. Then she felt her brother's hand on her shoulder again. "I'd like to see anyone even try to make me do something I don't want to do. Those days are gone forever."

The old man gurgled and gasped as he thrashed about in the big bed. Nealy watched him with a clinical interest. Her eyes narrowed when she saw drool leak from his mouth. God did work in mysterious ways, she thought as she remembered the day her father decided to take her drooling dim-witted child to the county orphanage. Spawn of the devil was what he'd called Emmie. She stood staring at him until he calmed down, then stretched out her leg and, with a booted foot, pulled over a straight-backed chair and sat down facing the bed. For long minutes she stared at her father with unblinking intensity until, finally, he closed his eyes.

"Okay, he's asleep now," Pyne said. "What the hell are you doing here, Nealy? We haven't heard a word from you in more than thirty years, and all of a sudden you show up just as Pa is getting ready to die. How did you know? Can't you let him die in peace?"

Nealy removed her Stetson and rubbed her forehead. She didn't really care all that much for hats, but she'd always longed to wear a pearly white Stetson, just like the Texans wore. These days she was into indulging herself and doing all the things she'd always longed to do but for one reason or another had never done.

"No, I can't let him die in peace," she said, her voice even now, calm. "He has to pay for what he did to me and Emmie." Her eyes narrowed as she watched her brother closely, wondering what he was thinking before she realized she didn't care. She really didn't give two hoots what her brothers or anyone else thought. "As to how I knew he was dying, I make it my business to know what goes on here. And you know why I'm here, Pyne. I want my share of this place for Emmie."

Pyne chuckled softly. "Your share? You just said you'd made it your business to know what goes on around here. So how come you don't know that Pa refused to make a will? There hasn't been any estate planning, Nealy. And neither Rhy nor I have power of attorney. The IRS is going to take it all. Whatever's left will be a piss in the bucket."

Nealy bridled with anger. Leave it to her gutless brothers to let their father go to his deathbed without so much as a power of attorney. "We'll just see about that," she said. "Call the lawyers right now and get them here on the double. Offer to pay them whatever they want. Just get them here. If we work fast, we can still get it all into place. As long as Pa's still breathing, there's a chance. Now, get on it and don't screw up, or you'll be out on the highway along with your brother."

Pyne stammered in bewilderment. "But . . . I can't. Pa wouldn't . . . "

Nealy stood up, took her brother by the shoulders, and shook him. "Don't tell me what Pa would or wouldn't do. It doesn't matter anymore. He's dying. There's nothing he can do to you, to any of us. Don't you understand that?"

Pyne Coleman stared down at his fit and *expensive*-looking younger sister. After all these years she was still pretty, with her dark hair and big brown eyes. Once when they were little he'd told her she looked like an angel. She'd laughed and laughed. Back then they had been close out of necessity. It was all so long ago. And now here she was, over thirty years later, just as defiant as ever and issuing orders like a general.

Nealy suffered through her brother's scrutiny, wondering what he was thinking. She was about to ask when Rhy stuck his head in the door. "You better come downstairs, Pyne, there's a whole gaggle of people outside. They said they were relatives, *family.* I didn't know we had a family. Do you know anything about this?"

Pyne didn't seem the least bit surprised. "I know a lot about it," he said, smiling. "Pa told me about them about a month ago, right before he had his stroke, but he didn't say anything about them coming here. I wonder what they want." He took Nealy's elbow and steered her toward the door. "I'll make you a deal. You make *our family* welcome while I make that phone call to the lawyers."

Nealy jerked her arm free, walked back to her father's bedside, and leaned close to him. Only after she was satisfied that he was still breathing did she follow her brothers downstairs. . . .

In the foyer, Nealy set her hat down on the telephone table and checked her hair and makeup. With all the skill of a seasoned actress, she worked a smile onto her face as she headed toward the door. Rhy wasn't kidding when he said there was a gaggle of people outside. But *family?* Whose family?

"Hello," she said. "I'm Nealy Coleman. And you are?"

PART I

1

Seventeen-year-old Nealy Coleman's chest heaved and rattled when she coughed, causing the housekeeper's faded eyes to grow wide with alarm. The toddler at Nealy's feet started to cry. Nealy reached down to pick up the little girl. "Shhh, don't cry, Emmie. Please don't cry," she pleaded hoarsely. The child whimpered in her mother's arms.

"Let me hold her while you stick your head under that steam tent I made for you. Land sakes, child, if you don't take care of yourself, you're going to end up in the hospital or the cemetery." The housekeeper reached for the toddler, who was barely two years old.

"All right, Tessie, but you keep an eye out for Pa. I've still got three horses to groom, and you know how he is. He doesn't like it when any of us get sick and can't do our chores." Nealy gave Emmie over to the housekeeper and sat down. "If you sing to Emmie, she'll stop crying."

Tessie walked around the kitchen with Emmie in her arms, crooning as she tried to calm the fretful child.

"Whatever you do," Nealy added, "make sure supper isn't late. Pa will take it out on me if it is." Nealy stuck her head under the towel and struggled to take deep breaths from the bowl of steaming mentholated water. She could hear the old woman singing off-key to Emmie. Something about a blackbird baked in a pie. If she wasn't so sick, she might have laughed.

Moments later Nealy heard the swinging door slam against the wall and ripped the towel away from her head. Her face dripping wet from the steam, she jerked around to face her father. In that one instant she saw everything in the huge kitchen: the coal stove and bucket, the stewpot on the stove, the old refrigerator, the clean crisp curtains hanging on the windows, her brothers Pyne and Rhy, and her hateful, angry father. So much for Tessie keeping an eye out.

The sound of rain hitting the back porch beat like a drum inside her head. Chills racked her body as she struggled to her feet. Afraid of what her father might do, she started to inch closer to Tessie and her daughter when his hand snaked out and pulled her back.

"What are you doin' lollygaggin' around in here when you have horses to tend, girl?"

Nealy threw her head back, lifted her chin, and met his angry gaze. "I wasn't lollygagging, Pa. I was waiting for the rain to let up."

Her father snickered in disgust. "Like hell you were," he said, looking at the bowl of water. "You got a slicker, girl. Now git to it."

Pyne stepped forward. "I can do her chores, Pa. Nealy's sick." Without warning, Josh Coleman swung his arm backward. Pyne took the blow full in the face. He reeled sideways, his hand going to his nose. Blood spurted out between his fingers. Rhy handed him a dish towel.

Tears filled Nealy's eyes. She staggered over to the coatrack by the kitchen door. Her hands were trembling so badly she could barely take the slicker from the peg. She turned around as she put on her slicker and looked straight at Tessie, begging her with her eyes to take care of Emmie a little while longer. The old woman nodded in understanding. Nealy cringed when she heard her father say, "Put that drooling half-wit in her bed and get our supper on the table, woman."

Outside in the pouring rain, Nealy trudged to the barn. Once inside, she collapsed on a bale of hay and fought to catch her breath. She turned fear-filled eyes on the barn door, and whispered, "Just this once, God, help me. Please."

Help arrived minutes later in the form of her brother Pyne. He touched his lips to her forehead. "Jesus God, Nealy, you're burning up. Lie down and rest, and I'll do what needs doing. Pa will never know. He went into his office with a bottle, and you know what that means."

Nealy curled up in a nest of loosened hay and put a horse blanket under her head. "I don't understand you, Pyne. Why do you let Pa treat you like he does? Why don't you stand up to him and show him what you're made of?"

Pyne looked up from cleaning April Fantasy's rear hoof. "You keep thinking I'm something I'm not. I don't have your grit, Nealy. I never have, and I never will. And Pa knows it."

Nealy sighed in resignation. It was sad but true. Pyne had no backbone whatsoever.

"He doesn't pick on Rhy, just you and me. I hate him. I hate him so much . . ." She broke into a fit of coughing. She felt like she'd swallowed a pack of razor blades. "I never felt like this before, Pyne. I think I must be dying. I see two of you. Who's going to take care of Emmie if I die?"

"Shhhh," Pyne said as he picked up the currycomb. "I'm not going to let you die, Nealy. As soon as I finish up here, I'll take you into the house and put you to bed. Tessie told me she's going to fix you a couple of mustard plasters and that you'll be right as rain in no time."

Right as rain, Nealy thought as her eyes started to close. *What's right about rain?* she wondered as she drifted off.

The barn door opened and banged against the inside wall. Nealy struggled to a sitting position and was relieved to see it was Rhy, not her father.

Pyne looked over the horse's back. "Rhy!"

Rhy looked at Nealy, then at Pyne, his expression full of disgust. "Pa's in rare form tonight," he said, picking up a hoof pick and a currycomb as he walked past Nealy toward the second stall.

Nealy didn't know what to think. Was Rhy going to help Pyne do her chores? Maybe he wasn't such a bad brother after all. Or maybe he wanted something. With Rhy, you just never knew.

"Hey, Rhy, you ever been horsewhipped?" Pyne asked.

Nealy knew that it wasn't so much a question as it was a prediction of what was going to happen if their father found out what they were doing.

"You know I haven't. If you're trying to scare me, don't bother. Pa isn't going to find out unless one of you tell him." He bent to pick up the horse's hoof. "I can tell you this, Pa's worse now than he ever was, and it's all *her* fault," Rhy said, pointing the hoof pick at Nealy. "Her and that illegitimate half-wit of hers have been the talk of the town for the last two years. Christ Almighty, we can't go anywhere anymore without folks whispering behind their hands."

Nealy bristled. "Just because Emmie hasn't talked yet doesn't mean she's a half-wit. Stop calling her that, Rhy. Please."

"Wake up, Nealy. For Christ's sake, Emmie's two years old, and she hasn't done anything but cry and grunt. Like it or not, sis, you spawned a half-wit, but worse than that you brought shame to this family and this farm. It's pretty damn hard for us to hold up our heads. Guess you didn't think about that when you opened up your legs." He tossed the hoof pick into the bucket. "You'd be doing us all a favor if you'd just pack up and leave."

"Rhy!" Pyne shouted. "You said you wouldn't say . . ."

"I know what I said," Rhy interrupted, his face transformed with rage. "But that was then, and this is now. I'm tired of living this way. Tired of the gossip, the whispers, the smirks. I'm tired of it all, ya hear? I've had enough."

Nealy bit down on her lower lip. So now she knew why Rhy had come out to the barn—not to help, but to tell her to leave. And since Pyne always wanted everything Rhy wanted, that probably meant he wanted her to go, too. But where could she go? What would she do? Even if she was almost eighteen, how would she take care of herself? How would she take care of Emmie? She tried to think, but her head was too fuzzy. Tomorrow she would think about it. Tomorrow, when she was feeling better.

A long time later, Nealy felt herself picked up and carried. She heard the familiar squeak of the barn door, then rain beat down on her face. It was cold against her hot skin. She heard her brother whisper something close to her ear but couldn't make out what he said.

A warm blast of air hit her when the kitchen door opened. She was on her feet a second later, the slicker sliding off her shoulders into a large wet puddle at her feet.

"Take her up to her bed," Tessie ordered. "As soon as I'm finished with the dishes I'll go up and tend to her." She handed

Emmie to Rhy. Her shoulders slumped as she faced the mountain of dishes that waited for her in the soapy water.

The moment they reached her room, Rhy dumped Emmie on the bed and left. Pyne set Nealy down on the edge of the bed, his face worried. His gaze raked the room as he looked for her flannel nightgown. He finally found it on the hook behind the closet door.

"Do you think you can get undressed by yourself or do you need me to help you?" His voice was not unkind; nor was it kind. It was cool and flat.

Nealy looked up at her brother. His demeanor had changed since Rhy had asked her to leave. "No, I don't need your help. I can do it myself," she said. When Pyne started for the door she added, "Thanks for doing my chores. I owe you one."

Pyne glanced at her over his shoulder. "No you don't. You would have done the same for me. But what Rhy said, Nealy . . . I hate to say it, but he's right. You might as well get it through your head Pa is never going to forgive you unless . . ."

"Unless I give Emmie up and put her in an orphanage," she finished for him. "I can't do that, Pyne. She's my baby, my child. Maybe she came into this world the wrong way, but it's my fault, not hers. I've done everything else Pa's asked. I quit school. I quit going to church though I haven't quit praying. I always pray. When I'm not sick, I work as hard as you and Rhy. Tessie says I work harder than most men. I keep up my studies here at home. And I take care of Emmie. I don't know what else I can do that I'm not already doing."

"You can go away," he said, then closed the door behind him.

Tears streamed down Nealy's face. She'd deluded herself into thinking Pyne loved her in spite of everything. The truth was he was just like Rhy, who was just like Pa—cold and heartless.

They'd always been that way, she realized with startling clarity. Emmie's birth had only magnified things.

The lack of love between her and her father and brothers was what had brought her to this point. Because she couldn't get any love or attention at home, she'd gone looking for it elsewhere. It was so easy to find. Too easy. He'd said the words, words she'd needed to hear, words that had lulled her into letting him make love to her. He'd offered her everything her father and brothers hadn't . . . love, comfort, joy, and promises for the future.

Lies. All lies, she realized now as she picked up Emmie and held her close to her breast.

Late the next afternoon, Nealy struggled to open her eyes and when she did she closed them instantly. Why were so many people in her room? She tried again and slowly opened one eye, thinking she must have imagined seeing the crowd of people. Maybe she was dreaming or delirious. But there they were—Pa, Rhy and Pyne. They were standing at the foot of the bed staring at her. The white-haired man with glasses was Dr. Cooper. What was a horse doctor doing in her room? And where was Emmie?

"Emmie? Emmie?" When there was no answer, she tried to crawl out of bed. It was Pyne who forced her back onto the pillows.

"Tessie has Emmie. She's got a low-grade fever and a cough," he whispered. Out of the corner of his eye he watched as the others left the room.

Nealy eyed him warily. After what he'd said last night, she didn't trust him anymore. But what could she do? She was too weak to move. "Am I dying, Pyne?"

"Don't be ridiculous. Doc gave you a shot and said you'll be fine in a little while. Listen, Nealy. You have to get better real fast. Pa's planning on sending Emmie to the orphanage in the morning. Once he does that, I don't know if you can get her back."

Nealy pushed the covers away and swung her legs over the side of the bed. Her face felt hot, her skin stretched to the breaking point. And yet her body was cold.

"What do you think you're doing?" Pyne asked.

"Taking your advice. I'm going to leave."

"But . . . You're too sick, and Emmie's coming down with the same thing."

Nealy ignored him. Chills racked her body as she gathered her warmest clothes and took them into the closet. Minutes later she emerged completely dressed. She sat down on the edge of the bed and was pulling on her boots when the door opened and

Emmie ran in. Tears streamed down Nealy's face as she hugged her. "I'll never let Pa take you away from me. Never." The toddler burrowed her head against her mother's chest. Nealy rocked her feverish daughter in her arms. She looked up when her brother came to stand in front of her.

"I knew you would react this way, so I came prepared." He reached his hand into his pocket, then handed her a neat roll of bills. "Tessie, Rhy and me . . . We scraped together all we could. It's almost $200. I wish it was more but . . . Wait a minute! I know where there's some more. Don't move till I get back," he said, excitement ringing in his voice. He was back within minutes holding a fat envelope. "There's four hundred dollars here. Tax money. I saw Pa counting it the other day. Don't say anything, Nealy. I'll deal with it later. Here's the keys to the truck. Tessie is packing up Emmie's things right now. There's not much time. Pa went to the barn with the vet, so if you're leaving, you best do it now. He made the call to the county orphanage last night, and they said they'd come for Emmie in the morning. I don't expect they'll go after you, but I covered the license plates with mud just in case." He reached into his other pocket and took out a napkin. "Doc Cooper left you some pills and gave me instructions to give them to you every four hours."

Nealy took the napkin from her brother's hands and opened it up. Staring up at her were five huge pills. "These are horse pills," she said, looking up at Pyne.

"Doc says what's good for horses is good for folks, too. He told me to cut them up in quarters. Just bite off a chunk."

Nealy stood up and tucked the napkin into her jeans pocket. "Thanks for the money and the pills." She used up another five minutes stuffing essentials into an old carpetbag that Tessie said had once belonged to her mother.

"You're welcome. It's cold out, but the heater in the truck is working, and it's gassed up. I'm sorry about all this, Nealy. I wish there was some other way to . . ."

"Forget it, Pyne," she said, cutting him short as she struggled to even out her breathing. "Pa is Pa, and that's it. Wherever I go and whatever I do . . . it's gotta be better than this." She gave the room a last look. "I love this place, Pyne. Maybe because I don't know any better or maybe because Mama is buried here. Then again . . ." She shook her head, unwilling to voice her thoughts. "Am I going to get a chance to say good-bye to Rhy and Tessie?"

"No. Rhy's in the barn with Pa and Doc, and Tessie is standing guard at the back door. She made up a food basket for you and Emmie." He took the carpetbag from her hand and opened the bedroom door. "When you drive out, coast down the hill and don't put your lights on till you get to the main road. Don't stop till you're far away from here. When you get where you're going, call Bill Yates and let him know how you are. He'll get a message to me. Can you remember to do that, Nealy? Jesus, I wish it didn't have to be like this. Make sure you remember to call now."

"I'll remember, Pyne. But I don't know where I'm going. Where should I go, Pyne?"

"Head for Lexington, Kentucky. Stop at the first breeding farm you come to. They'll take you in. You're good with horses, better than Rhy or I will ever be. Hell, you're better with them than Pa is. That's why he worked you so hard. He knew how good you were. You have grit, Nealy. Use it now."

"Good-bye, Pyne. And thanks . . . for everything," Nealy said, her voice ringing with tears.

"Go on, git now before Pa comes back from the barn," Pyne said gruffly. Then he did something that she would remember forever. He bent over and kissed Emmie on the cheek. "You take care of your mama, little one." He pressed a bright, shiny penny into her hand. Emmie looked at it and smiled.

Nealy held Emmie close as she negotiated the front stairs. "Pyne?"

"Yeah?"

"Emmie is not a half-wit."

"I know that, Nealy. Hurry up now."

Perspiration dotted Nealy's face and neck as she quietly opened the front door and headed for the truck parked in the gravel drive. After settling Emmie into a nest of blankets on the passenger side, Nealy climbed in and adjusted the seat. She saw Pyne toss her carpetbag into the back with some buckets and a shovel. Then she put the key in the ignition, but didn't turn it. The fact that she didn't have a driver's license suddenly occurred to her. She'd driven on the ranch and a few country roads, but she'd never driven on a major highway. If the state police caught her, would they send her back? Would her father tell them she stole the truck? Tessie would say she was borrowing trouble with such thoughts, and since she had all the trouble she could handle at the moment, she concentrated on the problem at hand, steering the coasting truck.

Nealy was almost to the main road when she stopped the truck to take one last look at the only home she'd ever known. SunStar Farms. Her shoulders slumped. Would she ever see SunStar's lush grassy pastures again? Or its miles of white board fence? Or April Fantasy, the stallion she'd raised and trained herself? Something told her she'd miss pasture grass, fencing, and a horse more than her own father and brothers.

Hot tears burned her eyes as she climbed out of the truck. She reached in the back for one of the empty oat buckets and the shovel. Moving off to the side of the road, she sank the shovel deep into the rain-softened ground, then filled the bucket with rich, dark soil. SunStar soil. That much she could take with her. She lugged the bucket back to the truck and hefted it into the truck bed. Her chest screamed with pain as she clamped a bigger bucket over the top to secure the dirt.

Gasping for breath, she leaned against the back fender and stared into the darkness. "They may think they're rid of me, but they aren't. I'll come back someday, and when I do, things will be different."

Nealy drove for hours, her body alternating between burning up and freezing. She stopped once to fill a cup with milk for Emmie and once to get gas. She took Emmie into the bathroom with her, careful to keep the wool cap pulled low over her face just in case anyone was looking for them. Satisfied that they had not attracted any attention, she climbed back into the truck. She gave Emmie some baby aspirin that she'd found packed among her things and broke off a quarter of one of the horse pills Pyne had given her.

Two hours later Nealy crossed the state line into Kentucky. She drove for another two hours before she left the main highway and headed down a secondary road with a sign pointing to Blue Diamond Farms. Maybe she could find work there, though why anyone would hire a sick teenager with a sick toddler was beyond her. On second thought, maybe she would be better off to find a cheap motel and stay there until they were both better.

Emmie tugged at her arm just as the truck bucked, sputtered, and died. Nealy steered it to the side of the road. She lifted the little girl into her arms and hugged her. The aspirin hadn't helped at all. Emmie was so hot she was listless. Fear, unlike anything she'd experienced in her short life, overcame Nealy. Emmie needed help—a doctor—a people doctor, not a horse doctor. She stared out the window and debated whether to take Emmie and walk down the road or cut across the field. If she cut across the field and couldn't make it, it might be days before anyone found them. With Emmie in her arms, she started down the road, only to turn around to get her bucket of dirt out of the truck bed. She could always come back for the rest of her belongings.

Twice she stumbled and almost fell but managed to right herself both times. She trudged on, the whimpering child clinging to her neck. "I can do this," she told herself. "I know I can do this." Like a litany, she said the words over and over.

The third time she fell she couldn't get up. Holding Emmie close to her she curled into the fetal position and cried. Then she prayed. And when she opened her eyes, she saw denim-clad legs and muddy boots. Through fevered eyes she looked up and saw the biggest, ugliest man she'd ever seen in her life. "Please, can you help me and my little girl?"

Nealy felt herself and Emmie being lifted, and somehow knew they were in good hands. "My bucket. Please, I can't go without my bucket," she said, when the giant took his first step. "I can't leave it. It's all I've got left." She felt him bend down, heard the click-clack of the handle, and closed her eyes.

Nealy went in and out of consciousness. She knew people were helping her, knew the hands were gentle. She could hear them talking about her and her daughter. Someone named Maud and someone else named Jess. She felt them take Emmie from her arms and didn't protest because the hands were good hands, gentle hands. "Please God," she prayed aloud, her voice scratchy. "Let this be a good place."

"This is a good place, child," the woman, Maud, said. Her

voice had a lilting Southern drawl. "Jess and I are gonna take care of you and your li'l girl. Is there anyone you want us to call? Do you have a family, child?"

Until now Nealy hadn't considered what she would tell people who questioned where she'd come from. She couldn't think about it now because she was in too much misery to concentrate. "No, ma'am. It's just me and my little girl," she said for lack of a better explanation. Later she would give them their names and tell them something about herself, something that was close to the truth. Later, when she could think more clearly.

"All right then. Don't you worry about a thing. Jess and me will take care of everything. You just close your eyes and go to sleep. The doctor is on his way."

"I need my . . ." Nealy's voice gave out.

"Jess is on his way now to tow your truck into the barn. As soon as he's through, he'll bring your things inside."

Nealy had to make the woman understand that it wasn't her belongings that were important to her. It was the bucket of SunStar soil. "No!" She struggled to raise up but Maud held her down.

"What is it, child?"

"I need . . ."

"Shhhh," Maud hushed her. "It's right here." She lifted the bucket for Nealy to see.

"Thank you, ma'am." And then she was asleep.

2

Nealy's eyes snapped open. She struggled to move. Where was Emmie? More to the point, where was she? Then she remembered. She let out a small hoarse cry as she felt a wet tongue on her cheek. "You're not Emmie, you're a dog!" she said, her eyes wide with awe.

Nealy stroked the dog's silky fur as she looked around. It was a pretty room, with flowered wallpaper and sheer curtains at the window. It looked like a girl's room. The bed she was lying on was narrow and comfortable, almost like the small bed she'd had back home. She looked down at the black dog lying on top of a double-ring wedding quilt. He licked her hand. "Are you my guardian?" she whispered as she scratched him gently behind the ears.

She saw her then, in the shadows of the room. The lady with the gentle hands, the one who'd reached out for Emmie. She was holding Emmie, rocking her on the rocker, and it sounded like she was singing.

The dog barked.

"Shhh, Molly, you'll wake the little one. How are you feeling, Nealy?"

"I'm not sure, ma'am. How long have I been here? Am I going to die? Is Emmie all right?"

"Mercy, child, so many questions. I guess you must be feeling better. You've been with us for eleven days. No, you aren't going to die, but it was touch-and-go there for a little while. You had pneumonia. Emmie is fine. Jess and I have been taking care of her. Molly stayed with you the whole time. She'd come and fetch us those first few days when you couldn't breathe."

Nealy continued to stroke the silky dog as she digested the

information. "Emmie has never been away from me before. Did she cry? Did she miss me?"

"Of course she missed you. She whimpered from time to time, but Jess could always make her smile. We'd bring her in here so she could see you. I'd rock her to sleep. She's a beautiful little girl. She looks like her mama. Right now you look a tad bony and hollow-eyed, but we'll fix that as soon as you can get up."

"I can pay you for my keep, ma'am. I can't be beholden to you. When I'm well, I can work. I'm good with horses. Do you think you might have some work for me? I can cook and clean, too. I can do most anything if you give me the chance."

"We can talk about all that later. First we have to get you on your feet."

"Ma'am, I need to know. I need to know there's a place for me and Emmie. I can't be having that hanging over our heads. It's going to be getting cold soon. I have to take care of her. There's no one but me to do that. I need to hear the words, ma'am."

"Honey, you and this sweet baby have a home here for as long as you want. If you want to work for me, I'll hire you. I'll pay you a decent wage. This can be your room if you want it. We have a room right next door for Emmie. Jess fetched a crib from town, but the tyke doesn't care for it. Likes to crawl in and out, so we set her up a real bed and got her some toys. Molly plays ball with her. She's happy. I'm going to put her in her bed now and get you something to eat. It's been a long time since you had real food. What would you like?"

"I'd like to see my daughter so I can kiss her good night. She was sick when we got here. Did you tend to her, too?"

"We did. The doctor came by twice a day. This little one did well on the medicine. She's fine now."

Tears blurred Nealy's eyes when she reached out to stroke her daughter's tangled curls. "She's not a half-wit, ma'am, she's not!" she said fiercely.

"Now why would you be saying such a thing? No one said this baby was a half-wit. Did someone say that to you?" Maud Diamond's voice quivered in outrage.

"Ma'am, I'd know if that was true, wouldn't I? I'm her mother. I never had a mother, so I couldn't ask the right questions. She doesn't cry much. I used to have a hard time trying to keep her quiet so . . . I think she understands. She should be saying words now, but she doesn't."

"When she's ready, she'll talk a blue streak. If she doesn't want to talk, she won't. Jess now, he never says three words if one will do. He grunts a lot. That doesn't mean he's a half-wit. As long as you stay in my house I never want to hear you say that word again. Do you understand me, Nealy? What's your last name? I'm going to need a name and a social security number for your work papers. And your birth date. Not right now but when you're better. Now what would you like to eat?"

"I think I might like an egg and some toast. My name is . . . Cole. Nealy Cole. I'm almost eighteen. My birthday is November 1. I promise never to use that word again. Did Emmie really miss me, ma'am?"

"Yes, honey, she did. I think she knew you were sick. As long as she could see you she was just as good as gold. I don't know if this is important or not, but she had this penny in her hand and wouldn't give it up nohow. I made her a little velvet bag with a drawstring, and she wears it on her wrist. She's about worn out the string opening it to make sure that penny is still there."

Nealy bit down on her lip. "Some . . . someone gave it to her. It was bright and shiny. She never saw a penny before. Thank you for making the bag for her. And thank you for taking care of us. I'll work hard for you, ma'am, so that you're never sorry you took us in. Do you still have my bucket? That bucket is important to me and Emmie."

Maud Diamond felt a lump start to grow in her throat. Tears burned her eyes as she turned to hobble from the room, her arthritic legs and back clearly visible to Nealy. "Everything is safe, honey. Don't you be fretting about anything now. All you need to do is get well and strong."

In the kitchen, Maud sat down at the table to stare at her longtime friend, companion, and farm foreman. "She's awake, Jess. She's going to be just fine. I think we got us a fine young filly here. That girl about broke this old heart of mine. We're keeping her. I don't much care if someone is looking for her or not. It's clear to me she lit out with that little one because things got out of hand. I want you to hide that truck of hers, and if anyone ever comes around here looking for her, you run them off, you hear me, Jess. Wherever you hide that truck, you hide that bucket of dirt of hers, too. We'll tell her where it is if she wants to know. What we have here, Jess, is a conspiracy."

The old man nodded. "You're in pain, Maud. Do you want me to fix you something to ease it?"

"I can stand it. You could make some eggs for Nealy, and toast. Tea would be good. I'll just sit here and watch you. Do you think she'll like it here, Jess? It'll be like us having a daughter and granddaughter to look after."

Jess Wooley grunted as he cracked eggs into a bowl. He was as tall as the sycamore sapling he'd planted outside the kitchen door to shade the steps because Maud liked to sit on them. A big man, Maud called him, with hands almost as big as fry pans. Gentle hands. Good hands. Some people, Maud included, said he was an ugly man. Maud always clarified that by saying he was so ugly he was beautiful, with twinkling blue eyes, snow-white hair, and dimples so deep you could stick a spoon in them. When he laughed, which wasn't often, the ground shook beneath his 260-pound frame.

"Jess, what do you think would have happened to Blue Diamond Farms if you hadn't rode onto my spread fifty years ago? I need to thank you again for stopping by that day. There I was with two stud horses, three mares, a run-down house, ramshackle barns, and only enough food to see me through a week at best. Didn't make one bit of difference that Pa had had a Derby winner years before. I'd just buried him that very morning. As I recall, I'd tipped the moonshine crock a few too many times. I was just about to lay down and die and there you were, big as life, jerking me to my feet and telling me to stop blubbering. You said nothing was so bad it couldn't be fixed. You fixed it all. I want to know, and I damn well want to know right now, this very minute, why you didn't move into this house with me. I want to know, Jess."

" 'Cause we weren't married. That's why. We've been over this a hundred times, maybe a thousand, Maud."

"I don't care. I want to hear it again. You slept in my bed. You never asked me to marry you."

"Did so."

"You did not."

"Said we should make it legal."

"That's not a proposal, you horse's patoot."

"Is to me."

"I wanted fancy words. Pretty words."

"Actions speak louder than words."

Maud watched as Jess slid the eggs onto a plate, then settled everything on a tray. "A posy would look nice on here. Before you know it the frost will kill all those flowers, so it's best to pick them now."

"She's got *the touch*, Maud."

"I know. I could feel it in her. If the little one has it, then it's a good bet her mama has it, too. I appreciate you taking the tray up. When you come down maybe I will take some of that elixir if you don't mind."

"Don't mind at all. I made a fire. Wrap up on the sofa, and I'll bring it in when I get done."

"Jess."

Jess turned, his eyes questioning.

"This is a good thing we're doing, isn't it?"

"Yep."

"Good. That makes me feel a lot better knowing you agree."

"Always do, Maud."

Maud made her way into the comfortable living room. She did love a fire on cold nights. Who was she fooling, she loved a good fire any time of the day or night. She sank down gratefully on her favorite chintz-covered sofa. She wished she could swing her legs up and stretch out, but those days were gone forever. Until now, all she'd had to look forward to were more days of pain and misery. Even the first sight of a new foal couldn't erase the pain these days. Now it was going to be different. She leaned back, closed her eyes, and waited for Jess. Jess always made things better.

The dream came quickly because it was always there, hovering inside her brain, just waiting for the moment she closed her eyes.

"Don't get on that horse, Maud. He's not ready."

"Maybe he isn't, but I am. That's all that counts. He's just skittish because it's getting ready to rain. I can handle him, Jess."

"Maud, you aren't twenty-five years old. You're damn well sixty-five, and you don't belong on a horse anymore."

"If that was true, Jess, I'd lay down and die. I was ready to do that the day you came riding onto Diamond property. Don't be saying that to me, or you'll jinx me."

The moment the words sailed past her lips, Stardancer reared up on his hind legs and lunged forward, snorting his disdain for the woman on his back. He tossed his head backward, his mane flying into Maud's face. She gripped the reins tighter just as he reared up a second time. This time she grabbed for his mane and hung on for dear life. Unable to shake the load on his back, the horse snorted again and took off at a full gallop. Maud blinked as she saw the split-rail fencing come into view. Stardancer flew over the fencing, tossing his rider into the air. She landed hard on the post dividing the fence sections. She heard her bones snap at the same moment she heard Jess's wild shout, and then her world turned black.

"You sleeping, Maud?"

"Not anymore, Jess. How is she?"

"She's fine. She ate a little, wobbled to the bathroom, and now she's sleeping. She did look in on Emmie for a second. Molly's sleeping on the bed with her. It's all gonna work out, Maud. Here's your elixir."

Maud smiled. Four ounces of Kentucky bourbon with a dash of lemon was Jess's idea of an elixir. She had one in the morning, one at noon, and one in the evening. On more than one occasion she had some in between times. Sometimes it dulled the pain, and sometimes it didn't.

"How bad is it tonight, Maud?"

"It's bad, Jess. A broken back isn't something you recover from. If it wasn't for this blasted arthritis settling in my joints and between the vertebrae in my back, I'd be fine. Maybe I should look into some of those newfangled surgeries they say work for joints."

"Maybe you shouldn't," Jess said curtly. "Let's just sit here and watch the fire. That game show you like is on tonight. It's your turn to spend the money this evening." It was a game they played every Monday night. They took turns pretending they were the winning contestants, and then discussed how they would spend their winnings.

"I think maybe I'd do some decorating now that we have young people living with us. You know, bright colors, fresh carpets, new draperies. A pony and a cart for Emmie. Maybe we should think about putting in a swimming pool. I always liked the water."

Jess clucked his tongue. "Let's take it a little slow. There's nothing wrong with this house or the furnishings. It's old, and it's comfortable. I don't think that girl upstairs has had much comfort along the way. I'd bet my last dollar she'll say she likes it just the way it is."

"Okay, then what should I spend the money on? We need to do some talking about our holdings, Jess. Seems to me people our age are dropping like flies. We need to do some of that estate planning. We don't want those government men coming in here and taking everything we worked for all our lives. We really do need to talk about this, Jess. Don't you be putting me off again. Neither one of us has kin."

"That means we have to talk about dying. I don't like talking about dying, Maud. We been over this before. I thought we agreed we'd leave our money to charity."

"I changed my mind." Maud's gnarled fingers plucked at the yellow-and-white afghan covering her. She'd made it one winter when she was down with the flu. Now she couldn't even hold the needles. "I'm not saying we shouldn't leave money to charity. What I'm saying is we need to maybe set up a foundation or something. We insure these Thoroughbreds for millions of dollars, and yet you and I only have a million each on our lives. If this place is going to continue after we're gone, then we need to make provisions for that. I'm going to look into it as soon as our guests are up and about. I want to know now if you're going to fuss and fret."

"You're an ornery woman, Maud Diamond. Do what you want."

Maud nodded. "Then I'd like another drink, Jess. Make it a double this time."

"That bad, eh?"

"Yes. It's going to rain. It's worse when it rains. God sent that child to us for a reason. You believe that, don't you?"

"Yep. I'm going to build up this fire. Wouldn't be a bit surprised to find frost in the morning."

Maud leaned her head back into the pillows. Was Jess right about the girl upstairs? Would she like the old, deep comfortable furniture? Would she curl up by the fire with the little one on her lap? What would she think of all the trophies on the mantel? Maybe this year she could talk Jess into setting up a real Christmas tree in the corner. She thought about her mortality then, because when the pain was bad like it was tonight she always thought about death.

Jess handed her the heavy cup with the wide handle. He watched her out of the corner of his eye as he stoked the fire, sweat dripping down his cheeks. "You never complain, Maud, why is that?"

"Because I did a damn fool thing. And because I didn't listen to you that day. Complaining isn't going to change anything. Sit down, Jess; this one is taking the edge off a bit. I was thinking, now that we more or less got ourselves a little family, I want a Christmas tree this year."

"You do, do you?"

"Yes. Are the horses all right?"

"You know they are. I'll take a last look before I turn in. Maud, we got the best people in the world working for us. There's no call to worry. The way I figure it, we got one more crack at the Derby. We got us two already. One more will round it out nicely."

"We need to think about some schooling for that girl upstairs. Maybe on the weekends."

"I'm talking about Kentucky Derby winners, and you're talking about schooling. If you don't beat all, Maud Diamond."

"I want to know more about that young girl, Jess. I think it might behoove us to hire on a private investigator to look into her background. We might need to know what we're up against down the road. She doesn't have to know. I'm looking at it as protection for her. Not for us. Make sure you understand that, Jess. Somehow or other, those two sneaked into this old heart of mine. Didn't think that could happen. Horses and dogs and, of course, you. That's all I thought I had room for. The same thing happened to you, Jess, so don't try to deny it."

"Wasn't going to."

Maud reached out for Jess's hand. She did her best to squeeze it. "We're coming into the home stretch, Jess."

"You're getting maudlin. Time for bed. I'll walk you up and get you settled in before I check on the horses. Another thing. Tomorrow, when you start making all your phone calls, call that place and order the chair rail. If you don't do it, I will. I want it set up and installed by the end of the week. My knees can't take these stairs anymore."

"All right, Jess."

"You'll do it."

"I said I would. New wallpaper. This is twenty years old. Looks like baby-poop yellow. I'll call about that, too."

Jess held on to Maud's arm, his finger going to his lips. "Shhh." He led her to the half-open door of Emmie's room. Maud's hand flew to her mouth as she listened to the tormented voice of the young girl.

"Shhh, Emmie, not a sound now. I know you understand what I'm telling you. I want you to be a really good little girl for Miss Maud and Mr. Jess. This is a wonderful place, and they said we could stay here. Mama's going to work hard, so they aren't ever sorry they took us in. Someday we'll go back home but probably not for a real long time. I'm going to buy you a pretty dress and some shiny black shoes. I'm your mama, so I have to do those things. I want to do that for you. I'll be getting a wage. Pa never gave me two cents, so the money Pyne gave me is the first real money I ever had. It's just a loan. Someday I have to pay it all back. I know you don't understand everything that's going on. Maybe when you get older I can explain it to you. Pa was going to send you to the orphanage, so that's why we lit out like we did. I couldn't let him take you away from me. He was just going to rip you away from me like I had no claim to you. I'm just a girl, not of age, so he could do anything he pleased. I hate him for what he did to us. I'll never forgive him as long as I live. Remember now, you have to be a good little girl and do what Miss Maud and Mr. Jess say. You have to remember not to wet your pants or mess in them. You're a big girl now. If we're both good, maybe they'll let us stay here forever and ever. Wouldn't that be the most wonderful thing in the world? I'll sing you a song now, but you have to close your eyes and go to sleep. Do you have your penny?"

The little girl held up her wrist and wiggled it. Nealy hugged her as she started to sing, *"Hush little baby . . . "*

3

Nealy held her daughter's hand as she walked up the long driveway that led to the house where she'd been living for the past four weeks. She held up her hand to shield her eyes from the bright sun. A moment later she offered up a small prayer that she would never have to leave this beautiful place. Her eyelids started to burn with unshed tears. She'd found such goodness here, such love. Not just for herself but for Emmie as well. Her heart swelled with love when she looked down at the small child tugging at her leg. She laughed when the toddler sat down in the middle of the driveway and crossed her legs. It was obvious she wasn't about to move. She pointed to the house where Maud Diamond was sitting on the porch. She waved, the little velvet bag with her shiny penny secure on her wrist.

Following her daughter's example, Nealy sat down, too, and stared at her new home. It was so beautiful, so unlike the stark place she'd lived in till now. She squinted against the sun to stare at the beige-and-gray fieldstone that made up the house with all the diamond-shaped windows that sparkled in the bright sunshine. It was old, the stones almost smooth to the touch. She knew that for a fact because she'd walked all around the big house, touching the stones she could reach. Some of them felt like marble, some felt like satin. Maud said the house had character, and she was right. But it was the windows, patterned after marquise diamonds, that she loved the most. They glistened and sparkled like precious gems. Maud said when it rained they looked like diamonds with flaws. Nothing would ever convince Nealy that anything at Diamond Farms was less than picture-perfect, from the bluegrass lawns that resembled a well-maintained golf course to the morning glories climbing up trellises all around the house. They were every color of the rainbow, and Maud called them her own personal rainbows. The confederate jasmine climbing up and around the outside lighting gave off a heady aroma that delighted her senses. Even from this distance Nealy could smell it and savor it. She loved the scent almost as much as she loved the pungent smells emanating from the long row of barns. For one wild moment she thought her heart was going to burst with happiness that God had allowed her to find this place for Emmie and herself. She couldn't help but wonder what the winter would bring. Would she think this place was beautiful when the bluegrass died off and the morning glories turned brown? Another few weeks and these beautiful Indian summer days would be nothing more than memories. But it was the first memories that were the best, the ones to hug to your chest, the ones to savor. Nealy knew in the years to come, nothing, no matter how grand, would ever erase her memory of her first sight of Blue Diamond Farms.

"Time to go, honey. I'll race you to the house. The winner gets a cookie!"

Emmie struggled to her feet. She smiled up at her mother before she waddled up the long drive, her pudgy legs pumping furiously. She would scramble up the four steps that led to the beautiful front porch where Maud Diamond waited for them, then bury her head in the old lady's lap. Maud's gnarled hands would caress the springy blonde curls as she struggled to lift the child onto her lap. She'd rock her in her old wicker chair and croon a lullaby until she fell asleep.

"Is she too heavy for you, Miss Maud?" Nealy asked.

"Not in the least. She's soft and warm, and smells the way a little one should, all powdery and clean. I never had a child to rock. I like the way it feels when I hold her close."

Nealy sat down at Maud's feet and hugged her knees. "Can I get you anything, Miss Maud? Tea, coffee, or a soda pop?"

"If I drink any more coffee, I'll float right off this porch. Just sit and talk to me, Nealy."

"I love this porch!" Nealy said. She waved her arms about to indicate the hanging ferns dangling from long white chains and the potted flowers on wicker stands and in colored clay pots. "I hate knowing all these beautiful flowers and plants will be withered in a few weeks. I hate it when something dies."

"There's a season for everything, child. As you grow older, you'll appreciate it more. My pa once told me the seasons reflect one's life, and he was right. Spring is when you're born, summer is when you grow and bloom, autumn is when you begin to age, and then winter is the final season. When I was younger, I wanted summer all the time. Now I hate the winter because I'm at the end of my life. I guess God has a reason for everything. One can't wish her life away." Her voice was so sad-sounding, Nealy wanted to get up and hug her. She stayed where she was. Affection was something she wasn't used to giving, except to Emmie.

"Was your father a nice man, Miss Maud?" Nealy asked.

"Yes, he was. He was fair and just, and he would whack my behind when it was needed. But he knew how to hold me close, and he always knew just the right words to say to me when things didn't go right. He worked me real hard when I was young because he knew someday I would be running Blue Diamond Farms. I loved him with all my heart. Now, tell me, what do you think about my idea to redecorate the inside of the house come winter."

"Are you asking for *my* opinion, Miss Maud?" Nealy replied. "No one has ever wanted my opinion before. I don't know much about decorating."

"Child, I would truly value your opinion. I know young people like bright colors and pretty things. All the furnishings are old and worn. They suit Jess and me, but we thought you and Emmie might want to pretty things up a bit."

"Oh, no, Miss Maud. I love your house just the way it is. Please don't change it for me and Emmie. She loves that chair in your living room. She likes to curl up like a little rabbit in the corner. The inside is like what you said the outside is, full of character. When I was younger I used to look in the Sears Roebuck catalog and pretend I was going to furnish our . . . a house. I'd cut out curtains and rugs and chairs, then I'd paste them on paper. The rooms always looked like your rooms, quiet and comfortable. If you're asking my opinion, then my opinion is you should keep it just the way it is."

"That's just what Jess said you'd say. I guess we'll keep things the way they are for now. Emmie is asleep, Nealy. Do you want to take her upstairs?"

"I've never seen her so happy. She loves being outside and going down to the barn. She never touches anything," Nealy added hastily. "She understands everything we say. I just don't know why she won't talk."

"Time, Nealy. In time we'll know. She's still young. Some children don't talk until later on, like around three or four." Maud wondered if what she said was the truth. Where the little one was concerned she tended to make things up as she went along to drive the misery out of Nealy's eyes.

"I hope so, Miss Maud. I'll put Emmie in her bed, then I'll fix us a cup of tea. Would you like that?"

"Only if you add bourbon to it."

Nealy smiled as she reached for her daughter. "I can do that. Jess showed me how to fix your tea and coffee."

"Did he now?"

"That man purely loves the ground you walk on, Miss Maud."

"I love the ground he walks on, too, but there's no need to be telling him that."

Nealy laughed. "I think he already knows it."

"Scat," Maud growled.

Nealy returned fifteen minutes later with a tray holding two cups of steaming tea. Alongside Maud's cup was an extra shot glass full to the brim with bourbon. "I told Emmie she could play in her room until I came back to put her to sleep. Let it cool a bit, Miss Maud, or it might slip out of your hands. I love it here on the porch. It's so quiet, so peaceful. I don't feel all jittery inside anymore. I worry, though, about how I'm ever going to repay you and Mr. Jess. The doctor said I could start working next week. When are you going to tell me what my job is going to be? I want to be thinking about it, so I don't make mistakes."

"Jess and I worked out a schedule for you. You're going to work in the office and learn the book end of things for two hours in the morning. Then you're going to work for two hours in the barn with the horses. Miss Emmie is going to go to our little preschool two miles down the road. We started it about eight years ago for the workers' children. We have a lot of husband-and-wife teams here. It's one of the best things we ever did. The children love it. The teacher is certified. She can work with

Emmie one-on-one. When the preschool lets out, the teacher is going to come here and tutor you so you can get your high-school diploma. You need to have that today, Nealy. Later on, if you're interested, we can talk about college. The rest of the day and evening is yours to spend with Emmie and Jess and me if you want. You can study your lessons after Emmie goes to sleep. Why are you looking at me like that, child?"

"Because . . . I . . . I told you I was strong. I can work like a man. No, that's not true, I had to learn to work like a man. I can carry my weight. I'm used to getting up at five o'clock and working all day. Hard work is good for you."

"Yes, hard work is commendable. However, you're a young girl," Maud said, as if that explained everything. "For now, this is the way it will be unless you have some objections."

"I'll do whatever you want, Miss Maud. I'm real good with the animals. I'm not half as good with schoolbooks. I'll try real hard."

"That's good enough for me, child."

"I can't get over how pretty everything is. This porch is like one of the pictures in your magazines. Did you fix it up your-self?" Nealy asked as she pointed to the wicker chairs and tables and all the colorful clay pots full of flowers.

"My pa loved flowers. Most men would never admit to lov-ing flowers. He used to have a greenhouse and he would putter around in it. He enjoyed growing things from seeds. He always had the bushiest ferns, the brightest geraniums, and the bottle-brush plants were so full and lush and colorful. All the workers liked to come up here and sit and chew the fat. Pa did like to chew the fat. He'd hand out beer but never more than two to one person. The workers loved him as much as I did. When he died, I didn't think I could keep up this place, but with Jess's help, I did. Blue Diamond Farms is the second-largest breeding farm in Kentucky. Next year I'm going to have Jess or one of the others take you to Keeneland for the yearling sale. Before I die, I'd like to have one more Derby winner. Pa had one in his day, and Jess and I have had two. I don't want to go to the hereafter without another Derby winner under my belt."

Nealy's heart raced inside her chest. She couldn't go to Keeneland. Her father went every year to the yearling sale, along with her brothers. But next year was a long way off. Better to pretend she was okay with the trip right now, so she wouldn't disappoint Miss Maud. She nodded in agreement because she didn't trust herself to speak.

Maud watched the girl out of the corner of her eye. She'd just said something that upset Nealy. She watched as she squirmed in the wicker rocker, the toes of her boots digging into the fiber of the porch carpet. "It's not something we have to decide right now. It's not until July. Anything can happen during that time. You might be needed here. We'll talk about it again. This is very good tea, honey."

Nealy sighed with relief.

She heard the sound, knew instantly what it was—a runaway horse galloping across the lawn and heading for the main road. She was a whirlwind as she heaved herself out of the rocker and over the railing of the fence. She hit the ground running as she raced after the runaway. She whistled sharply the way Pyne had taught her—just loud enough, just shrill enough so the horse could hear and try to puzzle out what the sound meant. The horse slowed imperceptibly, giving Nealy just the few seconds she needed to race up to her, grab her mane, and hoist herself onto her back. "Easy, girl, easy. That's it, calm down. I'm not going to hurt you. Good girl, good girl," she whispered, as the mare finally slowed to a trot. "Looks to me like you were born to run, little lady." Nealy slipped off the horse's back and walked forward to cup the horse's head in her two hands. She stroked her head, loving the feel of the animal against her hands. The horse calmed immediately as Nealy rubbed her nose against the horse's nose. "See, now we're friends. You are one beautiful girl. I don't think I've ever seen one as pretty as you. Pa had some beauties but none to compare to you. Come on now, act like a lady, and I'll walk you back to the barn. No? I see, you want to give me a ride. Okay, but don't you buck me off, you hear? Ladies don't do things like that," Nealy whispered as she hurled herself onto the horse's back.

It felt good, wonderful really, to be riding again. This was where she belonged.

"Did you see that, Maud? Did you see that? On my best day I

could never have done what Nealy did, and I don't think you could have either."

"I know, Jess. I know. Oh dear, Emmie must have seen from the window. There she goes. She's seen her mother, and she wants her. Fetch her, Jess."

"No need. Watch, Maud. I think we're about to see something neither one of us is going to believe."

They watched as the little girl toddled out to the edge of the lawn and waited for the horse and her mother to come abreast of her. Nealy leaned over. "Want to go for a ride, Emmie?" The little girl's head bobbed up and down.

The old couple on the porch watched as Emmie reached up and tried to wrap her arms around the animal's head. When her small arms couldn't circle the horse's head she buried her face against the horse's leg. The velvet bag dangled from her wrist. The mare whickered softly. A second later, Nealy had leaned down and lifted the little girl up. Emmie was holding on to the horse's mane. The couple watched until both riders and horse were out of sight.

"And we paid Adam how much to break that mare, Jess?" Maud said carefully.

"There's going to be some mighty red faces down to the barn about now." Jess grimaced as he fired up his first cigar of the day. "I think I'll mosey down there for a look-see."

"You do that, Jess. Bareback no less. Fancy likes her. She likes the tyke, too. I think they both have the touch, Jess. You were right about that."

"Me? I thought you were the one who noticed it first. You, me, the same thing. Finish your tea. I'll be right back. Don't even *think* about walking down to the barn. I'll give you a full report when I get back. Do we understand each other, Maud?"

"You aren't my husband, Jess. Stop telling me what to do."

"Gonna be. We're getting married next week."

"When were you going to tell me, Jess? Why?"

"So we can adopt that child when it's time. I already called a lawyer. He's looking into it."

"She has kin, Jess. Maybe we're moving too fast here. It won't be easy."

"No, it won't. I'm prepared. We'll do whatever we have to do. When I fall asleep at night, I keep seeing that little one's face. Whatever it was that made her light out with the young'un had to be serious. God knows where they could have ended up. You need to prepare for the possibility of trouble. We'll do our best to make it work. It's only been four weeks since they got here, but I can see how you love those two. I do, too," Jess said.

"Married, eh?"

"Yep. Thought we'd do it out by the corral. What's your feeling on that, Maud?"

"Well . . . I . . . the corral will be fine, Jess. I'll ask Nealy to stand up for me, and Emmie can throw the rose petals."

"You're getting carried away. This is just going to be one of those 'I do' things. Nothing fancy now. No geegaws and frills. You hear me?"

"The whole damn farm can hear you, Jess. If it's my wedding, then I say what goes and don't go. You do your end, and I'll do my end. A party. A barbecue. Just our people. Don't take that away from me, Jess."

"Okay, won't take that away from you."

"Jess, you sure know how to melt a woman's heart. Go on down to the barn so I can sit here and think about how we turned into two jackasses at our age."

A sharp pain the size of a lightning bolt roared up Maud's spine. She gasped at the same moment she reached for the shot glass full of hundred-proof Kentucky bourbon. She downed it in one quick swallow. The pain was getting worse with each passing day. She closed her eyes and waited for the liquor to take the edge off the pain. She wondered if tomorrow or the next day would be the day when she would no longer measure out the fiery liquor an ounce at a time. When would she be forced to swig from the bottle, a week from now, two weeks? She shuddered at the thought. "I wonder if I'll be sober enough to attend my own wedding," she mumbled as she lowered herself into the old, comfortable rocker.

She prayed then because she didn't know what else to do.

4

The moment the minister said "I now pronounce you man and wife," Nealy clapped her hands with happiness. Emmie stretched out her arms to Jess, a huge smile on her tiny face. She hugged him with all the strength she could muster in her little arms. A second later she blew kisses to Maud, who burst out laughing.

Chet Lincoln reached for his harmonica and did a perfect rendition of "Here Comes the Bride."

Nealy tapped her toes and clapped her hands until Maud signaled it was time to go up to the big house, where the barbecue was under way. She looked around at the smiling faces. Every single person who worked the farm, from the lowliest groom to the foreman, was in attendance. She knew most of them now, and they seemed to like her as much as she liked them. When they realized she loved horses and knew her way around the stables, they included her in their own little world. It didn't matter that she lived in the big house, and it didn't matter that she didn't share her private life with them. She belonged, it was that simple.

Nealy could feel her neck start to itch. That meant someone was either watching her or staring at her. The hair on the back of her neck always stood on end when she knew her pa was standing in the shadows watching what she was doing. It was the same kind of feeling. She turned around to peer through the milling crowd of workers who were making their way up to the main house. She saw him out of the corner of her eye—Jack Carney, the man who expected to take Jess's place when he stepped down. Nealy didn't like him, but then it wasn't her place to like or dislike him. He knew the farm, knew the horses, and had been with Blue Diamond Farms for a long time. She waved listlessly as she turned to follow the crowd. Wylie, Jack's son, fell into step with her. She didn't much care for him either. In her opinion he was too rough with the animals, too uncaring. Once she'd seen him try to shoo Emmie away as if she were one of the barn dogs. She didn't like that either.

"Nice wedding, doncha think? Kind of silly to be getting hitched at their age, but still it was nice."

"You're never too old to get married," Nealy said.

"So are you here for the long haul or are you just passing through? No one seems to know, and you don't give up a whole lot. Why is that?"

"Maybe because it's none of your business, Wylie." Nealy stopped walking and turned to face Jack's son. "Look, I don't like you, so I'm not going to pretend I do. I don't like your rough handling of the horses. I just want you to know I'm going to be watching you. You drink at night, too. You know drinking isn't permitted. And, no, no one told me that, I saw you myself. The others cover for you because of your father. I won't do that, though, so keep it in mind."

"Do we have a tattletale here?" Wylie sneered.

"I guess we'll just have to wait and see, won't we?"

"I think you're pretty goddamn uppity is what I think."

"And I think you're a horse's ass," Nealy said quietly. "Now, get away from me. You make my skin crawl."

"Just who the hell *are* you?" Wylie sneered again.

"I'm the one who has eyes in the back of her head. I told you, keep away from me. You don't want to take me on, Wylie. I'm here to work with the horses just the way you're supposed to work but don't. I think that sums it all up." Without another word, Nealy dug her new shoes into the thick grass and sprinted for the backyard, where the barbecue was under way. She skidded to a stop next to a smiling Maud, who was graciously accepting wedding gifts and hugs from her farm family.

She looks tired, Nealy thought as she led her to the nearest chair that was heavily padded with cushions. "What can I fetch you, Miss Maud?"

"Nothing, honey. Jess is bringing me something. What did you think of my wedding?"

"I thought it was beautiful. Jess loves you so much. Are you happy, Miss Maud?"

"Very happy, child. I didn't think this was ever going to happen. Now I am Mrs. Jess Wooley. I even have a paper that says so. I guess it doesn't get any better than that. What about you, Nealy? Are you happy?"

"Miss Maud, there are no words to tell you how happy I am. You bought me this beautiful new dress and these shoes I'm having a hard time walking in and all those things for Emmie. She looks like a little angel. I always wanted to get her a pair of shiny black shoes. She does love them. Jess showed her how to spit on her finger and rub the dirt off the toe."

"Tonight when she's sleeping you have to change the penny in her bag. Jess got some shiny ones yesterday at the bank. I suspect you'll want to save the . . . original one. I can put it in the safe for you if you like. I saw her staring at it, and I could just tell she couldn't understand why it was no longer shiny. Later, when she's older, you'll be able to make her understand. I love that child, Nealy. So does Jess."

"And she loves you both, too. If you don't need me, Miss Maud, I'm going to get Emmie some supper and get her ready for bed."

"Run along, child. I'm going to sit here and visit with my friends."

Nealy wound her way through the wedding crowd to the back door leading to the kitchen. When she felt her daughter tug on her skirt she looked down and smiled. "It's a party, Emmie. For Miss Maud and Mr. Jess. They got married today. That means they love each other and are going to be happy forever after. It's so pretty here, isn't it, honey? Look out over the land at all the split-rail fencing. It just goes on for miles and miles. Kind of like forever. Everything is so spic-and-span, the grass is like the stones in Miss Maud's ring. She said it was an emerald. I hope we never have to leave here. I'm going to say a prayer every night and ask God to let us stay. I'm going to tell you a secret, Emmie. I hardly ever think about Pa or the boys. They're family, but they didn't act like a family. Someday when you're all grown-up, we'll go back to Virginia so you can see where you were born. This is home now."

The little girl laid her head on Nealy's shoulder. "I love you, Emmie," Nealy whispered in the little girl's ear. She was rewarded with a squeezing hug from the toddler. "I hope someday I can hear you say those same words to me."

I love you, Mama. Lots and lots. A whole bushel.

Nealy stared out the office window at the long row of barns directly in her line of vision. She wished there was a magical way she could get through her chores here in the office so she could go to the barn and work with the horses. While she didn't hate her duties in the office, she didn't like them much. She wanted to be with the horses, doing what she did best. She clucked her tongue as she sat back down to complete the morning's work sheets. She was able to do the payroll now, but while her bookkeeping skills had improved over the past month, they still left much to be desired. She did keep a tidy office though, according to Maud, who popped her head in from time to time to see how things were going. She sighed as she stacked a neat pile of sales slips. Deposits really. They flew out of her hand when the black dog named Molly tried to leap onto her lap. "I couldn't have asked for a better diversion, Molly," Nealy giggled. "If I could train you to pick them up and file them, we would be in business. I know, you miss Emmie. So do I. This school is good for her. She's learning sign language. I have to learn it, too. I'm afraid you're going to have to get off my lap now so I can tidy up the office, then you can escort me to the barn."

The black dog slithered to the floor and lay down, her big head resting on her paws as she waited for Nealy to gather up the sales slips. She didn't move when strange sounds erupted from the young girl's mouth, but her ears stood straight up. She did stir when she saw Nealy reach out to the chair she'd been sitting on. When her head dropped between her knees, Molly was on her feet, racing down the hall to the kitchen where Maud was sitting at the kitchen table. She barked once, tugged on Maud's skirt, and raced back to the office.

Breathless with the effort it cost her to hurry down the hall to the office, Maud took in the situation at a glance. "Nealy, honey, what's wrong?"

Nealy raised her head, her face whiter than the shirt she was wearing. "Nothing, Miss Maud. I just felt a little dizzy. I'm fine. Really, I am. I think I just need some fresh air. Would you mind if I went down to the barn? Later this afternoon I can finish up in here if that's all right with you. I was almost done anyway." She stacked the sales bills into a neat pile on the corner of her desk.

"Run along, child. Take Molly with you. It is warm in here. Jess says I keep it much too warm. I guess he's right. I like what you did with this office. It's actually pretty now, with the green plants and the hanging basket by the window. This was my father's desk. A real antique like me. The chair was his, too. It just fit his big frame. I never bothered to change things. Didn't seem right because a person dies you throw away their things. Emmie's drawings on the file cabinets add just the right touch. Go on, I'm just going to sit here a moment and think about how I used to run in here when Pa was working at his desk. Memories are a wonderful thing. Be sure to wear your jacket. It's cold outside. And button it," Maud called to Nealy's back as the girl sprinted off, Molly on her heels.

"Let's just see what we have here to cause my girl to go white-faced," Maud muttered to herself as she riffled through the sales slips. She knew what it was the moment she held it in her hands: Josh Coleman, SunStar Farms, Virginia. Nealy Cole. Nealy Coleman. The old man had two sons and a daughter. One of the meanest, orneriest men she'd ever come across. She hated doing business with him, but Jess said business was business and personalities didn't belong in business. He also said Coleman's money was as good as anyone else's. He was good to his animals, Jess said. In Jess's eyes, that said it all. Maud wondered what he would say when she told him about this little episode.

Maud leaned back in the comfortable chair and closed her eyes. "Pa, I never called on you before. I always figured if you were dead, you were dead, and as far as I know the dead don't come back. That's about as blunt as I can be. Like you, I don't hold any truck with spirits and junk like that. As I recall, Pa, you didn't even believe in angels. Jess and me . . . it's possible we just opened up a can of worms. I can't let that girl go. Or the little one either. I've been racking my brains for days now trying to figure the best way to do things. Whatever I want to do will be okay with Jess. You'd like that man, Pa. He's just like you. Guess that's why I picked him. Got myself married and even got gussied up for the occasion. When the pain gets real bad, Pa, I can't think real clear. Course I'm half-liquored up, so that explains it. I think what I'm trying to say here is I could use some help. I need to know I'm doing the right things. Another thing, Pa. When I get there, I'm going to be bringing you another Derby winner. If you're going to do something, give me a sign. Could you do it now so I can go back to the kitchen to finish my tea?"

Maud looked around. When nothing happened, she shrugged. "Figured that," she mumbled. "It's all horse pucky, that spirit stuff. There probably aren't any angels either," she continued to mutter. She heaved herself to her feet and for a few blessed moments felt no pain at all. The walk down the hall, while painful, was easier than her earlier walk to the office. She wasn't sure, but she thought she felt gentle hands ease her down onto the kitchen chair. Was this the sign she'd asked for? She sat quietly, motionless, hardly daring to breathe while she waited for the pain to take on its own life or ease up. She heaved a sigh of relief when she realized the pain was bearable, the kind aspirin worked on. Maybe today was going to be a good day after all. Later, if she felt good enough, she would make a trip down to the barns to see the October foals.

Nealy let her breath out in a loud *swoosh* the minute she entered the warm, moist barn. She inhaled almost immediately, savoring the pungent smell of hay, warmth, and manure. She loved it, felt at home.

She took everything in at a glance, much the way she'd done back home in Virginia. She knew her duties and the time allotted to each. The barns ran on schedules and she had to run on the same schedule. She ran, her jacket flapping with the breeze, to the stallion barn with its shady overhang and oversize stalls. She knew the barn held twenty-five, sometimes as many as thirty stallions a year. Unfortunately not all the stallions were Blue Diamond studs. Maud had told her earlier that Blue Diamond Farms had an excellent reputation as a breeding operation. People paid handsomely for the privilege of standing their stallions at the farm. As she walked under the overhang, she touched and caressed each stallion curious enough to see what she was about. They knew her now and always whickered softly when she stroked their beautiful heads. "On my way back, you each get an apple," she whispered.

Outside she watched the hot walkers take their horses in a counterclockwise walk around the walking ring. It took forty minutes of walking and then a pause for the horses to sip water, at which point, the overheated horses would be back to normal, resting pulse.

She headed for the paddock where Danny Clay, the stud groom, would soon lead Private Dancer to his stall. If she hurried, she could have the stall ready for the stallion by the time Danny got there. All it took was new straw, a shaking of hay, fresh water, and a measure of grain mixture that Jess had concocted for this special stallion. With little grass at this time of year for grazing, Jess had left orders for extra feed for Private Dancer. Being on active stud duty, it was her job to make sure the horse was given preferential treatment, which wasn't hard to do since she'd developed a rapport with the huge animal. She longed to mount him just to see if he'd let her on his back, but she knew she would never take the chance unless Jess or Maud said it was okay to do so.

Nealy worked in earnest, breaking into a sweat as she forked hay into the stall. She tossed her jacket over the railing and never gave it another thought. She finished just as Danny led the snorting stallion down the middle of the barn to his stall. Nealy stood quietly to the side, waiting to see if the big stallion would pay attention to her. He snorted, reared back, and came down prancing and pawing the concrete. He tossed his head to the side, jerking free of Danny's hold, trotted over to the stall, picked up Nealy's jacket, and backed up until he was abreast of her. His big head bobbed up and down, his signal that she should take the jacket. She did. She slipped it on. "You're just an old softie, Dancer," she whispered. "How'd you know it was mine, huh? Did it smell like me?" While she talked her hands were busy rubbing and stroking the big animal. "C'mon, now, show me you appreciate this. A little love and devotion go a long way. We both know that." The stallion's body quivered as he used his big head to nuzzle Nealy's neck, making her laugh in delight. "Look what I have for you!" Nealy held out an apple from her pocket. Dancer nodded before he lowered his head to take the apple from the palm of her hand.

"I don't know how you do it, Miss Nealy. That horse won't take anything from me or Wylie. The truth is, this animal hates Wylie, and Wylie is afraid of him. Maybe Dancer senses his fear. He's gentle as a lamb right now. He lets me handle him, but he won't cozy up to me the way he does you."

"I'm a girl, Danny. He knows the difference. You have to talk softly, and your hands have to be gentle. Why am I telling you this, you already know it?"

"I do, but it doesn't work for me. And Dancer is my favorite. This big guy is so highly valued as a sire he's made the leading sires list for his progeny over three hundred times. One of his foals, Lead Dance, was undefeated. His next foal goes to SunStar Farms in Virginia. I heard they're going to be paying some big dollars for the foal."

"I'd like to talk to you more, Danny, but I have other stalls to get ready," Nealy said, her body going all jittery at what the groom had just said. "You're sure about his foal going to SunStar Farms?"

"Yep."

"Do they come to pick up the foal, or does Miss Maud transport it to Virginia?"

"It's one of those either-ors if you know what I mean. SunStar does a lot of business with Miss Maud. Can't say I much care for the man, but he's good with the horses. Runs a respectable breeding farm. Has two sons if I recall rightly. Met them once or twice. The old man is the boss, those boys of his never say a word. You best get a move on, Miss Nealy. Starbright is heading this way, and right behind him is Perfect Pa."

"Yes sir, right away, Danny."

Nealy worked tirelessly until she heard the bell at the end of the barn chime the hour. Time to head up to the house to wash up and sit down for her lessons. Emmie would be home soon. She looked forward to story hour, with milk and cookies. Nealy sighed. One day the lessons would be behind her, and so would the office routine. Now that she was eighteen, she would be of

age in three years. The day she turned twenty-one, she would
no longer have to fear her father. But would she still live in fear
that Emmie's father would somehow find them and reach out
for her? As unlikely as that was, she still couldn't rid herself of
the fear. When, she wondered, would she ever feel safe?

She thought about her brothers then. What were they doing?
Did they ever think of her? Were they better off without her?
Surely they must miss her a little. Now that she was out of their
lives they would have to take up the slack and work harder and
put in longer hours. Or did they feel getting rid of her was
worth getting their reputations back? Probably so.

Nealy's shoulders slumped. *Everything happens for a reason,*
she told herself as she headed for the bathroom to wash up.

5

Nealy tiptoed down the steps, feeling her way in the early-morning darkness. In the kitchen she reached for her jacket, opened the door quietly, and slipped out. This was her favorite time of day—right before the sun rose. She wrapped her arms about her chest to ward off the November cold as she walked out to the road, the same road she'd stumbled onto one rainy day five years earlier. God had been watching over her and Emmie that day. A day she would never forget as long as she lived. She threw her arms into the air and whispered, "Thank You, thank You!"

Perched on the split-rail fence, she strained to see in the darkness. She wanted to burn it all into her memory so she would never, ever, forget it. Not that she would. All she had to do was close her eyes, and she could see everything. She knew every rock, every pebble, every blade of grass on Blue Diamond Farms. She knew each one of the eighty-seven employees by name, knew their families, knew about their secrets, their hopes, and their plans. They were her family now, a family she loved and cherished. The horses were part of her life, too. God, how she loved those magnificent creatures. She closed her eyes, trying to calculate the number of nights she'd spent in the barns, sleeping on straw and covering herself with horse blankets when there was a problem with one of the Thoroughbreds. Those were treasured times because the horses trusted her, recognized her voice and her touch.

Life was wonderful.

Years ago she'd accepted the fact that her daughter, normal in every other way, was never going to speak. What was it the specialist said? "There is no medical reason that we can find as to why your daughter doesn't speak." He'd used words like *trauma*, *fear, anxiety,* and a few others that made no sense to her at the time. Emmie was seven now, and so beautiful Nealy often felt tears burn her eyes when she looked at her. They all had learned sign language, Maud, Jess, her, and some of the workers at the barns. There were times she swore even the horses understood the little girl's flying fingers.

The moment the sun started to creep over the horizon, Nealy jumped off the fence and headed back toward the house.

Today was her birthday, a time when she always reflected on her young life. Maud and Jess would be waiting in the kitchen for her. How kind, how astute they were. If they didn't know, then they sensed she needed these early minutes to herself out by the road. They never mentioned it, never said anything other than, happy birthday, Nealy. Later on there would be a big dinner, a cake with candles, presents, and so much love and affection she would get dizzy absorbing it all. She was loved. Her daughter was loved. What more could she possibly want or wish for? Absolutely nothing, she answered herself.

From the back porch, Nealy could see the fireplace blazing. The kitchen would be warm and toasty. That had to mean Carmela the housekeeper was up and preparing breakfast. Emmie would be getting ready for the special school she attended; Maud and Jess would be sitting at the table waiting for her. Carmela would be frying bacon, brewing coffee, and stirring batter for blueberry pancakes.

Nealy opened the door to silence. She sniffed. Where was the coffee, the sizzling bacon? Where were the others? She looked down at her watch and frowned. Where was Carmela? She called her name, knocked on the housekeeper's door. When there was no response she cracked the door and called out a second time. She opened the door wider, saw the unmade bed, but there was no sign of the housekeeper. She closed the door just as she heard a car screech to a stop in the driveway alongside the back porch. She ran to the door, her heart hammering in her chest.

"Dr. Parker! What's wrong? Why are you here?"

"It's Maud, Nealy. Jess called me. Where is she?"

Speechless with fear, Nealy could only point to the second

floor. The doctor took the kitchen stairs, two at a time, Nealy galloping behind him.

Emmie ran to Nealy, her eyes full of questions. "I don't know what's wrong, honey. I was outside, and when I came in there was no one in the kitchen. Do you know where Carmela is?" Emmie pointed to Maud's room. "Listen to me, Emmie. I want you to go downstairs and make some coffee. You know how to do that. Make some toast and wait for me. I'm sure Miss Maud just has a bad cold or maybe a bad bellyache. Do what I say, and I'll be right down. It's going to be all right." She waited until Emmie was at the bottom of the stairs before she ran to Maud's room.

She saw the huge sleigh bed, the colorful quilt, and the woman lying propped up against a mound of pillows. Nealy Diamond's eyes burned at the sight of Maud. Surely this caricature of the adoptive mother she loved with all her heart wasn't Maud Diamond. Her face was pulled to the side, her right eye closed, the lid drooping way past her bottom eyelashes. The right side of her body was hiked up as though she'd tried to curl into the fetal position, the left side almost as rigid. Drool oozed from the corner of her mouth. A sob caught in Nealy's throat as she made her way to the side of the bed. The doctor gently pushed her away. She found herself standing in the doorway next to Carmela. She heard a sob, and knew it wasn't her own. Jess. She heard the word *hospital*, heard Jess's vehement negative response.

"What happened, Carmela? Is Miss Maud going to die?"

"I don't know, Nealy. Mr. Jess came and got me right after you left the kitchen. I didn't see you leave, but I heard you. I'd just built up the fire when he came rattling down the steps. It's a stroke. People live after a stroke, Nealy. Sometimes they don't, but sometimes they do."

"She can't die, Carmela. She just can't. Jess won't know what to do without her. I won't know what to do. Emmie . . . Emmie won't . . . understand. The farm, the horses, everything will fall apart without Miss Maud. She's the glue that keeps us all together. I should do something. I need to do something. Tell me what to do, Carmela."

"You keep going, Nealy. You can't fold up. Jess is going to need you, and so is Emmie. You have to be strong. You do what Maud would do. Tell me what to make for breakfast. Then you have your work, Emmie has to go to school. You need to write down what you want me to make for supper. You have to go down to the barns and tell the others. You have a lot of things you have to do."

"Those are just things. I meant I want to do something for Miss Maud." Nealy reached out and grabbed Carmela's shoulders. She stared deep into her eyes. "Tell me she isn't going to die, Carmela. Tell me. She said she won't die till she gets another Derby winner. She told me and Emmie many times she can't go to meet her pa in heaven unless she has a third Derby winner in her hand. Say it, Carmela! Damn you, say it!"

The old housekeeper straightened her apron, her usual rosy cheeks pasty white. She tried to straighten her plump body as she stared Nealy down. "I can't tell you that, Nealy. Now, tell me what to make for breakfast."

Nealy stared at the woman, who was almost as old as Maud. Her face was lined and creased the way Maud's was. She wore wire-rimmed spectacles, whereas Maud preferred to squint or use a magnifying glass, saying eyeglasses were ugly. Where Maud's hair was thinning, Carmela's was thick and curly, fashioned into a long braid that hung down her back almost to her waist. Her hands slammed down on her plump hips. "I need you to tell me what to make for breakfast, Nealy."

"Pancakes."

"Fine. I can make pancakes. How many?"

"How many? Fifty. Sixty. That's a good round number. Lots of coffee," Nealy said, rubbing her temples.

"Who's going to eat sixty pancakes?" Carmela demanded, but Nealy was already halfway up the kitchen stairs to the second floor. "The barn dogs and cats, that's who," she mumbled.

Nealy found herself standing outside Maud's room. Everything was suddenly different now. Even the sunshine was gone. An omen? She wished she knew more about death and the dying process. She wanted to cry so bad she pinched her arms to stop the tears. Jess didn't need to see her cry. She was supposed to be strong. She wondered if Maud could hear or understand whatever it was the doctor was saying to Jess. It didn't look like Maud had moved even an inch. Jess looked different, too. Right now, right this minute, he looked *old*. He also looked brittle, like he was going to crack wide open. He turned, saw her, and motioned her to enter the room.

Nealy advanced, tears rolling down her cheeks. She stepped into his arms and howled her misery. He didn't try to stop her. Instead, he stroked her hair and let his own tears roll down his weathered cheeks. "We talked about something like this maybe happening someday. Maud said she didn't want to go to a hospital. I agreed. Dr. Parker is going to send us some nurses who will take care of Maud around the clock."

"I can do that, Jess. I want to do it."

"I know you do, child; but you have Emmie, and the farm still has to run. You can't do everything. Maud wouldn't want that. She'd want you to do what you do best, work with the horses."

"How can I do that, Jess, when my heart is here with Miss Maud? Tell me how."

"I can't tell you how, child. You have to find your way yourself. I'm going to have to make some decisions, too. We'll talk later. For now I'm going to stay here with Maud until the nurse gets here. Dr. Parker says she isn't in any pain. I'm going to hold on to that. See Emmie to the school bus and get on with your chores."

"But . . ."

"There are no buts, Nealy. This is the way it has to be. Get on the loudspeaker in the barn and tell everyone Maud has had a stroke. Tell them . . . tell them I'll let them know when she can have visitors. Now, git to it, girl." He hugged her tight to take the sting out of his words.

It was nine o'clock before Nealy tucked a tearful Emmie into bed. Exhausted with all the crying she'd done, Emmie slipped into sleep almost immediately but not before she tucked her velvet bag under the pillow.

Nealy sat on the edge of the bed for a long time, trying not to cry. Everyone was acting as if Maud was dead, while in fact she was alive and breathing. She couldn't die. She just couldn't.

Nealy offered up a prayer, kissed her daughter good night, and walked down the hall to Maud's room. She could see into the dimly lit room, where the nurse, in her starched, white uniform, sat reading. She'd always thought of Maud's room as a pretty room, with the overlarge sleigh bed that had once been her father's. Crisp organdy curtains hung from the diamond-shaped windows. There were no blinds or shades on any of the windows at Blue Diamond Farms. Maud wanted it that way. She said she liked light, not half-light. Privacy was something she never thought of. Besides, she'd said, who can see way up here to the second floor? Two wing chairs stood against the far wall. The blue one was for Jess and the burgundy one was Maud's. Both had matching footstools, and both were situated so Maud and Jess could watch television late at night if they wanted. A few lush green plants stood in the corners, just to fill up the space, Maud said. Other than a dresser that was almost bare and two night tables, there was nothing else in the room.

When Nealy had first arrived, there were no pictures on Maud's bedroom walls, but there were pictures now. One of her wedding to Jess, the rest of Emmie at different stages. Emmie sitting in her pony cart, Emmie at the wedding, Emmie with her first short haircut, Emmie and Molly, Emmie in a bathing suit running under the sprinkler and, the best of all, Emmie riding Wind Dancer, her very own pony. There was one picture that Maud said she treasured above all else, a picture of her with Emmie in her arms, sleeping together in the wicker rocker on the front porch. *It was a nice picture*, Nealy thought. *Probably because we all felt safe and peaceful.* Maud had always understood that.

"How . . . how is she?" Nealy whispered to the nurse.

"The same. She's sleeping. You look very tired, honey. Why don't you turn in? If there's any change at all, I'll call you."

"Can I kiss her good night?"

"I don't see why not."

Nealy walked hesitantly over to the bed. There were so many things she wanted to say, but her tongue felt thick in her mouth, and the words wouldn't come. She tried not to cry, but tears pooled in her eyes and rolled down her cheeks. She reached for Maud's hand and covered it with both of hers. She was stunned at how cold it felt. She wanted to crawl into the big bed the way she did with Emmie and hold her close to warm her clear through. She leaned over and kissed the old lady's dry cheek. She looked up when she felt Maud's eyelashes touch her cheek. "You're awake! I came in to say good night. I don't know if you can hear me. Can you, Miss Maud?"

When there was no response, Nealy moved to the foot of the bed where Maud could see her better. Her hands and fingers moved furiously. *Blink if you can understand what I just said, Miss Maud.* A smile ripped across Nealy's face when the old lady blinked. Nealy's fingers spoke a second time. *Do you want to see Jess?* Blink. *I'll fetch him.*

Nealy raced down the steps and into the living room, where Jess sat staring at the fire. "Come quick, Jess. Miss Maud wants to see you. I signed for her and told her to blink if she understood. She did. I asked her if she wanted to see you. She blinked. Hurry, Jess, before she falls asleep again."

Nealy's heart sang with joy when the old man lumbered across the room and up the kitchen stairway.

"You have to stand at the bottom of the bed so she can see you clearly, Jess," Nealy said, stepping aside for Jess to take her place.

Twenty minutes later, the nurse urged them to leave. "She needs to rest. The shot I gave her is starting to work, but she won't relax until you leave. I'll call you if she wakes."

Nealy had to drag Jess out to the hall and back down the steps. "It's wonderful, isn't it, Jess? We can communicate with her now. Emmie is going to be so happy. Maybe tomorrow will be better. You didn't eat any dinner, Jess. Let me fix you a sandwich. I'll sit with you in the parlor. Carmela made a chocolate cake. I'll cut you a slice, and coffee would go real good now, wouldn't it?"

"I'm not hungry, but go ahead and fix me something if it will make you feel better. We need to talk, Nealy. Serious talk."

"Are you going to ask . . . are you going to ask us to leave, Jess?" Nealy asked, fear written all over her face. She started to shake while she waited for the old man's response.

"Good God Almighty, girl, where did you get an idea like that? We adopted you, girl. You belong to us, to Maud and me.

You belong here. The only way you and Emmie can leave here is if you want to leave. You're the child and Emmie the grandchild Maud and I never had. Now go fix me that sandwich while I build up the fire. We'll be nice and cozy. Don't bring me any coffee, though. Bring me Maud's bottle."

Nealy returned to the parlor with a thick ham sandwich on fresh homemade bread, a dish of pickles, and a slice of dark chocolate cake. The bottle of bourbon was half-full. She placed it on the end table along with a glass. While Jess ate, she poked at the fire, her thoughts whirling inside her head. What did Jess want to talk to her about? Did it have something to do with Emmie or with Maud? She wished he'd gobble his food so she could relax. She turned around, sat down on the hearth, and hugged her knees. When he finished the cake, Nealy sighed with relief.

With her gaze fixed on the man across from her, she blurted, "What did you want to talk to me about, Jess?" She sucked in her breath as she waited for whatever he was going to say.

"A lot of things. Some of them important and some not so important. Maud and I were talking just the other day about sitting down with you and explaining things. This isn't the best time in the world, but things happen. Sometimes so swiftly, there's no time to prepare for the right time. Maud wanted to do the talking, the explaining, but now it looks like it's me who is going to be doing it. I told her that upstairs. She . . . she seemed to relax a bit once I did that.

"First things first. What do you think about me turning things over to Jack Carney? He's a good man. Not my favorite person in the world, but he's been with us just about all his working life. His home is here. Maud led him to believe he would be taking over at some point. He's well paid, as you know. I know you don't much care for him or his son. What I'm asking is, can you work with him knowing he's in authority?"

"No!" The single word shot from her mouth like a lone bullet.

"Could you work with him if he answered to you and only you? That means you'll be stepping into Maud's shoes. What I mean, Nealy, is, Maud and I decided that you will inherit Blue Diamond Farms. You and Emmie. Everything we have between us will go to you and your daughter with the exception of some special bequests and gifts to a few charities. You will be a very wealthy woman one day."

"Oh, no, Jess, I can't accept that. You must have kin somewhere. All I want is to be allowed to stay here and work. I never thought . . . never dreamed. No. It's not right. I can't accept such generosity."

"It's not up to you. Everything is all set up. Maud wanted it done years ago, right after you got here. She said you were the one who would carry on Blue Diamond Farms. Said you were the one who would give her another Derby winner. I agreed. It's done, girl. It's not a yes or a no. All our people, the workers, the families, yes, they love it here, but it's a job to them. They do a day's work and get a day's pay. Yes, they're loyal, and for that we're grateful. But there isn't one who loves this place or understands it like you do. I've seen you look at the land, at the fencing, at the animals with the same kind of love in your eyes as when you look at your daughter. Maud saw that. We're comfortable with our decisions. I know it's going to take some getting used to. Money is a powerful thing, Nealy. That's one of the reasons why Maud made you learn the business end of things.

"When Emmie comes of age, she'll take her place right alongside you. Won't matter one whit if she can talk or not. She has the touch like you do. We can't let that slip away. And before you can give me an argument, Maud and I know who you are and where you came from. That's why we waited until you were twenty-one to adopt you. We had the best lawyers we could find to make all this legal. One of these days, the girl's pa might rear up and try to make some claims. Won't work," Jess said emphatically. "Got it sewed up tight as a drum. Are you absorbing all this, Nealy?"

"Yes, I think so. I guess I'm overwhelmed that you would think so much of me and Emmie."

"We love you, that's the difference. I've never seen Maud so happy. The day you got here was the day she came alive, even with all the pain she was feeling. Maud is going to die, Nealy. I don't know when, but it will happen. I won't be long for this world once that happens. Don't go bawling on me now. I'm telling you facts so you can be prepared. When I draw my last breath, I want to know I left things in good hands. Say something, girl."

"I love you, Jess Wooley. I'll do my best to measure up. Emmie will, too. What happens if . . . if . . . Miss Maud . . . dies before I can bring in another Derby winner?"

"Nothing will happen. She'll know. Maud knows you won't let her down. Now, let's get back to Jack Carney. He's not going to like taking orders from you. Put him in his place early on. If he gets out of hand, boot his ass out of here. That goes for Wylie, too. Never could cotton to that kid. He's a sly little weasel. Keep him on the straight and narrow, and if he gives you even an ounce of trouble, get rid of him. Can you do that?"

"Yes, sir, I can."

"Good. There's more on the financial end we need to talk about. We set up trusts for you and Emmie. No one can ever get their hands on the money. There's a handsome brokerage account. You could live in luxury until your dying day and never touch the principal. These things have nothing to do with the business accounts. It will be damn near impossible for you to run this farm into the ground. Everything's been taken care of. There's a fund for wages for the next five years, funds for everything under the sun. We need to set up a meeting with the broker, who is going to educate you on the different holdings. Maud was . . . is insistent on that. You ask all the questions you want until you understand everything. Now, is it okay if I drink from this bottle?"

"Only if you let me have the first drink," Nealy shot back.

"Done!" Jess said as he handed over the bottle.

6

Nealy watched with tears in her eyes as the ambulance attendants wheeled Maud into the house and then into Carmela's small apartment off the kitchen on the first floor. The housekeeper had moved to the second floor a week after Maud's stroke. It had been Jess's idea to switch the rooms, saying it would make it easier on everyone. Nealy had done her best to take away the hospital atmosphere of the room with the hospital bed, medication bottles, charts, and the nurse herself by bringing down the pictures from Maud's room and rehanging them. She'd gone to the florist in town and had brought back some green plants the doctor frowned on, along with some knick-knacks the nurse said she wasn't dusting. Emmie watered the plants and dusted every other day. The florist delivered fresh flowers daily. There was nothing she could do about the sick smell to the room except open the windows from the top for a little fresh air.

Today was, according to Jess, the last time he was subjecting Maud to the ambulance trips to the local hospital for weekly testing, citing Maud's fear of hospitals. "What will be will be." Maud had blinked her acceptance of his decision early on, he'd said. The consensus now was that everything that could be done had been done, and the only thing left to do was to see to Maud's comfort.

Three long, agonizing weeks had passed since Maud's stroke. While her condition hadn't worsened, it hadn't improved either. The doctor stopped by daily. Jess said he didn't know why, since he didn't do a thing except take Maud's blood pressure. "He's doing it for the money," Jess had said sourly. Nealy decided he was probably right.

Nealy's gaze sought out Jess, who was hovering near the hospital bed. To her untrained eye, he had gone downhill steadily since Maud's stroke. His once-robust frame seemed shrunken now, his steps slower, his face almost as gaunt and haggard as Maud's. Nealy knew he wasn't sleeping, and he barely ate enough to keep him alive. On more than one occasion she'd woken and tiptoed into Maud's room in the middle of the night to see him sitting by the side of the bed, whispering or talking to his wife with his fingers.

Satisfied that Maud was settled and comfortable, the nurse in attendance, Nealy reached out to Jess, and whispered, "Let's go for a walk, Jess. Just once around the house. You need some fresh air, and it's snowing out. You know how you love snow. Emmie's down at the barn, and this is our quiet time. Maud is sleeping. I don't think she would want you to be giving up, and you are giving up, Jess. Please don't let Maud see that."

"She's not going to get any better," Jess said as he slipped into his denim jacket. "I always thought I'd be the first to go since I'm older. I'm having a hard time with this. Nothing seems to matter anymore. Why is that? The farm should count, the horses should count, but they don't. I don't give a good rat's ass about another Derby winner. Maud doesn't care anymore either. I know she doesn't. She wants to die. I see it in her eyes. What in the damn hell kind of life is blinking to communicate? She can't hear, she can only see out of one eye, and she can't talk or eat and is fed through her veins. Why doesn't God take her?"

Nealy shivered. "I don't know the answer, Jess. I guess He wants us to keep her a while longer. You aren't thinking what I think you're thinking, are you?" Nealy demanded as she grabbed the old man's arm and swung him around to face her. He slipped in the wet snow, but her young arms held him steady until he was upright.

"It's what Maud wants, Nealy." His voice was so flat, so dead-sounding, Nealy grew light-headed.

"No!" The single exclamation exploded into the frosty air. "Don't even think about that, Jess. They'll lock you up. You can't ... Damn it, no! Oh God, you aren't ... you weren't ... Jess, no!" Nealy cried. "I can't do this alone. I need you. Emmie needs you. Please. Don't ... Maud isn't of sound mind right now. You aren't either. I'll tell. I swear to God I'll tell."

"It's what Maud wants. I always do what she wants. I can't stand seeing her like she is. She isn't my Maud anymore. She doesn't even look like herself."

"If . . . if . . . you do . . . anything, I swear to God, I'll take Emmie and leave. I will, Jess. I've never been alone before. I need you. Emmie needs you. I think Maud looks forward to Emmie's visits to her room. Promise me."

"Can't do that. Don't you be badgering me now. Shouldn't you be fetching Emmie from the barns?"

"Emmie knows the way to the house. She's been coming and going for years, and you know it. If you want to be alone, just say you want to be alone, I'll go back to the house. The snow is pretty, isn't it?"

"Maud always loved the first snowfall of the year. Snow don't make me no never mind. I like warm weather." He reached out to shake the snow from a yew branch as much as to say, see, I told you I don't like this white stuff.

"Maybe I'll make Maud a snowball and take it up on a plate for her to see it. I can ask the nurse to wheel her bed over to the window so she can see the snow falling. What do you think, Jess?" Nealy asked.

"Don't bother. Here comes Emmie. Take her up to the house. I'm going down to the barns. How's the filly doing?"

"She's doing just fine. She isn't the one, Jess. I'd know if she was. I thought you didn't care."

"Don't." He returned Emmie's exuberant hug before he walked down to the barn. Nealy felt her heart thump in her chest at the way he shuffled and his shoulders slumped. She had to shift into neutral now and take care of her daughter.

Nealy looked at herself in the mirror. She couldn't ever remember looking this bad before. The dark circles under her eyes were almost as dark as her eyes themselves. There were hollows in her cheeks that hadn't been there prior to Maud's stroke. Pulling her dark curly hair back into a ponytail seemed to accentuate the hollows. Maybe she should let her hair down, but if she did that, it got in her way. She was more tired than she'd ever been in her life, even when her pa had worked her eighteen hours a day. It was the lack of sleep and eating on the run that was making her look like a ghost of herself, according to Carmela, who clucked her tongue and chased after her with plates of food she only picked at. She simply wasn't hungry. Sleeping was something she used to do but not now. She spent half the night in Maud's room watching Jess while the nurse dozed in her chair.

She walked up behind Jess's chair and placed her hands on his shoulders. She sniffed. He was wearing the same clothes four days in a row. Carmela had told her all he'd eaten in the past days was half an apple and some saltine crackers. It was alarming how much weight he'd dropped. His shoulders felt bony to her touch.

"Go to bed, Nealy. You look worse than I feel."

"In a little while, Jess. I'll just keep you company. Do you want to play checkers? I know how you and Maud loved a good game after supper."

"No. Don't like those things they have on her. Know she doesn't like it either. They're scratchy. Maud always liked . . . Maud likes fine things. She had this special nightgown she loved more than anything. She'd wash it out by hand and hang it on the line. It had little rosebuds that were silky-feeling around the neck and arms. She'd always iron it after she took it off the line. It was thin and fine and you could . . . you could see through it. Now they have *diapers* on her."

Nealy didn't know what to say, so she said nothing. She continued to massage Jess's shoulders.

"Maud used to like to paint her toenails. She had this varnish she said was called Strawberry Whip, and by dang it did look like the color of strawberries. She couldn't do that anymore after the accident. Oh, she could have gone to the beauty salon and they would have done it for her, but she just didn't like people doing things for her. She was . . . is a stubborn woman."

"You're stubborn, too, Jess," Nealy said, wondering where this conversation was going.

"True. We got along. Her breathing is different today. Did you notice that, Nealy?"

"Yes, I noticed."

"Means her lungs are filling up with fluid. Seen it happen too many times not to recognize the sound. Not a good thing."

"Let's go downstairs and get some tea, Jess. We could go outside for a breath of fresh air. It's so hot in this room you can't breathe."

"Maud likes it warm. You go ahead. I'll stay here."

"In that case, I'll stay, too."

"You should fix yourself a mint julep. Kentucky is known for their mint juleps. You're old enough to drink now."

Nealy forced a smile to her lips. "No thanks."

"What will you do when we're gone, Nealy?"

"I don't know, Jess. I've been thinking about that. The best answer I can give you is I will do my best to run this place the way you and Maud did."

"You won't be going home then?"

Nealy fixed her gaze on the opposite wall, where a picture of Maud, Jess, Emmie, and herself hung. One of the workers had taken it the day Emmie went off to first grade. They were all waving, smiling, and saying "cheese" for the benefit of the camera. So long ago. "No, I won't be going back." She refused to use the word home in reference to where she'd once lived. "This is home for me and Emmie, Jess. That other place, that was just a house. There was no love there."

"We never talk about that, Nealy. Do you want to?"

"Only if you feel a need for me to talk about it. I sent back all the money my brother loaned me and I called like I said I would. I know you know who my pa is. How did you find out? Didn't we talk about this that first day when Maud had her stroke?"

"Guess we did. My memory ain't what it used to be. Looked at the registration in that truck you drove here. It was all there. No need to talk about it. Maud said if you lit out, then you had a good reason. We heard you talking to Emmie one night, and you said your pa was going to send her to an orphanage. That made Maud's mind up right there on the spot. Mine, too. I think Maud loved you and that child as much as she loved me. Do you see how I'm talking in the past tense?"

"It doesn't matter, Jess. I know what you mean. Carmela made vegetable soup today and fresh bread. I'm going to fetch you some."

Jess shook his head. "If I eat it, it will just come back up. Nothing will stay down these days."

Nealy rubbed her eyes. She could feel Maud and Jess slipping away from her. Her stomach started to churn, and her eyes burned unbearably. She knew he was deliberately starving himself to death, and there was nothing she could do about it.

"I'm going upstairs to check on Emmie. Then I think I'll get a breath of fresh air. I won't be long."

"I'll be here. Take your time. Won't do anything, so stop worrying. Don't think I don't know how you've been watching me like some evil-eyed hawk."

"Was I that transparent, Jess?"

"Yep."

Nealy nodded as she backed out of the room. Outside in the frosty air, she sucked in a lungful, held it, then expelled it in a loud *swoosh.* When she felt her body cool down she sat on the steps and stared into the star-filled night. She knew in her heart that Maud's days were numbered. On the other hand maybe there wouldn't be days, just hours. Was there a way to prepare for death? If there was, she didn't know how to go about it. Obviously Jess knew, and that's why he hadn't budged from Maud's room. Wearing the same clothes for four days in a row had to mean something.

When the cold, nippy air made her shiver, she got up and headed for the second floor, where she stopped at Emmie's room to look in on her. She smiled. She always smiled when she looked at her daughter. How happy she was these days. How contented. How would the child handle Maud's and Jess's deaths? She had to admit she didn't know. She bent over, smoothed back the springy, blonde curls before she kissed her gently on the cheek. She closed the door softly behind her and headed to Maud's room.

She felt like a Peeping Tom, a thief, as she went through Maud's dresser drawers and closet. Where was the nightgown with the rosebuds Jess had described? If it was a special nightgown, Maud would have saved it even if it was worn-out. She finally found it at the bottom of the cedar chest that stood at the foot of the huge sleigh bed. She felt awkward and guilty going through Maud's things. The chest held mostly mementoes of her father and a few faded photographs of Jess. The nightgown was on the very bottom of the chest, wrapped in three layers of tissue paper and tied with a pink-satin ribbon. Jess was right, it was beautiful, gossamer thin, the rosebuds perfect little swirls of pink satin. Did Maud wear this the first night she spent with Jess? She held it to her cheek. It smelled musty, with a hint of jasmine, Maud's favorite scent. She folded the gown and wrapped it back up before she replaced everything else in the chest. Her heart heavy, she walked into the bathroom, where she opened the linen closet. Where would Maud keep nail polish and polish remover? She moved towels and linens, soap, tissues, and finally saw a box covered in gold leaf on the top shelf. There it was, Strawberry Whip nail polish. Four bottles that had never been opened. That meant it wouldn't be stringy and gooey. She stuck one of the bottles in her jeans pocket. She dropped to the floor and started to cry then, hard sobs racking her body, her fists pummeling the floor until she was exhausted. It was all she could do to get to her feet and stagger downstairs.

The kitchen clock read 3:10 when she put coffee on to brew and filled the sink with warm soapy water. Her touch was reverent when she placed the gossamer gown in the soapy water. While the gown soaked to get rid of the musty smell, she drank two cups of coffee.

An hour later she rinsed the gown, rolled it in a towel to get most of the water out of it, and set up the ironing board. With the tip of the iron she ironed each tiny rosebud, then the gossamer material. When she was finished, she bent over to sniff the garment. The musty smell was gone, but the faint scent of jasmine still lingered. From the pantry's middle shelf she plucked a wad of pale pink tissue paper to wrap up the gown. It would be ready when it was needed. The clock read 5:20.

Nealy walked on weary legs back to the second floor, where she showered and dressed. Would she be able to make it through the day? She prayed that she would.

It was four o'clock when Danny Clay, the stud groom, happened to look into the stall of Stardancer, the stallion that had thrown Maud years ago. His eyes almost popping from his head, he called out to the other grooms in the barn, who came on the run. They gaped, too, at the sight of Nealy sleeping in the straw under the big stallion's belly. "Someone needs to go up to the main house and fetch Jess. There's no way we can get her out of there. How in the hell did she get in there in the first place? And why would she go in there at all? That horse is not one to mess around with. Her head's right behind his front hooves. One move and she's a goner. We need to get her out of there, and we need to do it *now*."

Stardancer whickered and stepped daintily forward. He lowered his massive head and snorted. Satisfied that the sleeping girl was all right, he moved another step forward. Clay and the others watched, fascinated, as the stallion moved sideways and then forward again until he was clear of the girl entirely. He lowered his head again and nudged her shoulder. When she didn't move, he nudged her again, harder this time, so she would roll over. She woke as the prickly straw tickled her face. A moment later she was on her hands and knees, struggling to get up. When she fell back down, the stallion used his head again to boost her upright. She clung to his neck until she was on her feet. A sea of faces stared at her. She stared back. "Don't you have work to do? Why are you all standing here staring at me?"

Danny Clay's voice verged on hysteria. "Of all the damn horses on this farm to go to sleep with, you pick the one who would just as soon stomp you to death as look at you. How do you think I could explain that to Jess or Miss Maud?"

"I know all about this horse. Watch this," Nealy said as she swung herself onto the stallion's back. "See! This animal would no more stomp me to death than any other one. It was your mistake to ignore him all these years after Miss Maud's fall. He's your prize stallion, and you're all too damn dumb to know it. Now get back to work, this isn't a holiday! Another thing, I wasn't sleeping. I was resting my eyes."

She could hear them muttering as they went back to what they'd been doing earlier. She slid off the stallion's back and proceeded to stroke his head. "You're the one, Stardancer," she whispered. "I know it. I feel it. You are going to make it happen for Miss Maud. Your next foal is going to be my Derby winner. I'm going to breed you with Little Lady. I'm going to train the foal myself. With your help of course. You know what I'm saying. I know you understand. Show me. Show me you understand." She giggled and laughed outright when the stallion nudged her until she was in the corner. She stood on her toes and hugged him. "We'll do it, too. That's a promise."

"What in the hell is going on here?" Jess roared. "What are you doing in there, Nealy? I told you to stay away from that stallion. He's the one . . ."

"I know, Jess. I also know he's *the* one! He is, Jess. I can feel it. I can feel it in him, too. He knows. He's just waiting."

"No. Not this one. Never this one. Do you hear me? Not this one!"

"Yes, this one. Even Emmie knows he's the one. You have to accept it."

"Never! I'll have him shot dead."

"No you won't. You could no more harm an animal than I could. He's not the reason Maud is dying. Are you going to help me, or are you going to fight me on this?"

Jess turned to leave the barn. "Do what you want. I don't care."

"Maud knows! I told her a week ago. She said it was okay. I saw a spark, Jess, when I told her."

"I'll never believe that. Maud would never give her blessing to this horse. Never in a million years."

"She did, Jess. Emmie was with me when I asked her. She saw Maud's response. Ask her when she gets off the school bus. Better yet, go up to the house and ask Maud yourself. I think you know I would never lie to you. While you're up there, how about taking a shower. You smell worse than these horses."

"Smart-ass girl!" Jess said as he stomped his way from the barn.

"Takes one to know one," Nealy shouted. Stardancer pawed the ground. "He's just talking to hear himself. We'll make it happen. Just you, me, and Emmie. You wait and see. You are going to be the proud papa of a Derby winner, Stardancer!"

7

From her position on the back porch, Nealy watched Jess leading a bay colt to the yearling barns. She smiled. The colt was the picture of pure excitement. His eyes were wide and his sinews prominent from his recent exertion. Nealy guessed Jess was bringing him in from one of the pastures before going upstairs to see Maud.

What would Stardancer and Little Lady's colt be like? Was there really any doubt? He would be a champion, of course, with speed, courage, and heart. Lots of heart. She refused to entertain the idea that Little Lady might deliver a filly. It amazed her that she'd lived and worked around Stardancer for five years and hadn't realized his potential until a few months ago. How could she have been so blind? She was almost certain it was Jess's dislike of the horse that caused her to ignore him. If one of the grooms hadn't mistakenly put Stardancer in the wrong stall, she might never have gotten to know him.

She wished she didn't have to wait so long to breed him. March seemed a long time away, but if she wanted the foal to be born in January or February, she would have to be patient. From here on out, she promised herself, she would personally keep a record of Little Lady's estrous cycle and make it a point to exercise Stardancer herself at least once a week. Now, though, it was time to start thinking of other things and to go indoors.

The kitchen was fragrant with the smell of spices and cooking. Despite her lack of an appetite, Nealy's mouth began to water. "Why are you doing all this, Carmela? Who's going to eat that twenty-five-pound turkey and all those pies?" She eyed the long counter, with its pared vegetables and scrubbed sweet potatoes. She noticed Maud's fine china and silverware sitting on the opposite counter. Everything had been washed and polished. She'd noticed a huge bowl of fresh flowers in the dining room earlier. The linen tablecloth with twenty-four matching napkins that had been Maud's grandmother's rested on the sideboard. "Are we having company I don't know about?"

"Now, Miss Nealy, you know we do this every year. It's a tradition. No, we're not having company, but the employees asked if they could come by to see Miss Maud. We have to have something to offer them. If they eat it, fine; if they don't, that's fine, too. It's the way it is," she said curtly. "I thought I would bring trays to Miss Maud's room for all of you. The nurse has to eat, too, you know. It is Thanksgiving, Miss Nealy."

"I know, Carmela. It's just that there doesn't seem to be a whole lot to be thankful for this year. I didn't mean that the way it sounded. Of course there is. It's just that . . ."

"She's still here! That means business as usual. This is the way we do things. You know how particular Miss Maud was when it came to the holidays. She was always partial to Thanksgiving and Christmas. After you and Emmie got here, she was downright prickly when it came to using the good stuff and fancy cooking. Like I said, it's a Blue Diamond Farms tradition. Now, are you just going to stand there, or are you going to help me? I really don't need any help, so the decision is yours."

"I guess I'll just take my feet and go upstairs if it's all the same to you. You washed the curtains! Everything is so clean and shiny. I'll tell Maud."

Carmela made shooing motions with her hands to indicate Nealy should leave the kitchen. Nealy obliged. In the dining room she sat down on one of the twelve chairs surrounding the table and stared at the flowers. Yellow roses with gobs of baby's breath and delicate, green fern, Maud's favorite flowers. She herself was partial to tulips.

Nealy reached into her shirt pocket for a cigarette, a disgusting habit she'd picked up several years ago. She didn't smoke much, only when she was under pressure, like today. She'd spent the entire morning in Maud's room, listening to her ragged breathing. She knuckled her eyes to ward off the tears that were threatening to overflow. Surely God wouldn't call her today, Thanksgiving, of all days. She puffed furiously, the left hand holding the heavy coffee mug shaking uncontrollably. She set it down carefully, then crushed out her cigarette in a crystal dish on the sideboard. Her hands were still shaking. She sat on her hands the way Emmie did sometimes when she was being reprimanded. *Shift mental gears, Nealy,* she told herself. *Think about something else. Since today is Thanksgiving, think about changing into something other than Levi's and boots. Emmie, too. Maybe some makeup. A little perfume. Think about dressing up like a girl for a change.*

Maud and Jess had been so happy. And now this. It wasn't fair. Good people like Maud and Jess should live forever.

Maybe she should think about her burgeoning bank account. Maybe she should think about how well Emmie was doing in the special school. Or maybe she should think about her brothers and her father. In that order, her account at First Nation Bank was robust, and so was Emmie's account. She'd literally saved all her money from the day she arrived at Blue Diamond Farms and was put on the payroll. She had $64,833 dollars in her account while Emmie had $9,011. Maud had been overly generous with the salary she'd paid her and the bonuses at Christmas. Emmie's was mostly gift monies and her allowance, plus the bonuses Maud insisted she get at Christmas, too. She could buy herself a car or truck if she wanted. She could take Emmie on vacation someplace, maybe Hawaii. She knew she wouldn't do any of those things simply because there was no need to do them. Emmie would absolutely wilt if she wasn't around the farm and the horses. She was a straight A student. Her penmanship was exquisite. Her thirst for learning was unequaled. She whizzed through her homework and never asked for help. She had one friend, a young boy who could speak but couldn't hear. Emmie doted on Buddy. They wrote notes to one another and played together on alternating weekends. Jess approved of Buddy and his family. And, like Emmie, he lived to be around horses and the barns. If Emmie ever thought about her grandfather or her uncles, she never mentioned them. That was another life. It was probably better this way, Nealy realized.

She didn't want to think about her father or her brothers, though she did wonder from time to time if either Pyne or Rhy had married.

Nealy focused on the dining room she was sitting in. Maybe

it was time to change the wallpaper and do a little painting. Just to lighten things up a bit. The wallpaper was cracking in the corners and peeling away at the baseboards. Maybe something bright and lively, with some fresh green plants. New curtains instead of the heavy maroon draperies that matched the cushions on the twelve chairs. Maybe, if Jess gave the okay, she could take up the forest green carpeting and have the floors sanded and varnished. Then again, they rarely used the dining room. Maud always liked to eat in the kitchen, where it was warm and cozy, saying the dining room was for company or special occasions. On the other hand, maybe she should leave it alone and wait till the wallpaper fell off.

Nealy stood and turned on the lights. She did love the crystal chandelier over the table. It sparkled now; Carmela must have cleaned it recently. The pudgy housekeeper was a whirling dervish when it came to cleaning for the holidays. The house was always in an uproar, with buckets, rags, and the smell of furniture polish everywhere. Maud hated it. She preferred the smell of cinnamon, coffee beans, and orange peels that Carmela kept in the warming oven.

Nealy sighed. She would get dressed up. For Maud. She'd wear the lavender-wool dress Maud had helped her pick out last year for Christmas. She'd wear the pearls Jess gave her the year before. After all, it was Thanksgiving.

She heard the commotion the minute she stepped off the top step onto the second-floor hallway. She knew the doctor was being summoned, knew by the look on Emmie's face. Jess was nowhere to be seen. "What?" she screamed. Emmie just stared at her, tears streaming down her cheeks.

It was Maud's time.

"Quick, Emmie, you have to help me. Listen to me, honey. There's something we have to do for Miss Maud. Quick now."

Nealy raced into her room for the tissue-wrapped nightgown and the Strawberry Whip nail polish. She shoved the nurse out of the way and struggled, with Emmie's help, to get the scratchy hospital gown away from Maud's withered body. It seemed to Nealy that Maud was easier to handle as she slipped the nightgown over her head and smoothed it down over her wasted body. When Maud's head rolled to the side, Nealy gasped. She bent over and placed her ear against her chest. Satisfied that she was still breathing, she spoke quietly, gently as she pushed the covers to the foot of the bed before she twisted off the cap of the nail polish. She dipped and swirled the tiny brush as the nurse clucked her disapproval. "Did anyone call the minister?" Nealy demanded.

"Mr. Wooley said he was going to do that. This is highly irregular. The woman is dying. Why are you painting her toenails?" Her voice was so cold, so emotionless, Nealy fought the urge to slap her.

"Does it matter?" Nealy said quietly as she gathered her daughter close. She looked down at Emmie, and whispered, "I want to do something. I don't know what to do. I was going to get dressed up but . . . I thought . . ."

Jess rushed into the room, the minister behind him. The doctor was third in line as he lumbered into the room. He took his position on one side of the bed, the minister on the other. Jess pushed his way to the bed and reached for Maud's hand. Nealy heard the strangled sound, certain it came from Maud, but in reality it came from Jess as he looked down at the bright shiny penny in his wife's hand.

"Oh, Emmie, you gave Maud your penny! Oh God!" Nealy said. Her hands flew to her face as she tried to comprehend her daughter's generosity, then wondered if she should mention that the original penny was locked up in Maud's bedroom safe. She decided it really didn't matter.

Emmie's fingers worked furiously. *To help her feel better when she gets to that strange, new place. Like when Uncle Pyne gave it to me when we came here.*

Emmie's fingers continued to move. *Look, Mama, Miss Maud made a fist. That means she knows she has the penny. She's holding it tight in her hand.*

Nealy was sure it was a spasm. Through her tears, she thought she saw Maud smile. Another spasm? A grimace? And then she was still. Nealy bit down on her lip.

Emmie tugged at her mother's shirtsleeve. Her fingers moved quickly. *Aren't they pretty, Mama?*

"What's pretty, honey?"

Emmie worked her fingers again. *The angels. They're carrying*

Miss Maud. They're all smiling. They look like pictures on the Christmas cards.

Jess gasped at Emmie, his eyes wide, his mouth hanging open. "What did she say?" he asked, his voice gruff with unshed tears.

Emmie walked over to the old man and reached for his hand. She pulled him outside into the hallway. Nealy watched as her daughter slowly and carefully worked her fingers for Jess's benefit. *The three angels took Miss Maud. They all smiled, even Miss Maud. They were all gold and white. Miss Maud wiggled her toes. I could see the polish on her toes. The angels smiled when she did that. Miss Maud could move her arms and legs. She waved good-bye. Did you wave good-bye, Mr. Jess?*

"Yes," Jess croaked.

She took my penny with her. She opened her hand, and I saw it. She wanted me to see it.

Nealy felt a chill wash through her body as she watched Jess walk back into the room and over to the bed. He reached for Maud's hand and pried it open. Nealy gaped, her jaw dropping. The penny was gone.

"I need to be alone with Maud for a bit, Nealy. Take Emmie into the kitchen. See the doctor, the minister, and the nurse to the door. I'll take care of things here."

"Jess . . ."

"Shhh. It's all right. Everything is all right now."

There was little Nealy could do but obey Jess's instructions.

The minute the door closed behind the threesome, Nealy herded her daughter into the kitchen. Carmela was sitting at the table crying. Emmie dropped to her knees and laid her head in the housekeeper's lap. Nealy put her arms around her and sobbed.

It was four o'clock when they watched the hearse carrying Maud's body drive away.

The employees came then, one by one, never more than two together because Maud's first rule had always been, never leave the horses alone. They picked at the lavish Thanksgiving spread, drank the mulled cider, then left silently.

At nine o'clock, the dining room had been cleared, the leftover food put away, the dishes washed and dried. Carmela poured fresh coffee into thick mugs. They sat quietly staring off into space.

Maud was gone.

It was a beautiful dream, one she didn't want to end. He smelled sweet as fresh hay and was frisky and playful as she led him out to the paddock. She cupped his head in her hands and gently blew into his nostrils. "Now you will always have my scent," Nealy said quietly. "Come along, we're going for a walk. Oh oh, here comes big daddy. He wants to make sure I take good care of you. I think he's just being nosy. It's not time for you to run yet. I know you want to, but you can't, and this certainly isn't the place to do it. No, no, he can't run. Stop that! Don't let him run, Stardancer. He's not ready. No!" It was an iron command that was ignored. "Damn!"

She couldn't do a thing but watch as the stallion raced across the fields, the colt a furlong ahead of him. She screamed for them to come back as she fought to control her anger.

She jerked to wakefulness instantly, aware that she'd just had a horrible nightmare. She rolled over in the darkness only to find herself pulled upright at the same moment the lamp on her nightstand came to life. "Emmie, what's wrong? Are you sick? What?"

The angels are here again. They're going to take Mr. Jess. They said Maud needs him.

"Emmie, you just had a bad dream. Come on, I'll take you back to bed. I'll stay with you till you fall asleep. It's been a bad day for all of us," Nealy said. "I had a bad dream myself."

No. It's not a dream, Mama. They're waiting for you. They said they can't take him till you get there. Hurry, Mama, they're waiting. We need to say good-bye to Mr. Jess. I went into his room. They came to get me, Mama. They woke me up.

Nealy sprinted down the hall to Maud's old room. The door was open, the lamps glowing softly. Jess was sleeping quietly in his bed. She heaved a sigh of relief. "See, honey, Mr. Jess is sleeping. Shhhh, we don't want to wake him."

Emmie tugged at her mother's sleeve and then pointed upward to a beautiful golden glow directly over her head. Nealy sucked in her breath as she looked at first one lamp and then the other. There was no way either lamp could create the kind of glow she was seeing. She started to shake and shiver at the same time.

See, Mama. Aren't they pretty? Hurry, we have to say good-bye.

Nealy ran over to the bed and shook Jess's shoulder. When there was no response she shook him harder. Her fingers went to the pulse in his neck. Thin and thready, barely there. "Wake up, Jess. Oh, God, Jess, wake up. Please wake up."

Say good-bye, say good-bye! He can hear you, Mama. They have him, Mama. He's laughing at me. He's waving good-bye. Look, Mama, he blew us each a kiss. Look, there's Miss Maud, her hand is stretching out to touch his. Good-bye, Mr. Jess.

"Good-bye, Jess," Nealy wailed as she crumpled to the floor. "Emmie, go downstairs and fetch Carmela."

From somewhere off in the distance Nealy swore she could hear the words, "Good-bye dear Nealy, good-bye."

It was a small, private funeral, with just close friends and family. Maud and Jess were laid to rest alongside Maud's parents in the family cemetery, which was opposite the stallion cemetery. Four of Blue Diamond Farms' prize stallions rested there.

Nealy had been here with Maud and Jess to bury Wind Drinker, one of the farm's champion stallions, who had died at the grand old age of thirty. Maud said it was the most peaceful place on the farm. Her father and his father before him had planted oak trees that were as big and round at the base as the bourbon vats Kentucky was known for. Moss dangled from the branches, creating a shady haven for visitors. Iron benches fit snugly around the trees, affording those resting there a clear view of the wildflowers that bloomed in the spring and summer. Now, though, it was barren and dismal.

It would be up to Nealy to order the simple crosses to go over the graves. She would have to ask the stonemason to make sure they were the same as those of Maud's mother and father. Suddenly she wanted to run and hide from the world. She couldn't do that. She had responsibilities, and she had promises to keep. Tears rolled down her cheeks. She made no effort to stop them.

Emmie reached for her hand and used her left hand to point upward. Nealy raised her tear-filled eyes. The November sunshine was so bright she had to shield her eyes to peer through the trees. At the top of the tree line she thought she saw a wide band of gold that stretched from one end of the cemetery to the other. She looked down at her daughter.

It's the angels, Mama. A lot of them. There's one for you and one for me. They're our guardian angels. Can you see them, Mama?

"I wish I could, honey, but I can't. I can see the light, but that's all. Can you see Maud or Jess?" she whispered.

No, just the angels. They only came to tell us everything is all right and not to be sad.

"They told you that, Emmie?"

No, I can read their thoughts, and they can read mine. You believe me, don't you, Mama?

Did she? Was it wishful thinking on Emmie's part, or was it her way of coping with the loss of two people she loved so dearly? Yet, she'd seen the strange light twice. "Yes, honey, I believe you."

When Nealy walked away from the cemetery, her eyes were dry. In her heart she knew Maud was in a better place, free of pain and misery, and Jess was with her. She had to accept it and move on from there. She thought about Carmela and some of the employees' wives back at the house, setting out food. She thought it barbaric that food and bourbon would be served after a funeral, but what did she know? She would suffer through it, and somehow she would manage. Right now, though, she needed to do something. "Emmie, go up to the house and see if you can help Carmela. I'll be up shortly." The little girl nodded and scampered off in the direction of the house.

Nealy headed for one of the old barns. She stood looking at it for a long time before she made her way to the side door and opened it. Inside it was dry and moldy-smelling. Cobwebs and all manner of rodent life lived inside, she was sure of it. There was no electricity, but she could see the outline of her father's truck. Whatever had been wrong with it that day so long ago was still wrong. The tires were flat now, and it was more rusty than ever. It wasn't the truck itself she was interested in but the bucket in the back of it. She picked her way carefully through the gloom and peered inside. The dirt was still in the bucket. SunStar dirt.

So many times she'd wanted to ask Emmie if she remembered that long-ago day when they left SunStar, but she never had. She was always afraid to bring it up for fear Emmie might not have remembered, and then her words would trigger that hateful day. Yet she remembered Pyne giving her the penny. How strange. She remembered that clearly, and that was all that was necessary. She ran her hands through the dirt and felt surprised when she didn't feel any emotion at all. It was dirt. Pure and simple. She dusted off her hands and left the old barn. She didn't look back.

His name was Will Jenkins and he was Maud and Jess's attorney. She'd met him only once, years ago. His brother Lawrence Jenkins had handled the legal adoption. She hadn't known him well either.

"Would you care for some coffee, Mr. Jenkins?" Nealy said, ushering the old attorney into the library.

"I don't much care for coffee, but if you were to offer me some bourbon I would be amenable to that."

"Make yourself comfortable. I'll fetch it. I don't know much about Maud's personal business, so I'm afraid I won't be of much help. However, I know the business records inside and outside. I can bring those books to you if you want them."

"That won't be necessary. The bourbon is all I need. Don't actually need it. Want is more like it. Don't bother with the ice." He was gruff and as taciturn as Jess. Cut from the same cloth, Maud would have said.

Nealy set the squat glass in front of the attorney and watched as he took a healthy swallow before setting it back on Maud's desk.

"Do you know why I'm here, Nealy?"

"Not really. I suppose it has something to do with the farm and Maud's and Jess's deaths. The doctor said he would bring the death certificates by later on in the week. I can bring them in to your office if you need them."

"I'm here to read you Maud and Jess's will. Are you familiar with it?"

"No, sir, I'm not. I didn't even know they had wills."

"They did. Since Maud died first, she left everything to her husband. Jess in turn left everything to you and Emmie. That's the bulk of it. You and your daughter are the legal heirs. There are bequests to Carmela and some of the employees. There are several foundations and trusts, but we can go into that another day. Everything here now belongs to you. This house, all the horses, everything. Everything is substantial." Nealy stared at him blankly.

"Substantial," the attorney repeated. Nealy continued to stare at him.

"What that means is you are a very wealthy woman. And so is your daughter. You really stepped into it, young lady, when they adopted you."

Nealy bristled. "I don't think I like what you're implying, Mr. Jenkins. I didn't ask to be adopted. Maud wanted to do it, and so did Jess. It didn't matter to me. I would have loved them both no matter what. Maybe you had better clarify just exactly what substantial means." She thought back to the conversation she'd had with Jess right after Maud had her stroke. Everything was to come to her and Emmie was what he'd said.

"Try this one on for size, young lady. How does forty-seven million sound?"

Nealy grew light-headed. "Dollars?"

"Dollars," the attorney said smugly. "There's almost that amount again in the trusts and foundations. And that's after estate taxes are paid. You are one very lucky lady. I need you to sign some papers."

"Not today, Mr. Jenkins. Leave them. I'll look them over and sign them when I'm ready to sign them. I'm in no hurry."

"Probate . . ."

"I don't know what that is. Right now I don't care what it is. I don't want to be bothered with this right now. Everything is going to stay the same even if I do sign those papers, so there is no rush. I want to make sure I understand everything."

"Wages, salaries . . ."

"I have a power of attorney where the business is concerned. There's enough money in the account to pay wages for five years. I'll see you out. I'll call you or drop off the papers when I get a chance."

"This is highly irregular," the old man squawked, his glasses jiggling on his pointy nose.

"Irregular or not, that's the way it is."

"Don't you want the money?"

"Not really. All I ever wanted was for Maud and Jess to love me, and they did. Anything else is a bonus. No, I really don't care about it. Good-bye Mr. Jenkins," Nealy said, holding the door open. She slammed it shut the minute the attorney was out on the big front porch.

Nealy leaned against the door. "It's true, Maud," she whispered. "All I wanted was for you and Jess to love me and Emmie. You didn't have to do all this. You really didn't."

She couldn't begin to imagine what the future held in store for her and her daughter.

8

Nealy jammed her hands into the pockets of her shearling jacket as she trudged across the frozen ground. She removed her right hand a second later to swipe at the tears rolling down her cheeks. Today was the one-year anniversary of Maud's and Jess's deaths. On top of that there was a full moon, and the horses were restless. And if that wasn't bad enough, a freak, freezing cold front had rolled across the entire state of Kentucky and was supposed to last another five days. Emmie was acting strange of late, and nothing in her own life seemed to be going right, either.

Things simply weren't working out. The first months after Maud's and Jess's deaths had been spent in shock. She'd not changed her routine, had done everything by rote, and then, when reality set in, had toughened up and tightened the reins on the employees. They resented her. She'd heard all the rumors, thanks to Wylie Carney and his father Jack. Jack referred to her as the twit that stepped into the golden pile of horse shit. Wylie was insolent and hateful. He showed up for work when and if he felt like it. He was now on his third warning. One more false move, and she would have to exercise her authority and show him the road. But if she did that, Jack Carney would come down hard on her. He'd rally the other employees, and then she would have a revolt on her hands. Jess had had such faith in the man—faith she had yet to see justified. All she knew was that he was overpaid and underworked and condoned his son's bad behavior. It would all come to a head first thing in the morning. That meant there would be no sleep for her tonight.

Thanksgiving be damned. She thought about the dinner Carmela was preparing for Emmie and herself. She'd be lucky if she could force down a dinner roll. If only there was someone she could talk to, someone she could confide in, someone who would have the answers to all her questions; but there was no one. She was on her own.

She'd wanted to continue to be one of them, but it hadn't worked. It didn't matter that in her heart and mind she felt she knew more than they did. It didn't matter that she worked just as hard, maybe harder than any of the others. She was the stranger who had wandered in and not only stayed but ended up owning one of the most lucrative, most prestigious horse farms in the state of Kentucky.

There wasn't one man whom she could call friend or ally except maybe Danny Clay, and if Jack Carney rallied the men and there was a walkout, where would he stand? She had to admit she didn't know.

She saw her daughter running toward her, heard the horn on the minibus that belonged to the church signaling a pupil had been discharged from Bible class. She knew something was wrong by the way Emmie was running. There were tears on her daughter's cheeks. Emmie never cried.

"Whoa. Easy, Emmie. What's wrong?"

They came to get Buddy at church, she signed. *His parents got killed. A big truck hit their horse van. It killed Blue Boy, too. You have to get Buddy and bring him here. Can you do that, Mama? It's Thanksgiving.*

Nealy cringed. "Let's go into the house where it's warm so we can talk. I'll call the house. Of course we can bring him here. Who told you this, Emmie?"

Mrs. Adler. She was crying. The police called her. Hurry and call, Mama.

Nealy shrugged out of her jacket and hung it on the rack by the back door next to Maud's plaid lumberjack coat and Jess's denim jacket. She hadn't been able to bring herself to discard either garment. She probably never would.

Nealy dialed the number for the Owens farm and waited until the housekeeper picked up. She explained who she was and offered to pick Buddy up so he could be with Emmie. When she hung up the phone she said, "Mrs. Carpenter said it's okay to bring Buddy here. His uncle is on his way, but he lives in Ohio, so he probably won't get here till tomorrow. That's all I know, Emmie."

Will he go away, Mama? Will they take Buddy away? Don't let them do that, Mama. Buddy's my friend. They won't want him because he can't hear. You want him, don't you, Mama? Why does everybody go away? Please, Mama.

"Honey, Buddy's family will make the decisions. I don't have any authority to . . . to . . . I can ask, but that's all I can do. Put your jacket back on and we'll drive over to the Owens farm and get him. Carmela, we're going to have another guest for dinner. Will you get one of the rooms ready for Buddy?" The house-keeper nodded.

Nealy stood outside the kitchen door, her heart thumping in her chest. Bitter cold air swirled about her. She was glad she'd put on long johns under her jeans. Her breathing was ragged, great puffs of air escaping her lips as she ran to the barns. Inside she stomped her feet, grateful for the warmth. She inhaled deeply before she felt her shoulders relax. Her watch told her it was exactly five o'clock, the time of day when the farm came alive. She thought about the children sleeping in the house. She thought about the tearful dinner the night before, and how Buddy had clung to Emmie for comfort. She squared her shoulders as she walked the length of the stallion barn. She nodded to Danny Clay and the other grooms before she checked on Stardancer. She pulled a wrinkled apple out of her pocket and held it out. "It won't be long now, Dancer. Come January you are going to be a proud daddy. Things are looking good. Dr. Franklin doesn't anticipate any problems." The stallion nuzzled Nealy's neck and daintily pawed the ground. "This is not going to be a good morning. I'll be back a little later and work you myself." The stallion snorted, picking up on her anxiety. "Behave yourself now till I get back," Nealy whispered.

"It's five-fifteen, Danny! Get me Wylie's time sheet. Don't even think about giving me an argument." The minute the big man slapped the time sheet into her hand, Nealy said, "I'm going up to the house, but I'll be right back. Pack up his gear and whatever else belongs to him. Tell Adam I want him to escort Wylie off the property when and if he shows up."

"Nealy, do you know what you're doing? Jack isn't . . ."

Nealy's eyes narrowed. "Ask me if I care, Danny? Be careful, or I'll be asking for your time sheet as well. That goes for the rest of you. Now get a move on. These horses need your assistance."

Nealy stomped her way to the house, her eyes watering with the cold. Inside she poured herself a cup of coffee and carried it to the office. Still wearing her jacket, she pulled out the payroll checkbook, computed Wylie's hours, and wrote out his check, along with a second check for two weeks' severance pay. She stuffed them in an envelope, folded it, and jammed it into her hip pocket. She was about to close the checkbook when she thought about Jack Carney. Jack would push her to the wall if she allowed it. Well, that wasn't going to happen. She sat down, pulled out the adding machine, and worked the numbers. Satisfied that she wouldn't be shortchanging the manager, she wrote out two more checks. Just in case. The second envelope went into her jacket pocket. It was a quarter to six when Nealy entered the barn a second time. She stomped her way past the whispering men, aware of their eyes on her back. She didn't stop until she was next to Stardancer's stall. She unlatched the gate but leaned against it. She had one ally. Dancer didn't like Wylie.

She waited, a smile on her face as Dancer nuzzled her neck.

Wylie Carney entered the barn at twenty minutes to seven, one hour and forty minutes late. A cigarette dangled from the corner of his mouth. Nealy watched as Danny Clay whipped it from his mouth and stomped on it. Smoking in the barns was reason enough for instant dismissal.

"Adam, give this to Mr. Carney and escort him to the road," Nealy said, handing over the envelope containing Wylie's checks. "Make sure you lower the bar so he can't come back on Blue Diamond property. If you make me say it twice, you might as well join Mr. Carney. What's it going to be?"

"Do what the lady says. Don't make me drag you out of here, Wylie," the big man said, his face beet red.

"I think we should call my father in here," Wylie sneered. "Fetch him, Adam!"

Her arm on the stallion's gated door, Nealy took a half step forward. "There's no need to call your father, Wylie. Adam does what I tell him to do, not what you tell him to do. It's your choice to go quietly or not so quietly. Either way, your employment here has come to an end. You've got a week's wages and two weeks' severance pay."

The sneer this time wasn't so pronounced. "I think my father will have something to say about that."

"Maybe, maybe not. It's the way it is. Adam, show him the road."

"What's going on here?" a deep voice boomed.

"This . . . *lady* just fired me, Pa. She's running me off. She can't do that, can she, Pa?"

"Not if she wants me to keep working here."

Nealy whipped out the second envelope from her jacket pocket and handed it over. "No problem, Jack. Here's your check and your severance package. I was generous with you because Jess would have wanted me to. Clear out your gear and your belongings. You have one hour. Adam, see that it happens. Not one second longer."

The farm manager stomped his foot like an angry child as he cursed everyone in the barn. "It's no more than I expected from a *woman*. Old Jess must be spinning in his grave."

"I doubt that. He was the one who told me it might come to this. Don't go thinking you're not expendable, because you are."

"Pa, are you going to let this . . . this *female* do this?"

"It ain't over till it's over, son."

"You're using up your time. I'd hate to have you arrested for trespassing, Jack."

The moment the barn door closed and the other grooms went back to work, muttering among themselves, Danny Clay walked over to where Nealy was standing. "Christ Almighty, Nealy, do you know what you just up and done? Now what's going to happen?"

"I just up and fired two pieces of deadwood. Look me in the eye, Danny, and tell me father and son pulled their weight. I have eyes, I've seen how you and the others covered for them, taking up the slack. All Maud or Jess expected from their employees was a day's work for a day's wages. They were good to all of you. Damn good, and you know it. The minute I took over this farm all I've had are problems, and you damn well know it. I get by on three hours of sleep because I walk these barns at night because I can't trust my employees. Jess wasn't thinking clearly that last year. If he had been, he would have seen what Jack was all about. If you have anything else to say, now is the time to say it. Until I can replace Jack and Wylie, things are going to be a little tense. You all might have to work more hours, but you will be compensated. I've been fair with you, and I expect you to be fair with me. The road goes both ways out of this farm."

"This isn't going to be the end of it, Nealy."

"This is the end of it, Danny. You probably don't know this, but Ann and Richard Owens were killed in a car accident yesterday. There's a brother coming from Ohio to see to things. The housekeeper seems to think he's going to sell off the Owens farm. Their people will be looking for jobs. So, you see, this *is* the end of it. Is there anything you want to add?"

"No, *ma'am*," Danny said smartly as he offered up a sloppy salute.

Heart pounding, Nealy stared him down until he turned away. The stallion behind her whickered as she locked the gate. "I'll be back," she whispered.

She knew their eyes were boring into her back as she walked from the barn, her head high, her back ramrod stiff. "It had to be, Jess. There was no other way," she muttered.

Nealy looked at her watch at the same moment she closed the door to the office: 1:30. She ached from head to toe. *One of these days,* she thought, *I'm going to have to get more than three or four hours sleep a night.* Even with a hot, fragrant bath she knew she wasn't going to be able to sleep. Warm milk with a shot of bourbon wouldn't work either. Maybe if she skipped the hot bath and took a brisk walk outside, even if it was just around the house, she might sleep better. On the other hand, maybe it wasn't exactly a prudent thing to do. While things had been quiet since she'd fired the Carneys, she knew in her gut that Danny Clay was right; she hadn't heard the last of Jack and Wylie. So far there had been no revolt, but morale wasn't high. She was seeing surliness and open defiance, two traits she refused to tolerate. All she had to do was weed out the instigators, and maybe things would get back to normal.

Outside, Nealy buttoned her jacket and waited till her eyes adjusted to the darkness before she lit a cigarette. She decided she was too tired to walk around the house. Instead she walked over to the split-rail fence and perched on the top rail to stare ahead of her into the darkness. She thought about the boy sleeping soundly upstairs and wondered what was going to happen to him. Things had moved quickly at the Owens farm where Peter Owens, Buddy's uncle, arrived to see to things. Ann and Richard had been buried, the horses sold off, the farm put up for sale. Emmie had been right when she said Peter Owens wouldn't want Buddy. He'd actually sighed with relief when she'd told him Buddy could stay as long as he wanted. He'd agreed that the special school the youngster attended was the best, and it would be a shame to uproot him. When she'd told him child support wasn't necessary, Peter had agreed to sign on the dotted line, giving her temporary custody of the boy. The word *temporary* had not been defined. Nealy hoped it meant till he came of age. Perhaps then she could legally adopt him the way Maud and Jess had adopted her and Emmie. The monies from the sale of the horses and farm would go into a trust fund for Buddy when he turned twenty-one. Peter Owens had left then, as quickly as he arrived, leaving behind a skeleton crew to see to things, men who had signed on with Nealy when the Owens farm was sold.

The boy was adapting nicely, and the two children were inseparable. For that, Nealy was grateful. Yes, he grieved, and yes, he cried, but at the end of the day he had Nealy to hug him, tuck him in, and kiss him good night, and it was Emmie he had breakfast with and Emmie he rode with on the school bus, and together they helped in the barns and did their chores cheerfully. Time would heal his wounds the way they'd healed hers and Emmie's. For now she had a son, and she was growing to love the ginger-haired, freckle-faced boy almost as much as she loved Emmie.

She should be thinking about Christmas and maybe decorating the house. A party of sorts for the employees if she could find the time. Presents to be bought. A tree to set up and decorate. Last year, she and Emmie had agreed not to bother with Christmas. They'd gone to church, though, said their prayers, visited the stallion cemetery, eaten dinner, then slept the rest of the day away. This year she had to be concerned with Buddy and what he would expect. Just the thought of what the holidays entailed made her shoulders slump.

Back in Virginia, Christmas had been little more than another day. Work still had to be done, the horses seen to. There was always one gift, usually an article of clothing, for each of her brothers and herself. Now that she understood the financial workings of Blue Diamond Farms, she had to wonder what her father did with all his money.

Nealy hopped off the fence and found herself suddenly caught in a pair of bright headlights as a car stopped within inches of her body. Her heart started to pound as she tried to see past the blinding light. She moved quickly to the side of the road at the same moment the occupant stormed out of his car, his arms flailing, his voice angry and blustery. "You trying to get yourself killed! I could have killed you, you know! Who in their right mind is bouncing off a fence at two o'clock in the morning? Are you some kind of weirdo? Never mind, of course you are; otherwise, you wouldn't be out here in the middle of the night. You almost gave me a heart attack. Well, aren't you going to say something? Stupid female. Why do I get them all?" the man said, throwing his hands in the air.

"And you are . . . ? You're trespassing. I'm not a weirdo, but I can see how you might think I am one. My mind was someplace else. I didn't see your lights, and I didn't hear the sound of your car. I apologize for that. I'm glad you didn't have a heart attack, but you almost gave me one, so that makes us even. I'm also glad you have good brakes. I repeat, you are trespassing."

"Hunter Clay. Danny Clay is my father. He works here. I'm on Christmas break. He removed his baseball cap to run his fingers through a shock of dark curly hair. "I've been driving for two days. This car is worth about two hundred bucks. I have eighty dollars in the bank and a fortune tied up in law books thanks to my dad and Maud. I have one more quarter to go and then the bar. I grew up here. I was sorry to hear about Maud and Jess. They were like grandparents to me. Never saw you before, so I jumped to conclusions. Guess you're the new owner. Why don't we start over. I'm Hunter Clay. My friends call me Hunt."

"I'm Nealy Diamond," Nealy said, extending her hand. "I didn't know Danny had a son."

"Dad's like Jess. Never says two words if one will do. I lived with my mother in Syracuse until she died when I was ten. I came here then. Mom didn't like horses and refused to live here. They never got divorced. Dad came to see us twice a year. Listen, do you think we could continue this discussion tomorrow? Today really. I'm dead on my feet and need some sleep."

Nealy stared at him as he moved closer to the car door and stood outlined in the light from the headlights. For one wild, crazy moment she thought she was looking at Emmie's father. She blinked, and the vision vanished. Solid was her first thought. Spectacular, muscular body. Dark chocolate eyes and a cleft in his chin. He smiled then. There the likeness to Emmie's father disappeared.

"Did I pass?"

"Yes. How long are you going to be here?"

"Six or seven weeks. Is that going to be a problem?"

"How would you like to work for me while you're here?" She rattled off an obscene amount of money and wondered where the numbers came from and why she was being so generous with someone who had almost run her over. It was his turn to blink.

"You got yourself a new groom, lady."

"Good. Be in the stallion barn at five. I'll see you then."

"That's in . . . *three* hours."

Nealy turned. "You lawyers are soooo smart. You can count, too. Better get cracking. Five o'clock rolls around real quick. Don't even think about being late. I just fired the last guy that showed up late. *And* his father."

"That must have been Wylie and Jack! Okay, you just impressed me. That had to take some guts!"

"You could say that." Nealy grinned as she walked away.

Hunter Clay watched as Nealy sashayed her way over to the house and up the steps into the house. "Uh-huh," he mumbled as he settled the baseball cap more firmly on his head. "Five o'clock it is," he said as he climbed back into the rickety car.

Nealy walked into the kitchen to hang up her jacket. Hunter

Clay. She opened the refrigerator and pulled out a bottle of soda pop. Hunter Clay. She shivered when she remembered how much he looked like Dillon Roland. Dillon Roland, who had threatened to kill her if she ever accused him of being the father of her child. He'd said other things, too. Ugly, hurtful, threatening things. In the end, when her father threatened to beat her within an inch of her life, she'd said she'd fallen asleep in the barn and some vagrant had wandered in and attacked her.

Dillon Roland, whose father was very wealthy, was married now to the daughter of one of the town's most influential citizens. He also fancied himself a country squire and owned two magnificent horses he had bought at Keeneland two years ago. He'd been quoted as saying when the time was right he'd run the Derby. *All good things come to those who wait*, Nealy thought as she climbed the steps to the second floor.

Hunter Clay.

9

Nealy sat in the truck at the end of the driveway, the engine idling as she waited for the school bus to discharge Emmie and Buddy. She craned her neck to look upward. It was going to snow. She could feel it in her bones.

At breakfast that morning she'd announced that it was only one week until Christmas and time to get a Christmas tree. Emmie had been enthusiastic, but Buddy showed little emotion. She crossed her fingers and hoped the boy would get into the swing of things and join whatever festivities she could conjure up.

Today, a weekday, she'd taken the entire day off and gone into Lexington to shop for gifts, wrapping paper, and Christmas decorations. She still couldn't believe that she'd actually played *hooky*. Usually when she had shopping to do, she waited until Sunday, but this time she'd made an exception. It was a first. And it felt good. So good, in fact, she was looking forward to doing it again.

Tonight, after tallying up the receipts, she wondered if she would still feel good. She'd purchased two bicycles, a blue one for Buddy and a lavender one for Emmie, fishing poles, Rollerblades, a motorized scooter with a sidecar for Buddy and a sleek custom-designed motorcar that resembled a golf cart for Emmie. They would be delivered tomorrow while the kids were in school.

With the last of her purchases in hand, she'd headed for the truck only to stop short in front of a store window to stare at a dress. In her life she'd never seen anything so glamorous, so rich-looking, so elegant, and so trashy all at the same time. Maud would have loved it. She had marched into the store and asked for a size 2, praying they would have it. They did.

She had been on her way to the dressing room when she checked her watch and realized it was later than she realized. "Can I return this if it doesn't fit?" she asked the salesclerk.

"Of course. Just save your receipt."

She had the clerk take it up to the register and whipped out her checkbook. Where was she going to wear such a dress? she wondered. She never went anyplace. And even if something did come up, would she have the guts to wear it? It was so . . . so . . . *sexy and slutty-looking.*

While the salesclerk slid the dress between layers of tissue paper, she pointed out a pair of silver shoes with three-inch heels and two straps across the instep that she thought would complement the dress. Nealy agreed and said she'd take a pair. She grinned all the way home.

What fun she'd had. While Carmela was preparing an early supper, she could write out the Christmas bonus checks just the way Maud had done for years and years. Then, when dinner was over, they could go hunting for the Christmas tree. It was more or less a tradition Maud had started the first year she and Emmie had come to Blue Diamond Farms. A tradition Nealy hoped to continue forever.

Christmas was a time for giving, and Maud and Jess had been generous with all their employees. Nealy had no intention of discontinuing the tradition in spite of recent difficulties. Each of the employees would receive the same bonus they'd received last year. Carmela would get a round-trip plane ticket to California to visit her elderly sister along with her usual bonus. "This Christmas thing isn't so hard," Nealy mumbled.

She climbed out of the truck the moment the school bus pulled to a stop. She held out both her arms to the children and hugged them. "There's nothing like the last day of school before Christmas vacation," she said, signing at the same time for Buddy's benefit. "And guess what! This evening after supper we're going to have us a big adventure. We're going to cut down our very own Christmas tree!" She hated the pinched look that came over Buddy's face. "Listen, honey, your mom and dad wouldn't want you to be sad. They would want you to remember them with love and joy."

But I miss them, he said, his fingers slow to form the words.

"I know you do. Emmie and I miss Maud and Jess, too. But we're happy for them because they're in heaven with the angels."

Are my mom and dad with the angels, too? he asked, his face brightening with hope.

"You bet they are, Buddy."

How do you know there are angels?

It was Emmie who replied. *Because I've seen them,* she said, then smiled up at her mother.

Nealy smiled back. "Come on, last one in the truck is a rotten egg!"

The youngsters climbed into the back of the pickup, their arms waving in excitement. The resiliency of youth, Nealy marveled.

After supper and with only an hour left until sundown, Nealy loaded up the children, a tarp, and saw, and drove to the pine grove on the north end of the farm. It took them all of fifteen minutes to find the perfect tree, another fifteen minutes to cut it down, and a few more minutes to drag it back to the truck. All in all it had been much easier than Nealy had anticipated.

I think, Nealy said, her fingers moving rapidly, *the challenge is going to be getting this monster into the house and into a tree stand. Emmie, fetch Carmela. We're going to need all the help we can get. Buddy, get the tree stand out of the back of the truck. I'm thinking we should put the tree in the stand out here and then drag it by the stand into the house.*

"It's too big to go through the door, Nealy," Carmela gasped.

"Nonsense. We just have to ... shove it. You and I will pull from the kitchen and Emmie and Buddy will shove from this side. Maybe we need to take the door off," Nealy muttered twenty minutes later.

"What we need is some men to do this," Carmela grumbled.

"No, we do not need men to do this. We are going to do it ourselves. I will get this tree in the living room if it kills me. I'll just saw off some branches from the bottom. No one looks at the bottom anyway."

"Why did you choose such a big tree, Nealy?"

"It didn't look that big in the field. Actually, it looked kind of puny. Okay, okay, I'm sawing. There, I took off four branches. Now *push!*"

"It still won't go through the door," Carmela gasped.

"So I'll cut some more branches. There, four more off the sides. Now dammit, *push and pull.*"

"I quit!" Carmela stormed. "I have to get back to the kitchen. My advice is shove this tree back outside and go to Masons and buy an artificial tree that comes in a box."

"I will do no such thing. Carmela, you can't quit. You're an institution at Blue Diamond Farms. This is a mission now. I am going to get this tree into the living room. I mean it."

They watched, their jaws dropping as Nealy hacked and sawed, sweat dripping down her cheeks. "There! Now, *shove!*"

A moment later, Nealy and Carmela tumbled backward, pine needles and bits of branches flying everywhere. Emmie and Buddy grinned down at her from their perches inside the tree.

"Didn't I tell you this was going to be an adventure? See, we got it into the house. We didn't need a man to do it either." *No offense, Buddy,* she signed. "What we're going to do now is *roll* it into the living room, at which point the four us will somehow manage to stand it upright. We can do this. I know we can," Nealy said.

"There are pine needles in the vegetable soup," Carmela shouted from the kitchen.

"You should have put a lid on the pot. Pick them out. Flavor is flavor," Nealy said as she struggled to roll the tree into the living room. "We need you now, Carmela!"

"It's too tall," Carmela said, disgust rising in her voice.

"I can see that, Carmela. I'll just cut the top off." *Buddy, fetch the ladder from the pantry.* "It's a simple matter. I'll just saw off that big part up there at the top."

"That leaves you with a bush," Carmela snapped. "There's going to be sap in the soup. I don't like sap in my soup."

Nealy gritted her teeth. "Yes you do. We all love sap in our soup. Not another damn word, Carmela, until this tree is up and decorated. This is not a bush," Nealy said grimly. "Hold the ladder while I saw." The moment the top of the tree thumped to the floor, Nealy hopped off the ladder.

"Nice bush. I don't think I ever saw a Christmas bush before. Most people have Christmas *trees* in their houses at Christmas. Do you decorate a bush the same way you decorate a tree? I find this very interesting," Hunt Clay said, amusement ringing in his voice.

"Shut up! How did you get in here? Do you want something?"

"The kitchen door was open. I really had a hard time making my way in here. Your kitchen looks like a bomb hit it. My father wants you to come down to the stallion barn. He said Stardancer is acting strangely. Do you need some help here?"

"You can pick the needles out of the soup or you can start cleaning up the kitchen. Which do you prefer?" Carmela snapped.

Nealy looked at her hands, which were sticky with sap. "Of course he's acting strangely. I didn't take him to visit his partner. I'll do it as soon as I clean up."

"It's a fat pine bush."

"It's a tree! See, there's the top. I had to saw it off. Don't use that word around me ever again." *You kids put the lights on, just connect the strands and be careful on the ladder. I won't be long,* Nealy signed, stomping her way to the kitchen, Hunt Clay on her heels.

Nealy surveyed the kitchen. Clay was right, it did look like a bomb had hit the entire room.

"Why didn't you just get a smaller tree?" Hunt asked as he stepped over a pile of branches.

"Because I cut this one down. *I* cut it down. That's *I* as in *me.* I do not like to cut down trees. It takes years and years for trees to grow. So, why would I do that? I accomplished my mission. I now have a Christmas tree in my living room. This is the end of this conversation. If you clean up the mess, you can stay for supper."

"I don't much care for pine needles in my soup. Thanks anyway. This is your project, you created it; therefore, you should clean it up. That's the way it works."

"Smart-ass," Nealy seethed as she rubbed soap on her hands at the kitchen sink.

"Takes one to know one," Hunt chuckled as he made his way

over the debris to the door. "Do you want me to close the door? Oops, it can't close. I think you knocked it off its hinges. Yep, that's what you did all right. The door is cracked. All the way to the base. You might have to get a new door. Yeah, yeah, you're going to need a new door."

"Will you just shut the hell up. Go on, do whatever it is you were doing before you got here. I've had all the advice I can handle for one day."

"Testy aren't we? I'm going. Good luck with the door."

Nealy reached for her jacket, stuffing her arms into the sleeves as she walked through the door.

"Cranky, too," Hunt said, his breath fogging the air as he walked ahead of her.

"No, I'm not, but if you keep it up, I'm going to get real pissy."

They made their way to the stallion barn, side by side in complete silence. The breezeway between stalls was well lit. Nealy looked into each stall as she passed and received soft whickers of greeting. She knew each and every horse by name as well as pedigree.

Danny Clay came out of the tack room carrying a bucket of white oats, his special "feel better" blend. "I can't find anything wrong with him, but he looks kinda down . . . sad . . . if you know what I mean. So, I fixed him some oats, thinking that would cheer him up."

"Dancer doesn't need oats," she told him, unlatching the stall door. "He just needs me to visit him. I did something today I've never done before. I took the whole day off. I should have come out to see him as soon as I got home, but I had stuff to put away before the kids got out of school." She went into the stall and closed the door behind her. "Hey, big boy. I hear you're feeling kind of sorry for yourself." Stardancer nickered. "Well, I'm here now, so everything is all right." Nealy stood in front of him, rested his chin atop her left shoulder, and placed her hands on either side of his head, then rubbed his face. He immediately closed his eyes. "There now, feel better? Sure you do." Even when she moved her hands up to his ears, his eyes remained closed.

Danny and Hunt waited patiently outside the stall, talking softly.

"I dunno what she's got, but I sure wish I had it," Danny said, glancing over his shoulder to make sure he wasn't disturbing her.

"What do you mean?" Hunt asked.

"With anyone else that stallion is bad news, spelled t-r-o-u-b-l-e. But with her . . . . Well, look at him. She's got a special way with him . . . with all animals. It's almost like she can read their minds, know what they're thinking. On top of that, she can make them do damn near anything she wants them to."

"Interesting," Hunt said.

"Interesting? What kind of comment is that?" his father demanded.

"I don't know. It's just that she's not what I thought, you know?"

"No, I don't know," his father said. "What did you think she was?"

"Well, from all the talk, I thought . . ."

Danny nodded and guffawed. "You've been listening to Jack Carney's cronies. They're wrong, son. That girl in there is good people in spite of what you've heard."

Nealy came out of Stardancer's stall smiling. "He's better now," she said.

"You've spoiled him," Danny said.

"Maybe, but he deserves to be spoiled a little after all the years everybody ignored him. Thanks for sending Hunt for me. Good night, Danny. See you tomorrow."

"Night, Nealy."

Hunt followed Nealy through the breezeway into the open. "Hey, wait up," he called. "I want to talk to you."

"About what?" she asked over her shoulder.

She could hear him hesitate a moment. "About Stardancer. I'm curious about something my dad said."

She turned around and waited for him to fall in step beside her. "I'd invite you to have some dessert with us if you promise not to say anything about the Christmas tree." She gave him a challenging look.

He nodded. "Okay, I promise."

It felt good coming into the warm kitchen from outside. As soon as Nealy hung her coat on the hook, she peeked into the living room to see how Carmela and the kids were doing. A gurgle of laughter erupted from her throat when she saw the Christmas tree. Buddy was on the ladder with the tree topper, trying to tie it around the stump with a piece of Christmas ribbon. "It is a bush," she whispered to herself as she opened the door and went into the living room. "It's beautiful!" she said, her smile wide. Then she cocked her head to give it a better look. "Well, maybe *beautiful* isn't the right word. Let's say it's different. Very different. But I like it. I really like it! It's kind of like us. Not perfect, a little rough around the edges, but sturdy. Really sturdy."

"That's a profound statement if I ever heard one," Hunt said.

Nealy turned to look at him and saw that he wasn't making fun of her. His expression was serious.

"Milky Way bars for dessert," she announced, feeling suddenly uncomfortable and needing to escape. "The frozen kind." Nealy walked over to the children, hugged them, then signed, *You both did real good. See, this is something we'll remember for a very long time. Wash up and go to the kitchen.*

"I'll go get things ready," Carmela said, heading toward the kitchen.

Hunt touched her arm. "My dad says you've got a special way with horses, actually with all animals."

"I just pay attention to them, that's all." She bent to pick up an empty ornament box. "I know your father and some of the others think I was crazy to breed Stardancer with Little Lady, but they'll change their minds, just you wait and see. Their foal is going to be a Derby winner. And when he runs for the roses, Stardancer and Little Lady are going to be right there at the track watching him. Horses have feelings, emotions about their offspring, just like people. I don't care what the books say or those horse experts who think they know about horses. If people would just pay closer attention, they'd see what I've seen. Horses are not big, dumb, stupid animals like most people think. They aren't. Stardancer is the living proof. Go ahead, laugh. Everybody else does, so you might as well join in," Nealy said grimly, her jaw set in hard lines.

"You don't see me laughing, do you?" Hunt said quietly.

Nealy's tight expression eased. "No, I don't see you laughing. I guess I should thank you for that."

"In case you didn't know, I worked here part-time right alongside my dad until I went off to college, so I learned a thing or two about horses. I was here the day Stardancer threw Maud. Jess called my dad to get him after it happened. I was right there with my dad helping to quiet Stardancer. All the way back to his stall, Dancer kept twisting around to look behind him, as if he knew he'd done something he shouldn't have. So you see, it wouldn't surprise me at all to learn that horses are emotional, feeling creatures just like us, only different."

Nealy stared at him. An unexpected feeling of warmth surged through her. She'd been resisting Hunt's friendship since the day he'd arrived. Why, she didn't know. He was so easy to talk to, and he didn't laugh at her like the others did.

"So, you're going to be a lawyer," she said, deliberately changing the subject.

"Maud and Jess wanted me to make something out of myself, so they footed half the bill. All I ever wanted was to work here alongside my dad, grooming horses, watching them race around the track. It's what I lived for. But Dad was on Maud and Jess's side. He said anybody could be a groom, but to be a lawyer, now that was something special. He'd had enough disappointments in life, and I didn't want to be another one. So I went to law school, got good grades, and will graduate this May. I hate the law. Always did and probably always will. But I'm good at it."

"Wow, that ought to make for an interesting career. I can see you now, getting up every morning, going over your briefs as you absentmindedly sip coffee, putting on your fashionable dark gray suit and matching tie and walking into the courtroom and saying, "I object, Your Honor."

"Yep, you got it. And I'm going to hate every minute of it."

"I'm looking to replace Jack Carney," Nealy blurted without thinking. "You say you know a thing or two about horses, and I know you know a thing or two about handling people and about the legal system so . . ." She stopped to take a breath and to wonder what she was doing. "Do you think you could manage Blue Diamond Farms?"

"What?" Hunt's eyes were wide with disbelief.

"You'd have to report to me. If you think you'd have a problem with answering to a woman as your boss, say so now."

"I can't believe this. Are you serious?"

"There's something you need to know about me, Hunter Clay. I never say anything I don't mean. I'm serious, I'm dedicated, and I never give up on anything. Once I make a decision, and I make lots of snap decisions, I live with it. I got that tree . . . bush . . . whatever it is in here, didn't I? If you want the job, it's yours, but only after you finish law school. And you have to pass the bar exam. You can handle our routine legal affairs and save us outside fees. Your salary will be the same as what Jack was getting. It's more than generous. Jess set the pay scale a while back. The year-end bonuses are equally generous. We can talk about it when you're ready to sign on."

Without warning her feet left the floor and she was sailing through the air in a pair of hard, muscular arms. She could smell his aftershave and the overall clean smell of him. It was a heady combination. The kiss on her forehead burned. She was so flustered when he set her down she could feel her face start to burn.

"You're blushing," Hunt said. "I didn't know girls blushed these days."

"You . . . you took my breath away," she said, putting her hand over her heart to keep it from popping out of her chest. "Hey," she said breathlessly, "don't go getting any ideas now."

"God forbid!" he said, laughing. "You're okay, Nealy Diamond."

"So are you, Hunter Clay."

"C'mon, let's go celebrate with that dessert I promised you," Nealy said, linking her arm with Hunt's for the walk to the kitchen.

The twenty-ninth day of the New Year dawned clear and bright. Nealy knew when she woke that today was *the* day . . . the day her Kentucky Derby winner would be born.

Stardancer seemed to know, too. He was pacing in his stall when she arrived, and Danny said he had been excited all morning. "I want you to take Little Lady to the foaling stall in the new barn, then I'll help you take Stardancer over there and put him in the adjoining stall." When she saw his eyes narrow, she said, "Don't give me any flak on this, Danny. I know what I'm asking is against every Thoroughbred horse breeder's rules, but this is my farm now, and I make the rules. Think of it as an experiment."

"Okay, you're the boss, but don't blame me if something goes wrong."

"I won't, Danny. But nothing will go wrong. Will you please have faith in me just this once, okay?"

The new foaling barn had been built to Nealy's exact specifications just after Hunt had arrived. It wasn't for every mare, just for a few selected ones, and only one birth at a time ever took place. The stall was bigger than average, thirty square feet, to allow the mare and her attendants to walk around without running into each other. It was deeply bedded with clean straw, and the sides were padded so when the new foal fell he or she wouldn't be hurt. Every modern convenience, every comfort had been seen to, including a sleeping area and a small bathroom so the attendants had no reason to leave.

Hunt was the only one who hadn't raised his eyebrows at her plan. He understood her feelings and respected her instincts. "Do what your heart tells you to do," he had said. And that's what she'd done.

"Today's the day, isn't it, big fella?" Nealy asked from outside the stall. The stallion was far too excited to be bothered with hugs and pats. "Be patient a little while longer, okay?" She gave him a hug and a wave before she headed back to the house. Emmie and Buddy would be delighted with the news and equally delighted to learn that they wouldn't be going to school today.

Carmela had lived around Nealy long enough to trust her instincts. With Nealy's announcement that today was *the* day, she'd made coffee in the twenty-cup coffeemaker and prepared an assortment of sandwiches and snacks.

The children taken care of, Nealy returned to the barn to

check on Little Lady. She knew the workers were hissing and whispering about her behind her back, knew none of the old-timers approved of her methods. No one would have questioned Maud or Jess; but she was still fair game, the twit who had stepped into the golden pile of horse shit.

Hunter and Danny were settling the mare into her new quarters when she arrived.

"She's looking a mite uncomfortable," Hunt observed.

Nealy laughed. "You would be, too, if you were carrying that big of a load around in your belly."

Dr. Ed Franklin blew into the new barn with a heavy gust of wind. He chucked his wool jacket, his muffler, and his cap onto the bench in the breezeway. "So, how's it going?"

The moment the words were out of his mouth, Little Lady's water broke.

"Time to get Stardancer and bring him over," Nealy said, taking Hunt's arm.

"You can't be serious," the vet said.

Nealy turned around. "I'm very serious. Why do you think I had this barn built? You knew this was my plan from the beginning. Why are you acting so surprised now?"

"If you bring that stallion in here, I'm leaving. I won't be a party to this . . . this . . . craziness."

Nealy's back stiffened. She swallowed the saliva in her mouth. What would Maud and Jess do? She had to admit she didn't know. "That's your choice." She thought about how much money the vet earned annually at Blue Diamond Farms. "Hunt, call Dr. Miller."

"Miller?" the vet shouted, his voice several octaves higher than normal. "You want that quack to attend Little Lady?" His angry eyes were as big as horseshoes.

"Thank you for coming, Dr. Franklin. Since we won't be needing your services any longer, we'll be sending you a final check at the end of the week. You have a nice day now."

The vet stomped out of the stall, grumbling as he went. "Crazy female. Hasn't a clue. Wait till the other owners hear about this!"

The moment Hunt completed his call to Dr. Miller, he raced after Nealy to help her bring Stardancer to his new stall. The stallion pranced through the breezeway to his now-familiar quarters. He was the picture of excitement, his eyes big and wide and his ears perked to hear every sound. As excited and as spirited as he was, he was manageable, a fact that Hunt commented on with surprise.

A large opening between stalls had been built so that the stallion could poke his head through and see everything that was going on with his mare and foal. For hours, Stardancer watched intently, hardly moving, never eating or drinking.

Little Lady's contractions had started about ten minutes after her water broke. The vet had arrived thirty minutes later and didn't voice an opinion one way or another where Stardancer was concerned.

An hour later the vet split the thick, rubbery silver-looking placenta. A few minutes later, Nealy saw the first sign of the foal—his two front legs. As the foal moved, the vet skillfully peeled the placenta away. Then the foal's nostrils appeared, and, a second later, its head was out, tucking against the mare's legs.

Stardancer whickered softly from the next stall. He had been so quiet, so still, that Nealy had all but forgotten he was there.

With a little encouragement from the vet, the foal slipped out of the mare's womb onto the straw bedding.

A colt, Nealy cheered in silence. But she had known it would be.

Emmie moved into place and immediately started wiping away the afterbirth and running her small hands over the colt's body.

Nealy watched her daughter with pride. "What should we name him?" she asked, speaking to no one in particular.

Hunt's brows drew together in thought as did his father's.

"He's going to be our Derby winner, you know. Mark my words, he's going to fly by every other horse in the field," Nealy said, signing at the same time out of habit.

Buddy stood up and faced Nealy, his fingers animated as he signed, *How about Flyby?*

Hunt cocked his head to look at the newborn as he made his first awkward attempt to stand up. "I like it," he said. "It has *meaning.*"

"Flyby," Nealy repeated, testing the sound of it on her

tongue. "There goes Flyby into the stretch," she said in her announcer's voice. "Look at him run, folks! He's flying!" She walked over to Stardancer and rubbed his majestic forehead. "What do you think, boy? Is Flyby okay with you?" The big stallion bobbed his head up and down.

Nealy laughed. "Tell me he doesn't understand. Just try and tell me," she said smugly. "Flyby it is!"

As if on cue, the colt stood up and gave a little whinny.

Nealy put her arms around his still-wet body. "It's a long way from here to the Derby, Flyby, but you are *the one.*"

10

Hunter Clay's dark eyes searched Nealy's face. "A penny for your thoughts."

Nealy blinked and looked up. "I was just sitting here thinking. I do that sometimes, let my mind drift wherever it wants." She squeezed the couch pillow she was holding. "Aside from a few little things, I've never been more contented with my life than I am right now. It's such a joy to watch Emmie and Buddy with the new colt. You saw how Emmie bonded with him the second he was born. It was her hands he felt first, and then mine. I think that bodes well for all of us."

"I think so, too," he said, putting his arm around the back of the couch, close to her hair.

"No one ever believed that big guy could be so gentle," Nealy said, referring to the tense moment when little Flyby had wobbled over to the windowlike opening where his sire watched. Everyone had held their breath when the big stallion lowered his massive head and sniffed the colt. The colt sniffed back, gave a little whinny, then darted back over to his mother's side and began nursing. "I'm glad I followed my instincts and didn't let anyone talk me out of letting Stardancer in on the birth. Now you just watch, from here on out those three are going to be a family." Nealy noticed that Hunt's eyes were riveted on her face as she talked.

"So, you think Flyby is *the one*, huh? The Derby winner?"

"I don't think he's the one, I *know* he is," she said, her voice ringing with confidence. She looked away, disturbed by the way he was staring at her, as if he could see inside her. "Maud's dream was to have another Derby winner. Her father had one and she managed to get two early on. I promised her I would bring another trophy home, and I intend to do just that with Flyby."

"If anybody can do it, you can. As far as I'm concerned, you've proved yourself and your theory beyond a reasonable doubt," he said, emphasizing the courtroom cliché. "Even Dad is starting to come around. I heard him use the word *miracle* in reference to Stardancer a few days ago."

Nealy blinked, then focused her gaze. Just the other day she had wished for someone to talk to, confide in and help her resolve her problems. It was beginning to look like her wish had come true. In the few days following Flyby's birth she and Hunt had spent countless hours together talking about anything and everything. He was easy to talk to because he was a good listener. She hadn't confided any secrets to him yet, but she knew that if and when she did, he would keep her confidences.

"Speaking of your father. Has he heard any more grumblings about the Carneys or Stardancer?"

"He's dealing with some nasty stuff from some of the men. They don't take well to change. The bottom line is they haven't forgiven you for firing Jack Carney. But it's what you did with Stardancer that's rocking the foundation of this farm. They feel you risked the life of that colt to satisfy your ego."

"That's not true," Nealy answered in a rush of words. "I don't have an ego."

Hunt moved his hand off the back of the couch and took hold of her braid and gently tugged it. "Hey, I know you don't, but that's because I know you and understand you better than they do."

A part of her reveled in his trust in her. She felt an unexpected warmth flow through her. "It's just that I think this breeding thing has gotten too clinical. The breeders are turning the horses into machines. I pray to God the day never comes when Thoroughbreds are artificially bred, like cows." Nealy felt an odd twinge of disappointment when he took his hand from her hair. She had secretly hoped . . . She wasn't sure what she had been hoping for, but she didn't dare think too hard about it. She had enough on her mind right now.

"I saw Wiley in town yesterday around four o'clock. He was drunk as a skunk."

Nealy shrugged. "I could care less what Wiley is doing as long as he isn't doing it on my payroll and my farm. I've got bigger concerns at the moment than Wiley Carney, Jack, and even the staff. I'm worried about Buddy. One day he's up, and the next he's down. The psychologist seeing him wants to increase his sessions. I think it's a good idea. He doesn't open up to me too much, but he talks to Emmie nonstop. Maybe I'm expecting too much too soon."

"He's a survivor, Nealy. He's grieving the way a child grieves. It wouldn't be normal if he didn't have some downtime. He's doing well in school. He eats constantly because he's a growing boy, so that has to mean something. He's got all kinds of male role models around here. When I come back at the end of the quarter, I'll spend more time with him. He's teaching me to sign, but he says I'm way too slow. There's a guy in one of my classes who works with the deaf. I'll get him to work with me, and when I get back here, I'll blow Buddy's socks off with how good I am." He laughed at his own little joke.

A smile found its way to Nealy's lips. In the short time Hunt had been working on the farm, he'd proved himself not only to be an ally but a genuinely good person. He worked tirelessly, never complained, and was good to his father. Whenever she saw Hunt joke with his father or put his arm around his shoulders, her heart ached. Never once had her own father joked with her or put his arm around her. Ditto for Pyne and Rhy. Maybe that was why she was always hugging Emmie and Buddy, because she'd never gotten any hugs herself.

Nealy's mind drifted off.

A few minutes later Hunt asked, "What are you thinking?"

She blinked. "Hmm? Oh, this and that." She grinned mischievously. "Maud loved to talk about the old days to me. She had a rapt pupil in me. I soaked it all up like a sponge. Being a woman in the Thoroughbred horse business made for some really tough times, and yet she survived and thrived. Every single person on this farm loved her." She looked away then, her eyes misty, and said, "I think they're all likening me to Maud, and I'm coming up short in their eyes." She could feel her throat closing up and knew she had to regain control. The last thing she wanted was for Hunt to think she was feeling sorry for herself. "Anyway," she said, taking a deep breath, "Maud told me that her father's death devastated her. She admitted to drinking more than a bit of his moonshine to help her get through the burial. She said when she came back from the cemetery, she sat down on the front porch steps and wondered what she was going to do. She figured she had enough food to last her a week but only enough hay to last the horses a couple more days and no money to buy any more. I guess she was ready to give up, auction off the horses, and let the farm go back to the bank.

"That's when Jess rode onto the property, took her in hand, and told her she couldn't give up, that she had too much to lose. He offered to help her pull it all together if she'd get off her butt and make him some supper." Nealy couldn't help but break into a smile. "Jess never struck me as being a knight in shining armor, but that's exactly what he was. Maud said he wasn't the music-and-roses type, but he made up for it in other ways.

"To think that Blue Diamond Farms is what it is today because of that chance meeting." She paused a moment before adding, "It kind of reminds me of that night when I was sitting on the fence and you drove up asking if this was Blue Diamond Farms."

Hunt's eyebrows shot up to his hairline.

His reaction amused her. "Now don't be jumping to conclusions. I'm not suggesting that you're my knight in shining armor, and I'm certainly not down-and-out. It's just that I was feeling a little overwhelmed with all the responsibility, and then you came along and things eased up a bit."

"Glad I could help." His eyes brightened with pleasure. "Are you still feeling overwhelmed?"

Nealy chuckled. "Oh, yeah. While Maud and Jess were alive, the workers and I got along just fine. Now they resent me. I can't say I blame them, but it's not like I asked to inherit Blue Diamond Farms. I didn't. All I ever wanted was a home for Emmie and me. That's all, I swear," she said, crossing her heart. "Sometimes I wish they hadn't left it to me but maybe just provided for me and Emmie to stay on here. But then other times I think they may have known what they were doing after all. Nobody loves this place more than I do. Nobody cares more

about its future than I do. It isn't just a moneymaking Thoroughbred farm to me, it's a home.

"I want to believe I can handle the trouble I know is coming.
Maud and Jess had faith in me. I refuse to betray that faith. So,"
she said, dusting her hands together, "are you all set to leave in
the morning?"

"I'm packed. The car is gassed. But am I all set to leave? Physically yes, mentally no."

"Do you think that old car of yours will make it?"

"Maybe. Maybe not. If it doesn't, I might have to hitchhike.
I've done it before. Don't tell me that's worry I see on your face.
For me?" He pretended to be aghast.

Nealy rearranged her expression. She loved this gentle spar-
ring as much as he did. "Since you're going to be working here
come May, why don't you take one of the trucks? They were all
serviced right before the holidays. You're on the payroll, so that
means as far as our insurance goes, you can drive any of the vehicles."

He shook his head. "That would start more than a few
tongues wagging that you're showing favoritism."

Nealy thought a moment. "In that case, I insist. Besides, I
don't want your father worrying himself sick over you driving
that rusty clunker."

"Dad doesn't worry about things like that. He knows I know
how to survive. I was a Boy Scout and then an Eagle Scout. Got
all the knots to prove it and the badges, too."

"Then it's settled," she said, clapping her hands. "Take the
black Ford Ranger."

He grinned as he got up off the couch. "You're a persuasive
woman, Nealy Diamond." He walked to the front door, then
stopped before turning back toward her. "Nealy."

She came toward him, her legs wobbly as a new colt's. "Yes."

"I . . . just . . . what I wanted to say is . . ."

"Yes?" She hoped she didn't sound too anxious.

"You know, to say thanks. Dad couldn't believe your offer.
Hell, I can hardly believe it myself. I guess I want to know why.
Did I charm you? Did I say the right thing? What? Did you feel
sorry for me?"

Nealy's lips split into a grin. She liked this humble side of him. "None of the above. Blue Diamond Farms needs some more new blood besides me. You're Danny's son, and you said yourself you love it here. I know how that feels. Trust me, Maud and Jess would approve."

"Then I guess I'll say good-bye now. See you in May."

"Good-bye, Hunt. Drive safely."

He took a step forward then stopped again. "Nealy?"

"Yes," she responded with a smile in her voice.

"If you don't mind, I'd like to kiss you good-bye."

Instinct told her if he kissed her, she'd never let him go. "Nah," she laughed. "I hate good-bye kisses. When you come back, you can kiss me hello."

"Yeah, that's good," he said, flustered. "Uh-huh, hello is better than good-bye anyway. You're probably right. Yeah, yeah. It's doable."

He looked so disappointed that she threw her arms around him and pulled him toward her. "I think maybe I'll make an exception this time," she said, pressing her mouth to his. When he backed away, she grinned, and said, "The keys are in the truck. See you in May."

Back inside the house, with the door closed and locked behind her, Nealy leaned against the wall and slowly sank to the floor. Her heart thudded inside her chest, and her stomach felt fluttery. She wondered if she'd just done a stupid thing, but if something felt good and right, how could it be stupid?

Delighted with herself, she rolled across the foyer floor, grinning from ear to ear, until she saw Carmela standing above her.

"Is there a reason why you're rolling around on the floor, Nealy? Isn't it clean enough for you?" She reached down to grasp Nealy's hand to pull her to her feet.

"You know what, Carmela? I just kissed Hunter Clay. I kissed him, not the other way around."

The housekeeper pursed her lips, the topknot on her head jiggling with suppressed laughter. "Is that a fact?"

"Yes. And it was great, too. He tasted kind of minty, like maybe he'd just brushed his teeth, and he smelled good, like new leather."

"Imagine that."

"You're making fun of me, aren't you?" Before Carmela could answer, Nealy went on. "That's okay. Go ahead and laugh if that's what you want. I don't care. I enjoyed it. I mean I *really* enjoyed it." She twirled around and headed for the stairs. "Guess I'll go check on the kids."

"Wait a minute, Nealy. Before you fall head over heels there's something I want to say. I know it's none of my business but . . ." Carmela sighed. "I guess I just have to spit it out. I don't want to see you break that boy's heart. I've known him since he was a little boy, and he's a fine person. Maud and Jess were mighty sweet on him. They even paid half his way to send him to college and law school. It's a fine thing you did, offering him the job as farm manager. He'll do a good job because he loves this farm and the horses. But what I'm telling you is that you can't mix business with pleasure. You best be remembering that."

Nealy felt the fine hairs on the back of her neck start to ruffle. "All I did was kiss him! I'm not stupid, Carmela. Who said anything about breaking his heart?"

"Yes, I know, but when people fall in love they sometimes do stupid things," the housekeeper mumbled as she straightened the throw rug with her foot.

Nealy climbed two steps, then turned and leaned on the banister. "I'm not saying I'm going to do anything foolish or stupid, but why was it okay for Maud to fall for Jess and it's not okay for me to fall for Hunt? Just answer me that."

"Times were different. You have more at stake than Maud ever did. You have a highly successful Thoroughbred farm, a daughter, and now Buddy. You don't want to be doing anything that will fall back on those children."

Nealy refused to make the connection. "My God, it was just a kiss. I'm sorry I mentioned it. And I'm sorry I rolled on the foyer floor. I'm goddamn sorry about everything, okay?" she exploded. "Good night, Carmela."

Carmela returned to the kitchen, reached for the cup of coffee she was never without, and went out to the back porch. The moment she took a deep breath of the cold night air she spotted Danny Clay headed her way from the barns.

"Is Hunter still here?" he asked.

Carmela shook her head. "He left a few minutes ago, a very happy man I imagine."

"Yeah, he's all wound up about finishing school, passing the bar, then coming back here to work."

"That's not what I meant. Nealy kissed him. Just after he left, I found her rolling around on the floor having herself a grand old time."

"Jesus God!"

"It's just like Maud and Jess all over again. It's history repeating itself, Danny."

"It's not a bad thing, Carmela."

"It's too soon, though. Much too soon."

"Well, there's nothing either you or I can do about it, so there's no sense worrying. What will be will be."

At three months old, Flyby had already surpassed Nealy's expectations. He was a bright-looking chestnut colt with a distinct blaze and one white stocking. His conformation was nearly perfect, and his pedigree was as good as it got. But would he prove to be a runner? Only time would tell.

Since his birth he had been housed with his dam and his sire in the new barn. Nealy had decided not to test her "family" theory on any other horses until things settled down around the farm. She assigned Danny and two other loyal grooms to take care of her little horse family, allowing no one else near the barn. What the others didn't see, they couldn't talk about.

It was Emmie's job to take Flyby on long daily walks around the farm. It was important that he get used to being haltered and led. Little Lady and Stardancer watched their offspring from their individual stalls. Buddy was enlisted to act as farrier and put a file to Flyby's little hooves, getting the colt used to lifting up his feet and feeling the tickle.

Once the daily training was done, Emmie and Buddy took Little Lady and Flyby out to one of the paddocks to exercise and graze while Nealy took Stardancer running around the track. It was almost a criminal shame that Stardancer had never had a chance to race and all because of one mistake and a basketful of misunderstandings. The stallion was too old now to run for the roses or any other race. The Kentucky Derby was for three-year-olds. Generally, horses didn't race at all after they turned four.

If only she could turn back the clock, she knew in her gut Stardancer could have run the Derby, maybe even won it. Out on the track, when she gave him his head, he could still outrun most of the two-year-olds breezing with him.

Nealy threw her hands in the air in disgust. "I hate this! I hate this, Carmela! Help me here!"

The housekeeper jammed her hands onto her ample hips. "I have no idea why you are so stubborn. I told you a year ago to hire someone to help out here in the office. It would make your life so much easier. You could free up three or four hours a day to do other things. It isn't like you can't afford it. Just tell me why?"

Nealy lowered her head in frustration. "Because . . . because I told Maud I could handle it. I have. I am. It just takes so damn much time."

"Probably the reason it takes so much time is because you hate it so much. I think you're your own worst enemy."

"You're right. I'm going to call an agency right now, then I'm also going to place an ad in the *Leader*. When are you leaving to visit your sister?"

"Right now she's busy with all her church activities. She doesn't sound like she cares if I visit or not. Maybe I won't go at all. Don't much care for Seattle. Too cold and rainy for me even in the summer. Are you upset that I haven't gone?"

"No, of course not. I guess that a plane ticket wasn't such a good Christmas present after all. I'm sorry, Carmela. Turn the ticket in if you like. It won't hurt my feelings."

"You would all starve to death if I left. Those young ones are always eating. I had a whole plate of fried chicken in the refrigerator yesterday, and today it's all gone. Those kids ate it last night."

"I *can* cook, Carmela, believe it or not. I don't think we'd starve to death in two weeks."

The elderly housekeeper laughed, then waved Nealy away. "You better make your phone calls. You might make the paper's deadline if you call now. Split pea soup for lunch."

"Sounds good. I'll eat later."

"You always say that," Carmela sniffed. "It's no wonder

you're such a puny little thing, all skin and bones like those poor undernourished jockeys. By the way, I was wondering if you wanted me to clean up Jack Carney's quarters and fancy it up a bit for when Hunter gets here?"

"Why would he want to stay there when he can stay with his father? Danny has plenty of room."

"A man needs his privacy. Two grown men living together isn't going to work. One wants to go to bed early, the other doesn't. One wants to listen to the radio, one doesn't."

"All right, I get the point. But you better check with Danny to see what he thinks first."

"I'll do that," the housekeeper said happily as she exited the small office.

The woman from the agency arrived two days later in a sleek silver Corvette that spit gravel behind it as it roared up the driveway. The car skidded to a stop by the front steps leading up to the house. Her name was Arabella Consuela Magdalena Smith. Carmela announced her arrival in a breathless voice.

Nealy raised her head and immediately jumped to her feet, her eyes wide in disbelief. "Uh . . . hello . . . Miss Smith." She was a vision. Of what, Nealy wasn't sure.

"Hi, doll!" Arabella said flippantly. "The agency sent me. Here's my résumé and my references." She glanced around. Her eyes were the color of the Mediterranean, and they sparkled and glistened. "Boy, this sure is a small office. Don't you have a bigger one? When things get slow, I like to turn on the radio and dance. With the door closed, of course," she said, smiling to show exquisite pearly white teeth.

"I'm afraid this is all we have at the moment, Miss Smith." Who was this woman?

"Call me Smitty. Everyone else does. I guess it will have to do if this is all you have. My hours are nine to five. Three weeks' vacation, twelve sick days, and no weekends. I'm a hard worker. I expect a bonus at Christmastime. Ten percent of my salary. That's fair. I don't negotiate. Simply don't believe in it. My work speaks for itself. I have initiative, and I use it."

Carmela made a strangled sound in her throat. Nealy risked a glance in the housekeeper's direction but immediately returned to the voluptuous Arabella Consuela Magdalena Smith. Nealy was out of her depth, and she knew it. She'd never hired anyone before. Hunt didn't qualify since she'd offered him a job when he hadn't been seeking one. Was it possible the agency had told the woman the job was hers?

Nealy eyed the woman in front of her, waiting for her gut instinct to kick in. She was tall, perhaps five-foot-nine or -ten. Proportioned perfectly, with the longest, shapeliest legs Nealy had ever seen outside of a horse. Her hair was thick and black, and it went in all directions. *A well-preserved forty if she's a day,* she thought. Tawny skin, very little makeup, beautiful eyes, with thick, lustrous lashes. Maud would have called them bedroom eyes. She almost said, let me see your teeth again to see if they were real, but then the woman smiled and she knew they were real because one of them was slightly crooked.

"You're trying to figure me out, right? Portuguese with a splash of Spanish and Irish. My father was a dentist." She smiled again to show off her father's handiwork. Nealy blinked, then nodded nervously.

"Do you . . . always . . . what I mean is do you normally dress this way or is this your . . . interview outfit?" *My God, did I just ask that?*

"I always try to dress my best. This is pretty much the way I go to work. I wear a lot of black, slimming, if you know what I mean. If you think this is too conservative, I can find other things to wear."

Nealy eyed the woman's outfit. She was wearing a skintight *rubber* suit that was in actuality buttery-soft leather, dark stockings, and high-heeled boots that went up to mid-calf. A handbag the size of an overnight travel bag hung from her shoulders.

"We're pretty informal around here," Nealy said. "You can wear jeans and shirts if you like." Damned if that didn't sound like the job was a done deal. She heard Carmela croak with surprise. "Do you know anything about managing an office?"

"Just call me the paperwork queen. I can type 120 words a minute or as fast as you can talk, and I'm a filing whiz. I can do payroll, payroll taxes, monthlies, quarterlies, and annual reports. I can even do your taxes."

Nealy's mouth dropped open. After a moment, she asked, "Do you like horses?"

"Doll, I love horses. That's how I got that fancy set of wheels out there. I win all the time because I don't allow myself to get in over my head. But if you mean do I *like* horses as in do I like to be around them, yes, as long as they don't get too close. I got bit in the butt once as a kid and haven't forgotten the pain and the humiliation." She glanced around the room again. "I wish this office was bigger. Do those windows open? Can't you knock out a wall or something?" she said breezily.

Nealy didn't see where the problem was. She liked cozy little places. "Well . . . I . . . I guess I could look into it." Nealy glanced over at Carmela, then back at Miss Smith. "Why don't you go into the kitchen with Carmela and have some coffee while I go through your résumé and check your references."

Miss Smith gave Carmela a thorough once-over. "I'll take it with a shot of bourbon just the way Maud used to take hers. You aren't a true Kentuckian if you don't drink bourbon."

Nealy's eyelashes flew up in surprise. "You knew Maud?"

"Sure did. Knew Jess, too. I was sorry to hear they passed on. Nice people. Good people. I used to sit in their box at Derby time. Course I was younger then. My daddy was Maud and Jess's dentist. Years ago, Maud used to play poker with my mama."

Nealy closed the folder. "You're hired," she said, feeling as if a huge burden had been lifted from her shoulders. "Now, let's discuss your salary. Carmela, fetch Miss . . . Smitty some coffee, please. The way Maud drank it."

An hour later when the Corvette roared back down the driveway, Carmela snapped, "I can't believe you hired that . . . that . . . *floozie.*"

"Don't judge a book by its cover, Carmela. Her résumé is impressive and her references impeccable. And it sounds to me like Maud and Jess liked her. That's enough for me."

"If her references are so good, why is she looking for a job, huh?" Carmela raised an arthritic finger and shook it at Nealy. "Mark my words. There's going to be trouble with that one."

"I'll deal with it if it happens. If you don't like her, stay out of her way. You certainly are cranky today, Carmela."

Carmela didn't bother to reply but marched out of the room, her shoulders stiff, the empty coffee mug in her hand.

11

Nealy's smile was as big as all outdoors as she leaned against the paddock's white, board fence. Two days ago she'd stirred things up all over again by making another unorthodox decision to put Flyby, Little Lady, and Stardancer in adjoining paddocks. She knew that with almost any other stallion she would be taking a huge risk, but not with Dancer. More often than not, a stallion would go after a colt with the intention to kill it, but Dancer had proved to be that rare exception. He wasn't the least bit aggressive. That trait alone gave her all the confidence she needed to test and prove her theory that the little family could bond together. Now the threesome grazed and exercised in sight of each other.

Nealy loved watching the colt and his dam, loved being near Dancer in the adjoining paddock. She remembered how the colt had first wobbled up on his skinny legs, and now he was dancing in the meadow. At times it seemed like he could float like a butterfly. He was curious and playful, but after his frolicking he always returned to his mother's side, where it was safe. "You want out there, don't you, big boy?" Nealy whispered as she craned her head backward so the stallion could hear her. She turned around and slipped him a wintergreen mint. He snorted his thanks. "There are at least three dozen pairs of eyes watching us today, and I can feel every one of them on my back. This whole place is in an uproar since I got my trainer's license. I told Danny to spread the word earlier. There isn't one person here who thinks I'm capable of training your son for the Derby and going on to a Triple Crown. Well, maybe that isn't exactly true. Hunt and Smitty think I'm capable. And I suspect it causes some friction between Danny and his son. I don't think Danny likes it that his son is his immediate boss. You're listening to me, aren't you?" Nealy grinned as the stallion turned his head slightly, his ear tuned to her every word. He twitched his lips to ask for another mint.

For long moments she sat looking out over the paddocks thinking about how far she'd come and how far she still had to go. "It's a beautiful May day. Three more days till Derby Day. The year after next, when Flyby is two, he's going to start winning races," she said, tapping her finger against Dancer's forehead. "Maybe next year I'll go to the Derby. We'll have to see how it goes. This whole damn industry is talking about us. That means you, too, Dancer. They said what we did was unorthodox, dangerous, and a whole bunch of other stuff. We have Dr. Edwin Franklin and Jack Carney to thank for that." Nealy turned until she was eye level with the stallion. She caressed his head, his eyes, his ears. "Just remember this, I know what you're going to do before you do it. Okay, now, I'm going to open the gate. Go see your son, Dancer."

Nealy's eyes filled as the stallion trotted over to the mare and colt. He whickered playfully as his big head nudged Flyby. Little Lady looked on, but she stood at attention. Satisfied that her offspring was all right, she trotted over to the fence where Nealy was standing and waited patiently for her wintergreen mint. It was Emmie who had started the tradition of sharing her candies with the horses, and now they expected it. Dancer even knew which pocket she kept the candies in. If she was too slow in handing out the treats, he would nose her until she reached into her shirt pocket and handed it over. "And they said it couldn't be done," she whispered to the mare. "There's no stronger bond between animals than an offspring. I know Dancer will never hurt you or the colt. I know this. Even if something spooks him, he won't harm either of you. That baby of yours does like to frolic. Go on, mama, join in," Nealy whispered.

Nealy leaned back against the fencing, her elbows hooked over the sides as she watched the horses frolic in the pasture.

"I never thought this could be done," Hunt said, hopping over the fence. "I'm seeing it, but I'm still having a hard time accepting it."

"Wait until he's old enough to go through his paces. Just a few more months. Dancer and Little Lady will be right there with him. It's going to work. A while back," Nealy said, "I read that during the sixties, Forli, an Argentinian stud had accidentally been put in the same paddock with Sir Gaylord, Secretariat's half brother. When the groom discovered the error, he panicked and thought he was going to have a stallion fight on his hands. Instead, he found Sir Gaylord standing quietly and looking bemused. It seems Forli had decided to meander into the shade and had rolled up at Sir Gaylord's feet to go to sleep. So you see, there are exceptions to every rule. I got my trainer's license, Hunt."

"That's great, Nealy. Dad's nose is a little out of joint, but he'll get over it. He might not show it, but he does respect you. Are you taking in the Derby this weekend?"

"No. It's not my time yet. Are you going?"

"Nope. My boss keeps me hopping. No time. Smitty said she's going. She's putting down some serious money on a horse called Windstar and a few others. Windstar has been trained by Cal Metzer out of SunStar Farms in Virginia."

"Is that right?" Nealy felt her heart skip a beat.

"Yep. Carmela gave Smitty a hundred bucks to bet on him for her."

"Really. The odds are nine to one on Windstar. He doesn't have a chance at the roses. The trainer is too rigid, and so is the owner. You better tell her to change her bet."

Hunt blinked at Nealy's blunt, flat tone. "Okay. I've been out of the loop too long to know what the competition is. So, tell me, how is Smitty working out?"

"Like a dream, Hunt. She's everything she said she was. She's fast, thorough, efficient, neat, and she runs a tight ship. She doesn't imbibe till four o'clock. What she does off the clock is not my business. She runs these tallies daily. I know what every stable in the area is doing and when they're doing it. She even did the paperwork for my license. Carmela hates her for some reason I can't figure out. She's witty, she's charming, she's incredibly personable. She told me a rumor today that the Owens farm has been sold. I dread having to tell Buddy. Supposedly the new owners are recruiting and paying better than we do. She said the scuttlebutt is Jack Carney is going to be lord on high, and Wylie will be right there with him. Some big-time New York stockbroker fancies himself a gentleman horse breeder. All kinds of money. They're all going to Keeneland in July and snapping up every horse in sight."

"Smitty told you all this?"

"Early this morning. By the close of the day it will be a fact. So far she's never been wrong."

"Sometimes she reminds me of my mother. I think it's the hair. I like her. She's a bit like you, Nealy. She says what she thinks and gets right there in your face to say it. Just out of curiosity, if it comes down to it, where *are* you going to get these women who *might* be working here?"

Nealy's eyes narrowed. "Does it matter? Women are not prairie flowers. So get that idea right out of your head. Why do you men think we can't do what you do? Women are born nurturers. Because your minds are closed, that's why," Nealy said, kicking out at the fence. "I damn well hate that attitude. I won't tolerate it either. But to answer your questions, Smitty is on top of it if it should come to that."

"I guess it's your intention, then, to bend the rules and if necessary, break them. Uh-oh, what have we here?"

Nealy burst out laughing. "Charlie, what are you doing here? How'd you get out of the house?" She bent down to pick up Emmie's new pup, a seven-pound Yorkshire terrier named Charlemagne. Charlie for short. He wiggled loose and ran across the paddock. He ran straight for Flyby and started to bark. The colt reared back while his mother pawed the ground. Dancer watched the dog's activities but didn't move. And then they were off, Charlie racing forward and backward as he tried to catch Flyby's tail.

"Not a good idea, Nealy," Hunt grunted.

"Who says? You don't see Dancer or Little Lady getting bent out of shape, do you? Flyby now has a friend, not an equine friend, and that's okay. It's okay for him to play, Hunt. Look, it's just like it is with people—it's all about family, closeness, warmth, nurturing. Yes, it's a business, but these animals are flesh and blood. They have feelings, they have affection, they try to please us. What's the problem? I admit I don't know everything, but I damn well know what feels right."

"But Nealy . . ."

Nealy put her finger against her lips. "I don't want to hear 'but Nealy' anything. This feels right." She burst out laughing when she saw Charlie get in the pounce position and shoot toward Flyby. The colt darted away from him, jumping like a fawn through the grass, his little tail sticking up in the air like a flag.

Nealy burst out laughing as she watched Charlie run in circles in front of Flyby. This was a whole new experience for Flyby, and she wanted it to be a good one. Charlie wagged his tail. Flyby twitched his.

Stardancer and Little Lady stood back, watching.

Suddenly, Charlie bolted and ran through Flyby's legs toward the opposite end of the paddock. The little colt tossed his head and took out after him, kicking up his heels.

"My God, they're *playing*," she whispered. "They're actually playing, and mama and papa are okay with it."

The colt stopped and bent his head for a closer look at his excited playmate. Satisfied, he was off again, Charlie behind him.

Nealy sprinted to the center of the paddock, where she scooped Charlie up into her arms. She nuzzled him before she held him out to the colt. Little Lady crowded next to her. She gave the Yorkie a gentle pinch on his tail to make him bark and at the same time breathe into the colt's nostrils. "Good, now you have his scent. Time for you to go back to the house, Charlie. We need to have a little talk with Emmie about how you escaped."

She was still giggling when she escorted Dancer back to his own paddock. Out of the corner of her eye she could see Hunt push his baseball cap back on his head, and then scratch it. She knew he was dumbfounded. She continued to giggle and smile as Charlie yapped and yipped inside her shirt.

It was seven o'clock when Nealy settled her barn family for the night. It was quiet, too quiet for this time of night. Her gaze swept through the barn and the adjoining ones. There was no sound of any kind to be heard. Even the horses were quiet. She wondered where Hunt was. Probably studying for the bar. Something was going on. She could sense it, feel it in her bones.

She ran then, first to one barn and then the other. When she finally saw the angry mob, she pulled up short. They were gesturing, cursing, and stomping their feet. Hunt was out in front, trying to talk over the high-pitched angry voices, his father at his side. Should she interfere? Hunt was the farm manager and supervised the workers. As the owner, did she dare approach? What would Maud have done? She would have waded right in and stood next to Jess. Then again with Jess running things, something like this never would have happened.

She waited, knowing they could see her. She strained to hear what Hunt was saying, but she could hear only sound. If she couldn't hear him, how could the others know what he was saying?

It was Danny Clay who walked away to return with a double-barrel shotgun. He fired off a shot into the air and was rewarded with instant silence. "You have a spokesman, get him up front. Hunt speaks for Blue Diamond Farms. Now take it from there," he shouted.

Nealy kept her distance as she listened to the angry comments of her workers. *This place ain't the same since Maud died. 'Fore you know it, there will be curtains in the barns. Got nothin' against women, Maud was a hell of a woman. My pa and his pa worked for her pa. Thought I would be here till I died. These newfangled methods don't sit right. Can't go into town without someone jawin' about the craziness here. They're layin' down bets how soon we go into the ground. Them two young'uns spook us all. It ain't right. That damn stallion thinks he's a man.*

It went on and on until Nealy clapped her hands over her ears. Tears burned her eyes. She was back in Virginia listening to her father spew his venom.

Like hell! She sprinted off to the crowd.

"Pack your gear and get out! Now!" Nealy's arm snaked out to grab the shotgun from Danny Clay's hand. "You have twenty minutes. One minute longer, and you will be trespassing. There will be no severance pay, no vacation pay, and your health insurance will be canceled as of eight o'clock tomorrow morning. Get all your vehicles out of here and don't ever come back. You're traitors and backstabbers, and I don't want people like that working for me. Move! The clock is ticking."

Nealy gritted her teeth at the ugly comments. Hunt grabbed her when her knees started to buckle. "Do you have any idea of what you've done?" he said.

"Yeah, I fired them before they could quit. That's what Jess would have done. I'm not going to collapse over this. Maud said things always happen for a reason. I guess this is one of those things. Do you know how many are staying?"

"All Dad's people. About twenty-one or so. You're losing about sixty-five employees. I can work around the clock, but I'm not a magician. Neither are you, Nealy. The others can do double shifts, but they won't be able to keep it up. You're going to have to hire new people as soon as possible."

"I know that. You don't approve of what I did, do you?"

"There you go again trying to read my mind. Hell, I would have run them off ten minutes earlier if I knew Dad had a shotgun. You're right about something else, too. Jess would have done the same thing, and so would Maud. Dad knows that. That's why he and the others are still here. The old-timers don't take kindly to new ways or to young blood. You and I are the young blood in case you haven't noticed. Go back to the house and explain what happened. Carmela rang your dinner bell a half hour ago. We can handle things here for tonight. I'll see you in the morning. Like you said, four o'clock rolls around real quick. Get a good night's sleep."

"Five o'clock," Nealy said wearily.

"Four o'clock," Hunt said.

"Okay, four it is. What's this going to do to your studying routine?"

"Not to worry, I'll ace it. Graduated second in my class."

"Smart-ass."

"You should know," Hunt shot back.

When she got near the house, she was stunned to see Smitty's Corvette still parked out front. She frowned. "Now what?" she muttered.

She was even more surprised to see Smitty in the kitchen. The tension was so thick in there that Nealy almost gasped aloud. Charlie leaped out of Emmie's arms and hopped into Smitty's lap and immediately tried to chew at the dangling silver bracelets hanging off her arms. The tension eased a bit with the dog's antics.

"What's wrong, Smitty? Why are you still here? Kids, go wash up for dinner."

"This," Smitty said, holding up a copy of the *Lexington Herald-Leader*. "They gave you the front page, doll. Actually, they gave you the *entire* front page. They're taking shots at you. I told you it would happen, but I thought they would at least be fair about it. They're pissing me off now."

Nealy washed her hands in the kitchen sink. "That paper is the least of my problems. I just fired sixty-five people. Maybe more. I ran them off. Maud and Jess would have done the same thing. It's this *woman* thing. It's always this woman thing, and I'm getting sick and tired of it. How archaic can you get? Don't they understand it's the horses that count, it's the horses that are going to suffer? They were going to walk anyway. I just beat them to the punch. Danny Clay, Hunt, and Danny's crew are the only ones staying on. I have to find some help. We'll be okay for a few days, but we can't work twenty-four hours a day, seven days a week. I'm going to keep Emmie and Buddy out of school; both of them are so far ahead in their classes it won't make much difference. They can walk the mares, clean stalls, and wash them down."

Smitty uncrossed one long leg, stared at the tip of her shoe, then wiggled it seductively under Carmela's nose. "This couldn't have happened at a worse time, sweetie. Do I need to remind you this is Derby weekend? You know what it's like on a Derby weekend. It's worse than Mardi Gras. What do you expect me to do?"

"Find me some help. In the meantime, you and Carmela are going to have to pitch in down at the barns."

"No, no, no, this girl does not walk around in horse shit. These shoes are made for hardwood floors and carpeting. No, no, no."

"Yes, yes, yes. How can you sit there in your designer clothes and tell me no, Smitty, when the whole damn state of Kentucky is out to get me because I'm a woman? A woman who just happens to own a Thoroughbred horse farm. You're a woman, for God's sake. You aren't going to let them get away with it, are you?"

Nealy hoped her appeal on behalf of womanhood would spur the office manager to help. It was then that Nealy did something that she almost never did . . . she lit up a cigarette in the house.

"No, I'm not," Smitty said. "I'll take one of your cigarettes if you don't mind, honey. Carmela, could I have another splash of bourbon, and some ice would go real good."

"Why don't you just get up on those fancy shoes and get it yourself? The meat loaf is about dried out, Nealy."

"So I'll put ketchup on it. Do you know anyone, Carmela?"

"A couple of cousins. I'll call them. I'll be glad to help out, Nealy. Just tell me what you want me to do. I won't be cooking any six-course dinners if I'm working the barns. Everything will be on the fly."

"Sandwiches are good. So are hard-boiled eggs. We aren't going to starve. The horses come first. Smitty?"

Nealy leaned against the kitchen sink sipping at a cup of coffee Carmela shoved into her hands. Smitty would be worthless or next to worthless working with the horses. How could someone who wore stiletto heels, gallons of perfume, and skintight clothes muck a stall? Today Smitty was attired in a skintight zebra-print jumpsuit that zipped up the front. A wide silver belt around her waist jangled when she walked. Black snakeskin shoes with skinny heels added the finishing touches. Nealy sighed wearily as she watched her newest employee spill bourbon into her glass.

"If I agree to your cockamamie idea, will you knock out the wall?"

"Yes."

"And get me one of those little bar refrigerators so I don't have to keep coming in here and bothering Saint Carmela?"

"Yes."

"Since you're being so agreeable, how about an easy chair with a good reading lamp."

"I'll do better than that. I'll give you the guesthouse to live in until things get back to normal. What do you say to that?"

Smitty studied her bright red fingernails as if they held all the answers. "Okay, that sounds good. Short-term only."

"Agreed. Then let's eat. We can plan strategy when we're finished."

Four o'clock in the morning. Three days after the Run for the Roses, Nealy struggled to get out of bed. While her mind was willing, her body protested every step of the way to the shower. She turned on the cold tap and danced under the needle-sharp spray until she was wide-awake. She then turned on the hot water until she thought her skin would pop from her body. It was agony to pull on her jeans and boots, even more agonizing as she struggled to pull on a sweatshirt she would shed by mid-morning.

Breakfast was hard-boiled eggs that were cooked the night before, bananas, and a huge cup of coffee.

Carmela sat down at the kitchen table. She looked like death warmed over. "I've never been this tired in my life, Nealy. In case you haven't noticed, I'm an old woman. I can't keep up this pace any longer. When do you think you're going to be able to get some help?" she demanded.

"We're doing everything possible," Nealy said, her mouth full of banana. "Now that Derby weekend is over, people might be looking at the help-wanted ads. Smitty is working on it. She does have a way of getting things done. I wish you'd be a little kinder to her, Carmela. She's a good worker, and I don't want to lose her. Actually, Carmela that's not a wish but an order."

"My friend's daughter went to high school with her. She's a tramp, Nealy. A loose woman. She's been married a couple of times, both times she got handsome settlements. It was in the papers. People talk. She doesn't have to work. She's rich, and she's broken up several marriages. She's always the *other woman*," Carmela said spitefully.

"Is that what this is all about? Get over it, Carmela. Life goes on. The past is over. Today is what counts. We can't depend on tomorrow because tomorrow never gets here. I don't give two shits about Smitty's personal life. All I care is what she does here at the farm. As far as all that other stuff goes, maybe you should come right out and ask her to tell you about her life. I'll bet her version is totally different from the one you just gave me. Don't you get it, there are two sides to everything? If there is one thing I don't need right now, it's friction, and you should never repeat gossip."

Nealy turned to fill her coffee cup. She saw Smitty standing outside the kitchen screen door, tears in her eyes. "Coffee's ready," she called. "You heard, didn't you?"

"It was hard not to hear. Yes, I was married twice. My first husband died way too early of a heart attack. He had a handsome insurance policy. My second husband had a penchant for young girls. As you know, he was also a pillar of the community. I was willing to tell anyone who would listen what a lowlife he was. Unfortunately, the man had more money than I, and, as I said, a sterling reputation. My attorneys said no one would believe me, so I kept quiet. That's why my divorce settlement was so outrageously high. I did not break up anyone's marriage. I did date one man who had a wife who lived up north. He neglected to mention that when I met him. When I found out, I showed him the road. I am not nor have I ever been the other woman in anything. I am who I am. If you think poorly of me, that's your problem, not mine, Carmela. Then again maybe if you'd fix yourself up a little, I might be jealous of you. You are kind of dowdy. You could use some highlights in your hair. You need to pluck those eyebrows, too. They look like a bush over your face. Get yourself one of those Wonder Bras and some nail polish."

"Enough!" Nealy roared.

"Look, doll, you asked. I came to work just the way I was supposed to. You two were talking about me like I was some *floozie*. What do you expect? I'm out there busting my ass for you because we're all women, and I don't want to let you down. I'd appreciate a little respect."

"You have mine, Smitty. Any luck?"

"Hell yes, I've had luck. I spent the entire night combing this town from one end to the other. I lucked out with two old codgers that were hotwalkers who kept up their licenses. They both knew Maud and Jess. I sent them down to the barn. I got us some college kids for routine stuff, and I snared three guys from the Boudreau Farms. Nice guys, hard workers. They have families, and they don't screw around. Fully licensed."

"That's it? Smitty, we need more help. No one is answering the ad. What's that van doing out there? Where's your Corvette?"

"It's like this, sweetie. I recruited from the Night Gallery. I got you some women who are willing to give this a shot. You're going to be paying them very well, and when you get a full working crew you will be giving them a bonus. A substantial bonus. I agreed to all this in your name."

"What's the Night Gallery?"

"A brothel. The girls are ladies of the night."

Nealy choked on the coffee in her mouth. Carmela pretended to swoon.

"Will you two get off it. Those girls know what hard work is. This will be a piece of cake for them. They're tough. They don't whine, and they don't cry. Maybe if we're lucky we can get them on their feet and off their backs. You keep saying all you want is a day's work for a day's pay. Well, doll, this is your chance to put up or shut up. I handpicked these girls for you. I used to do Miz Jones's books for her. Lots of book work with a brothel. She gives her girls pension plans and health insurance. That makes it all as good as legal as far as I'm concerned. What's it going to be?"

Nealy cleared her throat. "Take them down to the barns. Have Danny show them what to do. I wouldn't mention, unless you have to of course, what they did . . . do for a living."

Smitty burst into laughter, "Are you kidding? Danny and the others are on a first-name basis with most of them."

"Oh."

"Uh-huh," Smitty grinned. "You can bring me down some coffee. Where do you want me to park this van?"

"It's fine where it is. I'll bring the coffee. I have to wake Emmie and Buddy, then I'll be down."

"I can't believe you're giving the go-ahead to this," Carmela challenged, her face dark with anger.

"Look, Carmela. In this world you do what you have to do. Like I told you before, I don't give a good rat's ass what Smitty did before she got here, and I don't give a good rat's ass what those women in the van did . . . do. I am really starting to care about your pissy attitude. I don't like it one bit. Prostitution is the oldest profession in the world. I can't change that. Maybe all of the women or some of them will want to find another way to earn a living. If I can help in doing that, fine. If I can't, that's fine, too. Now, it's time to paste a smile on your face and get your ass down to the barn and start giving me your day's work. I'm not going to go around on the matter with you again. We have a situation here, and we're doing the best we can under the circumstances. And, last but not least, I expect you to apologize to Smitty."

"Maybe I should just quit," Carmela muttered.

"Maybe you should. They probably need a cook over at the Owens farm. I'll give you a good reference."

Carmela burst into tears as she ran from the kitchen. Nealy threw her hands in the air as she stomped her way to the second floor. It was barely four-thirty in the morning, and already she was looking forward to evening, when she could fall into bed.

12

~

The Keeneland Select Yearling Sale in Lexington was not your ordinary horse sale because ordinary horses weren't sold at Keeneland, just the best of the best. Blue Diamond Farms was sending three colts this year, all full pedigrees laced with champions. From the time of their arrival until the day of the sale, the yearlings would be inspected by dozens of prospective buyers, who would check them closely to make sure they were sound and in good health.

"Yo, Nealy! Today's the big day, right?" Hunt shouted from the doorway of the barn.

Nealy had overseen loading the three yearlings into the horse van. Charlie had supervised. "Yep," she said, glancing around. "I'm almost finished here. Just some tack to put away."

"Smitty is going with me and Dad in the truck. She said she's always wanted to attend one of the auctions." Hunt took off his hat and wiped the sweat from his forehead with the sleeve of his shirt. "Damn it's hot today. I'll be glad to get going so I can turn on the air-conditioning."

Nealy squinted against the sun as she looked at him. "I hope everything goes all right. I have to admit I'm a little nervous."

"I wouldn't worry. We're sending three of the best yearlings this farm has ever produced. Three young princes whose bloodlines go back to the kings of Thoroughbred horse racing. I'm thinking they ought to bring in close to two-and-a-half million dollars."

Nealy hadn't been thinking quite that high, but she was glad Hunt was. "Smitty tells me Mr. Goldstein is going to be bidding on all three of our colts. I have to tell you, it makes me damn mad that not only did he buy Buddy's parents' farm, he hired all the employees I fired, and now he wants all our horses. I keep asking myself what Maud would do, and I can't come up with an answer." She flung her hands out in frustration.

"Maybe that's because there is no answer. We go to the Keeneland sales to sell horses, Nealy. It shouldn't matter to you who buys them."

"Ordinarily it wouldn't. But in this case . . . the reason he wants *our* horses is because Jack Carney told him they were the best. And you know how I feel about Jack Carney." She made an ugly face to express her dislike.

"Yes, I know."

"It doesn't seem right to call the Owens farm the Goldstein farm," she said, using the toe of her boot to make a pattern in the dirt. "I can't get used to the name change. Smitty tells me Mr. Goldstein is a nice man and dedicated to getting the farm back on its feet and training champions. She also said his wife used to be a high-fashion model. Smitty knows everything about everybody. She's a virtual font of information." Nealy raised her eyes to find Hunt watching her. "Why are you looking at me like that? Is something wrong?"

Hunt blinked, caught off guard. "No, I was just . . . No. Sorry," he said. He cleared his throat. "Everything's going great. I signed on another dozen men, all licensed, family men who don't have any axes to grind and are comfortable working for a woman. It's a slow process, but we're building." He nodded his satisfaction. As Nealy started to secure the doors on the horse van, Hunt asked, "Have you been reading the papers lately?"

Once the latch was securely in place, Nealy gave Hunt her full attention. "No. Who has time to read newspapers? Certainly not me. What are they saying now? If it's something that's going to make me worry, don't even think about sharing it with me." When there was no immediate response, she tilted her head to stare up at him. "What?"

"You've become famous, or should I say infamous? In any case, you're big news. People want to know who you are, where you came from, that sort of thing."

Nealy shrugged. "So? What else?"

Hunt crossed his arms and stared at her. "I just want you to be prepared. Because you're successful, they'll try to tear you down. That's the way those newspaper people work. I wish to hell you'd gone to the Kentucky Derby. You could have put out some of the gossip fires. Not going to Keeneland is going to fan the flames. One reporter has already hinted that you might be hiding something."

"Yeah," she said, laughing. "I'm a secret chain-saw murderer. And at night I work at the Night Gallery. Be sure to pass all that on. And be sure to spell my name right," Nealy said, looking Hunt full in the eyes. She had told him once before that she didn't care what other people thought about her. She'd meant it then, and she meant it now.

He gave her a big smile that showed he approved, albeit reluctantly. "If you don't mind, I think I'd just as soon say nothing at all. They're just waiting for something to sink their teeth into, and I don't want to slip up and be the one to give it to them." He walked around the van and stowed his gear in one of the outside storage compartments.

Nealy picked Charlie up in her arms and was on her way back to the house when she had a thought. "You want some gossip to spread at Keeneland, Hunt?" she called from across the driveway. "Something that will make those reporters sit up and take notice?"

"Depends," he said as he hooked his thumbs under his belt in a nonchalant pose.

"Tell them I'm riding Flyby in the Derby two years from now."

Hunt's mouth dropped open. "You can't do that! You're a woman! You're the horse's trainer, not his jockey, Nealy."

"Who says I can't do that? And of course I'm a woman. I'm glad you noticed. But my gender has nothing at all to do with my ability to be a jockey. I'll go to the wall on that if I have to."

"But . . . You can't!"

Nealy could feel herself bridle with anger. "Don't you ever tell me what I can and can't do, Hunt. Just after I arrived here, Maud told me I could be whatever I wanted to be if I worked hard and if my heart was in the right place. I believed her. I still believe her. Flyby is my chance to fulfill my promise to Maud." She walked over to the colt and ran her hand across his withers.

"I don't know if he's Triple Crown material or not. It's simply too early to tell, but, by God, he *is* a Derby horse. He may be only five months old, but I'm telling you, he was born to run."

Hunt clenched his teeth. "I swear to God you are more ornery than Maud and Jess put together. Cranky, too. A real curmudgeon."

Nealy's hands flew to her hips. "Listen, Mr. Sunshine," she said, regarding him with amusement, "just do what you're paid to do and shut up about all the rest."

"Yes, sireee, ma'am," he said, saluting smartly. He walked toward her. "I guess it's out of the question to ask for a kiss?"

Nealy's eyes brightened with pleasure. "I never said that." She watched as Hunt tilted his head forward, eyes closed. At the last second, she stepped away and the kiss landed on Charlie's furry face. She howled in laughter and doubled over.

"I'll get you for that!" Hunt reached for Charlie and set him down on the ground. The little dog immediately grabbed his pant leg and tugged it, growling ferociously.

"Charlie!" Nealy scolded him before she bent over to pick him up. "Be good now." She set him on Flyby's back, where he dropped his head onto his paws and pretended to go to sleep.

Hunt scowled as he eyed the dog. "That," he said, "is highly unorthodox."

"According to you and everyone else around here, everything I do is unorthodox. Ask me if I care?" she challenged.

Smitty and Danny walked toward them.

"Let's hit it," Danny said as he stuffed his duffel bag into the van's storage compartment and got into the backseat.

Hunt climbed into the driver's seat and Smitty into the passenger seat.

"Have a good trip," Nealy said, waving as Hunt started up the engine.

Hunt turned his head and winked at her. "I'll deal with you when I get back."

"Promises. Promises," Nealy responded.

Nealy opened Flyby's stall and walked him inside, noticing that one of the grooms had already filled his feeder. While he ate, she sat down cross-legged in the straw and stared straight ahead of her, her mind racing. Could the reporters trace her background? Even if they did, and they published the information, would it hurt her? So what that she was an unwed mother? So what that she'd run away from home at seventeen? So what that she'd landed on Maud and Jess's driveway and they'd taken her in and adopted her and Emmie? So what?

She wondered what her father would do when he discovered her whereabouts. "There's nothing he can do," she said, talking to Flyby, who was munching his hay. "I'm well past the age of consent and my own woman now." She thought about her father, about how he'd treated her. Prior to getting pregnant, what had she done to deserve his hate? She thought about his bitter Derby defeat. Windstar had come in fifth. Pyne and Rhy were probably paying for the defeat. She almost felt sorry for them. Almost.

Once her brothers discovered she owned Blue Diamond Farms, would they come crawling to her to help them? They could forget that. And what would Emmie's father do? So many questions, and she couldn't begin to answer any of them.

She shivered as Smitty's advice rang in her ears. "Don't talk to the press. Ignore them. Stay out of the limelight. When you don't say anything, there is nothing for them to feed on." For that reason she no longer answered the phone herself but let Smitty pick it up and screen the calls. For that reason, too, she decided not to go to Keeneland.

Out of sight, and, hopefully, out of mind.

Nealy leaned forward and hugged her knees. "This is where I belong," she whispered to the colt standing in front of her. "I think I would die if I had to leave you and the others. Maud said God smiled on me when he gave me the feelings I have for all of you. She said I was special, but I don't know for sure what she meant by special. My feelings, my understanding, my hands?"

She cupped the colt's head in her hands and talked softly to him as she breathed into his nostrils.

It was the end of October, Halloween to be exact. The days were cool and brisk. As Nealy approached the barn, Flyby pawed the ground, snorted, then whinnied . . . his way of pleading for her to take him out of the stall.

Flyby was nine months old now and weighed 750 pounds, nearly the weight of a yearling. If he kept going, he would be every bit as big if not bigger than his sire, who stood 16.2 hands tall. Wherever Flyby was, Charlie was there, too. The two were inseparable. When Charlie had spent the night at the vet's after being neutered, Flyby refused to eat. He'd even refused the treats he dearly loved. A knot of fear formed in Nealy's stomach at the thought of what would happen to Flyby if something happened to Charlie. She prayed the little dog would have a long and happy life.

"So you want to run, do you?" she asked, rubbing Flyby's velvety muzzle. "Well, it just so happens you're going to get your chance. Today, when I take your father for a breeze, I'm going to take you, too." She had been waiting for this day for a long time. She knew that, once again, she would be doing something unorthodox, but she had long since stopped worrying about such things. There was no law that said a colt couldn't be breezed. As long as she took it easy and didn't strain him or tire him, everything would be fine.

Head high, tail arched, Flyby proudly pranced beside his sire out to the track. They were a unique pair, father and son.

Nealy took it slow, first walking Flyby around the track, then trotting him for a couple of furlongs. He didn't fight the lead but kept pace. Anyone watching him could see he was having a wonderful time.

"This is your future, Flyby," Nealy told him, as they passed the practice starting gate. "Starting right now you're on your way to being the number one Thoroughbred in the country, maybe the world."

A trio of grooms bellied up to the fence to watch the colt being put through his paces. As if by magic, word of what was happening spread throughout the farm. Within minutes, the fence was lined with Blue Diamond Farm employees, as well as Emmie and Buddy.

Nealy saw them all out of the corner of her eye and smiled. This crew was so different from the others. She could almost feel that they were rooting for her.

After Flyby's little workout, she handed him over to Danny to hold while she and Stardancer breezed with more serious intent. Late next year she would start entering Flyby in some prep races, so the sooner she started learning the ins and outs of being a jockey, the better. She was determined that no one was going to ride Flyby but her.

One of the exercise riders, an ex-jockey, came onto the track. "You've got a good seat, Nealy, but you need to bend your legs more," he said, as she rode past him. "Attagirl. Keep your head low. Good!"

She urged Stardancer into an even faster pace and flew past the crowd of watchers. She knew she had a long way to go, but this was a start. A damn good start. "Show them, Stardancer. Show them what you could have been!"

Stardancer ran full out, his long legs eating up the ground. Nealy had never felt such exhilaration. Her heart banged against her chest at the thrill of it all.

"Way to go, Nealy," Hunt shouted, as she walked Stardancer to the track's exit. "I take back everything I said. I was wrong. You can be a jockey. You *will* be a jockey."

Nealy beamed at him. "Thanks, Hunt. It means a lot to me for you to say that."

On her way back to the barn, Nealy remembered tomorrow was her birthday. She'd always treated it as just another day, but this time she felt like celebrating. What would happen if she took the day off? *Could* she take the day off? Maybe she could take the night off instead and go into town to a movie. A grown-up night out. Maybe Smitty would go with her. Or she could ask Hunt. No, he might think it was a date. Then there was the question of what to wear. She thought about the elegant, trashy dress she'd bought at Christmas but had never worn. Knowing she had no fashion sense to speak of, she knew it wasn't suitable for a movie.

It was late in the afternoon when Nealy trudged up to the house for fresh coffee. On her way back she stopped in the office to see what Smitty was up to. "I think," she said, taking a quick sip, "that coffee runs in my veins instead of blood. Have you seen Carmela?"

"Not since breakfast. She said she was going into town to get her hair done. Is something wrong?"

"No, everything is fine. As a matter of fact, it's great, thanks to you." Nealy sat down in the armchair in front of Smitty's desk.

"Me? I didn't have anything to do with what you did today. You did that all by yourself, girl."

"I don't mean that. I meant great because of what you've done for Blue Diamond Farms. I'm serious, Smitty. I don't know what I would have done without you. Your Night Gallery recruits were some of the best employees I've ever seen. I was sorry they didn't want to stay on, that they preferred . . . you know . . ."

"Don't judge, Nealy. Accept. Thanks to their . . . ah . . . contacts, you now have a permanent working crew. It all worked out."

"Yes, it all worked out." Nealy stared into her coffee mug. "Let's just hope everything else works out."

Smitty pushed a copy of the *Leader* across the desk and pointed to an article at the bottom of the front page. "You've become one famous lady. The newspapers love you. I'm keeping a journal on it all. Someday you might want to write your memoirs."

"I doubt that," Nealy said, pushing the newspaper back across the desk toward Smitty without even glancing at the article. "So how's the new office now that the wall is out?"

"Real good. At least I can move around." To illustrate, she pushed her chair away from her desk and stretched her legs out in front of her. "See?"

"Yes, I see," Nealy laughed. She had to admit that enlarging and remodeling the office had been a good idea. As for the old furniture, Maud's father's desk and chair, she hadn't been able to part with them, so she'd had them taken up to the attic and covered them securely with old washed-out horse blankets.

Smitty pulled herself back up to her desk and clasped her hands in front. "I know how much you hate all this publicity stuff, and I don't blame you, but I think you need to know it's probably going to get worse before it gets better. You're a hot topic, Nealy, especially now that you let it out that you intend to ride Flyby in the Kentucky Derby. That gave the press two tidbits of information, and it's only natural that they're going to want more." She leaned forward, and whispered, "Why don't you tell me whatever it is you're hiding before I read it in the newspaper?"

Nealy took a quick breath. "Hiding? You mean my past? You mean you didn't figure it out yet. I thought nothing got past you."

Smitty raised a perfectly arched eyebrow. "I'm a good listener, and I know how to keep my lip zipped. Sometimes it helps to talk about things. That way those things don't settle between your shoulder blades and weigh you down."

Nealy stood up and started for the door. With her hand on the doorknob, she said, "If you have a few minutes, I'd like to show you something."

Smitty flew out of her seat. "I have all the time in the world. I have this great boss who lets me do what I want."

"It's raw out, put on a jacket." Nealy shrugged out of her denim jacket and handed it to Smitty. "Here, wear mine, I'll wear Maud's," she said, grabbing the coat off the hook.

A gust of cold wind blew the women's hair as they made their way to the vehicle barn.

Once inside, Nealy led Smitty to the back. "That's my father's truck," she said, pointing to it through a curtain of cobwebs. Nealy walked around the truck and looked into the driver's seat. Even after all these years she could remember how lost and alone she'd felt driving aimlessly through the rain to anywhere, nowhere. "My pa said I had shamed the family by getting pregnant. He'd never liked me much in the first place, but after Emmie's birth, he liked me even less. I worked hard, damn hard, to prove that I was worthy of his love, but it didn't do any good. Then I got sick, really sick, and went to bed. One of my brothers told me Pa was going to send Emmie to the orphanage the next morning. Pa hated Emmie, said she was a half-wit because she couldn't talk." She pulled a long painful breath. "With a little help from my brother, I took that truck and lit out. I had no idea where I was going. I just drove. All I had were the clothes on my back, Emmie, and the money my brother swiped from my father's desk drawer.

"Blue Diamond Farms is where the truck broke down, and so did I. Jess found me wandering around on his driveway and brought me inside with Emmie. They told me later that I almost died." She put her hands to her face. "I loved them, Smitty, with all my heart, and when they offered to adopt Emmie when I turned twenty-one, I said yes. They said it was all done legally but . . . Emmie . . . I don't know if her father will ever come forward or not. He threatened to blow my head off with a shotgun if I ever said he was the father. I lied to Pa and said a vagrant attacked me in the barn. Emmie's name on her birth certificate said it was . . ."

"Coleman?"

Nealy's mouth dropped open. "You know?"

"Not everything, but I was able to piece some things together, which is what worries me. If I could do it, so could someone else."

Nealy shrugged. "As far as I'm concerned, it doesn't matter anymore, Smitty. I'm well beyond my pa's reach. Emmie is a concern, though. Then again, maybe not. Her father is a respected businessman with a family of his own. I doubt he'd want to stir things up. It would ruin his image."

"What about *your* image?"

"My image? People already see me as someone who does things in an unorthodox way. How is getting pregnant at seventeen and running away from home any different? So they bring up my past? I can deal with it. I learned a lot from Maud and Jess. Maud said no one can hurt you unless you allow it. Well, Smitty, I damn well won't allow it." She walked to the back of the truck and pulled out the bucket of dirt. "See this? When I was leaving SunStar that night I stopped in the pouring rain and filled it with SunStar dirt. I wanted to take something from home for Emmie. It's just dirt but . . . Emmie doesn't even know it's here. I keep asking myself why I'm keeping it, and I can't find the answer."

"What about your brothers, Nealy?"

"Even though Pa's in his eighties, I imagine he still rules them with an iron hand. They were petrified of him, just the way I was. You know what's sad, Smitty? I can't ever remember seeing them smile. Or Pa. I know I never did. I never knew my mother. I don't know if Pyne or Rhy remember her. I'm glad she's dead because I don't think she could have stood up to my pa. He probably worked her to death the way he tried to work me. He worked me like a dog, Smitty. When I left there I was like some beaten, tired old junkyard dog. I came here into sunlight, warmth, love, and found substitute parents. Loving parents.

"I won't go to Keeneland because my pa and brothers go there. We sold them quite a few horses. My pa even came here once to pick one of them up. I think it was the third year I was here. Maud and Jess closed off this place like it was one of those hostage movies. They gave him what he wanted and hustled him out of here so fast his head must have been spinning. At the time I didn't know how Maud knew, but Jess told me later the truck's registration papers were in the glove compartment. She never let on to me she knew. Jess didn't either until Maud was dying. Sometimes I regret that we never talked about it. Smitty, I was so young, so green back then. Hell, I didn't even have a driver's license and didn't know what a social security card was. According to my brothers, what I did know was how to open my legs and shame the family. With a half-wit. That's my story." She smiled as she put the bucket back into the truck bed. "Listen, tomorrow is my birthday. Would you like to go to a movie with me tomorrow night?"

"Ah, gee, Nealy, I have a date. But I might be able to break it."

"No, that's okay. Maybe I'll take the kids into town for ice cream or something."

"Why don't you ask Hunt? I think he's kind of sweet on you."

"I can't do that," she said, wondering what she was afraid of. "Hey, you know what? Remember that first day you came out here and applied for the job?" At Smitty's nod, she continued, "I almost didn't hire you that day. You were so . . . so . . . in command, so confident and sure of yourself. I wish I could be more like you. I can be like that with horses but not with people. How did you get that way?"

"By being stomped on once too often. So what made you hire me?"

"You said you knew Maud and Jess and spoke so highly of them. I'm sorry I didn't knock that wall out sooner."

"Yeah, me too."

"Don't let them get me, Smitty."

"Listen, doll, they'll have to get you over my dead body. As long as you approve of how and what I do, it will all work out. Just trust me, okay?"

"Smitty, do you think I can do it? Win the Derby, I mean?"

Smitty swung around, a fierce look on her face. "Doll, if I didn't admire your spirit and your guts, I would have been out of here a long time ago. Don't you ever second-guess yourself. If it can be done, you'll do it. You aren't upset about the movie, are you?"

"No. I'm not even sure I wanted to see a movie. It was more like I was supposed to do something on my birthday, and a movie seemed like the thing to do. Maybe I'll ask Carmela to bake me a cake so Emmie and Buddy can blow out the candles. By the way, Smitty, what's the scuttlebutt over at the Owens . . . sorry, the Goldstein farm?"

"They don't have one good trainer. Jack's been scouting. It's a tough business, as you well know. Did hear there is a little dissension over there, but what it's about I have no idea. Eventually, I'll find out. I'd like to stand here and talk, honey, but I want to clear my desk before I leave for the day. I want to do some shopping on my way home."

"Smitty?"

"Hmm?"

"Thanks for everything."

"Anytime. You just hang in there."

Nealy sat for a long time at the kitchen table drinking her coffee. She bowed her head once and offered up a prayer of thanks. Whatever the future held for her, she would do her best to be worthy of it.

13

Nealy rolled over, opened one sleepy eye, and saw the glowing red numbers on the bedside clock. Today she didn't have to get up at three-thirty or even four-thirty. Today was her birthday. If she wanted to stay in bed all day, she could.

Not in this lifetime, she thought a moment later. She'd made a promise to Maud and a commitment to herself, and she would honor them both. For the next two years, come rain, shine, snow, or sleet, she would keep Flyby and herself on a strict training schedule. As far as she was concerned, she had a lot more to learn about being a jockey than Flyby had to learn about being a champion racehorse.

At four-thirty, she came down to the kitchen and stopped just inside the door to stare in shock at the elderly housekeeper. "Carmela, why you look . . . you look wonderful. That hairstyle is very becoming. I like your dress, too. What's come over you?"

Carmela blushed like a girl. "I treated myself to what they call 'the works' yesterday. I realized I let myself go. Sometimes it takes someone like Smitty to wake a person up. I don't think I could ever dress as . . . flamboyantly as she does, though."

Nealy's brows knitted in confusion. "I'm getting the feeling you think you're in competition with her. But why?"

Carmela lifted her shoulders and sighed. "You might as well know. I've been seeing one of the grooms, Vince Edwards, for a couple of months now. He's a few years younger than me, in his late sixties, but he doesn't seem to think that's a problem. He's a good man, and I think I'm falling in love with him; but I don't know if he feels the same about me. All I know is that he can't take his eyes off Smitty whenever he sees her outside. It's not her fault. Smitty is what Smitty is, and there's obviously no changing it. But I wanted him to look at me like that, so I decided to fix myself up."

Nealy couldn't have been more surprised if Carmela had told her she was going to become an exotic dancer. "Well, you certainly did. You look like a new woman, a woman about ten years younger, I might add."

Carmela's eyes widened. "Really?"

Nealy headed for the coffeepot. "Really," she said, anticipating her first taste of the dark, rich brew. As soon as she'd taken a few sips and felt human again, she turned and gave Carmela a hug. "I'm happy for you, Carmela. I hope it all works out. Remember, the only person you have to answer to is yourself." Nealy sat down at the table and sipped her coffee, savoring the flavor. She drank coffee off and on all day long, but it never tasted the same as that first cup in the morning. "Listen, do you think you could find time today to make me a little birthday cake? Emmie and Buddy will expect one after dinner." At Carmela's nod, she continued. "Just put one candle on it. No, put two, one for each of the kids to blow out."

"What about dinner? You want anything special?"

Nealy pursed her lips, thinking. "No. I don't want anybody fussing. Just a regular dinner and then the cake."

"Chocolate or vanilla?"

"Chocolate. Chocolate frosting, too," she said, mentally counting the calories. Tonight she would splurge, but after that she would have to start a strict diet. This morning when she stepped on the scales she weighed 122 pounds, ten pounds over the ideal weight for a jockey. Over the weekend she would have to have a long talk with Carmela and see if they couldn't come up with a new, low-fat way of eating. Considering Carmela's new love interest, it seemed reasonable that she would also be interested in losing a few pounds. As for herself, she had two years to lose the weight, but she suspected it would be a struggle because she loved to eat.

She would also have to start some sort of rigorous exercise program to build strength, endurance and power. A good jockey needed to be a good athlete first. Shoemaker had been called one of the greatest athletes ever to sit astride a horse. Laffit Pincay, Jr. was built like a miniature Venice Beach muscleman. Nealy had done hard physical labor all her life, so she wasn't a softy, but she also wasn't nearly as fit as she needed to be. In the few times she'd raced Stardancer against the stopwatch, she'd learned that it was no easy thing to control a half-ton horse who was flying around the racetrack at forty miles an hour.

"I'm going to take this little cup of coffee with me down to the barn. After you put the kids on the bus, will you please bring me another cup? I'll be in with Flyby." She turned in mid-stride. "Oh, and, don't wear an apron, Carmela." She winked to make her point. Carmela laughed but nodded. "Happy birthday, Nealy."

Tessie, still the cook at SunStar Farms, set a platter of blueberry pancakes in the middle of the table. Another platter of bacon and sausage followed, along with a bowl of melted butter and one of warm syrup.

"Today is Nealy's birthday!" she said, looking boldly down at her employer.

"Is that supposed to mean something to us?" Josh Coleman growled without looking up.

"It means it's your daughter's birthday." When there was no response, she turned her gaze on Pyne and Rhy. "It also means it's your sister's birthday." They, at least, had the good grace to look up. "I'd like to send her a birthday card, but I don't know where to send it," she said in spite of the old man's scowl.

"It's a day like any other day," Josh said with a mouth full of food. Tessie could only stare at him. Why she continued to work for the Colemans she didn't know. Yes, she did. The money. If it wasn't for the money, more than she could make anywhere else, she would have left a long time ago.

Pyne pushed his plate toward the center of the table and rested his arms on the tabletop. "How long's it been now, seven years, eight? I've lost count." He paused for a moment, then continued in a sad voice. "All I know is that Nealy was what made this farm work. She had the touch. I know it, Rhy knows it, and you should know it, too, Pa."

"That's enough out of you, Pyne. One more word, and you'll feel the back of my hand. Eat your breakfast and get on down to the barn."

Pyne started to back his chair away from the table. He didn't want to be around in case his pa's temper exploded.

"Pyne's right, Pa," Rhy said. "Windstar could have won the Derby if Nealy had worked him. There were a lot of races our horses could have won if Nealy had worked them. Ever since you drove her away, this place has been going downhill. And it isn't the horses' fault. God knows you've bought the best of the best."

"Shut up!" the elder Coleman shouted, the veins in his neck bulging. In a fit of rage he upended the table, leftover food, melted butter, and sticky syrup scattering in all directions.

Tessie turned around to see father and sons leave the room at the same time, the elder Coleman in one direction, the two brothers in another. "That's just dandy," she grumbled, looking at the mess she now had to clean up. "Just dandy."

Pyne stormed to the stallion barn ahead of his brother. "I hate his fucking guts," he shouted, his fists boxing the air. "Why in the hell do we put up with his shit?"

Rhy's face was alive with rage. "Because we want to inherit this place when he dies."

"I wish that would be soon. If he keeps working us the way he does, we'll go before he does." Pyne slammed his right fist into the palm of his left hand. "I remember Nealy asking me why I let him treat me the way he does, why I didn't stand up to him and show him what I was made of. I told her it was because I didn't have her grit, but that's not true. You just made me realize why . . . we're greedy bastards. We both put up with his shit because we want his money. I don't like what that makes us, Rhy. I don't like it at all."

"Then leave," Rhy said, sitting down on a hay bale.

Pyne sat down across from him. "Nealy was the one with the guts," he said. He leaned forward, rested his elbows on his knees, and looked down at the ground. "I think about her all the time. I think about the way he drove her out, and I think about our part in it." Terrible regrets assailed him. "I never told you this before, but I don't think it was a vagrant who attacked our sister. I don't think she was attacked at all. I think she was sleeping with someone we all know, like maybe Dillon Roland. He was over here a lot back then."

"Dillon Roland?" Rhy seemed surprised.

"Yeah, old Dilly Dally himself. Don't you remember? He had himself a whole stable of good-looking girls through high school, and he was always in one kind of trouble or another. He also had a daddy who went around cleaning up after him. I'm not saying he's the one for sure, Rhy. I'm just speculating." He got up and meandered over to the first stall. "I sure wish I knew what happened to her. It couldn't have been easy for her, toting a kid around."

"If you knew where she was, would you go after her?"

"Yeah, I would," Pyne said without hesitation. "We never should have let her go in the first place. We may have been just kids ourselves, but we should have stood up to Pa for her." He leaned his head back and laughed out loud. "Pa thought she'd come crawling back, but I knew she wouldn't." He looked out the end of the breezeway. "For months after she left, I'd see him looking down the road. Even now, after all these years, I catch him staring at the road with a funny look on his face. This morning before you came into the kitchen, I caught him looking at the calendar." When Rhy gave him a doubting look, Pyne nodded. "Yeah, I did. The son of a bitch remembered it was her birthday. Now, I'm going to ask you the same question you asked me. Would you fetch her back if you knew where she was?"

"No. Wherever she is, it has to be better than here. God knows anything would be better than here. Maybe she'll get in touch with us someday. I'd like to see how she turned out, her and the kid."

"Emmie," Pyne said. "The kid's name is Emmie. And she wasn't a half-wit."

"I know that. Look, for whatever it's worth, I'm sorry I said the things I did to her. I was just sick and tired of Pa being mad at Nealy and taking it out on me. As for . . . Emmie . . . she was actually a smart little kid, but what I could never figure out was if she could cry, why couldn't she talk? There was nothing wrong with her vocal cords." He shrugged. "Hey, come on, we've got work to do."

Pyne nodded and looked through the breezeway to the road. "Happy birthday, Nealy, wherever you are," he said gruffly.

"Yeah, happy birthday, sis," Rhy said.

* * *

Nealy made the rounds one last time before heading up to the house for dinner. She stopped at Stardancer's stall to give him loving pats to his back. "Flyby and me, we had a good day today, big guy. He's doing better than I have any right to expect. He's got heart, that son of yours." She rubbed Stardancer's sleek neck and felt him relax. "I've been wondering," she whispered, "how's it going to look, me being the owner, trainer, and jockey to Flyby? I know there's no rule that says I can't be all those things, but that's not going to stop people from making a fuss." She hugged the big horse. "I've got so much to learn. So very, very much. I pray every night that I don't foul things up." Stardancer whickered as if to tell her everything would be all right. She threw her arms around his neck and hugged him. "What would I do if I didn't have you to talk to, huh? C'mon now, show me you understand everything I just said."

When Stardancer bobbed his head up and down, Nealy laughed. She knew the horse didn't *really* understand. He was just reacting to the tone of her voice and her own body gestures. Still, it was fun to pretend that he did. "See you in the morning, big boy. Don't you open this gate either, Stardancer. You can visit Little Lady and Flyby through your stall window." She wagged her finger at him.

Stardancer whinnied. It sounded like laughter to Nealy's ears.

Nealy's good humor turned sour when she opened the kitchen door. There were no fragrant smells, no cake sitting on the table, no dinner cooking on the stove. And on top of that, Emmie and Buddy were nowhere in sight. She looked down at her watch. Seven o'clock. "Carmela! Emmie! Buddy!" Damn, where was everyone? She called out a second time and then a third time as she made her way to the living room at the front of the house.

"Surprise!"

Nealy grabbed the back of an armchair and blinked at the crowded room.

Emmie ran up to her. *Are you surprised, Mama?* she signed, jumping up and down. *Smitty did it all. Carmela helped, and so did me and Buddy. Are you happy for your birthday?*

Nealy lowered her head and wrapped her arms around her daughter. "I'm more than happy. I'm delirious!" She looked at the crowd of people filling the living room and foyer. "Thank you, I . . . I had no idea . . ."

"That's why it's called a surprise party," Smitty said, coming forward. She was elegant in a fire-engine red ensemble that looked like it had been melted onto her.

When Nealy turned around, she saw even more people spilling into the dining room and hallway. All her employees, and all the temporary ones that had worked for her earlier in the year smiled at her. Even the girls from the Night Gallery were present. Any one of them could have passed for a banker's secretary. She hugged them all as others shook hands, clapping one another on the back, their faces wreathed in happy smiles.

At the end of the well-wishers' line, Nealy threw caution to the winds and planted a kiss on Hunt's lips that rocked him back on his heels.

Smitty watched the exchange and winked at Nealy. "Attagirl," she said, laughing.

An hour into the party, Smitty whistled for everyone's attention. "It's time to give Nealy her present! C'mon," she said, grabbing Nealy's hand. "We have to go out on the front porch to see it." Everyone followed. "It's from all of us," she said, opening the door. "Every single person here tonight contributed because no one knew what to give a woman who has everything. We hope you like it. Emmie, honey, turn on the porch lights so your mama can see what love and respect can buy."

The second the light went on, Nealy gasped.

Emmie tugged on her mother's arm to get her attention. *Do you like it, Mama?*

Nealy stared openmouthed at a life-size sculpture of Flyby. "Oh, honey, what's not to like? I love it," she squealed.

Smitty walked down the steps, waving her arms this way and that. "This is our way of saying we know he's going to be successful when he makes his run for the roses. We didn't have enough time to get it cast in bronze before your birthday, so it has to go back. But only temporarily."

Nealy's hands framed her face as she said, "I don't know

what to say. It's . . . it's . . ." She swiped at her eyes with the sleeve of her flannel shirt.

"Nealy Diamond speechless! Now I've seen everything," Hunt quipped. "Let's drink a toast to Flyby. And then a toast to Nealy to celebrate her birthday!"

"Hear, hear!"

Nealy turned around to face her friends and employees. A smile trembled over her lips. "I swear, this is the best birthday ever. Thank you. Thank you all for everything."

At eleven o'clock, as soon as Nealy had said her thank-yous to the last guest, she sat down cross-legged on the front porch to stare at the sculpture of Flyby.

"That's quite a statue," she said, cocking her head from right to left to view it from different angles. "It looks just like him, every detail. How'd the artist do it?"

"Smitty told me to take a picture of Flyby and that the artist would do the rest. I wish you could have seen me. I'm not much of a photographer. Luckily for me that horse is a ham. If I didn't know better, I'd say he actually posed for me. Anyway, the picture was all the sculptor needed. She worked around the clock to get it to this stage for your birthday. When it's finished it will be magnificent. We thought you might want to use it to build a sort of monument at the farm's entrance."

"That's a great idea, Hunt. I love it. But . . . What if Flyby doesn't win the Derby?"

"Are you kidding, Nealy? He can't lose. Not with you training and riding him."

Nealy turned her gaze on Hunt and was taken aback by the deep emotion she saw shining in his eyes. The possibility that he was in love with her both excited her and frightened her. "I . . . I hope you're right," she stuttered.

"Nealy, I want you to know . . . I mean, I think you should know . . ." He threw up his hands in exasperation. "I'm making a real mess of this," he said, standing up.

Nealy reached for Hunt's hand and let him help pull her up. When he took her into his arms, she didn't resist. Instead, she gave herself up to the moment. She felt his hands in her hair as he pulled her to him, felt his lips against hers. Sweet and gentle, hot and demanding. A kiss that demanded other things.

"Oh, Nealy. There's so much I want to say to you. So much I want to do . . ."

"Then say it and do it," she whispered against his lips.

He pulled back from her to look into her eyes. "Are you sure?"

"I'm absolutely positive."

"Where?" he whispered huskily. "The barn?"

"No. No," she said, aching for his touch. "The manager's house, your house."

A long time later, with the fire reduced to smoldering embers, Hunt groaned as he nestled Nealy more comfortably in his arms. In the whole of his life he had never felt what he was feeling now. He forgot she was his boss, forgot everything but the woman in his arms. He wanted to say something to her, something to let her know what he was feeling, but the words wouldn't come. He sighed when Nealy burrowed deeper into the nest of his arms. "Is it all right not to talk, just to feel?" he whispered into her sweet-smelling hair.

Nealy sighed. "Ummmm."

"Are you cold? The fire is dying down." He shifted his weight until she was stretched out alongside him. He loved the feel of her naked body against his, loved the feel of her warm skin against his hands. He wanted her. Again.

His mouth was gentle, his touch delicate, as he explored and caressed. He could feel her passion quicken, and he calmed her with his touch and soothed her with words known only to lovers.

He was gentle, so very gentle, evoking in her a golden warmth that spread through her loins and tingled her toes. His movements were familiar, reassuring, his touch on her naked breasts light and lingering.

He gentled her with a sure touch and a soft voice, quieting her whimper with his mouth and yet evoking moans of passion with his caress. When passion flamed again, it burned as pure as the fire that had warmed them earlier.

Hunt cradled Nealy in his arms, his expression full of awe. Nealy had matched his ardor, and without reservation given herself totally to him. How beautiful she was in the dim glow of the room, how gentle she could be, and then she could become a raging riptide, swirling and crushing his volcanic outpourings until the molten lava and thundering waters were a marriage of one.

Nealy's last conscious thought before closing her eyes was to wonder if she was falling in love with Hunter Clay.

And then they slept, entwined in each other's arms.

14

Nealy looked across the front pasture, shielding her eyes from the early-morning sun. How many times had she stood here like this savoring the sounds emanating from the barns, smelling the clover, staring at the diamondlike droplets of early-morning dew on the velvety bluegrass Kentucky was known for? Hundreds? Thousands?

She jammed her hands into her pockets to stop them from trembling. Tomorrow, the first Saturday in May, was the day she'd knocked herself out for these last two years. Kentucky Derby Day at Churchill Downs. Tomorrow she would fulfill her promise to Maud and make her Derby-winning dream come true. And tomorrow Nealy herself would go down in history as the first female trainer to ride a Kentucky Derby winner.

She refused even to consider the possibility that she might not win because she knew she would. Flyby was ready. She was ready.

Nealy reached into her shirt pocket for her cigarettes and had to laugh at herself when she found it empty. Of course it was empty. She'd given up smoking over two years ago when she'd started her fitness program. Clasping her hands in front of her, she fought back the urge to go running down to the barns to ask one of the grooms for a cigarette. Smoking was forbidden anywhere near the barns, but there was a small area close to the largest where smoking was permitted.

At the sight of a television van parking along the fence outside the gate, Nealy forgot about her desire for a cigarette. Months ago Smitty had warned her that the closer it got to Derby Day, the more pressure the media would put on her to do interviews. "Get used to it," she said, "you're unique because you're the owner, trainer, and the rider of a Derby entrant, and you're also a female. That makes you big news, honey."

Nealy had done her history homework and knew the names of the three women who had trained Derby horses. In 1937 Mary Hirsch's horse, No Sir, finished thirteenth. Mrs. Albert Roth's 1949 entry, Seneca Coin, hadn't finished at all. The Derby of 1965 recorded Mary Keim as the trainer of the sixth place horse, Mr. Pak.

So far, not a single Derby winner among them. Not even one in the money. But after tomorrow . . .

When a second TV van parked along the fence, Nealy went back inside the house. Thank God she'd had the foresight to hire a twenty-four-hour security service to make sure no one except the employees got past the front gates. Reporters were obnoxious people who popped off questions they had no business asking. Smitty had told her that eventually she would have to talk to them, and Nealy had said she would . . . after she won the Derby.

In spite of her silence and reclusiveness, the newspapers had run numerous articles about her. It was no surprise that Jack and Wiley Carney were the two men the reporters quoted most. Jack accused her of breaking every unwritten rule that applied to the Derby. "She thumbs her nose at the establishment," he told one of the papers. "She hasn't done one single thing according to the book, and she's getting away with it because she's a woman!"

Nealy had figured that Jack would eventually find a way to get even with her for firing him and his son, but she'd thought he would do something more sneaky and underhanded than just bad-mouthing her to the media.

She'd been lucky, too, that so far Smitty's dire predictions of digging up her past had not come true. But tomorrow was another day.

Hunt came into the kitchen just as Nealy sat down to drink her second cup of coffee. Not a day went by that she didn't congratulate herself on hiring Hunt. He was a stickler about legalities. There was no doubt in her mind that he could recite every rule and requirement listed in the Jockey Club's *American Stud Book.*

"I saw the TV vans out in front," he said.

"That's why I came back in the house, so they wouldn't see me."

"You won't be able to get away from them after the race, you know."

"I won't want to then."

Hunt finished pouring himself a cup of coffee and sat down across from her. "Any doubts about tomorrow?"

"Not a one," she said without hesitation.

He smiled at her and winked. "You should be proud of yourself, Nealy. You're paving the way for other women who want to be in the Thoroughbred horse business."

Nealy wrapped her hands around her coffee cup, the weight of responsibility heavy on her small shoulders. "I'm getting really jittery, Hunt."

"You!" His voice rose in feigned surprise. "I don't believe it." He gave her a sideways look. "I heard on the early news that Knight Wing was scratched. Sid Calloway, his owner, didn't say what the problem was."

Nealy frowned. "That's too bad," she said with all sincerity. "From what I've seen Knight Wing is a good horse. And thanks for changing the subject, but it won't do any good. These are serious jitters. You'd be jittery, too. Most of it is because of those . . . *people,*" she mumbled. His look of question prompted her to explain. "You know, Jack, Wiley, people like them. Why do they want to see me fail, Hunt? Because I didn't follow their methods? Because I disregarded a few silly rules? Or because I'm a woman, and I'm upsetting the status quo?"

"Probably a little of all three," he answered, setting down his coffee cup. "But you have to rise above it, Nealy. You have to stop thinking about all that garbage. You have a single purpose here. Don't deviate by word or deed. You're in the clear. I checked on Flyby during the night. Stardancer, too. They're picking up on your anxiety. Knock it off, or you're going to be in big trouble tomorrow. Maybe you need a couple of laps around the track with Charlie. He's as hyper as you are."

"I know," she said, sighing. "Give me a couple of hours, and I'll get a handle on it. I thought I would go over to the cemetery and . . ."

"Talk to Maud and Jess?" He stood up and put his hand on the back of her chair. "Go."

Nealy put her hands on the table and pushed herself to her feet. "Make sure nobody disturbs me, okay? I've got a lot of talking to do."

"Not a problem. Talk all you want but keep track of the time. We've got a lot to do today."

Hunt walked Nealy outside and watched her walk across the acreage. God, she was just a tiny little thing, a little over a hundred pounds soaking wet. And yet she had magic running through that small body. Magic only animals understood. Why was she the one? What made her different? Even his father knew and understood Nealy's magic.

In that one split second he realized just how deep his love for Nealy went.

"You're up early, Smitty," Hunt said as he accepted the cup of coffee she held out. His third of the morning.

"I couldn't sleep. The whole media fiasco," she said, pointing toward the front of the property, where a dozen or more vans and cars were now parked alongside the fence. "This whole thing has knocked the stuffing out of me. Not to mention pissed me off. Why can't they leave her alone? Why do they have to hunt and peck and dig and poke? Do you know who I saw at the store in Frankfort yesterday? Sylvia Goldstein, that's who. She stopped me in the parking lot and asked me if Nealy was serious about riding Flyby herself. I told her Nealy was very serious and that she and her husband might as well scratch their entry because he didn't have a chance. She tried to look offended in her designer duds, but I wasn't buying it. Nothing offends that woman. When are we heading out for Louisville?"

"Around midnight. Even if we drive slow, we'll be there by one o'clock. We don't want to get there any earlier. Nealy doesn't want to give anything away."

"Funny," Smitty said. "Before we made the announcement that Nealy was going to ride Flyby in the Derby, the media didn't pay any attention to them. Not even at Santa Anita. I imagine they're kicking themselves sideways for scratching them as a flash in the pan." Smitty clasped her hands in front of her. "They

are going to win, aren't they, Hunt? Have you heard the morning line yet?"

"To answer your first question, yes, they're going to win. To
answer the second, Flyby is a long shot at eighteen to one. No
reason to think that will change."

Smitty started to cough and sputter as she gasped, "Eighteen
to one!" Hunt thumped her on the back until she could pull herself together. "If we play our cards right and they don't decrease
the odds, we could become overnight millionaires. I'm laying
down a bundle, and so is Carmela. How about you?"

"Only every cent I've got to my name. What do you think of
the nineteen-horse field? I heard Sid scratched his horse. Is there
even one colt who can give Flyby some serious competition?"

Smitty tossed the rest of her coffee onto the ground. "Maybe
one or two. My feeling is they aren't as good as the hype I've
been hearing."

"One of them being Nightstar, the Coleman horse from Sun-
Star Farms?" At Smitty's nod, Hunt said, "He's a fireball at the
gate, but I don't think he'll be able to maintain his speed in the
stretch. Ricky Vee is on him, but a jockey is only as good as
the horse he's riding. Leisure Boy, the Dillon Roland horse, is on
a par with Nightstar. His trainer is okay but no great shakes. I
don't much care for his jockey either." The honking of a horn interrupted him. He turned around. "You going out there to talk
to that pack of ghouls?"

Smitty gritted her teeth. "I suppose. Otherwise, they might
get unruly and storm the gates. But I think I'll make them wait a
little while, until it warms up some more, to about ninety. I want
to see them all wilted and snarly."

"Well, be careful, and don't let them get to you," he cau-
tioned.

"Trust me, they won't get within three yards of me. I'm taking my cattle prod, and if they get too close, I'll hold it up and
threaten them." To demonstrate, she raised her arms and shook
it threateningly.

Hunt pretended to look frightened. "You've got me scared."

"Nothing like a cattle prod to give a woman a sense of power.
Now, Carmela, she doesn't need a prod. That lady has a mouth
on her that would burn rubber, and she uses it, but only to pro-

tect Nealy. Speaking of Nealy," she said, "is she as nervous this morning as she was last night?"

"Uh-huh, but she'll be fine. She went over to the cemetery to have a nice long talk with Maud and Jess."

Smitty gave Hunt a thumbs-up and walked back to the office. She knew he was in love with Nealy. Everybody who worked on the farm knew it. Hunt wasn't very good at keeping his feelings off his face. Nealy, however, had a poker face. You almost never knew what she was thinking until she told you . . . if she told you.

Reflecting on her conversation with Hunt, she wondered if Nealy had told him anything about her past . . . that tomorrow she would be running for the roses not only against her own father but against Emmie's father. If that wasn't enough to make a body nervous, she didn't know what was. Smitty sighed. Sometimes she wished she didn't know as many secrets as she did.

She looked at her watch. She'd wait until around noon to go out to beard the hordes of tabloid reporters and legitimate journalists. She checked her outfit in the mirror behind the door and gave herself a nod of approval. She'd taken extra pains today with her grooming and dress, knowing she would have the media to contend with. The scarlet-leather skirt Nealy referred to as rubber clung to her ample curves. The matching silk blouse showed more curves and a deep cleavage. The short flight jacket trimmed in gold was eye-boggling, as were the dangling earrings that tinkled when she walked. She lowered her head and shook her hair before she pawed through it with her fingers. It stood out from her head like a bush.

Charlie in her arms, Nealy walked to the barn. Just one more day. She shrugged. "We're okay, Charlie," she said, cuddling the little dog. "That talk with Maud and Jess helped a lot. I'm centered now and ready to take on the world. Even my father. Today will be the first time I've seen him in years. But thanks to Maud and Jess, he can't hurt me anymore. I wonder if Pyne and Rhy will be there. Of course, they will. As for the esteemed Mr. Dillon Roland, aka Mr. Son-of-a-bitch, I doubt he'll even recognize me. And if he does, so what? I'm beyond his threats."

Charlie licked her face. "That's right, Charlie, and what I need to do is concentrate on one thing and one thing only: Flyby. Now scamper over there and let Flyby know things are okay. I want to spend a few minutes with Stardancer." She moved out of the sunlight into the shade of the breezeway and heard Stardancer whicker to Little Lady through the wrought-iron bars on her stall. "Stardancer, dammit, you promised to stay in your stall until I could come and get you. You have to stop doing stuff like this. You make me nuts sometimes." Hands on hips, Nealy walked toward the stallion. "What do you think you're doing, big guy? C'mere," she said, coaxing him toward her with a mint.

Nealy leaned against the stall door, watching the stallion as he chewed the mint, then rolled back his lips in ecstasy. She giggled, her voice low and calm, then handed him over to Danny to take out to the paddock.

As soon as he was out of sight, Nealy opened Little Lady's stall. "Come on, mama, let's hit it," she said, unlatching the door. The mare stood still while Nealy haltered her. Then the two of them left the stall and walked side by side through the breezeway. Nealy grinned from ear to ear as she watched Charlie scampering ahead. He yipped and yapped and almost turned himself inside out in his excitement.

Just yesterday Smitty had told her Nightstar's barn buddy was a chicken named Rosalie and that Leisure Boy had bonded with a pygmy goat named Lucille. She snorted. A dog, at least, was respectable. Charlie helped to make things work.

Nealy took a deep breath and realized she was calm. She held out her hands to see if they trembled. Not a tremor. "Yesssss."

Flyby whinnied as Nealy and Little Lady passed his paddock. Because she couldn't risk any chances of injury, she had Danny put him in a paddock by himself today. As always, the sight of him made her heart skip a beat. God, how she loved him. She knew in her gut he would run until he dropped if that was what she wanted. He could do the mile and a quarter and barely break a sweat. Aside from the word *beautiful*, the only word to describe him that came to mind was *magnificent*.

Like his sire, he had developed into an impressive-looking horse who stood at 16.3 hands, slightly taller than Stardancer. Even standing still he gave off an aura of power and speed. His bright chestnut coat gleamed in the sun, reminding Nealy of Emmie's penny.

She could tell by looking at him that he knew something was different today. The routine he'd lived by for the past two years was suddenly over. Day in and day out, from the moment his training began, without missing a day, Nealy had talked to him as she would to a human being—told him what she was doing, what she expected from him—and he seemed to understand. And always, at the end of the day, there were rewards, the apple, the mint, Charlie barking his approval, and then what she called her cuddle time . . . time she spent in his stall sitting in the corner and talking, sometimes laughing, sometimes crying as she shared her joys and miseries.

After tomorrow it would all be over, all the hard work, the sleepless nights, the worry and fretting.

"Nealy, I brought you another cup of coffee," Hunt said, coming up behind her. "The crowd out by the road is growing. It might not be a bad idea for you to go out there and give an interview or say a few words."

"Why?"

"So your words are on record. Pick one of the reporters, invite him or her into the house, and have Smitty tape it. That will eliminate any misquotes."

"I wouldn't know what to say, Hunt."

"Say what's in your heart. Tell them why you and only you could ride Flyby."

She took a deep breath and gave him a pained look. "They probably think it's all about money. But it isn't. It was never about the money. It's about a promise, a payback, and proving that I was put on this earth for a reason."

Hunt wiped a speck of dirt off her cheek with his thumb. "Then that's what you should tell them."

"They don't care about that stuff," she scoffed. "All they want to do is ask who I am and where I came from. And how a nobody like me became the heir to one of the biggest Thoroughbred breeding farms in Kentucky."

For a moment Hunt said nothing. His gaze drifted past Nealy to the barns beyond. "Maybe you should tell them."

Nealy gasped. "It's none of their business. It's nobody's business but my own."

"Yes, but better you tell them and set them straight with the facts than let them find it out on their own and exaggerate the truth." He playfully punched her chin. "Just think about it, that's all I ask."

"Are there any women reporters out there?" Nealy queried, getting up.

"I'm sure there are."

Hand in hand, they walked out of the barn. Nealy squinted into the sunshine. There was so much she wanted to say to Hunt, but now wasn't the time. As Jess had always said, "Why mess with something when it's working just fine?" Was she destined to end up like Maud and Jess? Their lives paralleled hers in so many ways. She squeezed his hand. "I have to wonder if I would have made it this far without you and Danny."

He wanted to tell her no, she wouldn't have, but it would have been a lie. Nealy didn't know the meaning of the word *fail*. It simply wasn't in her vocabulary. "Of course you would have. Dad and I were just on the periphery. Everything you've accomplished, Nealy, you've accomplished by yourself. You think Flyby was born to run for the roses, and I think you were, too. I believe that in my heart," he said, thumping his chest.

"That's one of the nicest things you've ever said to me, Hunt," she said, smiling up at him, loving him for the very special man he was. No other man would have put up with her stubbornness. She knew she wasn't an easy person to deal with. Sometimes she could barely deal with herself.

His arm snaked around her back and he pulled her to him. "I'd say a lot more if you'd let me. Like, will you marry me?"

Nealy laughed. "Is that a proposal?"

"Yeah, it is." He bent his head and touched his lips to her forehead. "What's your answer?"

Nealy's stomach fluttered, and she felt light-headed. "Yes . . . but," she said, pushing back from him just a little, "not right now." She saw his look of disappointment, and said, "I do love you. I didn't think it was possible, but you sneaked into my heart. It's just that . . . I don't want to rush into anything. Will you wait?"

She knew his answer before he said it.

"I'll wait, Nealy."

They headed for the house. In the kitchen Nealy asked, "If I do an interview, should I let them take a picture of Flyby?"

"Why the hell not! It will be on the front page tomorrow morning. If you're going to do it, do it now, so they can make their deadline. And Nealy, don't tell them to kiss your ass if they tick you off, okay?"

"I'll think about it," she said, standing on tiptoe to kiss the tip of his nose. "By the way, thanks for the silks. But purple? It's not exactly my color."

"Purple was Maud's favorite color," he said. "Besides, it stands out from all the others."

"Good thinking!" She kissed him again, this time full on the lips.

Hunt groaned. "You shouldn't do stuff like that if you can't carry through."

"Who says I can't carry through? We've got all day . . . and tonight," she said, flashing him a big smile. Then she twisted away from him and pressed the intercom on the telephone. "Smitty, you there?"

"Yep, I'm here. What's up?" she returned.

"Hunt thinks I should pick one of those reporters and give an interview. He said it will make the headlines of the morning paper."

There was a moment of silence, then, "I think he's right."

Nealy looked over at Hunt. "Okay, but only with a female reporter. If she has a cameraman, she can bring him, too, but no one else, got me?"

"Gotcha! I know just the gal. Her name is Dagmar Doolittle."

When Nealy choked into the speaker, Smitty said, "I swear to God, that's her name. She's a big Swede. Hell, she's bigger than life, and she's been out there every morning with those vultures. She'll give you a fair shake if you open up. She has never written a negative thing about you. She just stated facts as she knew them. You want her, she's yours."

"Okay, Smitty. Go get her."

Smitty was right. Dagmar was a big woman, but she was amazingly graceful. She was also refreshingly intelligent, unlike some of the female reporters Nealy had seen on TV. There was a spark in her eyes that Nealy immediately related to.

"To what do I owe the pleasure of this interview?" Dagmar asked, looking as if the ax was about to fall directly on her head.

"You're a woman. I'm a woman. Smitty tells me you're fair. I consider myself a fair person, too. I can give you forty-five minutes, so we need to talk fast. I'll let you take one picture of Flyby providing you put him on the front page of your paper. Smitty is going to tape the interview so there won't be any misquotes. If you're okay with that, we can move right along. Let's be clear on one thing, this is about a horse, his rider, his owner, and his trainer. It is not about my personal life. Okay?"

"Absolutely. What are my chances of getting an exclusive in the winner's circle when they drape your horse with the blanket of roses?"

Nealy laughed, the sound ricocheting off the walls of the kitchen. "The interview is yours because you said 'when' not 'if.' You get the Preakness and the Belmont if I run Flyby, too. Deal?"

"Deal."

"What the hell kind of name is Dagmar Doolittle?"

"You don't want to know, honey. Maybe sometime when I know you a little better, we can share secrets."

"Don't count on it," Nealy and Smitty said in chorus.

15

Derby Day!

Nealy sucked in her breath and moved quickly. She hadn't had one moment to herself since she, Hunt, and Danny had pulled in at the back gate of Churchill Downs at two-thirty that morning. From then on she'd had an endless stream of things to do, not the least of which was getting Flyby and Stardancer comfortably settled in their assigned stalls in barn number twenty-six.

Now, finally, everything was done. Flyby and Stardancer were resting from their midnight run from the media hounds and would soon enjoy a good breakfast of clean white oats. Nealy had brought Stardancer along to be Flyby's lead pony. Normally only geldings escorted the runners in the post parade, but because of Flyby and Stardancer's unusual relationship, father and son got special permission to ride together to the post. Another unorthodox note in the long list of unorthodox notes.

From there on in, the horses could be left in Danny's capable hands. He still had to brush away the accumulated sawdust from the trailer ride, bathe them both, then braid Stardancer's mane and tail with purple and white ribbons. It was a long-standing Derby tradition for the lead ponies to be decked out in their finest livery.

During the ride to the track, Nealy and Hunt had talked about taking Flyby out to the track for a morning workout, but decided against it because of the media. Instead she would walk him around the barns, talking to him softly, trying to explain what these new goings-on were all about. Later she swore he understood everything she said.

With Charlie leashed and at her feet, Nealy hurried down the length of the long shed row toward the racetrack. These few minutes, just prior to sunup, might be her only chance to get a good look at the famed twin spires of the venerable Churchill Downs.

Mist rose from the tubs of warm water the grooms were carrying to bathe their charges. A cat meowed, and a hen clucked. The smells of leather and liniment, straw and manure filled the air. A wonderful memory to tuck away and cherish.

Then she saw it. Churchill Downs. The white spires shone like beacons in the predawn light. A light breeze moved the American flag that rose over the rooftop. She looked upward into the grandstand and imagined it as it would be later that afternoon, filled with more than a hundred thousand people. The thought made her feel light-headed and weak in the knees.

The sound of thundering hooves caught her attention. She looked to the left and saw a dappled gray horse galloping out of the clubhouse turn, toward her. She smiled as she watched him race past. Steam rose in foot-high vapors off his heated shoulders. Whoever he was, he was a plucky little colt, 15.3 hands max, with legs barely long enough to keep his tail off the ground. Yet he didn't lack for speed, and Nealy knew he would be a serious contender.

As of late the previous night, Flyby was still a long shot, though the odds had dropped from eighteen to one to ten to one. "A crackerjack colt," the evening paper had called him. "Owned, bred, and trained by Cornelia Diamond, whose unorthodox training methods have shaken the Thoroughbred racing world."

The media certainly had made a big deal about her being Flyby's trainer, even more than being his jockey. "Female trainer makes a run at history," one banner line read. "When Cornelia Diamond makes her run for the roses, she'll be challenging a male-dominated tradition." Nealy sighed. What could she expect? Horse training, like horse breeding, was dominated by testicles. And that made today's race all the more exciting.

If the reporters' estimations were right, thousands of women in the stands and at home would be watching her, rooting for her. By winning the world's most famous horse race, she would knock down yet one more door that had been previously closed to women.

Watching the dappled gray colt head into the quarter mile stretch made her positively itch to get into the saddle and get out on the track.

Hunt was sitting on a bench between Flyby's and Stardancer's stalls when she returned. She smiled as she waved her arms airily to show what she thought of her magnificent surroundings.

"How are they doing?" she asked.

"Better than me," Hunt answered. "Flyby's taking everything in stride. Absolutely nothing ruffles him. Nothing. You've trained him well, Nealy. He's the most adaptable horse I've ever seen." Hunt folded up the newspaper he had been reading and handed it to her. "There's going to be a lot of bullshit going down once people read this."

Briefly, their eyes met, but she couldn't read his expression. Resigned to seeing another embarrassing banner line, she slowly opened the paper, and gasped. "My God," she whispered, staring at the front page picture of Flyby. "This is . . . I mean it's . . . my God! It's the whole front page!"

"I'd say that woman who interviewed you really delivered the goods, wouldn't you?"

Still overwhelmed, Nealy could only nod.

Hunt laughed. He could count on one hand the times he'd seen Nealy speechless.

"Look at him, Hunt," she said, turning the paper back around for him to see. "Look at the way he's looking at the camera. What a ham. If I didn't know better, I'd swear he was smiling." Seeing the agreement in Hunt's eyes, she started to howl with laughter. "Tell me he isn't one kick-ass horse, Hunt. Tell me."

"He's one kick-ass horse, Nealy," he said, beaming up at her. "But if you think that's great, wait until you read the article. You won't believe it. I think you finally found an ally, maybe even a crusader."

Nealy folded the paper up and stuck it under her arm. "I'm not going to read it. At least not now. This is enough for me. More than enough. I love it, absolutely love it." Brows knitting, she glanced up and down the length of the shed row. "Where's your dad? And isn't it about time Smitty and Carmela got here with the kids?"

"They came while you were gone, and Dad took them out to breakfast. They'll be back in a little while. Wait until you see them. . . . Carmela and Smitty are wearing big, floppy hats with flowers and birds and the whole nine yards. I wouldn't be surprised if Smitty isn't carrying a lace hankie. And Emmie looks . . . well let's just say she looks like an angel." He leaned forward and grabbed her hand. "Sit down here with me. I have a feeling that as soon as that paper starts to circulate, there's going to be some curiosity seekers wanting to get a close-up look at you and Flyby."

Nealy leaned her back against the wall. "Wherever Maud and Jess are, I sure hope they're watching today. Do you believe in the afterlife, Hunt?"

He leaned back, too. "I don't know. I never thought much about it," he said, yawning. "As soon as my dad gets back, let's leave him in charge and head out for the hotel. He slept all the way here, so he's rested; but I'm beat, and I'll bet you are, too."

Thank God for Hunt. He was forever thinking about her wants and needs. He took better care of her than she did herself. "Sounds good to me. Meantime, Charlie and I want to have a little heart-to-heart with Flyby. Come on, Charlie," she said, patting her knees for him to jump up.

Nealy listened as the announcer's voice came over the speakers. "None of the horses running today have gone a mile and a quarter, and except for those going on to the Belmont, none of these horses will ever go the mile and a quarter again. When you handicap a race, you usually look backward to see the best performance. Not so with the Derby. You have to anticipate who is going to run their best race today . . . for that reason Celebration, General Don, Phil's Choice, and Texas Rich still have their best shot yet to fire.

"Phil's Choice is not the favorite on this first Saturday in May, but he's made it here, and that's all that matters. His owner is said to have made a nasty wisecrack to Cornelia Diamond at Santa Anita. He apologized, but Ms. Diamond would have none of it. She said her horse had more class and breeding than Phil's Choice or his owner."

"This is it, Nealy," Hunt announced, briefly taking her into his arms and hugging her. "Twenty-four minutes to post time. You look great. Purple is definitely your color."

"And yours," she said, referring to his coordinated shirt and cap.

"Nealy, I'm going to wish you luck even though I know you don't need it," Danny Clay said. His eyes were shiny and bright. She suspected unshed tears. She nodded as she bit down on her lip.

"I wouldn't be standing here if I didn't believe you and Flyby were going to win. Trust in him to know what to do. Give him his head and let him go would be my advice."

Nealy was shocked when he threw his arms around her and gave her a squeezing hug. She returned it.

Carmela and Smitty came forward, all smiles. Nealy grinned at their attire. They were the picture of Louisville's society ladies, with their crisp linen suits, wide-brimmed straw hats, and bow-trimmed shoes.

"Take this for luck," Smitty said, handing her a lace-trimmed hankie. "It was my mother's, and she was one lucky old lady."

Carmela stepped up to the plate and hugged Nealy. "Maud and Jess would be so proud of you," she whispered. "I'm proud of you, too."

Nealy swallowed.

Emmie and Buddy were next. Nealy hugged them both to her, then stepped back to talk with her fingers. *What do you say when this is over, we take a long vacation and go to Disney World?*

They broke into wide smiles and hugged her again.

Emmie's fingers said, *See you in the winner's circle, Mom.*

Count on it, baby!

The announcer's voice boomed over the PA system. "Riders up!" was the call in the paddock. Nineteen jockeys mounted their colts and got ready for the walk underneath the main stands and out into the sunshine in front of 151,000 people.

Nealy gave Hunt a quick kiss. "I love you," she said.

"I love you, too." He gave her a hand and helped her settle into the irons. "This is it, Nealy. God, my heart is pumping so hard it feels like it's going to bust right out of my chest. Does yours feel like that?"

"It did, but I'm calmer now."

The bugle sounded. "The moment is at hand," the announcer blared into the microphone.

Nealy mounted Flyby and walked behind Leisure Boy and Nightstar, the favorites to win. Her eyes narrowed slightly when she saw Ricky Vee look at her sharply. She smiled. The walk was longer than she thought it would be, under the main stand and out into the bright sunshine. The roar of the crowd thundered in her ears.

"We're now bringing you a live look at the walkover that starts in the barn and then goes out onto the track. Here comes Flyby with his owner/trainer/jockey, Cornelia Diamond, along with the Blue Diamond Farms manager, Hunter Clay. A little while ago we tried to get a few words with Ms. Diamond, but we weren't successful. As the only female jockey riding today, she opted to stay away from the jockey room and the media. She's wearing purple silks, her mother's favorite color. Her mother, by the way, was the late Maud Diamond of Blue Diamond Farms, a two-time Derby winner. As another point of interest, and a first-time-ever occurrence, Flyby is being escorted out onto the track by his sire, Stardancer. Flyby is Stardancer's only colt, but after today his stud services may be in great demand."

Riding next to Nealy, on Stardancer, Hunt listened as the announcer rattled off the gate numbers. Flyby was in fifteen. Three of the last five Derby winners had rocketed out of that same gate. Today would make four. His mind raced as he imagined how the race would be run. Serendipity would go to the front early, and that could be a negative because there was going to be a lot of other speed in the race. Vegas Heat was the mystery horse, with the best jockey in the world riding him. Saturday's Warrior won the Breeders Cup Juvenile with odds of thirty to one. He had an excellent pedigree for the mile and a quarter. He could save valuable ground on the first turn if he ran true to form. Nightstar, Flyby's biggest competitor, was bred to go long.

Would Phil's Choice be able to make the distance? He wasn't a long-distance runner. Saturday's Warrior was a month of May foal and the youngest horse in the race. He had four starts and three wins. Did he have a chance? General Don had a terrific stride, but he'd lost out to Vegas Heat in the Blue Grass in front of 145,000 fans. Celebration had everything going against him today. He hadn't won a graded stakes. Still, if he picked up his feet, he might make a respectable finish.

Hunt mopped at his sweaty brow. He asked himself the question every owner, every trainer, and every jockey were asking themselves right this minute: How was the winner going to get to the finish line? Speed. A lot of speed. Crusader and Serendipity were going to get out early, with Texas Rich coming out of seventeen. Trying to get positioned right behind him would be Leisure Boy, Phil's Choice, Saturday's Warrior, and General Don. By the time they made the backstretch, the front runners would be getting a little tired. Leisure Boy would come up on the inside and Phil's Choice on the outside. Saturday's Warrior would be right there, too. At the top of the lane Saturday's Warrior and Leisure Boy would slug it out, and Phil's Choice would start to drift. Then Flyby would make his move, with Nightstar making a run for the rail. As they hit the finish line, it would be Flyby taking over and Leisure Boy chasing but unable to keep up. Nightstar and Saturday's Warrior would be in there for second place with a photo finish.

Nealy looked across at Hunt. "What's the matter? You look a little green around the edges. Is something wrong?"

He licked his dry lips. "I just ran the race in my head."

Nealy laughed. "Flyby won, of course."

"By three lengths."

"Wow!" She leaned over and wrapped her arms around Flyby's neck. "Did you hear that, boy? You won by three lengths."

"Six minutes to post time," the announcer called out. Nealy listened. His words seemed to run together. "The late Native Dancer was a horse with thunder in his stride and victory in his heart." There was a pause, then, "The one name that's been heard around the world is Flyby. At this minute he's as famous as his owner, trainer, and jockey. Here at Churchill Downs we're calling her a phenomenon. The big question is, will she win the Run for the Roses? Ladies and gentlemen, please rise for the playing of 'My Old Kentucky Home.'"

When the last note sounded, Nealy leaned over, and whispered in Flyby's ear, "Do your best! That's all I ask."

One by one the horses were led into their gates. The sound of the metal door clanging shut behind them echoed in Nealy's ears. The number 13 horse put up a fuss, and extra help was needed to get him into the gate.

When it was Flyby's turn, Nealy gave Hunt a wink, then rode into the gate unassisted. "Good boy, Flyby, you're such a gentleman."

Four more horses to go.

Nealy pressed down in the irons and prepared herself for that most important moment when the gate would open. "I'm saying a prayer, boy," she whispered. "For both of us."

One minute to go.

"Maud," she whispered, "this would be a good time for you to let me know you're watching this. Some little thing, a breeze on my cheek, a sound, something," she said, holding out her hand, palm up. A heartbeat later she stared into her open hand. A bright shiny penny stared up at her. "Dear God." With seconds to spare, she popped the shiny penny into her mouth and under her tongue.

The bell rang, the gates opened, and the horses flew out.

"And they're off in the Kentucky Derby!" the announcer roared over the loudspeaker. "Flyby got away cleanly and moved to the left right at the start. Serendipity takes the early lead, and Crusader is on the inside as he challenges early. Celebration is third on the inside, with Nightstar fourth. General Don is fifth and Crusader is in the sixth position. Then comes Phil's Choice, seventh. On the outside, Texas Rich is eighth and caught wide. Leisure Boy is between horses. As they round the clubhouse turn Crusader moves to the front. Serendipity goes to the outside and challenges Nightstar for position. Saturday's Warrior in blue and yellow moves up from behind and makes his play. General Don is fifth, with Phil's Choice tucked in at the rail and sixth at this point. Texas Rich gains speed and challenges Flyby for the first position."

Nealy couldn't hear anything except the thundering of hooves beside her and behind her. Out of the corner of her eye, she saw Texas Rich gaining ground but wasn't worried. Flyby hadn't even begun to show what he could do. Even when Texas Rich passed her, she wasn't worried.

Nealy bent low over Flyby's neck to talk to him. "Take it easy, boy, you'll get your chance. There's some racing room on the inside. Let's go for it," she urged, reining him left, closer to the rail.

Hunt stood at the finish line, watching, praying. Over the crowd's roar the announcer called out the order. "In the middle of the track comes the favorite, Nighstar, the Coleman horse, and he's making his run for the roses. On the far outside is Phil's Choice. General Don swings to the middle of the racetrack. Down the stretch they come in the Derby," the announcer screamed into the microphone, spurring the crowd to even greater excitement. "Texas Rich takes command by a head. Celebration on the inside. But here comes Flyby with huge strides, gobbling up ground and getting the lead."

"Go! Go! Go!" Nealy shouted, her heart thumping hard against her chest. She could feel Flyby make his move and knew she was knocking at heaven's gate.

Hunt slapped his racing form against the rail. "Go baby, go! Go!" he shouted.

The announcer screamed again, "Here comes Crusader, his colors showing the way. On the outside Serendipity is coming off the middle, and here comes Phil's Choice, but they can't catch Flyby, who is flying!"

"This is it!" Nealy said, using her voice and hands rather than a whip to let Flyby know what she wanted. "I can smell those roses!" she bellowed at the top of her lungs.

"And it's Flyby running for the finish, two lengths, four lengths, six lengths ahead. Here's the finish! Flyby wins by eight lengths and makes racing history for his owner, trainer, and jockey, Cornelia Diamond. What a punch that horse has! Texas Rich gets the place spot." Nealy stood up in the irons and felt Flyby slow down. He'd won. He'd truly won. The roses belonged to Flyby.

And then she was in the winner's circle surrounded by her family, track officials, and the media. "How'd it feel, Miss Diamond?"

Nealy looked down at the man holding the microphone. "There's no other feeling like it in the world," she told him. "He's a great horse. I never doubted him for a moment."

"How did it feel going out?"

"Great. He took off like a rocket. I didn't push. I was comfortable, and so was he. We just waited for our time, and he found it and knew exactly what to do."

"What do you have to say to all those people who said you couldn't do it?"

Nealy stuck her finger under her tongue and pulled out the penny. "I'd say they need to be more open to women involving themselves in the Thoroughbred industry and that they shouldn't be such stick-in-the-muds where their training methods are concerned. I might be the first, but I sure as hell won't be the last. Quote me on that."

The shiny penny clutched in her hand, Nealy watched as the blanket of red roses was draped across Flyby's withers. "For you, Maud," Nealy whispered, her eyes filling with tears. "I never break a promise. Tell Jess I hope I made him proud."

She jumped off Flyby and handed him to his groom.

Minutes later, back at the barn, Hunt threw his arms around Nealy and kissed her soundly. "You're quite a woman, you know that?"

She blushed.

"I'm so proud of you," he said, beaming. "What you said in the winner's circle . . . that was really good, Nealy. You didn't exactly thumb your nose at them, yet you said what needed to be said."

The moment Nealy spotted a gaggle of reporters coming toward her, she sent Smitty to fend them off.

"Emmie, come here," Nealy said, bending to her level. "I have something for you." She slowly opened the palm of her hand. "Just before the starting gate opened, Maud gave me this to give to you. It came all the way from heaven. I think she wanted you to have it back."

Tears rolled down Emmie's cheeks as she reached for the shiny penny.

In spite of Smitty's efforts, the owners, trainers, and jockeys came one by one to express their congratulations. It was the politically correct thing to do. In turn, Nealy was gracious and polite.

And then came the moment she had dreaded. "Fine horse you got yourself there, Miss Diamond."

Nealy would have recognized his voice anywhere. She turned, her heart thundering in her chest. She raised her head to look into her father's eyes and almost fainted in relief. His eyes, once eagle-sharp and bright blue, were now milky white. Cataracts.

"Thank you," she said gruffly.

"That was a fine race. I didn't think a girl could do it."

"You and a lot of others," she tossed back at him.

"Sassy little gal, ain't ya? You remind me of someone, but I can't think who at the moment."

"I guess I just have a universal personality."

"Are you taking him to the Preakness?"

"Wouldn't miss it for the world." She patted Flyby's mane. "We're going for the Triple Crown."

"I'll see you there," Josh Coleman called over his shoulder.

"Look for me in the winner's circle," she called after him. She watched him as he walked away and wondered how, after all these years, she could still despise the man. As far as she could see, he hadn't changed—not in looks and not in manner. Too bad. A change would have done him good.

A gentle breeze carried the scent of a familiar cologne.

"Excuse me, Miss Diamond," a smooth, sophisticated voice called out.

Nealy whirled around and gasped. Another phantom of her past.

The man extended his hand. "Dillon Roland, Leisure Boy's owner." Nealy jammed her hands into her pockets and saw the expression on his handsome face pinch with confusion. "I'm sorry to bother you, but I heard you're running the Preakness and the Belmont. I am, too. I wanted to meet my competition."

"If you'll excuse me, I'm really busy right now."

"I'd like to do some business with you and was hoping we might arrange a meeting."

"No thank you," she answered curtly.

He was incredulous. "I beg your pardon?" he stammered.

Nealy felt a wonderful sense of power. "I said," she said, looking him straight in the eye, "no thank you. What part of *no thank you* don't you understand? It means I'm not interested in doing business with you."

He stared at her. "May I ask why?" He seemed confused, unwilling to accept the fact that she wasn't interested in his offer.

"Sure. Your reputation precedes you, that's why. Now, if you'll excuse me. . . ."

When he made no move to leave, Nealy wondered if her rudeness hadn't done more harm than good.

"Have we met before? You look vaguely familiar," the debonair horse owner said quietly, his expression openly puzzled.

A little familiar? she wanted to ask. *We went to bed together, not once but several times. You told me you loved me and that you'd take care of me. Then, when I said I was pregnant, you threatened to blow my head off with your shotgun if I ever told anyone you were the father of my child.* "Not that I recall. I think I would remember someone like you," she said coldly. She turned her back on the man who was her daughter's father and walked away in search of Hunt.

"Let's get some food and some sleep, and then let's get these horses loaded. I want to go home."

On a cloudy, overcast day in June, Nealy and Flyby rode out of the winner's circle for the third time, a Triple Crown winner!

"It's stud heaven for you now, Flyby," she told him on the way back to the barns. "You never have to run again unless you want to. It's you and Charlie in the paddock from here on in. You did me proud today. What that means is you're the best of the best now. There's only a handful like you in the whole world. Blue Diamond Farms is now on the map. All because of you. Let's cool you down so we can go home where we belong."

PART II

16

Visually, little had changed at Blue Diamond Farms in the twenty-one years since Flyby brought home the Triple Crown. The Kentucky bluegrass was just as blue, the board fencing just as white, the huge bronze statue of Flyby greeting visitors at the entrance to the farm just as awesome, just as breathtaking.

Wealth and power were everywhere, but the owner paid it no mind. While the outward trappings remained the same, internal family changes had taken place, some for the good, some for the bad.

In late July, following the Triple Crown win, Blue Diamond Farms hosted a second wedding. Nealy and Hunt planned everything to duplicate Maud and Jess's wedding, right down to the hour they said "I do." A year later they were blessed with a son they both doted on.

Soon after Nick was born, Carmela went into semiretirement. Until she died five years later, she still cooked from time to time, but the day-to-day business of cooking and cleaning was left to a younger woman who lived off the premises.

Continuing the wedding tradition, Emmie and Buddy joined hands and hearts the year Emmie turned twenty-three. The couple lived happily on the farm in their own home a quarter mile away from the main house. Buddy assisted Hunt in managing the farm, and Emmie worked toward her goal of bringing a second Triple Crown win to Blue Diamond Farms. So far the right colt hadn't been born, but she remained optimistic.

The next three years brought nothing but sadness and grief. First Stardancer died and was buried in the stallion cemetery, then Charlie died and was buried next to Molly in the pet cemetery. The stonemason carved out an etching of his head crowned by a halo into the marble marker. The third death struck directly at Nealy . . . Hunt suffered a heart attack while haltering Flyby. It was Flyby's loud whinnies signaling something was wrong that brought Nealy and Nick running, only to discover they were too late.

Danny, Hunt's father, was so overcome with grief that he'd retired, packed up, and moved out of state. He called from time to time to ask how everyone was doing, but Nealy knew she would never see him again.

Smitty continued to run the business end of the farm with an iron hand. She had been the glue holding everything and everyone together after Hunt's death. She dried tears, offered her shoulder to cry on, and staunchly stood tall, her own grief hidden. Over the years she had become more to Nealy than just a business manager; she'd become Nealy's mother, sister, aunt, and best friend.

Life went on and Nick, Hunt and Nealy's son, turned twenty, and according to Smitty, was the spittin' image of his pa. He was tall, well over six feet, hard-muscled, sharp-eyed, and as handsome as a new spring colt. But it was his gentle ways, his soft voice, and most of all his special *touch* with horses that made him the apple of his mother's eye. She'd always thought Emmie had inherited her touch, but she'd been wrong. She wasn't wrong about Nick. And for that reason she was convinced that one day he would be the best horse trainer ever to come out of the state of Kentucky and quite possibly the whole United States. Nealy had taught him everything she knew, but there were some things that couldn't be taught, things that were instinctive. Nick had those instincts.

Physically, the years had been kind to Nealy Coleman Diamond Clay. She was still an attractive woman. Still as healthy and strong as ever. Hardly a day went by that she didn't take Flyby out for a breeze alongside whatever current pair of two-year-olds were being trained by Emmie and Nick. Even to the casual onlooker, the three of them riding abreast were quite a sight.

When Nealy had first come to Blue Diamond Farms there had been fewer horses in residence, about half of which belonged to Maud and Jess. Now there were 150, and two-thirds belonged to Nealy. In addition to acquiring horses, she had acquired the farm adjoining hers. It included a house, several outbuildings, and another eight hundred acres. This new acreage she used for retired stud horses and mares.

Nealy's unorthodox methods had made news once again after Flyby's Triple Crown win when she announced that she would put Flyby to stud only three times during the breeding season, thereby limiting his offspring to three foals a year. Other farms bred their champion stallions considerably more often, but Nealy was of the opinion that this overbreeding compromised the quality of the foals.

Even though Flyby's foals went for several million dollars each, money was not the goal. Money had never been a goal. It was quality, always quality.

It was spring again in Kentucky and just three weeks until the Kentucky Derby. Nealy sat on the front porch waiting for the sun to rise, coffee cup in hand.

"A penny for your thoughts, Ma."

She twisted around. "Nick!"

He laughed. "You always act so surprised when I come out here early in the morning to sit with you, but I've been doing it for years, ever since . . ."

"Since your dad died," she finished for him, and saw him nod. "Sometimes I think he's here with me and that I can hear him talking. It's just a feeling," she said, smiling. "There's nothing ghostly about it. You know what I mean. I still miss him as much as I did those first horrible days." She grabbed his hand and squeezed it. "He would be so proud of you. Do you miss him, Nick?"

Nick sat down in his father's old chair. "More than you know. You feel his presence here on the porch, and I feel it in Flyby's stall."

Nealy stared at the statue of Flyby out by the front gate and thought about Hunt, of how happy they'd been those first few years and how miserable they'd been later. She sipped her coffee.

"Do you think Grandpa will ever come back?" Nick asked.

"No, I'm afraid not. But be sure you call him every few days to let him know we're thinking of him."

"I will."

"What would you say if I told you I've been thinking about taking a vacation?" When she saw her son's mouth drop open, she couldn't help but laugh. "I know I've shocked you, but I'm serious, and what I want to know is . . . if I decide to go ahead and plan the trip, do you think you and Emmie can handle things here?"

"Ma, I'm not even going to answer that. You should know better than to ask. Where are you going?"

Nealy leaned back in her chair and crossed one leg over the other. "I have no idea. But somewhere. The only time I went anywhere was when I left Virginia to come here and when I took Flyby to his races, but I didn't even get to see New York the way a tourist would. Hawaii maybe," she said, shrugging her shoulders. The idea of palm trees and warm beaches sounded very appealing at that moment. "Your dad always wanted to go there, but we never could find the time. He wanted to go to the Orient, too. But that was in the early days of our marriage, and it was always *someday*." She stared into her empty coffee cup, thinking of all the things that should have been, could have been but for . . . "Maybe I'll just go into town and do some shopping," she said, pulling herself out of her melancholy. "Smitty has a birthday coming up. What do you buy for someone who has everything?"

"Ma, I don't have a clue. I saw an advertisement in the paper last week for some gift shop in Lexington that sells monogrammed toilet paper." At Nealy's look of surprise, he said, "Honest, Ma. Do you think people actually buy stuff like that?" He guffawed. "You could give her a trip to some faraway exotic place. Maybe send her on a cruise. I bet she'd like that. Better yet, why don't the two of you go together?"

Now it was Nealy's mouth that dropped open. "That's a wonderful idea, Nick!" How come she hadn't thought about that?

Nick scrutinized his mother. "Something's wrong, Ma. What is it?"

"Nothing," she said. "I just feel . . . I have this feeling . . . I can't explain it. I know something bad is about to happen, but since I don't know what it is, the feeling spooks me. Flyby is all right, isn't he?"

Nick knew not to discount his mother's feelings. She had an uncanny knack for predicting things before they happened. "He's fine." Nick stood up and clapped his mother on the back. "My mother the seer." He looked to the east and saw a snip of pink sky showing through the clouds. "It's going to rain. That's probably what's bothering you. I gotta get down to the barns. Let me know if you're going into town." He took the porch steps in two strides.

"Why?" Nealy called after him.

He turned around and regarded her with a sideways look. "Because you're my mother, and I want to know where you go and what you do."

"That's my line," Nealy laughed.

"You know what, Ma? I bet if you went into town and got yourself fixed up, you could probably scare up some good-lookin' guy to take you dancing."

"Go!" Nealy thundered.

"You have gray hair!" Nick shouted over his shoulder. "You're too young for gray hair!"

Nealy sighed. Gray hair. A sign of impending old age. Was forty-eight old? Obviously her son thought so. At twenty, she supposed forty-eight sounded ancient. That meant Rhy was fifty-two and Pyne was fifty. And her father was over a hundred. She wondered if he'd ever had his cataracts operated on.

If she went into the house and called SunStar Farms, who would answer? Damn, why was she suddenly thinking about her family? Were they the reason she was feeling spooked? She hadn't thought about them in a long time. Why today? Maybe Nick was right, and it was just the impending rain. He always said she wigged out when a storm threatened. Of course it wasn't true. It was just Nick's way of teasing her.

"Gray hair, indeed!"

"Nealy!"

Nealy turned to see Smitty at the screen door. "What are you doing up? I thought you said you were going to sleep in today. It's Saturday."

Smitty came out on the porch, her expression tight. "Your bad habits have rubbed off on me. I can't sleep past four-thirty anymore. Nealy, I . . ."

"What's wrong, Smitty?"

"Wrong? I don't know whether you'll think what I have to tell you is wrong or if you'll think it's right."

"Wrong, right, what are you talking about?"

"I woke up to the news on my radio. You know how those jocks like to give every bit of horse news there is. They said . . . what they said was that Josh Coleman suffered a stroke. Then they gave a rundown on his farm, his family, his career. . . . I thought . . . I thought you might want to get in touch with your brothers or something."

Nealy uncrossed her legs and sat forward. "Now why would I want to do a thing like that?" The fine hairs on the back of her neck started to prickle.

"Probably for the same reason you kept up with your family these past years by reading everything I put in front of you. If you want, I can find out more." When there was no response, she said, "It wouldn't hurt to make a few inquiries to find out what his condition is. After all, once he's gone, you may not be able to collect on that check of his you never resubmitted after payment was refused." When Nealy gave her the evil eye, she backed off. "Okay, okay, forget I mentioned it."

Nealy felt something like relief. Her intuition had been right. Smitty's news was the reason she felt so spooked. "What would you rather have for your birthday gift, a cruise or a roll of monogrammed toilet paper?" she asked, sidestepping the subject altogether.

"Yes to both, but it won't do you any good to try to change the subject on me. This is serious business. I think that if it's not already too late, you should pay your father a visit. Either make your peace with him or damn him to hell and eternity. Whichever makes you happy. Death is final. You won't get up to bat again." She looked Nealy straight in the eyes. "Do people really wipe their rear ends on monogrammed toiled paper? That seems so . . . decadent."

Nealy guffawed and stood up. "I'm going shopping."

"Shopping?" Smitty echoed, a stupid look on her face. "In all the years I've known you, you've never gone shopping. Shopping?" she repeated.

"I'm going to get my hair colored. Nick doesn't like the gray.

He said if I fixed myself up, some man might latch on to me and take me dancing. When my own kid tells me something like that, I think it's time I paid attention."

"I'll be damned."

"That about sums it up," Nealy said, heading for the house. "While I'm out, I think I'll go by the animal shelter and see about adopting a dog. I didn't have the heart to get another dog after Charlie crossed the Rainbow Bridge. But I think I'm ready now. How about you, Smitty? I know you love cats. Do you want me to get you a cat?"

"Why the hell not? Sure, get two. Get the least likely to be adopted ones, the ones they would put down first."

Nealy nodded. "Come with me, Smitty, and pick out your own cats. It's not like you can't get away from the office now and then. With that mess of people you hired, you don't have anything to do but stand around looking over their shoulders. One of these days, one of them is going to take a poke at you."

Smitty appeared to consider the idea. "I suppose I could . . . But first I want to know, are you going to think about what I told you?"

"Yes, but only if you go shopping with me."

"That's blackmail."

Nealy closed the screen door behind her. She knew Smitty would do as she asked. She always did. Nealy felt positively *brittle* as she walked up the steps to her second-floor bedroom. How was it possible that after all these years thinking of her family could make her feel like this? She didn't give a good rat's ass about her father or her brothers. No, that wasn't true, she amended. She did care some about her brothers.

She felt incredibly old when she sat down in Maud's rocker. All the old hatreds she thought she'd overcome long ago rivered through her. Maybe Smitty was right, and she should pay her family a visit.

The memory of her father coming up to her on Derby Day all those years ago still haunted her. Only now did she understand that what she'd felt was fear, pure and simple. Was she still afraid?

Both Smitty and Hunt had told her that if her father really wanted to find her, he could have, without any difficulty. "Blood,"

Hunt had said, "always wins out. Good, bad, or indifferent, family is family." She'd lost count of the times he had goaded her to go home and confront her family. He'd begged, cajoled, and pleaded. But she'd always turned a deaf ear.

The one major fight they'd had during their married life was about her father. Hunt said Nick deserved to know his grandfather and uncles. Emmie too. He said SunStar Farms was part of their heritage.

Nealy leaned her head against the back of the rocker and let the tears come. She could still remember every awful detail of the night she'd taken Emmie and driven away from SunStar Farms. She remembered the rain slashing down on her when she stopped at the end of the drive to dig up the bucket of SunStar soil. She remembered being so sick she thought she might die . . .

The morning of the day Hunt died, he'd asked her when she was going to shed the bitterness in her heart so she could be a real woman, the woman he thought she was when he married her. She'd given him a flip answer and told him if he didn't like her heart, then maybe it was time for him to move on. The look on his face . . . like he'd just been stomped on . . . made her feel ashamed, but she hadn't apologized. How she regretted that.

She cried until she couldn't cry anymore because there were no tears left to shed. She was wiping her eyes on the sleeve of her shirt when Smitty came into the room with a cup of coffee in her hand.

"That bad, huh?" she said, holding out the coffee cup.

"Yeah. That bad." She took the cup from Smitty's hands and sipped the steaming brew. "Tell me something, Smitty, did you know things weren't right between Hunt and me those last couple of years?"

Smitty sat down opposite Nealy in Jess's old chair. "Everyone knew."

Nealy nodded. She supposed she'd been fooling herself to think it was a secret. "I still don't know what he wanted from me, Smitty. I really think he fell out of love with me when he realized that the horses were my first love." Her breath shuddered as she let it out. "I never hid that from him. He knew who and what I was when he asked me to marry him." She looked away and waited until she could be sure her voice would be steady before asking, "Just out of curiosity, do you happen to know how many affairs he had?"

Smitty drew up her knees and wrapped her arms around her legs. "Three that I know of."

"Did his father know?"

She nodded. "They had more than one row about it. I was never sure if you knew, and I always wondered if I should say something, but it wasn't my place, you know?"

"Yeah, I know, and you're right, it wasn't your place. I suspected," she said, then shook her head. "No, that's not true. I knew, but I never confronted him. I suppose because I was gutless and didn't really want him confirming it. I didn't want to have to deal with it because once I did that I would have had to make decisions. I guess he died thinking I didn't know. I suppose that's for the best."

"Did you love him, Nealy?"

She took a few moments to gather her thoughts. "If you mean that bell and whistle stuff, no. He didn't rock the ground under my feet. I loved him in a different kind of way, and I never would have cheated on him, Smitty." She looked down into her coffee cup. "He said I had a bitter heart. One time he even said my heart was black. I wonder if Nick feels that way about me."

"That boy loves you with all his heart. Whatever his father was or wasn't, it has nothing to do with him or you. You know what you've always told me, get over it and move on."

"I know but . . ." A look of guilt crossed her face. "Smitty, I didn't grieve for Hunt the way I did for Maud and Jess. When they died, I thought my world was coming to an end. I remember when it was Maud's time, Jess wanted to lie down and die right alongside of her. I didn't feel like that when Hunt died. Good God, what's wrong with me? Maybe I'm not capable of loving anyone except my children, dogs, and horses."

Smitty jumped up, went over to Nealy, and pulled her out of her chair. "Come on. I made an appointment for you at the beauty shop. You have an hour. We'll get the cats and dog another time. Oh, and by the way, I also called your old home and pretended I was a reporter. I spoke to your brother Pyne. He said the doctor said your father isn't going to survive very long.

You probably shouldn't drag your feet on this, Nealy. By the way, didn't you tell me you have no other family?"

"Yes. Why?"

"Your brother said the family has been notified, and they're coming from all over the country."

Nealy stopped dead in her tracks. "Family? Are you sure you called the right number?"

"Of course I'm sure. I don't make mistakes, Nealy."

"Then Pyne was either drunk or delirious. We don't have any other family."

"Should I make plane reservations for this afternoon?"

"All right, Smitty."

"What about Emmie, Buddy, and Nick?"

"Make them for three. Buddy mentioned having to go out of town. And hire a car service to pick us up at the airport and drive us around."

"You're doing the right thing, Nealy."

Nealy laughed. "I hope you're right." She closed her eyes to ward off the dizziness she was feeling.

I'm going home.

Her heart fluttered in her chest.

Home.

The two brothers watched from the window as a black, stretch limousine crunched to a stop in the middle of the gravel driveway. In silence, they watched a uniformed driver get out and open the rear passenger door. Their jaws dropped when they saw a slender woman dressed in brown-leather boots, well-cut jeans, and white shirt emerge and look around. She reached a sun-darkened hand up to adjust her tinted glasses, then tipped the brim of her pearly white Stetson to reveal a mane of thick sable brown hair.

"Who the hell is *that?*" Rhy Coleman demanded of his brother Pyne.

Pyne's face screwed up. "How the hell should I know? But whoever she is, she's coming up to the porch. I think you should open the door."

When his older brother made no move to greet their guest, Pyne started toward the door, but it opened before he could reach it, and the woman blew in like a gust of wind. Without so much as a glance at the brothers, she headed straight for the stairway leading to the second floor.

"Hey! Just a damn minute!" Rhy shouted. "Who the hell are you to walk in here like you own the place?"

She turned to face them and grinned as she lowered her glasses. "Why, I do own it, Rhy, at least a third of it. Don't you recognize me, big brother?"

Rhy's eyes widened with shock.

Pyne walked toward her. "Nealy! Is it really you?"

"In the flesh," she said, thinking it funny that neither one of them had recognized her. She'd recognized them the second she'd seen them, not by the family resemblance but by the slump of their shoulders. Her grin vanished as she glanced back at the stairs. "Where is he?"

Pyne's head jerked upward.

Nealy nodded. "You two stay here," she ordered. "I have something I want to say to him, and I don't want either of you interfering. Understand?" When there was no response, she repeated her question. This time both brothers nodded. Nealy stared at her brothers and realized they were strangers to her and that she felt absolutely nothing for them—not love, not hate, nothing.

After all these years, here she was on Coleman land.

Shoulders stiff, back straight, she mounted the stairs with the same mix of confidence and caution she used when mounting her horses. At the top, she stopped and looked down at her brothers, who appeared to be debating whether or not to follow her. "Go about your business while I take care of mine."

Nealy hesitated only a moment outside her father's bedroom, then opened the door and walked in. The room was just as she remembered it, dingy gray walls, a few pieces of battered pine furniture and worn-out, roll-down shades covering the two windows.

Her nose wrinkled at the smell of dust, mold, and medication. Hearing a groan, she turned her gaze toward the bed and saw a mound of quilts . . . her father, the man who had sent her fleeing from this very house over thirty years ago.

A frail voice demanded to know who was there. Nealy

stepped up closer to the bed and heard a footfall behind her. Rhy or Pyne? she wondered. Pyne.

"Hello, Pa. It's Nealy."

The voice was stronger when he spoke a second time. "There ain't nothin' here for you, girl. Go back where you came from. You don't belong here."

"I don't want anything, Pa," Nealy said looking down at the load of quilts on the bed. They looked dirty or maybe it was just the lighting. Clean, dirty . . . what did she care? She pushed the pearly white Stetson farther back on her head so she could get a better look at the dying man.

"Then what are you here for?"

Nearly felt a hand on her shoulder and glanced back to see Pyne. The hand was to tell her to take it easy.

Like hell she would. Her father had never taken it easy on her. Not even when she was so sick she couldn't stand up. She removed his hand with her own and gave him a warning look. More than thirty years she'd waited for this moment, and neither Pyne nor Rhy was going to take it away from her.

"I came here to watch you die, old man," she said, looking her father straight in the eyes. "And I'm not leaving until I hear you draw your last breath. Only after I've danced on your grave will I leave. Do you hear me, old man?" She glared at him, her eyes burning with hate.

The old man's face became a glowering mask of rage. "Get out of my house!"

"Still ordering people around, are you? Well guess what? I don't have to take your orders anymore. I repeat, I came here to see you die, and I'm not leaving until you go to hell. That's where you're going, Pa. Hell!" There, she'd said what she'd come to say, but why didn't she feel a bigger sense of satisfaction? Why did she feel this strange emptiness?

"Pyne! Take this devil child away from me. Do you hear me?" the old man gasped as he struggled to raise himself up on his elbow.

"I'd like to see him try," Nealy said bitterly. Then she felt her brother's hand on her shoulder again. "I'd like to see anyone try to make me do something I don't want to do. Those days are gone forever."

The old man gurgled and gasped as he thrashed about in the big bed. Nealy watched him with clinical interest. Her eyes narrowed when she saw drool leak from his mouth. She stood staring at him until he calmed down, then stretched out her leg and, with a booted foot, pulled over a straight-backed chair and sat down facing the bed. For long minutes she stared at him with unblinking intensity until he finally closed his eyes.

"Okay, he's asleep now," Pyne said. "What the hell are you doing here, Nealy? We haven't heard a word from you in over thirty years, and all of a sudden you show up just as Pa is getting ready to die. How did you know? Can't you let him die in peace?"

Nealy removed her Stetson and rubbed her forehead. She didn't really care all that much for hats, but she'd always longed to wear a pearly white Stetson, just like the Texans wore.

"No, I can't let him die in peace," she said, her voice even now, calm. "He has to pay for what he did to me and Emmie. As to how I knew he was dying, I make it my business to know what goes on here. And you know why I'm here, Pyne. I want my share of this place for Emmie."

Pyne chuckled softly. "Your share? You just said you'd made it your business to know what goes on around here. So how come you don't know that Pa refused to make a will? There hasn't been any estate planning, Nealy. And neither Rhy nor I have power of attorney. The IRS is going to take almost all of it. Whatever's left will be a piss in the bucket."

"We'll just see about that," Nealy said. "Call the lawyers and get them here on the double. Offer to pay them whatever they want. Just get them here. If we work fast, we can still get it all in place. As long as Pa's still breathing, there's a chance. Now, get on it and don't screw up, or you'll be out on the highway along with your brother."

Pyne stammered in bewilderment. "But . . . I can't. Pa wouldn't . . ."

Nealy stood up, took her brother by the shoulders, and shook him. "Don't tell me what Pa would or wouldn't do. It doesn't matter anymore. He's dying. There's nothing he can do to you, to any of us. Don't you understand that?"

Pyne Coleman stared down at his fit and *expensive*-looking

younger sister. After all these years she was still pretty, with her dark hair and big brown eyes. Once when they were little he'd told her she looked like an angel. She'd laughed and laughed. Back then they had been close out of necessity. It was all so long ago. And now here she was, over thirty years later, just as defiant as ever and issuing orders like a general.

Nealy suffered through her brother's scrutiny, wondering what he was thinking. She was about to ask when Rhy stuck his head in the door. "You better come downstairs, Pyne, there's a whole gaggle of people outside. They said they were relatives, *family.* I didn't know we had a family. Do you know anything about this?"

Pyne didn't seem the least bit surprised. "I know a lot about it," he said, smiling. "Pa told me about them about a month ago, right before he had his stroke." He took Nealy's elbow and steered her toward the door. "I'll make you a deal. You make them welcome while I make that phone call to the lawyers."

Nealy jerked her arm free, went back to her father's bedside and leaned close to him. Only when she was satisfied that he was still breathing did she follow her brothers downstairs.

"Before I go out there and introduce myself, I want to reintroduce myself to you. In the world of Thoroughbred horse racing I'm known as Cornelia Diamond of Blue Diamond Farms in Kentucky. I own, trained, and rode Flyby, the last Triple Crown winner."

"You're Cornelia Diamond!" Pyne said in awe. "But how? I mean . . ."

"There's no time to explain it all now," Nealy said, heading toward the front door.

"Wait a minute!" Rhy said. "Pa said he shook your hand after the Derby win, but he didn't say it was you."

"I suspect he couldn't see me clearly because of his cataracts. More than nine years had gone by. I was the last person he ever expected to see."

"You never cashed the check for the two colts you sold us."

"I have it right here." She pulled the check out of her pocket and held it up so they could see it. "It bounced."

"I don't understand," Rhy said. "What are you doing here?

What do you want? Revenge? The past is gone, Nealy. Let it go. Show a little compassion."

"The way you all showed me compassion when you told me that I'd be doing you all a favor if I just packed up and left? Do you ever think about that night, Rhy? You and Pyne sent me packing so that you'd be spared Pa's wrath. Did you ever consider that I had nowhere to go, that I had a baby and very little money and nothing but that broken-down truck? Before that night, I had never even driven on the highway. My God, I didn't even have a driver's license." She took a step toward him, her eyes narrowed. "Why didn't you and Pyne stand up to him on my behalf? Why? Because you're cowards, that's why. Yellow-bellied cowards. And now look at you. Look at this place, this hellhole," she said, glancing around. "If you'd had any balls you could have made something out of yourselves and SunStar Farms."

Nealy walked over to the foyer, set her hat down on the telephone table, and checked her hair and makeup in the mirror. With all the skill of a seasoned actress, she put a smile on her face as she moved to open the front door.

"Hi," she said. "I'm Nealy Coleman. And you are?"

A well-dressed elderly woman stepped forward and introduced herself. "I'm Fanny Thornton Reed. I represent Sallie, your father's sister's side of the family. We're based in Las Vegas, Nevada. And this is Maggie Coleman Tanaka. She represents Seth, your father's brother's family. Their roots are in Texas. I talked to your father on the phone about a month ago and told him we were coming, but it looks like you weren't expecting us. Is something wrong?"

"No, it's just that our father never mentioned any other family. I thought . . . We all thought it was just us. Come in, please, and make yourself at home." As soon as they stepped inside, Nealy waved to the occupants of the limo. She excused herself. She had a moment of surging pride when her own little family walked toward her. "This is my beautiful daughter Emmie and my son Nick," she said. "Emmie uses sign language." She turned to her brothers. "These are your uncles, Pyne and Rhy. And those people you saw go inside are our long-lost relatives."

17

Twenty years ago I would have given up my soul to be sitting around a kitchen table with my real family, Nealy thought. Now that it was actually happening, she didn't quite know what to make of it all. Family or not, these people were strangers. For the moment, she would let them think she was simply a daughter who had married, moved away, and returned to visit her dying father. Later on, depending on the circumstances and her mood, she would decide whether or not to tell them she was the daughter who had had to flee her home and fend for herself and her child, the daughter who had survived and prospered in spite of everything.

These relatives of hers, she thought, all seemed quite nice, but there were questions in their eyes. Nealy had questions, too—like why had they come and what did they want?

She glanced around the kitchen. Everything was neat and clean but aged and pathetically out-of-date. The stove was the same, but the refrigerator had been replaced. There hadn't been a dishwasher when she lived here, and there wasn't one now. There had never been any knickknacks or things nestled in corners and no rugs on the floor. The kitchen was as bleak and ugly as her memories of that last horrible evening when her father had come in and caught her sitting down, inhaling medicated steam from a bowl.

She looked at her watch and saw that it was almost nine o'-clock. Time to think about heading to town and the hotel.

Nealy sat forward. "Let me see if I've got this right so far." She looked across the table at Maggie Coleman Tanaka. "You are my father's brother Seth's granddaughter. Your father was Moss Coleman, and your mother was Billie. Sawyer and Cole are your children. You have a sister named Susan who is a concert pianist but no one seems to know where she is. Your brother Riley died in Vietnam, and Riley junior is his son." She smiled when she said, "How am I doing?" At Maggie's nod, she continued. "Cole lives in Japan, Riley in Texas, and you're in Hawaii. Oh, and Sawyer lives in Hong Kong but is moving back to Texas."

"Yes, that's right," Maggie confirmed. "Cary Asante and Thad Kingsley will be here tomorrow. That pretty much covers the Coleman side of the family with the exception of the children, Sawyer's husband Adam Jarvis, my husband Henry, Cole's wife Sumi, and Riley's wife Ivy. Don't fret over it. We have all the time in the world to get to know one another. My mother was here once with her husband and with Fanny Thornton. That was a while ago, though," Maggie said.

Nealy blinked and looked at her brothers. What were they thinking about all of this? Like her, were they wondering what these people wanted? She wished she hadn't come, wished she was back in Kentucky on her big front porch sipping a cup of coffee. Of one thing she was certain, her life was going to change. But for the better or the worse? A tired sigh escaped her lips.

"And you-all are the Thorntons," she said, looking at the people sitting and standing to her left. "Our father's sister Sallie's family." She pointed to each one as she said their name. "You're Billie, you're Birch, and you're Sage. Sunny is at home because she can't travel. Fanny is in Europe with her husband number three, Marcus Reed, but is on the way back. You're Ruby and Metaxas. Sage's wife is Iris, Birch is divorced. We're an incredibly large family. How is it we didn't know about all of you before?"

Maggie acted as spokesperson. "Why don't we leave all the questions for tomorrow? It's been a long day, and we're all tired. What do you say that we plan on getting back together here tomorrow around noon? Will that be convenient for you and your brothers?"

"It's fine with me," Nealy said as she glanced at her brothers.

"Yeah, sure," Pyne agreed.

Rhy nodded, his action belying his expression of displeasure.

Chairs scraped backward on the old pine floor as people got up to leave. Everyone spoke in low, respectful tones as they filed out of the kitchen.

"I'm going upstairs to check on Pa," Nealy said to Pyne, who was holding the door open for the departing guests. "See everyone to their cars, will you?" She was about to head upstairs when out of the corner of her eye she saw Ruby staring at her. For some unexplained reason she felt compelled to go over to her. "Is there anything I can get for you or do for you, Ruby?"

Ruby's mouth was as pale as her cheeks. "Thank you for asking, Nealy, but no. We'll talk tomorrow. Just so you know though, Maggie was wrong, we don't have all the time in the world to get to know each other. At least I don't." She smiled then, and said, "I do have tomorrow, though." She squeezed Nealy's hand before dashing out the door. "Here I am, Metaxas. I'm coming. I just don't want to be rushed. It isn't that often I get to meet family. Good night, everyone," she called, waving. "See you all tomorrow."

Nealy stared after Ruby's retreating back, wondering what she'd meant, hoping it wasn't what she thought. She was about to go upstairs when she saw Emmie standing on the bottom step looking upward. "Do you want to go up and see your grandfather?" Emmie nodded and headed up the steps. In the second-floor hallway, Nealy reached for her daughter's arm to stop her. "You remember this place, don't you?" At Emmie's nod, she said, "I didn't think you would. You were so little back then. You don't have to go into the room if you don't want to. You can stay out here in the hallway or in the doorway. It's your choice, Emmie."

Is he really going to die? Emmie asked, her fingers signing.

"Yes. I don't know exactly when, but soon."

Are you sure, Mama? Are you really sure?

"Yes, honey, I'm sure." She turned her daughter around and took her back to the top of the stairs. "Go down and stay with Nick. I'll be along in a few minutes."

Nealy walked into her father's room and shut the door. The room smelled worse than it had earlier. At eleven o'clock, the night nurse would come and at seven tomorrow morning she would be relieved by the day nurse. The second day-shift nurse had called in sick.

Nealy could tell her father was awake by the way his gaze ricocheted around the room. He was probably hoping someone else was in the room besides just her. "I thought you'd want to know that your brother's and sister's families are here. A woman named Maggie said some of them had been here before and that they brought family photo albums for you to see. You never mentioned us having any family. Why is that?" She paused, waiting for him to answer.

"None of your business," he said in a voice so low she had to lean toward him to hear.

"Actually, I'm thinking it's because you were afraid we'd hightail it out of here. Pyne and Rhy hate you as much as I do, you know." She watched the play of emotions in his eyes and on his face. "We've got a little business matter to settle, you and me. It's about those two colts you bought from Blue Diamond Farms. It seems you forgot to pay me for them. But, of course, you didn't really forget, did you?" She hunkered down next to the side of the bed and looked at him on his own level. "If you thought you were getting away with something, think again. I had my lawyer slap a lien on SunStar Farms." She found joyous satisfaction in hearing him gasp. "It's just occurred to me that I was wrong thinking you didn't recognize me that day at the Derby. You did, and you hid it from me. You are one black-hearted, motherfucking son of a bitch, Pa. But you know what? I outsmarted you, old man. SunStar Farms will come to me and my daughter in the end. After I take the horses, I'll burn this place down to the ground. Then I'll rebuild it for Pyne and Rhy." Nealy saw the fear in her father's eyes and realized that the threats she had no intention of carrying out were having the desired effect. "You're drooling again, Pa." She clucked her tongue to show what she thought of that. "Why, I think you're afraid of me. That's good. How does it feel? Awful, huh? You don't know what's going to happen next. You almost want to die, but you're afraid to do that, too. Right now you're hoping I'll just disappear. Well, you can forget that unless . . . you tell me what I want to know." She clamped her mouth shut.

Nealy sat on the edge of the bed and picked imaginary lint off her pants. "You know I could make all this unpleasantness go away," she said in a nonchalant tone that belied her inner turmoil. "I'll make you a deal. I'll go downstairs and call my lawyer and tell him to cancel the lien, and then I'll take my kids and leave . . . *if* . . . you tell me one thing: why you hated me so much."

The silence that followed loomed between them like a heavy fog. She clenched her jaw to kill the sob in her throat. "All I ever did was work my ass off for you. From sunup to sundown. I never whined, and I damn well never cried. I said, 'yes Pa, no Pa.' I never asked for a thing. Never once. Then I made a mistake. I looked for somebody to love me. I was young, and I thought sex was love. I want you to go to your grave knowing Dillon Roland is Emmie's father. I'm going to get that son of a bitch, too. Your good friend, Cyrus Roland's son, told me he'd blow my head off if I ever told anyone that he had fathered Emmie." She pressed her hand against the mattress and leaned toward him. "You listening, Pa? This is your chance. Tell me why you hated me. And don't pretend that you can't talk because I heard you before, remember?" She waited, but when he didn't say anything, she got up. "You had your chance, and now the offer is off the table. I'm going downstairs now, and if you're lucky, you'll be dead in the morning when I get back here. And if you're not, I'm going to make your every waking moment a living hell."

Out in the hall, with the door closed behind her, Nealy burst into tears. She leaned against the wall, then slid down to her haunches. She cried for the would-haves, could-haves, and should-haves.

A long time later, outside in the moonlight, Nealy turned to stare at the house she'd been born in. Nick was at her side. "I always thought this house looked like the one in *Gone With the Wind.* You know, Tara. The Thorntons own a mountain and huge gambling casinos. Isn't that amazing, Nick? And the Colemans own the biggest cattle ranch in the state of Texas. They're into electronics, aviation, and all kinds of things. They're diversified."

"Are you trying to compare net worths here, Ma? If you are, I think you have a definite edge. Why didn't you tell them who you are? You let them think that you're as pathetic as your brothers. Why didn't you say anything? I need to understand, Ma."

Nealy wasn't sure how she should respond to her son. "I was

. . . I don't know. For one thing I was overwhelmed, and for another, that's not the kind of person I am. I've never been out to impress anybody with money or things. Maybe I'll say something to them tomorrow after I find out what they want. Is Emmie okay?"

"No, Ma, she isn't okay. What the hell happened upstairs? She came flying down to the kitchen shaking so bad she stumbled on the last three steps and fell. She jumped up, ran out the door, doubled over, and threw up. We need to get her out of here."

"I think she might remember the house, the second floor. She was the one who wanted to go upstairs, but I sent her back down. She didn't go into Pa's room. She didn't even look inside the room. It's probably just nerves."

"Let's talk about this tomorrow, Ma," Nick said as he reached for his mother's arm to lead her back into the house to collect Emmie. "It's late, and none of us had anything but coffee this morning."

"My God, that's true. Let's stop at a fast-food place and get some hot dogs and hamburgers and some of those greasy French fries that I like so much. We can eat them in the limo on the way back to the hotel. I don't want to think about this place any more tonight. Something's wrong here, and I'm not sure what it is. It's just one of those feelings if you know what I mean."

"I know, Ma. I can feel it, too."

Out of habit Nealy awoke at three-forty-five. She stared at the red digital numbers on the hotel clock and groaned. She rolled over but knew she wouldn't be able to reclaim sleep. She couldn't even call down for room service because the kitchen didn't open until six. If she really wanted coffee, she could shower, dress, and head out to an all-night diner. She'd sent the limo driver back and arranged for a rental car. It would be in the hotel parking lot, but did she want it? Would a cup of coffee really make her feel any better? Yes.

Nealy swung her legs over the side of the bed and headed for the shower. The others wouldn't be up until at least six. That would give her some time to drive around town to check on

things. Obviously she was going to need some kind of game plan. She'd come here on the fly, literally at the last second, with no concrete plan in mind. Now that there was a whole family to consider, she had to get her ducks in a row and decide how she was going to proceed.

Thirty minutes later, Nealy picked up the key to the rental car from the night clerk. She drove carefully, searching for landmarks, but either her memory was faulty or the area had changed drastically since she'd left. The diner she remembered was gone, in its place a 7-Eleven store with a drive-through window. She ordered a pack of cigarettes and a large coffee, then pulled off into a parking space. After fiddling with the lid, she burned her tongue on the first sip. She cursed ripely.

While waiting for the coffee to cool, Nealy fired up a cigarette, her first in more than a year, and blew a perfect smoke ring. She'd quit smoking nine times and nine times she'd taken up the disgusting habit again. "I guess I'm weak, no willpower," she muttered. She made a mental note to quit again when she returned to Kentucky. For the moment, with everything going on, she needed the crutch.

How garish everything looked. All the bright neon on the highway was blinding. She wondered if what she was seeing was anything like the lights in Las Vegas. She thought about her new family, wondered at the bewildered looks on their faces. Maybe when Fanny, the matriarch of the Thornton clan, arrived she would be able to make sense out of what was going on. Maggie seemed to be the matriarch of the Colemans. *That has to make me the matriarch of this branch of the family,* she thought grimly.

Nealy positioned the huge cup of coffee between her knees as she slipped the car into gear and headed out to SunStar Farms. She realized now this had been her intention all along.

Twenty minutes later she turned onto the long dirt road leading to the house and immediately flipped off the car's headlights, stopped, and got out. Her throat constricted as she stared at her old home in the moonlight.

She'd called Blue Diamond Farms home, but now she knew that no matter how much she loved it, SunStar Farms would always be her home. Hot tears burned her eyes as she trudged down the long road to the house. She stopped to stare at the moss dripping from the ancient oak trees. The year she'd left a storm had destroyed all the moss. She remembered that the trees had looked naked without it. It was back now, hanging in long, thick gray strands. In the last of the predawn light it looked silvery.

Nealy sat down in the middle of the road and crossed her legs. She stared up at the old trees. Neither she nor her brothers had ever climbed them. With their father's threat of breaking their legs if they even thought about it, they'd kept their distance. Everything her father had said back then had been a threat. She now realized that she and her brothers had lived in absolute fear.

It had been Smitty's idea that she come back to SunStar. She'd thought that it would do her good, that it would give her a chance to make peace with her father and thereby with herself. Nealy had bought in to that, and had come with the hope of finding answers and understanding; but she knew now that was never going to happen. Sometimes you couldn't go back and heal the wounds. They were too deep.

She saw Pyne come out onto the porch and stretch. Maybe, if she was lucky, she could salvage a relationship with her brothers.

"Nealy! What the hell are you doing out here in the dark in the middle of the road?" he called out to her.

"I'm just sitting here, Pyne. What does it look like I'm doing?" she called back. As he came closer, she said, "All these years, whenever I thought about this place, this is the picture that came to mind. The oaks, the white pillars, the fencing, the barns. I always wanted to plant flowers in the spring, but there was never time to do that. There was never time to do anything pleasurable." Pyne leaned against the fence, gazing down at her. "I've already told you that the check for those two colts Pa bought from Blue Diamond Farms some years back bounced. So I put a lien on this farm. I'm thinking he did recognize me that day at Churchill Downs, or else Ricky Vee told him it was me." She cocked her head and looked up at him. "What did he want from us, Pyne? Do you know?"

"I don't know, Nealy. I honest to God don't know."

"This new family. He knew about them, yet he didn't tell you or Rhy until a month ago. Aren't you wondering why?"

"There's a long story about how Pa and his brother Seth lit out from their home and never went back. They left six other siblings behind—Sallie, Peggy, and I don't know the rest of their names. Sallie was the oldest girl, and after she left home and made her fortune, she went back, buried their mother, and bailed out the rest of her brothers and sisters. Then she set about searching for her older brothers. She found Seth first, then Pa. I guess it made her plenty mad to find out that both of them were rich men, yet neither had gone back to help the family."

"If that's true, it's sad, Pyne. What makes a man so stingy and selfish that he would do something like that? When all is said and done, at the end of the day the only thing you can really count on is family. Maybe not in our family, but for most people that's the way it works." She took a deep breath and got up. "While I'm at it, I might as well tell you that Dillon Roland is Emmie's father. I lied to Pa when I said a vagrant attacked me. I had to. Dillon said he'd blow my head off if I told anyone." She got up and brushed herself off. "You know what's funny? The bastard wants one of Flyby's colts so bad he drools just thinking about it. My day is coming where he's concerned."

Pyne turned to her and put his hands on her shoulders. "For God's sake, Nealy, leave it alone. I wish to God you had never come back here."

Nealy pushed his hands away. "Right now I do, too. But I'm here. Tell me, what is it this new family of ours wants? Do you have any idea? They didn't know Pa all that well, so it can't be love."

"I don't know yet. I haven't bothered to ask. I guess we should just wait and see. It can't hurt."

Nealy shrugged. "How is Pa this morning?"

"Just like yesterday. The nurse is with him."

Nealy consulted her watch. "When is the lawyer coming?"

"Nine."

"Good. That should give us plenty of time before the Colemans and Thorntons come back." She turned to head for her car, then remembered something she'd wanted to say, something Nick had told her last night after they'd gotten back to the hotel. "Birch told my son Nick that when his mother and Billie Coleman visited here they thought there was something out of whack with the pictures in the family album. Now that I think about it, we don't bear any resemblance to this new family of ours. We don't look like Pa either. I don't know if we look like Ma because I've never seen a picture of her. Have you?" When he shook his head, she asked, "Don't you find that strange?"

"I never thought about it."

"Well, I'm thinking about it, and I'm thinking I might have stumbled across the reason Pa hates us."

Pyne looked at her as if she had a screw loose. "Which is?"

"That maybe we aren't his children. Where are the family records? I want to see them along with the books."

Pyne threw his hands in the air. "God, Nealy, why are you doing this?"

She answered quickly. "Because I need to understand. Only then can I get rid of this baggage I've been carrying around all these years. Last night I told Pa I would make it all go away if he would just tell me why he hated me. He wouldn't say a word. I find that very suspicious. Don't you want to know where all this hatred came from? More to the point, don't you care?"

Pyne's shoulders slumped. "Don't, Nealy. Leave it alone."

"Damn you, I can't. Why don't you understand that? Do you know what I think, Pyne? I think the moment that old man was taken upstairs after his stroke, you went through all his stuff, and you know the truth."

18

Nealy closed the brown accordion-pleated envelope. She had called Nick at the hotel and told him to rent a second car. They were on their way. Her fingers worked the dark string to tie it into a perfect little bow. When she finished, she started to shake as panic coursed through her body. She reached out to the corner of the desk to hold on to it when her head started to spin. *Focus,* her mind shrieked. *Focus on the calendar. Focus on the numbers. Take deep breaths. Long, deep breaths. It's not the end of the world. Yet. Focus. Don't look at the folder. Deep breaths, Nealy, long, deep breaths.* Twice she struggled to get out of her father's chair. Twice she fell back into the worn padding. She wished she could go to sleep and never wake up.

"What are you going to do, Nealy?" Pyne whispered.

"I honest to God don't know. Would you have ever told me? Were you going to tell Rhy? If you had destroyed this folder, no one would ever have known. I guess you thought Pa might get better and come down here again. Say something to me, Pyne. I need to hear you say something to me."

"What do you want me to say? I wouldn't have told either of you. What's the point at this juncture? More wounds? We can start clean when he passes on. You wanted answers. They're all there. And, yes, you're right, I didn't destroy the folder for the reason you stated. Pa asked me at least fifty times to bring that folder upstairs. I kept saying I couldn't find it. He did hide it pretty good, but I was determined. Before you can ask, I've only known for a few weeks. Now you know why I invited his family here. What are you going to do, Nealy?"

"I'm going to take my kids and go back to Kentucky. I can't think right now. Maybe not knowing was better than knowing.

Go get Rhy. Now, Pyne. We'll give him the short version and go on from there. Are you going to tell *them?*"

"Are you crazy, Nealy? Of course not." He opened the door and bellowed to his brother in the kitchen.

"What now?" Rhy asked as he burst into the office.

Nealy gave him the short version of the contents of the brown folder. She waited for his reaction. "Well that certainly explains a lot of things," was his only comment.

Nealy picked up the folder with both hands just as Emmie, who had just arrived, poked her head into the room. "We'll be leaving as soon as I . . . tell Pa good-bye. Do you want to wait here for me?"

I'll say good-bye, too, Emmie signed.

"Where's the lawyer, Pyne?"

"In the dining room. He's waiting for us."

Nealy made an unladylike sound as she turned her back on her brothers. "Where's Nick?"

He's coming. He wanted to walk around a bit first, Emmie signed.

Nealy looked at her watch. Ten minutes past nine. She marched up the back staircase, her back ramrod stiff, the brown folder clutched tightly in both her hands. Emmie followed her.

In her father's room, Nealy looked at the nurse. "Go downstairs and have some coffee. I'll call you if you're needed." She raised her index finger at her father to show him he wasn't to object. He was propped up in bed with a mound of pillows behind him. As she advanced into the room, he noticed the brown folder. Nealy swore later that he shriveled to nothing right in front of her eyes.

Out of the corner of her eye she saw Emmie's agitation, saw her face contort in horror as her hands flew up to her face the moment she had a clear view of her grandfather. "Go with Nick, Emmie," she said. "It's okay for me to be here by myself. I appreciate you wanting to be with me, but it isn't necessary. Tell Nick I'll be down shortly, and then we'll be leaving for Kentucky." Her daughter was frozen in place, her mouth half-open, her hands clawlike as she reached out. "My God, Emmie, what is it? What's wrong?"

"Maaaamaaaa."

Nealy caught her daughter as she swayed backward.

Emmie's first word in thirty-two years! "Pyne!" she shrilled. "Rhy! Come up here! Help me. Something's wrong with Emmie. Call the nurse. She took one look at Pa and let out a bloodcurdling sound. She called me Mama. God, Emmie, what's wrong? Use your fingers, tell me what's wrong."

Emmie used her hands and feet to scramble backward and out the door, where she collapsed again in the hallway. "What is it, Emmie? My God, tell me, what's wrong?"

Nealy watched her daughter's fingers move as her face turned ashen. Strangled sounds came from her lips. "No, no, don't tell me that! Emmie, you were so little. How can you remember? Yes, yes. God, no. Please God, no."

"Will somebody please tell me what the hell is going on here?" Pyne shouted.

Nealy gritted her teeth as the nurse checked her daughter. "She's had a fright of some sort. She's fine, ma'am. I'll take her downstairs and outside."

"Ma, what's wrong? What happened to Emmie?"

"Emmie said her first word. Go with the nurse, Nick. Stay with her but keep her outside. She spoke. My God, she finally spoke. I'll be down in a minute. My God, I can't think. This can't be happening." Nealy clapped both hands to the sides of her head. "This is a bad dream. I'm going to wake up any minute. Oh God, oh God!"

"Nealy, for God's sake, what happened?" Pyne continued to shout, oblivious to the old man propped up in the bed in front of him.

"I'll tell you what happened," Nealy said the moment the door closed behind the nurse. "Emmie said Pa tried to choke her when she was little. She said she was crying, and he grabbed her around the throat and told her if she ever made another sound, he'd kill us both. That's what happened just now. She saw him, and she remembered. She called my name. She said it out loud. Out loud, Pyne. It's the first word I've ever heard her say. She called my name."

"Stop being so damn melodramatic, Nealy. Pa would never do anything like that," Rhy said, but he sounded as if he didn't believe his own words. He stared at her, his mouth slack, his body shaking like his sister's.

"I took Emmie to every specialist I could find. They told me there was no medical reason why she didn't speak. Every single specialist said she had undergone some kind of trauma. For years I blamed myself. God Almighty, I never, ever thought of anything like this. It explains everything. Yesterday she wanted to know if I was certain Pa was going to die. She kept pressing me for confirmation. All those years of fear, and I didn't know. What does that say for me?"

"I'll never believe that of Pa," Pyne said feebly. "Emmie wasn't prepared to see Pa looking like that. Don't forget he was a lot younger when you left here."

"Why don't we ask him? Point-blank, Pyne," Nealy said. "Don't let that nurse up here unless you want the whole world to know about this."

The moment the nurse's feet hit the last step of the stairway, Nealy opened the door to her father's room. Her brothers followed her into the room. The man she'd thought of as her father all these years looked even more shriveled than he had minutes ago. "I guess you heard, Pa. These two fine upstanding brothers of mine find it hard to believe you would try to strangle my daughter. I imagine you thought you were safe because Emmie was too young to talk. On top of all that you had the gall to turn around and call my daughter a half-wit and these two fine upstanding brothers of mine agreed with you. If you weren't already dying, I'd choke the life out of you with my bare hands for what you put that child through. I'm not done with you yet either, you miserable excuse for a human being. We know everything. It's all here in this folder. Every stinking, lousy detail. You aren't our father. Seth Coleman was our father. You met up with him way back when and made a pact with that damn devil. He made a bargain with you. You took us off his hands for money. He gave you a handsome stake, and in return you took his woman and us three kids so his upright, sanctimonious family never found out he'd been having an affair for years with another woman. And all you had to do in return was feed us, put a roof over our heads, and work us to death. Then when you died, all you had worked for all your life, excuse me, what my brothers and I worked for, would revert to the Texas Colemans, your brother's *real* family. You agreed to all that and promised to keep your mouth shut and never tell anyone. We were trailer-park trash according to your brother. Not fit to mingle with his legitimate family. We were good enough for you, though, weren't we? Did you work our mother to the bone the way you worked us?"

"Pa, say something," Pyne pleaded.

"You didn't try to choke that baby to death, did you, Pa?" Rhy demanded, his face full of tortured disbelief.

The wizened old man in the bed nodded.

"It was a trade-off." Nealy went on, relentless now. "You took us off old Seth's hands and he gave you $110,000. Fifty thousand for Rhy, fifty thousand for Pyne, and ten for me because I was a worthless girl-child. When you get to where you're going, you son of a bitch, the devil is going to have a field day with you. I'm going to keep this folder. I no longer care if I see you take your last breath or not. Maybe God in His infinite wisdom will let you live for years and years and *years* in your present condition *so* you can contemplate what you did to the three of us." At the door Nealy turned to her brothers, who appeared to be rooted to the floor in shock. "You can come with me if you want to. My door will always be open to you both. I'll make you full partners at Blue Diamond Farms. It's your choice. It doesn't have to be right now. Take all the time you want. Say good-bye to our new family for me."

"Nealy, wait!"

"No. There's nothing for me here. There never was. The only thing I want from this place is our mother's remains. I'll have the grave dug up and move her to Blue Diamond Farms. As the only daughter, it's my right to do this. I take care of my own. Now if you'll all excuse me, I want to see to Emmie."

Nealy heard her name being called when she walked down the hall across from the dining room. She looked over her shoulder but kept on walking. The last thing she wanted to do was to talk to Josh Coleman's lawyer. "Miss Nealy, wait. This is about your father's will."

Nealy did stop then and turn around to confront the attorney. "I think you have me confused with someone who cares about things like that. Wrong time, wrong person. You have a nice day now." Having said all she intended to, Nealy went outside to where Nick was waiting for her.

"Ma, she's talking a blue streak. I don't understand what she's saying, but they're words. A good speech therapist, and she'll be fine. Do you want to tell me what the hell is going on around here?" Nick demanded.

"I came here for answers, and I got them. I feel like a thousand pounds have been lifted from my shoulders. We'll talk about this when we get home. All I want to do now is get far away from here. By the way, that old man up there on the second floor is not your grandfather, so don't feel bad about leaving."

Nick shoved his Stetson farther back on his head. He watched his mother adjust her own Stetson before he spoke. "Then that has to mean the old man is not your father."

"That's right. Isn't it wonderful? I don't mean it's wonderful he's dying, I mean it's wonderful that he isn't my father."

"I knew what you meant, Ma." Nick grinned.

Emmie threw her arms around her mother and jabbered a blue streak. "Whatever you're saying is music to my ears, honey. I'm so happy for you. God does move in mysterious ways," Nealy said, hugging her daughter so hard she squealed, a sound Nealy loved hearing. "Nick, take Emmie back to the hotel and pack your things. I have some other unfinished business to take care of. Get the first flight out of here, and I'll be home by midmorning tomorrow."

"Ma, what other unfinished business?" Nick demanded.

"Thirty-three-year-old business, Nick. I'm on a roll now. We'll talk when I get home. It's wonderful about Emmie, isn't it? I prayed every day of my life that this would happen. I'm sorry about the circumstances that brought it out, but I'm glad it happened."

"What is it, honey? You want to go back to the house! Why for God's sake?"

I have to do something. By myself.

"Okay, we'll wait here for you." Nealy's eyes questioned her son, but he shrugged to show he knew as much as she did.

Emmie walked around to the back of the house and let herself into the kitchen. She looked around, uncertain where the voices she heard were coming from. She walked tentatively down the short hall to the dining room, where her two uncles and a stranger were sitting at the table. They looked at her questioningly. Trembling, Emmie walked over to her Uncle Pyne and reached down to take his hand. She looked at the big, callused hand and smiled as she dropped a penny onto his palm and closed his hand over it. She nodded, smiled, and walked out of the room.

Outside in the bright May sunshine, Emmie raised her face to drink in the warmth from the sun. She spread her arms wide and laughed. And laughed. She laughed so hard, Nick had to run over and clap her on the back to stop her from choking. "What did you do, Emmie?"

I gave my uncle Pyne a penny, she signed. *It's been to heaven and back. I don't need it anymore. He does, though. He started to cry. Do you think he'll cry as much as I did?*

Nick stared helplessly at his mother, who was smiling from ear to ear. "Count on it, big sister."

Nealy hugged her daughter and son good-bye and watched until their rental car was out of sight. Now she had other business to take care of.

Since it was still early in the business day, Nealy had her choice of parking spots. She maneuvered the rental car into a spot under the overhang of a large oak, hoping the sun wouldn't be as strong in that particular spot. It would probably be stifling hot when she came back, but she would be able to live with that.

It was a new building, all brick and glass. There was no character to it at all. Just a clean-looking square building with four floors. The Cyrus Roland Building. She just knew the entire building was full of white-collar investment bankers with the senior Roland still active in the day-to-day business. The senior and junior members of the Roland family also belonged to every equine organization there was. They owned and boarded over a dozen horses in Kentucky that represented millions of dollars. No Derby winners, no Preakness winners, no Belmont winners. A few Blue Grass Stakes, one Santa Anita, but that was it. Nothing to light up a trophy room.

Nealy smiled as she hitched up her jeans, tucked in the pristine white shirt, and adjusted her Stetson before she slipped on a pair of Chanel sunglasses, a gift from Smitty on her last birthday.

At the entrance she looked around. The landscaping was lush and green, even fragrant. She found herself staring at her reflection in the glass and shiny brass that was everywhere on the first floor. It looked expensive. Cold, austere, and expensive. Perhaps even a tad intimidating to those without seven digits in their yearly income. Smitty had told Nealy a few months ago that Roland Investments had hit a rough patch with some junk-bond mess they were struggling to get out of.

Nealy opened the door, meandered toward the center of the huge lobby to a round marble desk, where a uniformed guard sat staring at monitors and an open car-racing magazine in front of him. "Good morning, sir," she said. "I'm here to pick up Dillon. Now don't you be calling upstairs and spoiling the surprise. Rolly and I are going to surprise Dillon today like he's never been surprised before. He's waiting for me, and you know Rolly doesn't have a lot of patience at his age. I'm Cornelia Diamond, sir."

"Rolly?" the guard said, a puzzled look on his face.

Nealy clucked her tongue. "Shoot, I keep forgetting everyone doesn't call Mr. Cyrus Roland Rolly the way family does. He's going to be a mite put out if you don't let me go upstairs right now."

"Your name isn't on the list, ma'am," the guard said.

"Shoot. Rolly is getting forgetful. Seems like every day or so he has one of those little senior moments everyone talks about. I spoke to him just ten minutes ago, and he told me to hustle right over here. I hustled. I'm here. I'll be sure to mention to Rolly how accommodating you've been. Things like this help when they start figuring out Christmas bonuses."

"Well, all right. I don't want to be the one upsetting Mr. Roland's surprise. It's the fourth floor. Take the private elevator to the right."

"Shoot, I know that, sweetie. You be sure to mark my name down there now. Rolly likes to know who comes in and out of his building. You are the sweetest man for helping me out like this. I'm going to tweak Rolly about not putting my name down on the expected list. Guess he was afraid Dillon would see it and spoil the surprise."

"I'm sure that's it. Y'all enjoy that surprise."

"Honey, Dillon is going to sit up and *purr* when he finds out," Nealy drawled.

She sashayed her way to the private elevator that led to Cyrus and Dillon Roland's private offices. Inside the elevator, Nealy looked around at the luxurious teakwood paneling and mirrored walls. She sat down on a petit point chair and gazed at her reflection. She looked scared out of her wits. She removed her sunglasses. She still looked scared out of her wits. So much for bluster. She put them back on.

Dove gray carpeting hugged her instep when she exited the elevator. The walls were mirrored, a perfect backdrop for the exquisite creature sitting behind a green-marble desk that was bare of everything except a phone, a marble nameplate, a message pad with an attached pen, and a crystal dish of M&Ms. Her thick blonde hair was stylish and piled on top of her head. *Hair extensions*, Nealy thought. No one could have that much hair and not be top-heavy. Her eyes were a compliment to her eye doctor. Lavender. The only other person she'd ever heard of that had lavender eyes was Elizabeth Taylor. Excellent contact lenses. Her teeth were pearl white, small, and perfect. It was obvious she'd made some dentist thirty thousand dollars richer. Nealy knew a thing or two about fashion these days, with Smitty's help. The exquisite creature wore Armani that draped flawlessly over her perfectly shaped body. Nips and tucks, sliced and diced, another forty grand. Rolex watch, diamond stud earrings, and extra-long, acrylic, squared-off nails with a French manicure. Emmie's only question would be, how does she wipe her rear end? *Very carefully*, Nealy thought. The marble nameplate on her desk said the exquisite creature's name was Felicity St. John.

Felicity smiled, a major feat in itself with her lacquered-looking makeup. Nealy noticed the woman staring at her jeans and boots. "Honey, I didn't have time to change. The moment my private jet landed, I had to skeddadle right over here. Tell Dillon I need to see him right away. Like this very minute," Nealy purred.

"Miss . . . Mr. Roland is in a meeting. He can't be disturbed. You don't have an appointment. Do you, Miss . . . ?"

"Well shoot! You just go in there and fetch him right out. I can't be tying up my pilot while Dilly is in there discussing stuffy old things like money. Hustle now. Airplane fuel is expensive."

"Mr. Roland left strict orders that he was not to be disturbed. He instructed me to keep all his calls on hold, Miss . . . I'm sorry. You really need to make an appointment."

Nealy reached into her hip pocket for one of her business cards. It was wrinkled and bent when she pulled it out. She leaned across the shiny green-marble desk and got a whiff of an incredibly expensive perfume. "Let me put it to you another way, Miss Felicity St. John. Either you get off that designer ass of yours and go in there, or I'll boot it through the goddamn door. That means like now. Don't even think about not doing it or the toe of this boot will find its way clear up to your *tonsils*. Now hop to it, honey, and give old Dillon my card while you're at it. By the way, Armani or not, lime green does not go with those lavender contact lenses."

Nealy grinned when Felicity St. John tripped over her own feet in her haste to plow through the thick carpeting leading to Dillon's door, where she knocked discreetly, opening the door at the same moment to slither inside and close the door behind her.

He should be out on the count of three, Nealy thought. *One, two, threeee.*

"Cornelia Diamond, if I do live and breathe. Now to what do I owe the pleasure of this little visit?" Dillon Roland threw out his arms in welcome. "I never thought I'd see the day you'd come calling on old Dillon Roland."

"I was in the area. Can we go somewhere to talk in private?" Nealy said, looking pointedly at the Barbie doll behind the desk, who was staring at her with venom in her eyes.

"I have a client in my office, but we were just finishing up. The conference room on this floor is available if you'll just give me a minute. Felicity, see to Miss Diamond's comfort." From the look on Miss Felicity St. John's face, she would rather have seen to a rattler's comfort.

"Certainly, sir," she said, showing off the pearl white teeth. "If you'll follow me, Miss Diamond. Can I get you anything? A soda pop, coffee, hemlock?"

Nealy smiled. "Cappuccino would be nice."

"Why . . . I . . ."

"Would you have to leave the building to get it? That's all right. I'll be here for a little while. You take your time now, you hear." Nealy flopped down on a chair whose petit point cushions matched the cushion on the bench in the private elevator.

The door opened soundlessly. Nealy half turned in her chair to acknowledge Dillon Roland's presence.

"Cornelia, may I call you that? And of course, I'm Dillon. I'm not a formal kind of person. My father is, but I'm not. Never have been."

Thinning hair, thick around the middle. Custom-made suit, pricey shoes. Rolex watch. All the trappings of wealth not to mention the elegant surroundings. In his youth, he'd been handsome and muscular. He'd recited beautiful poetry to her. Back then he did have a way with words. Back then she'd thought he had soulful eyes. Now they looked calculating and wary.

"Call me whatever you like. First things first. Wherever did you get that Barbie doll in the reception area?"

"My father hired her. She makes the place look good, and for that we pay her eighty grand a year. She reads trashy magazines all day long. When she hears the elevator coming up she shoves them in the drawer. It's hard to find good help these days. Now, what can I do for you, Cornelia?"

"You did say, did you not, that you would do anything to get one of Dancer's Flyby colts?"

"Yes, ma'am, I did say that, and I meant it. Short of murder that is. The price doesn't matter. Would you like me to call my father in here? He can back me up on my offer. He's quite elderly now, and his sole purpose in life is to get a Triple Crown winner. I'd like to give him that if it's possible. I know he would dearly love to meet you and shake your hand."

"Anything, Dillon, short of murder?"

"Anything short of murder. Name it and it's yours."

Nealy leaned across the table to stare directly into Dillon Roland's eyes. "You really don't remember me, do you?"

"Of course I remember you. I congratulated you the day you won the Kentucky Derby. I was so in awe of you I was slobbering over myself. Your horse was magnificent. My own was a slug in comparison. I tried to get near you at the Belmont, but it was impossible. A Triple Crown now, that's something to take home."

"I'm Nealy Coleman, Dillon. You're the father of my daughter, Emmie. Surely you remember the day you threatened to blow my head off with a shotgun if I ever told anyone. Now do you remember?"

Dillon slapped at his receding hairline. "Jesus H. Christ! I thought you looked familiar that day. I didn't connect the names. You look so . . . *different.* Listen, that was the scared kid in me talking back then. I would never have done a thing like that," he blustered. "We had some fun. It's all in the past. Are you telling me you're holding a grudge against me for that?" His face registered total disbelief at his own question.

"Yeah, Dillon, that's exactly what I'm telling you. Emmie's birth certificate reads Emmaline Coleman. I think it should read Emmaline Roland. She's thirty-two. She might want to have children someday. She'll need to know her medical background. Don't think about denying it, Dillon. Today we have DNA. It's a costly process, but I can afford it. That's all I want from you. Nothing more."

"But she's a . . . they said . . ."

Nealy's eyes narrowed. "Half-wit? Retarded? No. She's normal in every way. She talks a blue streak. I can produce medical records. She's married now. Emmie herself can file a lawsuit against you, make a claim, whatever. This, Dillon, is the 'anything' I mentioned earlier."

"For Christ's sake, Nealy, I have a family. My oldest son's wife is due to have a baby any day now. If this comes out, I'll never be able to live it down. That was over thirty-two years ago. If all you want is a name on a birth certificate, I can do that and have the records sealed. If you want me to go public, I can't do that. My wife would never understand. My father would never understand."

"Which part? The part where you were going to blow my head off or the part where you denied you were Emmie's father or the part where I impregnated myself? I see, all of the above. The courts are very lenient these days in such matters. Okay, time for me to leave."

"Does that mean you won't sell me the next foal from Dancer's Flyby?"

"Yep, Dillon, that's what it means. You really are a ring-tailed son of a bitch, aren't you? I guess I knew that when I came here. Oh, one other thing. Lordy, Lordy, how could I have forgotten? I'm moving all the Blue Diamond accounts. You know, you really are stupid, Dillon. I've been feeding those accounts to you little by little these past fifteen years. You have almost the whole ball of wax, and still you didn't catch on. You're up on it now, though, right? By the close of business tomorrow. Everything, Dillon. Don't leave any fractions either. I called my broker earlier. He positively salivated when I gave him his orders. Gee, I hope you manage to get yourself out of that junk-bond mess. See you around."

"Just a goddamn minute, Nealy. This is blackmail. That's against the law."

"So is seducing a minor. So are coercion and threats of bodily harm to said minor. I guess we'll see each other in court."

"Nealy . . ."

Head high, back and shoulders stiff, Nealy strode from the conference room and out to the reception area, where Felicity St. John was exiting the elevator, a paper bag in hand. "You're grossly overpaid," Nealy said as she stepped into the elevator.

In the marble-and-glass lobby, Nealy walked over to the guard and poked his arm playfully. "It went swimmingly. Thank you so much. You have a nice day now."

"You, too, ma'am."

Outside in the humid morning air, Nealy twirled around and around in the parking lot, not caring who saw her. Free. She was finally free of all of them.

Damn she felt good.

Real good.

19

Joshua Coleman was laid to rest on the third Saturday of May, just as the three-year-olds bolted from the starting gates at Pimlico. There were those who said it was an omen. Others said it was nothing more than a coincidence. Horse people, superstitious to the core, held to their belief and watched as Sharpshooter, Josh Coleman's colt, ran the distance to move into the winner's circle at the Preakness. Those same people whispered and speculated among themselves, saying old Josh was spurring the horse on from on high. The family said nothing, their faces and manner somber as they walked away from the cemetery. There was no joy in the win, no sadness at the burial.

It simply was.

The good-byes were subdued and quick. There were handshakes all around, promises to stay in touch, and then they were gone. Only Ruby and Metaxas Parish lagged behind.

"Is there anything we can do, boys, before we head on out? I know this isn't the time, then again, maybe it is, to congratulate you on your win at the Preakness. Ruby and I are both sorry your father wasn't here to see it."

Pyne jerked at the tie around his neck. When it wouldn't loosen, he stretched his neck and ripped at the tie. He threw it across the kitchen. "He wasn't our father," he said in a strangled voice.

Ruby looked at her husband in disbelief before she sat down on the kitchen chair. "Maybe you better explain that. Then again, if you feel it isn't our business, don't tell us."

"Well we have to tell somebody, so it might as well be you. Nealy liked you a lot, so I guess you're the logical choice for us to spill our guts. I'll give you the short version, and you can figure out the rest. Rhy, get out the bourbon."

When the bourbon bottle was empty, Pyne pushed his chair away from the table. "Nealy took the folder with her. The really weird part of it all is she wasn't angry. Relieved and sad, but not angry. Hell, when she first got here she was like some wild, raging bull. She stomped, she snorted, and she raged. She didn't spare that old man one thing. I don't know if she was right or if she was wrong. All I know is when she took her kids and left, all I had to show for it was a penny in my hand. Emmie said it had been to heaven and back, and maybe I needed it. I don't know what the hell that means. All of this," he said, waving his arms about, "supposedly reverts to the Texas Colemans. I don't know how that can be, but there was a paper in that folder that said that's the way it was supposed to be. They don't know it yet. Rhy and I want to talk to Nealy before we tell them. We didn't know Pa . . . Josh Coleman left a will until the lawyer told us that last morning when Nealy was here. He won't read it or tell us what's in it until Nealy comes back, and Nealy is never coming back here.

"Nealy isn't just Nealy, our sister. She's Cornelia Diamond, the richest woman in the state of Kentucky. She won the Triple Crown. She bred the horse, trained it, and rode it to three wins. Dancer's Flyby colts go for millions a pop. SunStar had two of those colts. Our own stud fees from their offspring are in the millions, too. Pa never paid Nealy for the horses. Plain and simple, he stiffed her. She retaliated but not right away. She gave him every chance and then some, and when he didn't pay, she slapped a lien on this farm and as near as we can figure, she charged twenty percent interest, so there has to be an outstanding debt of close to forty million dollars, maybe more. Then all the stud fees from those two colts come into question. When she's done collecting, there won't be anything left for the Texas Colemans. When she first came here, she said all she wanted was her daughter's share. That was a whole messy story, and I already gave you the gist of it."

"And you don't approve of any of this, is that what you're saying?" Ruby asked. "I understand your sister. The minute I laid eyes on her I knew she was special. I knew we would become friends. The first thing she said to me was, what can I do for you? I traveled the same road your sister did. I went through the same things she did, so I know where she's coming from. I want to go to Kentucky, Metaxas."

"If that's what you want, sweet baby, then that's what we'll do." Metaxas smiled at his wife.

"Our sister is a hothead," Rhy said.

"She can't be that much of a hothead if she managed to get where she is today," Metaxas said quietly. "She sounds like a pretty amazing woman to me. About that will. Why don't you, your brother, and your attorney go to Kentucky to read it. I can fly you there if you like. You need to settle things so you know where you stand. I'm no lawyer, but I do know things have to go to probate. I think you might have a problem with your accounts. When there are liens on a property, accounts can get frozen. You might not even be able to pay your workers. You need to put the legal wheels in motion."

Pyne stared at his brother. "You're the oldest, you make the decision."

"We can't all go. One of Pa's rules was one of us had to be here at all times."

"He's not here anymore, Rhy. You're the oldest. Now it's your turn to make the decision. What's the worst thing that could happen? You have a vet on the premises, your employees know their jobs. I'll fly you there in the morning and you'll be home in time to put the horses to bed. Why don't you think about it and call us at the hotel. We'll stay over and do a little sight-seeing. My baby here likes to see new things," he said, tousling Ruby's wild mane of hair.

"I liked your sister. She has grit. I could tell that right off. She's a good mother, too. I saw and felt that the moment I laid eyes on her. I was like that when I was her age wasn't I, Metaxas?"

"That you were, honey. Hell, you're still like that. We're staying at the Lansdowne since it's only forty-five minutes from Washington and Ruby wanted to see the Vietnam Memorial. If you decide to take me up on my offer, I can be ready to leave by seven. We can see ourselves out. Talk it over and give us a call one way or the other."

Pyne nodded. Rhy, stubborn to the end, muttered something that sounded like, "Yeah, okay."

Nick walked up behind Smitty, and whispered, "What's she doing?"

"She's just sitting out there with a cup of coffee and smoking cigarettes. She's having a bad time with all this. She knows she has to do something, but she doesn't know quite what that something is. The burial is today, and so is the Preakness. Your grandfather . . . whatever he was, has a horse running and is favored to win. Your uncles have a horse . . . you know what I mean, Nick. I think if both events were televised, your mother would opt for the Preakness."

"Maybe you should go out there and talk to her, Smitty."

"Maybe I shouldn't. I know when not to cross the line. That's the reason your mother and I get on so well. It works both ways. It's only been five weeks, Nick. She has a lifetime of reconciling to do. My advice is to leave her alone."

"Yeah, I guess you're right. Do you think she's rooting for Sharpshooter to win?"

"You bet she is. She's rooting for the horse, not the owners. Be sure you have that clear in your mind."

"I gotta get back to the barn. If you need me, call, okay?"

"You bet."

"You can come out now, Smitty," Nealy called over her shoulder.

"You know what I really like about this place these days is it runs itself. I didn't think that would ever happen, but it did. Beautiful day. I thought you were going to plant some flowers this morning, Nealy."

"I am. I was just sitting here thinking. What kind of person am I that I didn't go to *his* funeral. I've been asking myself questions since the day I got back here. I'm beginning to think Hunt was right about me. I have no heart. Somewhere along the way it eroded. I'm not a nice person. I can be mean and obnoxious. I'm arrogant and opinionated. It's my way or the highway. My God, how did I ever get to be like this? Maud and Jess must be spinning in their graves at how I turned out. How can you stand to be around me? For whatever it's worth, I sent

Felicity St. John a note of apology for my bad attitude. I told you about her."

"Nealy, don't be so hard on yourself. You did what you had to do to survive. In time it got you to this place. You have your answers now. It doesn't matter where you've been, baby, what matters is where you're going and how you get there. The past is gone. Don't try to go there. Tomorrow morning it's going to be a whole new ball game, as Nick says. Try thinking of it as the first day of your new life."

"Hunt . . ."

"It wasn't meant to be, Nealy. Hunt's gone. You're still here. You're rich, you're beautiful, you have two wonderful children. And you have me. What more could you possibly want?"

"Peace. Inner tranquillity. A purpose. Love. I'm forty-eight years old, Smitty, and I've never been in love in the true sense of the word. I want to experience that feeling. I want to feel some man's arms around me and know he cares more about me than he does himself. I want to fall asleep next to him and wake up before he does so I can just look at him and know he's what makes me whole. I want someone to care about me when I don't feel good. I want someone to hold my hand when we walk through the garden and I want him to pick me a flower and say I'm prettier than it is. I want to run barefoot in the rain with him. I want to do wild crazy things that only lovers do. There's a part of my heart, Smitty, that no one has ever touched. I want it to bust wide open so I can *feel*. I want to dream and sing and be happy. Is that so much to ask? Do you think I should advertise for someone like that in the *Lexington Herald-Leader?*"

"I don't think I would do that if I were you. Of course it isn't asking too much. It does, however, bring a question to mind. If you never leave here, if you hang out in the barns day and night, how do you propose to meet the man of your dreams? I get it, you're waiting for him to ride up here to the porch on his handsome steed, kind of like the way Jess did that day when he met Maud for the first time."

Nealy laughed. "Hunt rode up in the dark. For a while I thought he was the one. I never should have married him. I was too selfish back then. He wasn't selfish enough. Like you said, that's all in the past. How'd you get so smart, Smitty?"

"By hanging around you. I think it's time for you to join the social scene. You could set this whole state on its ear. Yeah, you, Nealy Diamond Clay. Why don't we organize a ball and give it some fancy name. Like, the Derby Ball, the Triple Crown Ball, something like that. We could charge outrageous amounts and donate all the money to some worthy charity. That's another thing, Nealy, you have all this money, and you don't donate or give anything away. You need to start doing that. It's called giving back. You could do all kinds of things like summer camps for kids where they can learn to ride, swim, play tennis, you could give out scholarships, you could do something for animal rights. Endowments. The list is endless."

"So you're saying I'm selfish *and* greedy."

"Pretty much," Smitty laughed.

Nealy stared at Smitty as though she had sprouted a second head. "You are absolutely right. Let's do it! But not till tomorrow. I need this last day to wallow. My God, where in the hell have I been all these years?"

"In a barn," Smitty snapped.

"Right again," Nealy giggled.

Nealy watched the sun creep over the horizon from her bedroom window. It was a treat to stand at a window and revel in the beautiful colors of early morning. Dawn. A new day. A new beginning. This day, whatever it would bring, would be of her choosing. Decisions or lack of decisions would either affect her life or not affect it. If she chose to stay by the window all day long, nothing in her life would change.

A new beginning. That meant she had to make decisions. She had to go through the accordion-pleated envelope and scrutinize each piece of paper, every single document, and then she had to act on her findings. She also had to make arrangements to have her mother's remains buried alongside Maud and Jess. *I wish I had known her for just one day. Just one single day. I'd give everything I hold dear to experience my mother's smile, my mother's touch, my mother's kiss. Did she smell like vanilla and homemade bread? Were her hands rough and callused? Did she smile? Did she sing when she did the laundry? Did she make pancakes on Sunday morning and big chocolate cakes for Sunday dinner?* She would never know. Never, ever. When she herself was dead and gone, what would Emmie and Nick remember about her? Maybe it was better not to know things like that.

Nealy walked into the bathroom and stared at her reflection. The gray in her hair was showing again. She made a mental note to look into having it frosted. She grimaced when she thought of Felicity St. John. She never wanted to look like the shellacked receptionist.

A new day. That meant it was time to shower and go downstairs for breakfast. She was hungry enough to start chewing on the doorknob.

She put on a daffodil yellow sundress that showed off her spring tan along with matching sandals that felt funny on her feet after all the years of wearing sturdy boots. She was halfway down the steps when she stopped. If she planned to go riding later on, she was going to have to change her clothes. "Damn," she muttered.

In the kitchen she looked at Smitty, who was sipping coffee and reading the newspaper. "I think we're going to hire a housekeeper, Smitty. There aren't any smells in here. There should be sweet smells, like cinnamon, fresh bread, and maybe an apple-pie smell. We both know you stink as a cook, and I'm even worse than you. I was hoping for pancakes or something like that. You know, hearty, to start off the first day of my new life."

"There's some frozen ones in the freezer. Just pop them in the toaster. A cook is a good idea. I hate cooking. I do like hanging out in the kitchen, though. It's so cheerful in here since we did it over. All that red and all those green plants. You just want to sit here and do nothing."

"I can't just do nothing. That's not in my makeup. I have a list. Each day I'm going to tackle at least two of those things. Emmie didn't call, did she?"

"Not this morning. Nealy, she is amazing. She talks nonstop, and she's getting quite good at it. Buddy says she talks in her sleep, but I don't know how he knows this since he's deaf. He said she wakes him in the middle of the night and practices her words on him. The whole thing is just amazing. Uh-oh, someone's coming. I hear a car."

Nealy looked out the kitchen window and gasped. "It's my brothers and the lawyer. Oh look, there's Ruby and Metaxas. Make more coffee, Smitty. Something must have happened."

"Are you going to just stand there, or are you going to open the door, Nealy? I swear, you do belong in a barn. These are guests coming to your home. Smile and greet them. You can fight with them later."

"I know that. I know that, Smitty. I'm just surprised that they're here."

"Hello," Nealy said cheerfully the moment she opened the door. "What brings you all the way to Kentucky? Coffee anyone? Oh, Ruby, I'm so glad you came. I've thought about you and your husband a lot since I got back here. Please, come in. Let's go into the living room or the dining room. There's more space in there."

"We're here for . . . the will," Rhy said.

"I thought he didn't have a will," Nealy said as she led the way into the dining room. "Since Pa wasn't our pa, what does his will have to do with anything?"

"I don't know. Mr. Avery Hollister, the attorney, has been very tight-lipped about it all. I know nothing more than you do, Nealy. Nice place you got here."

"Yes, it is nice. In some ways it reminds me of . . . home."

"Honey, Metaxas and I will stay in the kitchen until you finish your business."

"No, no. Stay right here. I'm sure we'll be done with this in a few minutes. Smitty is going to bring in some coffee. You're family now, Ruby. That means you belong. You, too, Metaxas."

"This is highly irregular," the attorney said huffily.

"Get on with it, Mr. Hollister. Family is family. It doesn't matter. Please, give us the short version. I think we already know what it says."

"I rather doubt that, Mrs. Clay."

"Wait a minute. How did you know my name? Clay is my married name. When did . . . Mr. Coleman make this will?"

"Two days after you won the Triple Crown. He marched into my office, proud as a peacock. Told me it was time to draft up a brand-new will. We did it right then and there. He came back and signed it one week later. A month later he updated it with your married name."

Nealy could feel her heart fluttering in her chest. She looked across the table at Ruby, who smiled reassuringly.

"I'll just gloss over the usual bequests. There aren't that many anyway."

"To Rhy Coleman, I leave the sum of one million dollars. To Pyne Coleman, I leave the sum of one million. To Cornelia Coleman Diamond Clay, I leave the sum of one dollar. To Emmaline Coleman I leave SunStar Farms in its entirety, with the provision that Rhy and Pyne live out their days at SunStar. It is my wish for them to stay on to manage the farm the way they see fit."

"I thought the farm was to revert to the Texas Colemans," Nealy gasped, her face full of shock.

"That's the way it was originally. However, Mr. Seth Coleman found himself in a financial bind some years back and asked Joshua for money. They cut a deal around the same time a sister named Sallie stepped forward to buy into Coleman Aviation. I was privy to those negotiations as well. SunStar Farms is free and clear, with the exception of your lien, Mrs. Clay. There is a sizable trust that can be drawn upon when needed."

Nealy looked at her brothers, who were staring intently at the attorney. "Emmie doesn't want the farm. She'll deed it over to you both. You can keep my dollar, too. Now that it's all been settled, why don't we send Mr. Hollister on his way and enjoy this little family visit."

"It's not that simple, Mrs. Clay," the attorney said. "You can say whatever you want, but until Miss Emmie tells me that's what she wants, the will stands."

"Yes, Mr. Hollister, it is that simple. My daughter doesn't want the farm. I'll call her to come over here right now. Did you ever hear that old saying, too much, too little, too late? This applies. My brothers worked their asses off from sunup to sundown, seven days a week, all their lives. They deserve that farm, and you're going to see that they get it all nice and legal-like. If you'll excuse me, I'll call my daughter and we can wrap this up right now."

In the kitchen, Nealy gaped at Smitty. "Did you hear all that?"

"I sure did. I'll call Emmie. Are you sure she's going to want to do this?"

"I've never been more sure of anything in my life. Tell her to hurry. Smitty, why do you suppose he did that?"

"Guilt! Remorse. I guess it was the only way he knew of to try to make it right. She'll be doing the right thing if she deeds it back to her uncles."

Back in the dining room, Nealy looked at her brothers. "Emmie will be here in about ten minutes. I'd like it if you stayed on for a visit, boys," she said, suddenly shy.

"We need to get back to the farm, Nealy, but I know I speak for Pyne when I say we'd like to come back without any baggage trailing us."

"My door will always be open to you both. I'll have my attorneys take care of the lien."

Pyne found his tongue. "You'd do that for us!"

"You're my brothers. I would do anything for you. You should know that without asking."

"Anything, Nealy?"

A chill ran up Nealy's spine at the word. "Well almost anything. What do you have in mind?"

"Ride Sharpshooter at the Belmont for us."

"Pyne, I'm out of shape. I was younger when I rode Flyby to his win, and I worked with him for three solid years. I don't know your horse. He doesn't know me. I don't know . . . I don't think . . . I was going to start this new life I've been promising myself. I was going to plant flowers, go to the beauty shop, start looking for some handsome guy to take me dancing, that kind of thing." Nealy looked away so she wouldn't have to see the disappointment on her brothers' faces. "Besides, I wouldn't be comfortable back there. What's wrong with Ricky Vee?"

"He's booked. You'd be riding against him at the Belmont."

"Three weeks isn't much time, Pyne. Okay, okay, but you bring the horse here. Just because I ride him doesn't mean he can win. This is a big gamble for you to take."

"You know Belmont. You rode it. I watched you win that race a thousand times. So did Rhy. Of course we didn't know who you were back then. You were the best!"

Nealy felt her chest puff out. In a million years she never expected to hear her brother say she was the best at anything. "Pyne, that was a long time ago. I'm forty-eight years old now. How would you feel about Emmie riding for you? She's her mother's daughter. I think she's as good, maybe better than I was back then. When can you have the horse here?"

"By tomorrow night. We want you, Nealy. I'm not saying your daughter isn't as good as you. Win, lose, or draw, we want you riding Sharpshooter."

Nealy's head whirled. "Then let's do it!"

Emmie breezed into the room, her face wreathed in a wide smile. "Where do I sign off on this?" she said, enunciating each word carefully.

Ten minutes later, Hollister closed his briefcase.

"I'm going to stay here with Nealy if she doesn't mind having me for a guest," Ruby said to her husband.

"Are you kidding? I would love it! Stay as long as you like."

"I'd like to see you work with the horse, and, Metaxas, I want to go to the Belmont."

"Sweet baby," Metaxas boomed, "we'll have the best seats in the clubhouse. I have a little business to take care of. Can you ladies survive without me for a few days?"

"Two at the most," Ruby quipped.

"Nealy . . ." Rhy struggled for words, his boots scuffing the carpet.

"Shhh. This is a new day. For all of us. We're family. If it's in my power to give you a Triple Crown, I'll do it. I don't think I've ever been happier."

Nealy's eyes were moist as she watched the foursome make their way to the car that waited for them.

"We have one day for you to give me a crash course in horse racing," Ruby said. "That's so when you're working with the horse I don't ask all kinds of dumb questions."

"This is so strange," Nealy said, reaching for Ruby's hand. "I feel like I've known you all my life. Isn't having family wonderful?"

"Yes, honey, it is. For a long time I didn't have one. I know what you're feeling. Now, let's go sit on that wonderful front porch of yours and *talk*."

20

〜

The sun rode high in the sky, bathing the landscape in a warm yellow glow, when Ruby and Nealy settled down on the front porch to talk. When the shadows lengthened and the light spring breeze ruffled the trees, the two occupants on the front porch barely noticed. Nor did they notice when sandwiches and fresh coffee were set down on the small table between the twin rockers as darkness fell. As the stars peeped into the velvety night, the two women continued to talk, hardly aware that daylight had turned into darkness. They were still talking when the sun rose on what Nealy referred to as the first day of her new life.

Nealy flexed her shoulders and stretched her neck. "I can't believe I'm not talked out. Do you realize, Ruby, we've been talking nonstop since eleven o'clock yesterday morning? And I have so much more to tell you, and I know you have things to tell me. But right now, I think we both need a shower and some breakfast. We have some of those things you pop into a toaster. We don't cook much around here."

"Then, honey, I have a cook for you. I pensioned her off when Metaxas and I moved to our island. I heard from her a month or so ago, and she said she's climbing the walls with nothing to do. She'll come here in a heartbeat if I call her. Metaxas will fly her here if you want."

"I want. I want. Smitty will be so happy. My son will be forever in your debt." Nealy turned suddenly shy. "There's something about you, Ruby Parish. I told you things I've never told another soul. You're the mother I never had. The sister I always wanted. You're my favorite aunt. Smitty is right up there, but it's a different kind of relationship. Maybe it's the family thing, blood ties. I don't know what it is or why I was drawn to you so instantly. It had nothing to do with . . . with your condition. I loved Maud Diamond with all my heart, but as much as I wanted and yearned for her to be a mother figure to me, it didn't happen. There was always something missing. Smitty is a friend. A wonderful friend. When you get to know her, you'll feel the same way. I wouldn't have made it this far without her help. I'm so glad you decided to stay on for a few days. Am I doing the right thing, Ruby?"

"Absolutely," Ruby grinned. "Believe it or not, the best thing that ever happened to you was when you left home."

"I keep telling myself the same thing. Most times it works. There's always that little part of you that says, what if. What I'm doing does feel . . . right."

"Always go with your feelings, Nealy. If it feels right, then it's right. It boggles my mind that you can race a horse. You're just this little bit of a thing. Those horses are *huge*. I can't wait to meet the horse responsible for all those winning colts. Do you know anything about your brothers' horse?"

"Everything I need to know. He's Flyby's progeny. I've kept up on each and every one of Flyby's colts. We have a chart in the office. I have airtight contracts and bills of sale. One wrong move, one wrong word, and a horse will come back to me at the speed of light. We drill that into the buyers from the git-go. They sign off on it willingly. I'm pretty good with horses. I'll know in a few days if he'll work with me. I cannot tell you how thrilled and delighted I was when my brothers asked me to take him on. Me! Me, Ruby! At that precise moment, I think I could have flown if I had flapped my arms. I've waited all my life for a moment like that. Come on, let's get you fixed up. You're going to need some coveralls and boots. Smitty can fix you up with a shirt and underwear. You're about the same size. For all I know she has a whole shopping bag of stuff for you in the kitchen. She anticipates. Three weeks isn't a lot of time."

"Three weeks can be a lifetime for someone like me. Each day, each minute is one to be tasted, savored, and held dear. Before you can ask, maybe three years if I'm lucky. It could be two. It could be four. Let's not talk about this, Nealy. I just want to enjoy being here without any worries. Metaxas is on top of everything. Is he not the wonder in wonderful? That man built an entire mountain for Fanny Thornton. I want to take you there, Nealy. I want you to see it all, and I'd like to be the one to show it to you. And we're going to get Billie Thornton to dress you up. When we're done with you, you are going to be one stylin' lady. I guess you can say I'm partial to the Thorntons considering, like you, I was born on the wrong side of the blanket. I don't know too much about the Colemans in Texas. They seem nice enough. I think it's one of those, if you need me, you can count on me, kind of things. Everyone is busy with their own lives. Sometimes they forget just how important family is. Unless you didn't have one like you and me, you can't really appreciate it. That's just my opinion." Nealy nodded.

They walked in companionable silence into the kitchen. Nealy burst out laughing. "See, I told you there would be a shopping bag out here. Betcha there are enough clothes for four days."

Ruby grinned as she pawed through the bag. "I'm going to help you and Smitty arrange that ball you were telling me about after the race. We'll put Metaxas in charge of the guest list. I swear, honey, that man knows everyone in the world. He calls the president George. *The* president, Nealy. Your eyes would pop out of your head at the famous people who have come to our island to get away from the world. You ride a horse to the Triple Crown for the second time and that world is yours, honey! You'll be one of the most famous women in the world!"

Nealy laughed. The sound was so contagious Ruby hooted right along with her.

"Ma! What's so funny? I never heard you laugh like that in my whole life. Come on, share," Nick said, opening the refrigerator.

Nealy continued to laugh. "I'm going to throw a party, and the president of the United States is coming."

"Oh. Do we have any of those pop-up things with the frosting on top? Do I need a date? I heard you're going to ride the Belmont, Ma. Smitty told me last night. She said you never went to bed. Is that true? You need eight hours of sleep, Ma. You better get that gray out of your hair before that race, or they'll be calling you the old lady riding Sharpshooter. The press will kill you."

"Go!" Nealy thundered as she tossed her son a banana.

Nealy watched as Ruby fished around in her handbag. "I want you to read this, Nealy. It was written by a woman named Teresa M. Walker. It's a poem titled, 'A Mother's Love.' I was so lonely when they sent me away to school. I know now that my mother loved me, and sending me away was the best thing for me, but I didn't see it that way at the time. This poem helped me. I know it by heart."

Nealy unfolded the wrinkled paper that was torn in several spots. She rather imagined the spots on the single sheet of paper were Ruby's tears. She read it, her own eyes moist.

A Mother's Love
A Mother's Love is important,
For every child to see,
To hold, to touch, to kiss their cheeks,
Her way for them to be.

A love that is so gentle,
A love that is so pure,
A love that only A Mother's Love,
Is felt and will endure.

She knows your every weakness,
She knows your every pain.
She knows A Mother's Love for you,
Has everything to gain.

You see her will to do what's right,
And hope you don't do wrong,
But if you do, A Mother's Love,
Forgives and just goes on.

Nealy dabbed at her eyes as she imagined Ruby as a young girl, cuddled in her bed with only a poem to comfort her. She held it out.

"No, you keep it. I don't need it anymore."

"Thank you, Ruby. I'll treasure this."

"You go ahead and shower. I want to call our old cook and

make arrangements. You are going to love her, Nealy. I swear, she is the best cook in the whole world."

"Okay, your room is the first door on the left. It has its own bath. Take your time, and I'll make us some coffee when I come down."

"I'll make the coffee, Nealy."

One of the five richest women in the world was going to make coffee for her. *Life is certainly strange,* Nealy thought. *Wonderful, but strange.*

They looked tired, Nealy thought as she stared at her brothers. Sharpshooter, however, was full of spit and vinegar as he backed out of the horse trailer.

"My God, he's a monster!" Ruby quivered as she hid behind Nealy.

"He is a big boy. He's awesome, isn't he?"

"He's got a good temperament, Nealy, but I have to tell you, he can pitch a fit with the best of them. Call us if you have any problems. We have to turn around and head back," Rhy said.

"I'll take good care of him. He's going into the barn and paddock I used when I trained Flyby. Have a safe trip home." She waited, not quite knowing what she was waiting for. When her brothers hugged her, she knew. "You're getting gray hair, sis," Rhy said.

Sis. Rhy couldn't have said anything more endearing. "The two of you gave me these gray hairs."

Pyne guffawed as he unhitched the trailer. "See you at Belmont, Nealy."

"Yeah, see you," Nealy said wistfully.

"They're so different now," Nealy told Ruby. "I can't believe they hugged me. Rhy called me sis and teased me about my gray hair. I think I hate that old man more for what he did to them than for what he did to me."

"Let it go, Nealy. Life is too short for hatred and bitterness. You're out of the darkness now and into the sunlight. Stay there. You are not that bitter, vindictive person any longer. Now what are you going to do with this giant?"

"I'm going to walk him to his new home, then I'm going to talk to him for a long time. I'll sleep in the next stall. We don't have a lot of window room here. Three weeks isn't much, Ruby. I want him to know I'm always there, right next to him. People say you can't bond with a horse, and that's pure horse shit. Pardon the pun. You *can* bond with a horse. Flyby and I are the perfect example. You just have to know how to do it. Watch this." Nealy extended her hand with a wintergreen mint in the middle. Sharpshooter took it, whinnied, and waited for more. She gave him a second one before she took his bridle and started for the barn. "You ever sleep in a barn, Ruby?"

"No, but damn close. I hung out in the chicken coops when the chickens got restless way back when. Metaxas is going to be lost . . . later on. I was wondering, Nealy, do you think you could see your way clear to selling us one of Flyby's colts? Metaxas has a birthday in January, and I'd like to give it to him for a present. We could board him here and you could train him. Oh, Nealy, wouldn't it be wonderful if I could give him a winner? It's about the only thing he doesn't have. All he does is good things for people and never asks for anything in return. He's one person you can count on no matter what. So, will you sell us one?"

"I don't think so, Ruby." Nealy smiled to take the sting from her refusal. "However, since we're family, I could *give* you one. Give, Ruby. Not sell. It would be my pleasure."

"Lady, you are one hell of a horse trader. I accept. Can I stay for the whole three weeks and go on to Belmont with you?"

Ruby Coleman Parish, one of the five richest women in the world, wanted to sleep in her barn and make coffee for her. "Ruby, you can stay forever. Metaxas, too. We're family now."

Twenty minutes later Ruby climbed the steps to the second floor. She was tired, but she wasn't exhausted, which was strange since she hadn't slept at all. She wondered if she should read something into it.

She looked around the small room. It was warm, cozy, and comfortable, all done up in soft, subdued colors. The rocker beckoned her. She'd noticed other rocking chairs in the house and couldn't help but wonder if Nealy or her predecessor was the one who liked to rock. She smiled at the huge yellow daffodil appliqué in the middle of the bedspread. Everything about these two families reflected either sun, stars, or the color yellow. Perhaps one day she would try to figure it out but not now. Now she wanted to think about Nealy and the instant rapport they'd found on the front porch.

She leaned her head back and closed her eyes as she tried to picture the opulent island home Metaxas had lavished on her. She'd never been able to make him understand she didn't want or need all the costly things he gave her. In the end she'd just given up because it gave him such pleasure to do things for her. Once she'd tried to tell him she got more pleasure out of rescuing animals from the pound so they wouldn't be put to sleep. The very next day the wheels were in motion to build and set up a five-thousand-acre animal sanctuary. He had the simple sign made before the architect finished the plans. It was plain, the way she was, the words just as simple, The Ruby Thornton Parish Home For Animals. She felt like crying.

"*Are you going to start to blubber, Ruby? You and Fanny are just alike. She blubbers, too. For good things. I was never able to understand that.*"

"Ash! Ash, is that you? How'd you know I was here? Back there on the mountain you said good-bye. I thought you weren't ever . . . you know, coming back."

"*I did say good-bye to Fanny because she didn't need me anymore. I keep tabs on all my family. You know that, Ruby.*"

"Yeah, well, I remember the day you told me to get out of your life. Are you here because you know about me and . . ."

"*You can't dwell on things like that. I learned the hard way.*"

"Easy for you to say, you're already dead."

"*Dead is dead, Ruby. You're still alive. I was stupid back then. Blood is blood. They don't come any better than you. I haven't forgotten how you saved my kids. That guy you married, he's one in a million. Stop worrying about what's going to happen. Live your life, Ruby. When it's your turn, I'll be here waiting for you along with a lot of other people.*"

"Ash, what do you think about this new branch of the family?"

"*They're okay. She's a spitfire. I've been watching her for a long time. It took you all long enough to hook up. Is anyone every going to look for Aunt Peggy? Now there's a project for you, Ruby. I think*" *you're going to learn a lot from each other. I guess you miss the family.*"

"Yes, I do. Everyone has their own lives. We come together for an event, a crisis, but other than that, I never get to see anyone. It's a damn shame when you look forward to a funeral just so you can see your family."

"*Ah, Ruby, if you had your way, you'd cluster all of them under one roof. I can see how Fanny rubbed off on you. The mountain is lookin' real good these days. Real good.*"

"Ash, do you know how long . . . ?"

"*Live, Ruby. Do what you want, but live. God, lady, you have it all. Do you have any idea what you can do before it's your time?*"

"We aren't talking horse races and balls, are we?"

"*In part. Keep a sharp eye, Ruby. The Colemans are in some financial difficulty. There's going to be some trouble there.*"

"Damn it, Ash, be more specific. Don't make me spin my wheels. Who the hell is Peggy?"

"*There's a severe drought in Texas. The oil wells are coming up dry. The Japanese stock market is down, way down. The coffers are almost empty. Fanny owns fifty-one percent of Coleman Aviation. Just tuck that away for future reference. Peggy is Sallie's sister. Did you forget?*"

"What does that mean, Ash? Don't just throw words at me like that. What is it I'm supposed to do? I don't ever remember anyone telling me about an Aunt Peggy."

"*You know how to fight, Ruby. You showed me that at the casino the first time we met. You have guts. Be prepared to use them.*"

"Does this all have something to do with Nealy and her brothers? Ash, don't let me hang here."

"*Avery Hollister is a jerk. Hell, he's not even a bad lawyer, he's a terrible lawyer. He's real sloppy with his paperwork, too. Listen, I gotta go, Ruby. I think you can handle things.*"

"Wait, Ash, don't go. What if I need you? Should I whistle, call your name? What?"

"*Ruby, you sound just like Fanny. When you need me, I'll be there for you.*"

"All right, Ash. Is this our little secret? I don't think I ever had a real secret before. Having one with my brother is kind of special."

"*It's whatever you want it to be, Ruby.*"

"Oh, shit! That means this is all a dream, and I'm going to wake up and start to cry all over again. Don't come into my dreams anymore. It's too sad. Oh, I wish this was real."

"Ruby, are you ready?" Nealy called from the hallway.

Ruby jerked upright. "I'm . . . I'm coming, Nealy. I think I must have dozed off for a moment. I was having this . . . nice dream about my brother. I'll be out in a minute."

"Take your time. I'll meet you downstairs."

In the bathroom, Ruby's bare toe touched something cold and hard. Staring up at her was a round gold medallion that said Babylon in the middle and underneath, the number 1000. The gold medallions were special. Everyone in Las Vegas knew about Ash Thornton's thousand gold medallions. Fanny had told her early on that Ash had a thousand of them made up to give to special people. Anyone entering Babylon with one of his gold medallions was to be given the red-carpet treatment. Translated, that meant the holder of the medallion was to be given whatever he or she wanted, no questions asked. To date, according to Fanny, all but two of the medallions had been redeemed. Fanny said she kept hers in her safety-deposit box and as far as she knew, Ash had the other one, but it was never found after his death. The number on Fanny's medallion was 999. Ash's number was 1000.

Ruby squeezed her eyes shut and then opened them immediately as she dropped to her knees to see the gold chip winking up at her. It wasn't a dream after all.

She finally had a secret.

"Thanks, big brother."

"My pleasure, Ruby."

She arrived in a swirl of dust and spurting gravel, the horn blasting on a brand-new, fire-engine red Jeep Grand Cherokee. She said her name was Willow Bishop, and she was there to *cook*. But not till her nine suitcases, four trunks, and her box of copper-bottom pots and pans were secured indoors.

"How old is she, Ruby?" Nealy whispered.

"Maybe twenty-two. I don't really know. Probably twenty. I told you, her mother used to cook for us. I never met Willow. She was away at school. Unfortunately for us, Angelina just

signed a contract to cook for the secretary of state. We have
Metaxas to thank for that since he's the one who got her the job.
She assured me Willow was a better cook than she was. Why,
Nealy, is it important? You don't have to be a certain age to cook.
Look at you, you're forty-eight, and you can't cook worth a
damn."

"Take another look at her, Ruby, and then think about Nick."

"She is pretty. Look at those dark eyes. A body could drown
in them. Nice figure, a perfect size eight, I'd say. Fashionable,
too. You do realize she only cooks and cleans up. No house-
work. Five hundred a week, room and board. You'll probably
want to give her a raise after the first week. I'd sign her to a contract if I were you. Don't worry about Nick. According to you,
all that boy does is work. If they hit it off, great. If they don't,
that's okay, too."

"I'm Nealy Clay, Miss Bishop. This is Ruby Parish. Your room
is off the kitchen, and it has a private bath. I'll give you the name
and phone number for the grocery store. Just call and have them
deliver whatever you want. They'll send me a bill. I'll send
someone up to carry your things inside. We like to eat dinner
around seven, lunch around twelve, and breakfast at six. Is that
okay with you?"

Willow smiled. "That's fine, ma'am. What I do is make up
menus the beginning of the week. I stick to them, too, unless
something special comes up. You can pencil in any changes
Monday morning. All I really need to know is, are you into
health-conscious food, are you hearty eaters, and how many
will there be for meals. I'll check your pantry, your refrigerator,
and get to work. Is there anything in particular you'd like for
dinner this evening? I'm not going to be able to do lunch with
what you have here," she said, opening the refrigerator and
frowning.

"She has a lot of those pop-up things you put in a toaster.
Some are even like pizza."

"You can die from that stuff," Willow said, wrinkling her
nose.

"As for dinner, surprise us. I do like desserts. Sweet desserts.
The gooier the better. Make enough so I can eat it before I go to

bed, too. Lately we've been more or less eating on the run around here."

"Not anymore," Ruby grinned. "I think we should get out of Willow's way and let her get started. I can't remember the last time I was up and dressed at this hour. Probably never. No, that's not true. I used to have to get up for the chickens. Do not ever serve me chicken, Willow."

"Yes, ma'am."

"All right, Ruby, it's time to start working with Sharpshooter. Get it in gear and let's go."

It was six-thirty when Nealy walked into the kitchen, with Ruby trailing behind. She was tired, so tired she didn't think she could take another step until she sniffed at the aromas emanating from the stove. She perked up immediately. "Do we have time to shower and change, Willow?"

"Absolutely."

"I'll set the table for you when I get done."

"That's not necessary, ma'am. I already did it. In the dining room. My food is not kitchen food. It deserves to be eaten on fine china in a dining room. I have three different wines for the meal. I washed everything since it had a thick layer of dust on it."

"Well . . . I . . . thank you. I like eating in the dining room. Fine china is good. Crystal and silver are just as good. Actually, I'm looking forward to this. I'm starving. How about you, Ruby?"

"I have never been so tired in my whole life." At Nealy's instant look of concern, she hastened to add, "It's a good kind of tired, Nealy. It's nothing to worry about. A shower, some clean clothes, and a fine dinner will work wonders. If I don't fall asleep after dinner, remind me to call Metaxas."

"He called five times, Miss Ruby. He said not to disturb you. He's going to call you after dinner."

"And dinner is . . ."

"Roasted Maine lobster with some very fine chanterelle mushrooms, a butter cognac sauce with fried leeks. I found a nice Corton Charlemagne, Bonneau du Martray. I also prepared a grilled rack of lamb with potato gratin, a mango-apple chutney, and mint aioli. I prepared a small dish of pan-crispy turbot with baby spinach, some teardrop tomatoes, and a bluefin tuna, bacon, and truffle hollandaise sauce. I did not make a lot of any one thing. I need to see what kind of appetites you all have. Miss Smitty said she would be joining you for dinner and said she likes to eat hearty. She said your son also has a big appetite. I kept that all in mind. Hurry now, as it will all be ready to serve momentarily."

"What's for dessert?" Ruby shouted as Nealy dragged her toward the stairway.

"Bonbons and petit fours with a minty chocolate marshmallow sauce."

Nick charged into the kitchen, stopped in his tracks, stared at Willow Bishop, sniffed the aromas that wafted about, grinned, and said, "Marry me now!"

"That's one way of keeping her in the family!" Ruby giggled. "Sign her to a contract, Nealy, as soon as we finish dinner."

"I knew it! I knew it!" Nealy sighed. "He's only twenty!"

"And you think, what? That he's a virgin?"

"No, I don't think . . . he might be . . . He doesn't really, you know, date."

"That you know of. Stop being a mother for a little while. Let him be a young man."

"All right. All right. Emmie sort of inched her way along. This is like *bam!*"

"Nealy, look at me. You're jealous, aren't you?"

"A little," Nealy said.

"Get over it. Quickly. For both your sakes."

"I'll try."

21

"Hey, big guy, how's it going?" Nealy said, crawling out of the straw in the stall next to Sharpshooter. "No work today. We're going for a long ride with just two stops for you." She fished a mint from her pocket and held it out. "I'm going to give you a whole bag of these if you take me into the winner's circle. D'ya think we can do it?" The colt reared back and snorted. "I'm going to take that for a yes. I think we're both lookin' pretty good. Ruby dyed my hair last night, so they aren't going to be calling me an old lady when we trot into the gate. Well, maybe they will, but they won't be able to call me an old lady with gray hair. You better not show me that pissy side of you when we get there either. We both know that doesn't work with me. Your daddy didn't get away with it and neither are you.

"It's a beautiful day for traveling. I don't know why, but I've always loved the month of June. For some reason the world seems different in June." As she talked softly to the colt, her hands were busy, rubbing and caressing his head, whispering in his ear, snorting in his nostrils and tickling him. Each time she laughed, Sharpshooter whinnied.

"The last time I traveled to New York, it was a day just like today. I woke up with a rocket in my stomach that morning. I think Flyby had one in his stomach, too, and they both exploded at the same time. Listen to me, this race isn't for me. I don't have to prove anything to anyone any longer. Smitty and Ruby are right, it's time for me to give back. I know this isn't exactly what they meant, but it's a start, and I want to give this win to Rhy and Pyne. Three weeks out of my life and two minutes to race you down to the home stretch don't amount to much unless you're counting time like Ruby and my brothers. There's only one little thing bothering me. Ricky Vee is going to be riding

Dillon Roland's horse. We can't let that bastard win. We're favored to win, but that can go either way. No one knows I'm riding you tomorrow. Rhy filled out the papers with another jockey's name. He'll be scratched at the last minute and my name announced. My brothers want it that way. I know it has something to do with Dillon, but guess what, I don't care. I hope you understand everything I said.

"If you were mine, I think I would give Ruby your first colt. Then again, maybe it should be Flyby's colt. Can you imagine anything more important than your daddy siring two Triple Crown winners? I guess it's going to depend on how well you do tomorrow."

Ruby rolled over in the straw in the stall to the left of Sharpshooter's stall. She blinked at the mention of her name, then listened shamelessly.

"In the three weeks that I've known Ruby, I have come to love her. I want to do something wonderful for her. And for her husband, too. She's so rich her husband planted a whole mountain, and you know what, she's sleeping in a barn and she makes me coffee. She's sick, too. If I could, I'd breathe my own life into her. I'd give her one of my organs if she needed it. I've been praying every night that the doctors can help her. I don't like time limits, so I am going to pretend she is going to be here forever. Okay, baby, time to go for your walk. No workout today. Okay, okay, one more," Nealy said, as the colt tried to stick his nose into her shirt pocket.

Ruby struggled to her feet, her eyes moist. The only person who had ever said such nice things to her was Metaxas.

"She meant every word she said, Ruby."

"Ash! Good morning. You're up early," Ruby quipped. "I know she did. I love that girl. Is she going to win, Ash?"

"I have no clue. Listen, Ruby, I thought I told you to stay on top of that legal crap. You promised you would."

"Ash, when have I had time? I told Metaxas to check up on it. He said he has a handle on all of it. Nealy needed me here in the barn. Did something happen? What?"

"There's a big powwow going down in Texas tomorrow."

"What does that mean to me, Ash? If you know what's going to happen tomorrow, how come you don't know who's going to win the race? Does that . . . powwow have anything to do with Nealy and her brothers?"

"It has everything to do with them. Now get on it, Ruby."

"First I have to find my husband. Do you know where he is?"

"Ruby, Ruby, Ruby. I don't know everything. I imagine he's having breakfast. Did you ever have a fried egg sandwich at midnight?"

"Almost every night of my life once I met all our family. It's Sunny's favorite. She's doing really well, Ash. Jake is . . . Jake. He talks about you all the time. He hasn't forgotten you either. I don't think he ever will."

"I have to go now, Ruby. Get a move on. You need to take care of this family. I'm counting on you."

"Really, Ash. I thought . . . Fanny . . . the kids. Why me?"

"Because I picked you, that's why."

"Are you going to be at the race tomorrow?"

"Damn straight I'm going to be there. You might want to think about giving Nealy your good-luck charm tomorrow."

"What good-luck charm?"

"The one I gave you. It's kind of special, Ruby. It doesn't mean you can't, you know, lend it out for special occasions like tomorrow. When you get it back, you keep it close to you, and you'll be fine. Do you hear what I'm saying?"

"Are you saying what I think you're saying?"

"Yeah, Ruby."

"Oh, Ash. Can I tell Metaxas?"

"I think he knows, but yeah, okay."

"I'll see you . . . talk to you tomorrow. I have to find Metaxas now."

She was off like a bullet, running like a young girl, shouting her husband's name as she raced to the kitchen where he was finishing his breakfast. She burst into the kitchen, her face flushed, her voice jubilant.

"Quick, Metaxas, come with me. I have to hurry, and there's something I have to tell you. Hurry, honey."

"Ruby, what the hell? Calm down. You know what the doctors said."

"Screw those doctors, Metaxas. I want you to listen to me. I don't have time to go through this twice."

"Okay, honey, spit it out!"

"I'm just going to blurt out all of this as I get undressed. I've been talking to Ash. He told me something so wonderful I can't believe it. You know the story of the gold medallions he gave out, right? Fanny has 999. Ash had the last one. Number 1000. They were all redeemed except Fanny's and the one Ash had. Fanny keeps hers in her safety-deposit box. They never found the one Ash kept for himself. I found it, Metaxas. Three weeks ago right there on the bathroom floor. I didn't tell you because . . . because I thought you'd laugh at me. Look, here it is," she said, opening the dresser drawer. "Ash told me not ten minutes ago that if I kept it close to me, I would be fine. He said I'll be okay. He said I'm not going to die. When you're up *there*, you have the inside track on things. He isn't the one who is going to let me live, it's nothing like that. What he meant was all the treatments, all the medications and therapy are working. It's like I can breathe again, come alive, and be with you."

"Ruby . . ."

"Don't say it, Metaxas. I believe him. I've been feeling so good lately. Tired but good. I sleep, I eat like a horse, and I just feel damn good." To prove her point, Ruby removed her denim shirt. Metaxas wanted to bawl when he looked at her naked chest, at the scars and the burns from the radiation and chemotherapy she'd had to undergo for her *double* mastectomy. "I never wanted you to see how ugly I was, that's why I always wore a tee shirt under my clothes. Now it doesn't matter to me. As long as I can live and as long as I know you can accept me and the way I look, I'll walk outside naked for the world to see. Metaxas, I'm okay. Do you hear what I'm saying?"

"Oh, God, Ruby," Metaxas said, gathering her into his arms. "That never mattered to me for one minute. It didn't matter to me when you lost all your hair either. You know that. I didn't fall in love with your hair or your breasts. I fell in love with *you*. Are you sure you weren't dreaming this?"

"I was not dreaming. This is not wishful thinking on my part. Honey, Ash was never here in this house. He told me to give the medallion to Nealy tomorrow for the race, but to take it back right away. I never asked you for anything, but the minute she gives it back to me I need someone to drill a hole in it, and then I want a heavy gold chain with a super-duper latch so I don't ever lose it. Can you do that for me? I know it isn't a challenge like planting a mountain or building an island. I really gotta hurry now, honey. You can do that for me, can't you? I look like a boy now, don't I?" Ruby said sadly as she peered at her flat chest in the bathroom mirror. She perked up immediately at the concern on her husband's face. "No more push-up bras for me."

Metaxas sat down on the edge of the bathtub and howled with laughter.

Fifteen minutes later, Ruby was dressed and ready to go, the medallion clutched in her hand. "Ash never said what would happen if I lost this," she said.

"You aren't going to lose it, sweet baby. I guarantee it. C'mere, give me a big kiss, and I'll see you in New York."

"Honey, Ash said there's going to be a big powwow in Texas tomorrow. He was upset with me because I wasn't on top of it. Do you know what's going on?"

"I think so. I'll know more tomorrow. I can't believe you're sleeping in a barn, honey."

"I love it. The rich smell of horse poop, there's nothing like it anywhere. It gets in your blood. Nealy said it would happen, and it did."

"Do you want me to buy you a horse farm, sweet baby?"

"No! All I want is to be able to come here and be welcome. Nealy said we could stay forever. She meant it, too. She loves me, Metaxas, she really does. I love mucking the stalls, I love doing all that stuff. Those damn chickens made all this possible for me. Horse dung is a lot different from chicken poop. See ya, honey."

Every emotion in the world crossed Metaxas Parish's face as he watched his wife run down the path to the barn. "If this is some kind of cruel joke, Ash Thornton, I'll find a way to get up there to wherever the hell you are and kick your ass all the way to hell. I never make threats I don't intend to keep, so keep that in mind," Metaxas said fiercely.

"*Oh yeah. Well, hear this, big guy. I never make promises I can't keep either, so you keep that in your mind. Chew on that one, Metaxas Parish.*"

"Son of a bitch! You are real! What I mean is, you really do talk to her."

"Only when she needs me. That was a real nice thing you did there in the bathroom. You're okay in my book. Now get off your ass and figure out what's going on in Texas before the dark stuff hits the fan."

"I'm on it!"

"Good. See ya at Belmont."

"Yeah, right. Hey, wait a minute . . ."

"You people down there think I have all the time in the world. I have things to do and places to go. I'm busy. What?"

"Thanks. I know it's just a word, but it's the best I can come up with."

"It'll do. I still owe you for replanting the mountain. When you have time, go fishing with Jake."

"You got it!"

At the airport, Metaxas headed for the first phone booth that came into his line of vision. He hoped he was on time. His shoulders squared off the moment he heard the voice on the other end of the line. "Metaxas Parish here. I have something to tell you, and I want you to listen very carefully. When I'm finished, I want you to do exactly as I say. I know it's going to cut into your travel time, but it has to be done immediately. Check everything twice, be sure there are no mistakes. You have to trust me on this and not ask questions. I want you to bring everything with you to New York. You know what they say, the first one out of the gate wins the prize. This is what you do . . ."

Riley Coleman stopped his car, the way he did each and every day, before he drove under the high wooden arch emblazoned with the name SUNBRIDGE. His practiced eye took in the miles of white rail fence stretching into the distance. Tall oak trees lined the winding drive, and on either side were expanses of dead brown grass. The whirl and swish of the pulsating sprinklers was silent these days because of the drought.

He eased his foot down on the gas pedal, the Bronco moving slowly down the driveway, Riley savoring the moment when Sunbridge came into view.

The great house, caressed by the sun, basked upon a gently sloping rise beneath the Texas sky. It was three stories of the palest pink brick and was flanked by twin wings, which were also three stories high, but set back several feet from the main structure. White columns supported the roof of the veranda, which swept along the entire front. There was a fanlight transom over the two huge oak front doors. The same design was repeated over each window on the top floor. Ornamental topiaries and crepe myrtle hugged the foundation, and a magnificent rose garden surrounded the house, complete with trellises and statuary.

It was a hell of a spread, Riley liked to say, and all of it his and Ivy's. One day it would belong to his son, Moss. Thousands of acres of prime land, where Thoroughbreds and cattle grazed contentedly. For now.

Once the land had been owned by Riley's great-grandfather, Seth Coleman. It was said that when he first saw it, he felt as though he could reach up and touch the sun. He had come from dark beginnings, and this great house upon the rise would bridge his past with his future. The name Sunbridge was entirely his own conception. Seth Coleman, according to all who knew him, was a ring-tailed son of a bitch who stomped on people, was cruel and vindictive, with a black heart. It was well-known in Texas circles that he was greedy and power-hungry and would stop at nothing to get what he wanted.

Riley brought the Bronco to a stop outside the front doors. He liked walking past the ethereally graceful rose garden and the feminine sweep of the clematis vine that surrounded the oak doors. He remembered how the house had looked before the tornado swept it all away. There had been shiny, dark wooden floors, massive beams supporting the ceilings, thick, dark Oriental carpets, and man-sized leather furniture. Each time he entered the old house, he imagined the smell of his great-grandfather's cigar smoke, the thudding of high-heeled cowboy boots, and the sound of boisterous men drinking hard whiskey. Now Sunbridge was full of sunlight, earth-tone furniture, white walls, and light oak floors. The smells were those of his wife and son. The sounds were popular rock, Ivy's and his son's laughter. The floor-to-ceiling walls were gone, replaced with half walls, so that the entire first floor was open and inviting.

He almost had it all, he thought as he opened the massive

oaken doors. As always, he stood stock-still and pitched his baseball cap toward his peg on the hat rack, the only thing to survive the tornado that had destroyed the house.

Normally he viewed his entrance into the house as a homecoming. A happy event. Today it wasn't so. He listened to the sound of voices coming from the kitchen. That had to mean the others were here. Sawyer, Maggie, and Cole, Cary and Thad. Counting himself, there were just four members left of the family, if you didn't count the wandering gypsy Susan and her children. While Cary and Thad were family, they weren't blood. Cole had called this family meeting. More than likely it was a crisis. These past years they only seemed to get together as a family when a crisis of some sort threatened either the family or one of them as an individual.

He dreaded walking into the kitchen, dreaded listening to whatever the problem was going to be. Hell, he had enough problems of his own—the severe drought, the oil wells that weren't producing, and some kind of sticky problem with the newest branch of the family.

There were hugs and kisses, handshakes and manly slaps on the back the moment Riley entered the kitchen. Someone handed him a bottle of beer. He looked around. *It must be a major crisis*, he thought. *Everyone looks worried.*

He waited. When the silence continued, he gritted his teeth. "Let's hear the short version," he snapped.

"I can give it to you in four words, the Japanese stock market," Cole said. Riley cringed. He was painfully aware of the deep decline of the Japanese stock market.

"Coleman Aviation sucks," Sawyer said sourly. "We're so deep in the red I doubt we can climb out. I hate to remind you all, but the Thorntons take fifty-one percent of everything. I'm getting a little sick of busting my ass for that branch of the family."

"I don't want to hear that kind of talk. The Thorntons bailed out Mam when she needed it, so hush, Sawyer," Maggie said. "Family is family. You know Mam's feeling on that."

"Mam isn't here now," Sawyer said coldly. "Riley, what do you have to say?"

"This is the worst drought ever to hit the state of Texas. My two water wells are almost dry. We're buying water for the cattle, and the price is prohibitive. We haven't had a gusher in four years. We're hemorrhaging money."

Cary Asante looked around the table. "What's mine is yours."

"I feel the same way," Thad said.

"I don't know what your assets are, but I suspect they won't come close to the kind of money this family needs. The offer is appreciated, though," Cole said tightly.

"What are our options?" Maggie asked. "Whatever I have independently is all yours if needed. Billie Limited is in the black. We can mortgage it or sell."

"I already exercised my one option. I'm mortgaged to the rafters. My plan was to call Cole for a temporary loan. I guess that's out of the question. I have six months before my notes are called at the bank. The day after, the whole kit and caboodle goes to the highest bidder. I haven't said anything to Ivy, so let's keep this between us."

"Where does that leave us?" Maggie asked.

Cole looked across the table at his mother. "At the edge of a very big, very dark black hole."

"The stock market will go back up. It always does. The drought can't last forever. I'll go to the Thorntons and beg if I have to. They've helped us in the past. I'm sure they'll help us again," Maggie said.

"Mother, that was in the old days, when a handshake worked like magic. It doesn't work that way anymore. We're talking interest in double digits. They're saying the drought could last another year. If Riley doesn't strike oil or if we don't get orders for planes in the next few months, we might as well pack it in," Cole said. His fingers worked and twisted his tie. In his frustration he yanked it so hard his entire face and neck turned brick red. "How the fuck did this happen?" he said in a strangled voice. "Usually one or the other of us has some ups and downs, but we never have them all at the same time."

"Everyone just calm down," Maggie said. "We can talk this out and come up with a solution if we all work on it."

Riley dropped his head into his hands. "I wish Grandma Billie was here. She always knew what to do."

"What exactly is that supposed to mean, Riley? I'm doing the best I can to understand what happened. No, I'm not Mam. You all told me you were capable of running things. I took you at your word. Now this. I offered to sell Billie Limited. That will fetch us some high millions. It's been operating in the black for years. Just in case no one has noticed, let me point something out to all of you. Anything us Coleman or Thornton women work at works. One hundred percent. Look at Nealy Coleman for God's sake. Mam did it. Fanny Thornton pulled it all together, and before her, Sallie Coleman Thornton did the same thing. This is no time to start blaming anyone for anything. We're a family, and we'll pull together. We made it work before, and we'll make it work this time, too."

"Aunt Maggie, I didn't mean . . ."

"Yes, Riley, you did mean it. You were comparing me to Mam, and I came up short in your eyes. If anyone else feels the same way, say so now."

"What time is it?" Riley asked suddenly.

"Almost four-thirty. Why?"

"Let's go into the den. I want you all to see something. Josh Coleman's horse, Sharpshooter, is running in the Belmont. If he bags it, SunStar Farms has itself a Triple Crown winner. This," Riley said, pulling a legal-looking brown envelope out of a kitchen desk drawer, "will explain it all. First we're going to watch the race."

Cole Tanner smacked both his hands, palms down on the kitchen table. "We're teetering on the edge of a black hole where we could all literally lose our shirts, and you want to watch a horse race on television. I-don't-think-so."

"You always were a goddamn hothead, Cole. Would it make a difference if I told you SunStar Farms and that possible Triple Crown winner now belong to Seth Coleman's, our great-grandfather's, estate? It's amazing when you sit down and actually think about what a horse like that is worth in stud fees. If he wins, we're talking hundreds of millions of dollars. Multiply that by Great-uncle Josh's other colts sired by Dancer's Flyby and what do you see? Do the math, cousin. The race is about to start any minute. Aunt Maggie, turn on ABC."

"Hold on a minute, Riley. What are you talking about?" Cole demanded.

"Look, we all know what a bastard our great-grandfather was. Well, he had good company. His brother was just as big a bastard. They tried to skin each other. It looks like, according to the papers in this envelope, our great-granddaddy was the bigger bastard. It's the answer to our present problem if we care to exercise our rights. There is a glitch, though. A serious one you and the others aren't going to like. It's one of those damned if you do, damned if you don't situations. I'm thinking the first one to lawyer up is the one who's going to win. Just my opinion, cousin."

Cole snorted. "Then that makes us just like our great-grandfather, doesn't it?"

"Yeah. Yeah, it does. You want to play with the big dogs, then you better be in the front of the pack."

"Look!" Sawyer squealed. "Nealy Coleman is riding the horse. They just said they scratched the other jockey."

Riley looked at his cousin Cole. He raised his eyebrows.

"Is this one of those things where we have to vote as a family?" Cole demanded.

"Depends," Riley said, sitting down on the floor, his eyes glued to the wide screen just in time to hear the announcer say, "Cornelia Diamond will be riding Sharpshooter today in the Belmont. For those of you who don't know, Sharpshooter's sire was Dancer's Flyby, a Triple Crown winner himself. Dancer's Flyby is owned, trained, and was ridden to the Triple Crown by Cornelia Diamond. The buzz here today at the announcement is mind-boggling. There is all kinds of speculation going on here today as to the reason for this last-minute switch up. And now a word from one of our sponsors."

"I can't believe a woman can ride in a race like this," Cary Asante muttered.

"Why not? Who says it has to be a male jockey? If she won a Triple Crown, and I don't even know what that is, it has to mean she's pretty damn good. She's looking real good to me right now. Anyone care to make a little wager? What, no takers? Sawyer?" Maggie said.

The ever-outspoken Sawyer grimaced. "It's a sucker bet. She's gonna win. Just look at her. Confidence oozes out of her. I saw that when we met in Virginia. She's my kind of woman. I just love trailblazers."

"I wish Billie was here to see this," Thad murmured.

"She's probably watching. Mam never missed a trick. She and Amelia are probably both up there chortling away," Maggie murmured.

"How can she see this race if she donated her eyes to me when I was blinded in that explosion?" Cary said brokenly.

"Oh, Cary, don't you see, she is seeing it, through you," Maggie said, putting her arm around Cary's shoulder.

"Billie was something, wasn't she?" Cary said quietly.

"One of a kind," Thad said.

22

Nealy looked around at the serious faces and smiled. "This horse is platinum. If anyone can run this race and win it, it's Sharpshooter. I'm just along for the ride. We're both going to give it our best shot. It's time for you all to go to the clubhouse and watch this big guy take me into the winner's circle. Go on now before he gets nervous. This is no place for him to pitch a fit."

"Nealy, take this with you. Emmie said it went to heaven and back, so maybe it will bring you good luck. If it doesn't go right, that's okay, too. Rhy and I just wanted you to know that."

"I couldn't believe it when Emmie gave you back the penny," Nealy said. "There are no words to tell you what that penny has meant to her all these years."

"I think I know. I want it back, Nealy."

Nealy nodded before she stuck the penny under her tongue. She remembered another time when she'd done the same thing in almost the same circumstances. That time the horse was hers. Would it make a difference today?

"You got room for one more, Nealy?" Ruby asked as she held out the gold medallion.

Nealy nodded and reached for the gold disc. Her eyes popped wide. "Is this . . . ?"

"Yes. Ash said to give it to you, but you have to give it back to me. Whatever you do, don't swallow it!" Nealy's head bobbed up and down as she slipped the gold disc inside her cheek.

"Good luck, Nealy," Metaxas said.

"Sis?"

There it was again. That lovely word from her brother. "Yeah, Rhy?"

"This guy is good enough to tie Flyby's record."

"I know that."

"Just let him rip in the stretch. Hell, if he wants to rip at the gate, let him go."

"Okay. Anything else?"

"Good luck." Nealy grinned. "You know what, it feels good up here. It's been a long time. See ya."

"What if she doesn't win, Metaxas? She's come so far. Done so much. Do you think . . . ?"

"You know what I think, Ruby. I think she's going to be happy with whatever happens. That's the kind of person she is. She gives it her best shot. That's all any of us can do."

"That night on the porch when we talked she said she got her strength from her own solitude. She said being alone fit her like a good pair of jeans. Isn't that amazing, Metaxas?"

"It sure is, honey. You're taking her under your wing, aren't you?"

"I am. It's time for her to live."

"God, I love you, Ruby."

"You got that guy ready to drill the hole in my medallion?"

"He's in the clubhouse with his portable jeweler's drill, just waiting."

"Now that's why I love you," Ruby giggled. "She's going to win, Metaxas."

Nealy worked the coins in her mouth to be sure she would be able to shout to the horse and not swallow them. "Easy big guy. Easy. We've been in and out of the gate a hundred times just the way your daddy did it. Do it like a gentleman. I want him to be proud of you. Don't look at those other horses. They're slugs compared to you. You have wings on your feet just the same as Flyby. I want you to use those wings. Here we go!"

She knew she had the lead the moment she broke from the inside rail, and she didn't let up. She was so far over Sharpshooter's head she thought she was going to sail off into the wind. "Fly baby, fly!" she screamed until her throat gave out, and still she screamed. "You have the lead! You got it! They're eating our dust." She didn't look to the right or the left as the colt reacted to the thundering hooves behind him. They were all behind her. Sharpshooter knew it, too, as he ripped down the stretch five lengths ahead of the others to equal his daddy's win.

The roar in the stands was music to Nealy's ears! "Wherever you are, Josh Coleman, I hope you saw that!" Nealy shouted.

She turned to see Ricky Vee coming up alongside her. That had to mean he came in second. Dillon Roland must be having a bird.

"Great race, Nealy," Ricky said. "Super horse. The minute I saw you fly out of that gate, I knew I didn't have a chance. You were so far ahead of me there was no way to catch up. You got yourself one hell of a horse there."

"He's not mine, he belongs to my two brothers." She offered her hand. The jockey nodded and shook it. "I'll ride with or against you anytime, Nealy."

"Nah, this is it for me. I'm getting too old for this."

"Don't say that. Don't you want a triple Triple Crown? One more and then you really make the old history books. Don't be so quick to hang it up. See you around, Nealy. By the way, I wasn't the one who told your pa who you were. I just want you to know that."

"Yeah, see you around."

Nealy suffered through the ceremonies, the interviews, the well-wishers. The coins safely in her hand, she led the new Triple Crown winner back to the barn, where her family was waiting for her. She held out both coins. Metaxas in turn held the medallion out to the jeweler standing next to him. Pyne stuck his penny in his shirt pocket and then buttoned the flap.

"Jesus God, sis, you did it! I still can't believe it. Saying thanks doesn't seem enough."

"It's enough, Rhy. This is some horse you got here."

"He's got his daddy's legs, that's for sure," Pyne said dreamily. "We got us an honest-to-God Triple Crown winner. I knew he was good, but I didn't know how good until I saw you let him go. He flew. He had the race from the git-go. I gotta tell you, sis, no other jockey could have ridden him to the crown. You did it. You brought it home for us."

"Not bad for a girl, huh?" Nealy said softly.

"Not bad at all," Pyne said.

"Rhy said to let him rip, and I did. He needs to cool down. Let's all work on him. He needs to feel both your hands on him. Here you go, baby," Nealy said, pulling a handful of mints out of her shirt. "You get 'em all."

"That's your secret!" Rhy said, eyeing the candies.

"Plus a few other things that shall remain secret. I'm going to miss him. You take care of him, you hear."

"You made history today, Nealy," Metaxas said happily.

"In more ways than you know. Uh-oh, here comes someone I don't want to deal with right now."

Nealy's brothers edged her out of the way as Dillon Roland approached. "Let us handle this," Rhy hissed in her ear.

"I want to be the first in line to make an offer for this stallion's first colt," Dillon Roland said. "Name your price."

"We would do this . . . why?" Rhy asked in a dangerously low voice.

"To make money, of course."

"If I had a rat chewing on my leg and you offered to buy it from me, I'd tell you to go to hell," Pyne said, just as Rhy's fist shot forward to land squarely between Dillon's eyes. "I'm just sorry I didn't do this thirty-two years ago, you son of a bitch!"

Nealy leaned over to peer down at the immaculately groomed horse owner. "I think you knocked him cold, Rhy. I didn't know you had it in you," Nealy said, her voice full of awe.

"I didn't think I did either. It was for you, Nealy. Pyne and I were never really sure he was the one until we read that contract you had Pa sign for the colts. None of Flyby's progeny can ever be sold to Dillon Roland or his associates or anyone connected in any way, shape, or form with Dillon Roland or under any other name, corporation, or holding company he might use. I don't know if that's when Pa figured it out or not. Hell, you know what he was like. He could have known from the beginning. You just never knew with him."

"I think he's coming to."

"What the hell was that for?" Dillon said, rubbing his head and blinking away tears.

"If I have to tell you, then you're dumber than I thought.

Now get the hell out of here. Just the sight of you offends my family," Rhy snarled through clenched teeth.

"Look, everyone, isn't it beautiful?" Ruby said, showing off the gold medallion with the double safety latch and a triple-braided eighteen-inch gold rope.

"Great race. Wear it in good health, Ruby."

"I will. I'll never take it off. Never."

"Did you say something, honey?"

"No. Just talking to myself."

"I have a surprise for you two lovely ladies. We are not heading back to Kentucky today like we planned. Instead, I reserved two luxurious suites at the Plaza in Manhattan. You two ladies are going to get 'the works,' you know, hair, massage, manicure, pedicure, whatever, and then we are going dining at a fabulous restaurant so we can celebrate. I've also taken the liberty of inviting a very old, dear friend. We are going to party and celebrate your good news, honey, and Nealy's superior win. Are you with me?"

"I'm your girl, honey. Wait a minute. All we have is what we're wearing. Did you . . . ?"

"Of course. Everything is waiting for you. Can we go now?"

"Nealy?"

"Just one minute."

They watched as Nealy walked over to the new Triple Crown winner. She wrapped her arms around him and kissed his long nose. "You made me real proud today, but the real glory is all yours. It's stud heaven for you now, big boy." She laughed in delight when the horse nudged her pocket. "How'd you know I had one left?" Sharpshooter tossed his head back and whinnied. To her brothers, she said, "You need to buy these mints by the case. Call me, okay?"

"You bet!"

"I'm all yours. A massage is going to feel soooo good. Oh, God, you want me to get in a limo when I'm full of mud and muck."

"Nealy, Metaxas owns the livery company."

"Is there anything he *doesn't* own?"

"There might be one or two things, but I don't know what

they are. Who cares? In my whole life I have never been this happy," Ruby said as she reached for Metaxas's arm. Nealy reached for the other.

"Let's go, ladies. Our carriage awaits!"

Nealy Coleman Diamond Clay's destiny walked into the restaurant as if he owned the place, which he did, and headed straight to the best table in the house. There were no menus at *La Petite*, and if a guest dared to ask the price of any dish he knew instantly by the frown on the waiter's face that he had committed a serious faux pas. Four dishes were served nightly, and the tables turned over once. The first seating was at seven, the second at ten. Their guest list was reserved six months in advance. *La Petite* was one of six high-end, outrageously priced restaurants owned by one Kendrick Bell and Metaxas Parish.

The introductions and amenities over, Nealy's insides were twanging, and her head was buzzing. This was definitely a man she would like to get to know better. A lot better.

"I'm sorry I'm late. I was upstate this morning checking on one of the other restaurants, and then this afternoon I took two guests to Belmont for the race. It was spectacular, even though I didn't win a lot of money. I knew Sharpshooter was favored to win, but I couldn't see myself betting on a horse ridden by a female jockey. I bet on the one that came in second. So did my guests. What is this world coming to? Females riding in horse races! My mother laid down a bundle on Sharpshooter and crowed all the way back home. No offense, ladies, but horse racing is definitely a man's game."

"Really," Ruby said.

"Amazing," Nealy said.

Metaxas opened his mouth to say something, then changed his mind when his wife kicked him none too gently under the table.

"Does that mean you think women should, you know, stay in their place?" Nealy queried.

"Well no, not exactly. There are some things women shouldn't do, in my opinion. Women are nurturers and mothers. I like women to be women. I like them to look like women and dress like women."

"Really," Ruby said.

"Amazing," Nealy said.

Metaxas played it cool and kept his mouth shut.

"Why is it I feel like I'm doing all the talking?"

"Because you are," Nealy said sweetly as she looked him square in the eye. He wasn't good-looking at all. His nose seemed off center and his jawline a tad too defined. His hairline was receding, but he had wonderful eyebrows and incredible dark eyes that were now staring at Nealy, a frown starting to build on his face. She knew somehow that he had a beautiful smile.

"I'm sorry, I do tend to monopolize conversations. What were you saying?"

"I agreed with you that you were doing all the talking. I understand you own this place."

"Metaxas is my partner. We own six other restaurants."

"I didn't ask you how many restaurants you owned. Actually it wasn't a question at all. Merely a statement. Now I'm going to ask you a question. Are your cooks women or men?"

"Men of course."

"Really," Ruby said.

"Amazing," Nealy said.

Metaxas continued to play it safe and kept quiet, his eyes full of misery.

"I've never eaten anything I liked that was cooked by a man. Have you, Ruby?"

"Never!" Ruby responded smartly.

"I think you'll like tonight's dinner," Kendrick said, looking to Metaxas for help. Metaxas fiddled with his cuff links and refused to make eye contact.

A devil perched itself on Nealy's shoulder and spurred her on. "I'm a steak and potatoes girl. With lots of ketchup on the side. Thick chunks of bread with big hunks of butter to sop up the juice. How about you, Ruby?"

Ruby winked at Nealy. "I'm a sopper from way back. I like my meat rare and bloody. Give me a triple-baked potato with sour cream, butter, bacon bits, chives, ketchup, and a dab of hot mustard. Do not ever serve me chicken. Honey, how about you?" Ruby prodded her husband.

Metaxas took the safe way out. "I'll have whatever you all are having. Ken, what about you?"

"Well . . . I was going to recommend . . ."

Nealy leaned across the table, a half smile on her lips. "Tell us," she said.

Flustered by Nealy's intent gaze, he mumbled, "I was going to recommend the duck roulades with avocado, pistachios, and pistachio armagnac sauce. We also have a tangerine duck that is quite good."

"Nah," Nealy said.

Ruby shook her head.

Metaxas stared at the chandelier.

"We also have a wonderful sautéed escolar with curry oil and apple mint couscous."

Ruby and Nealy shook their heads in unison. Metaxas stared across the room at a painting hanging on the wall.

"We do have a lovely curry-crusted lamb chop with a garlic wine sauce served with a potato shallot custard," Kendrick said, a note of desperation creeping into his voice.

"I don't care for lamb. If I'm desperate, I can eat it, but I'd rather not," Ruby said.

"I don't like curry, and I'm not crazy about lamb either," Nealy murmured.

Metaxas switched his gaze to the beautiful stained-glass window opposite their table.

"That just leaves our chicken dish, and since you don't care for chicken, I'm at a loss as to what to offer you. If there's something in particular you like, I'm willing to go into the kitchen to cook it for you myself."

"You cook!" Nealy asked in amazement.

"Doesn't everyone?" Kendrick shot back.

Metaxas felt like he was now on safe ground. "Kendrick is a five-star chef."

"Really," Ruby said.

"Amazing," Nealy said.

Metaxas clamped his lips shut as he stared down at the bowl of fresh violets on the table.

"If you are serious about the offer to cook for us personally, then I would like French oysters wrapped in spinach leaves as an appetizer. Go light on the paprika. A salmon and sorrel souf-flé for the main course with some braised mushrooms with pancetta and pine nuts and perhaps an endive custard. Don't forget the nutmeg. For dessert, I think I would like a fresh strawberry soufflé. I'll leave the wine selection up to you."

"I'll have the same thing," Ruby said guilessly. "Honey?"

"Sounds good to me."

"What am I missing here? The three of you look like you just put one over on me."

Nealy burst out laughing. Ruby joined in.

"Ken, this pretty lady sitting next to me isn't just our friend and family member. She's the one who rode Sharpshooter to the winner's circle at Belmont this afternoon. I think it's that tit-for-tat thing women are famous for."

Nealy smiled.

Ruby beamed.

Metaxas scowled at his business partner's miserable countenance. "This might be a good time for you to say something, buddy."

Kendrick Bell slipped off his chair onto his knees. He reached for Nealy's hand. "I'm sorry if I offended you. That wasn't my intention. I'm looking at you sitting here and you're so beautiful and so womanly and feminine, it's impossible for me to believe you . . . do what you do. I guess I mistakenly thought you need to be a hard-muscled man to handle a horse. If there was a crow here, I'd eat it. I want you to know you have my deep admiration, and I will never make a mistake like that again. Would you like to marry me?"

Nealy flushed a rosy pink. "I think I have to get to know you a little better. This city would suffocate me. I could never live here. I need wide-open spaces, and I need the horses. It probably wouldn't work," she said impishly. "You can come for a visit, and I'll teach you to ride." My God, she was flirting with a virtual stranger. And liking it. She took a moment to wonder how Nick and Emmie would like this man with the laughing eyes.

"I don't live here. I live in the mountains, where there are trees and grass. I just might take you up on your offer."

"Can we eat now?" Metaxas grumbled good-naturedly.

"Absolutely. How about three T-bone steaks grilled to perfection. Beef straight out of Texas, Coleman beef to be exact. Wouldn't serve anything else. Some potatoes and a nice crisp garden salad."

"Sounds wonderful," the trio said in unison.

"I'll head for the kitchen and put the order in. Any particular wine you'd like, or do you trust me to come up with one?"

"We'll leave it up to you," Metaxas said.

The moment the restaurateur was out of sight, Ruby turned to Nealy. "So, what do you think?"

"You mean other than being a typical man? Seems nice. What did you think?"

"He's a hell of a guy," Metaxas blurted, worried that his choice for Nealy was being frowned upon. "He'd give you the shirt off his back, and if you needed a dollar and he only had fifty cents, he'd borrow the other fifty for you. That says something about a man in my book. Plus, he's a hell of a good cook. He likes the outdoors. Good sense of humor. Has humility. He's rich, so he doesn't need your money. Hard worker. Very hardworking. Great smile. Did ya see those teeth? Perfect. Women faint over him. I can't figure out why some woman hasn't snapped him up. He's never married and he's more than eligible and he has no baggage. Fifty. Fifty is good. Still young. Works out. Likes sports. Loves to dance. Loves animals, especially dogs. Loves music. He's everything a woman would want."

"Enough, honey. I think Nealy likes him. You do, don't you, Nealy?" Ruby asked.

"No one is that perfect," Nealy sniffed. "He seems very nice. You two are matchmaking. Listen, my life is very good. Just because there isn't a man in it doesn't mean it isn't good or isn't what I want. There weren't any bells and whistles if that's what you mean. He doesn't do anything for me. I appreciate you trying, I really do. I can see by the look on your face that you're both feeling sorry for me. Please don't. I have new directions now. I don't need a man in my life to clutter it up."

"Is that what men do, clutter up women's lives?" Kendrick asked, coming up behind Nealy's chair.

Nealy flushed. "Some men do. That's just my opinion, of course." Damn, couldn't she do anything right? She'd just sabotaged what could have been the beginning of a nice relationship. Ruby and Smitty were right. She didn't know how to act. She'd been living and working with horses so long she no longer knew how to act with human beings.

Nealy knew in her gut the evening was ruined, and there was no way to salvage it. The beautiful emerald dress that made her feel like Cinderella, the gift from Metaxas, was now nothing more than a dress. The matching satin slippers were just shoes. The magic ball was simply a restaurant, and the prince turned into a frog way too early in the evening. She felt like crying. Just leave it to a man to ruin things.

"I would hate to think I was one of those men. By the same token, what about women who clutter up men's lives with their 'I want this, take me there, do this, and do that.' Now, that's what I call clutter."

"I'm not like that," Nealy said.

"I never said you were, miss, whatever your name is. We're talking generalities here, or at least I thought we were."

"You don't even know my name! One minute you're blasting women for doing something you think only a man is capable of, the next minute you're on your knees asking me to marry you and then you . . . you . . . *cook!* Cooking is women's work."

"Says who?"

"Says me, that's who. I wouldn't eat in this place if it was the last place on earth."

"It's easy to see what kind of palate you have. You like *ketchup.*"

He was making fun of her, and people were turning their heads to listen. Without thinking, she stood up, pulled back her arm, and whopped the restaurateur smack on the nose. "Kiss my ass," she hissed as she stalked from the room, her head high, her eyes bright with unshed tears.

"What the hell!" Kendrick said, blinking to ward off a wave of dizziness.

"She popped you," Metaxas said, his eyes wide with amazement.

"I think she broke my nose," Kendrick said.

"You need to apologize," Ruby said, getting up from the chair. "I'll go after her."

"Apologize for what? She's the one who hit me. I swear, I think my nose is broken. You're a man, what the hell did I do?"

Metaxas sucked in his breath. "Don't look at me for an answer. You're a great guy. How could you ruin something that was so perfect?"

"What? Tell me what? There was nothing perfect about this evening. Not one damn thing. People are staring at me. I own this damn place, and people are staring at me like I killed someone. They'll probably never come back. Goddamn it, Metaxas, say something."

Metaxas cleared his throat and took the high road. "I think, buddy, my wife is right, you owe Nealy an apology. I can't believe you forgot her name."

"Damn it, I know her name. Cornelia, Nealy Coleman Diamond Clay. She had me so rattled I couldn't think."

"You! Debonair bachelor that you are were rattled by that little slip of a woman? Now I've heard everything. Just in case you're interested, people aren't staring anymore. They're eating. So, what did you *really* think of Nealy?"

"This is the last time I'm letting you try to fix me up. Don't think for one minute I've forgotten the other disasters."

"It's your own fault," Metaxas said virtuously. "Never argue with two women. You argued. Admit it. I have to go now. Nealy's in Room 1207 at the Plaza in case you want to send flowers or a note of apology. We're leaving tomorrow."

"That'll be the damn day. Go ahead, go. Some friend you are. You got me into this. You said she was a gem among gems. That rare jewel one finds only once in a lifetime. That's what you said, Metaxas. And I believed you! She's a *zircon*."

"I can see myself out," Metaxas muttered.

"Don't come back," Kendrick shouted. He was rewarded with more sly smiles and knowing winks.

The day he apologized to that horse jockey would be the day they served ice water in hell.

Nealy knew from the dampness on her pillow that she had cried in her sleep. She hadn't done that in years. She rolled over and looked at the clock on the nightstand: 4:10. She slipped her legs over the side of the bed. What was that noise? She walked

through the luxurious suite of rooms to the door and against it. She jerked backward when she heard wh like a tentative knock. Alarmed that something was w Ruby, she undid the chain lock and dead bolt. Cauti opened the door. Startled at Kendrick Bell's appear stepped backward.

"It's four o'clock in the morning and you're knockin door. Plus, you're drunk. I know this because you sme distillery. How did you get here?"

"I walked!" Kendrick said. "I came to apologize. It' turn now," he singsonged. "That wasn't nice what you s my restaurant. I run a respectable . . . establishment," he cuped. "Ladies don't do things like that, and they don't say my ass' either. Even if I deserved it, which I did."

Nealy led Kendrick to the sitting room. "You're absolu right. My social skills are abominable. You're right about me a the horses, too. You got under my skin. I apologize."

"You rattled me. I don't know how to act around you. Tha never happened to me before. I just wanted you to like me. Yo can ride a horse in a race and win that race. You conquered a man's world. My mother thought that was the most wonderful thing in the world."

"Oh."

"Do you accept my apology?"

"Yes. Do you accept mine?"

"I guess so. Do you want to meet my mother?"

"The next time I come to New York."

"Okay. I'm going to go to sleep now on this couch. I won't bother you. You're very pretty for a woman your age."

"I guess that's a compliment. Thank you."

"I do like you. Metaxas doesn't think I do, but I do. Did I say that right?"

"Uh-huh."

"I can't do this anymore. I don't want to do it anymore. This was supposed to be the charm. It is . . . I think it is. Is it? I apologize for saying you were a zircon."

Nealy grinned. Whatever he was talking about was Greek to her.

23

On a hot, sultry day in mid-August, two things—one good, and one not so good—happened at Blue Diamond Farms that forced Nealy to stand at attention and look to the future.

On her way from the barn to the house for a late lunch, she stopped to watch the cloud of dust shooting backward from an approaching unfamiliar black car. She waited for the car to stop and the driver to climb out. He looked around, and said, "I'm looking for Emmaline Owens and Cornelia Clay."

"I'm Cornelia Clay. Emmaline is my daughter. What can I do for you?"

"Accept this," the man said, slapping two sets of legal-looking papers into her hand. Before she could voice a question, the man was behind the wheel of his car and backing up the long driveway. A process server.

"Whatcha got there, Ma? Who was that guy?" Nick demanded.

"He was a process server. I guess someone is suing me and Emmie," Nealy said, placing the papers into her son's outstretched hand. "Just give them to Smitty and let her deal with it. God, it's hot, isn't it?"

"It's going to get a lot hotter," Nick said as he scanned the papers in his hand. "Ma, you're right. You and Emmie aren't just being sued, you're being *sued*. Big-time. The Colemans, et al. of Texas are suing for your old homestead. I think this is a little out of Smitty's league."

Nealy pushed the Stetson farther back on her head, then removed her dark glasses. "They're *what*?" Outrage rang in her voice.

"You heard me. You better call your brothers. This is serious stuff, Ma."

Nealy raced into the house just as a second vehicle drove up. A tall figure got out, looked around, then headed toward Nick. "I'm Kendrick Bell. I'd like to see your mother if that's possible," he said, extending his hand.

"By any chance are you the guy who was supposed to take my mother dancing a few months ago and never showed up?" Nick asked as he gave him the head-to-toe once-over.

"Yeah, I'm the guy. I came to apologize."

"A little late, aren't you? This is not exactly a good time," Nick said, slapping the legal papers against his leg with loud thwacking sounds. "Come along, but I'm telling you, my mother isn't in the best frame of mind right now. Would you like to stay for lunch?"

"I'd like that very much. You look like your mother. This is a very nice farm from what I can see."

Nealy didn't bother to turn around when the screen door closed behind Nick and Kendrick. One hand was in her hip pocket, the other gripped the phone in her hand so hard, her knuckles were white. She still wore the Stetson, something she never did in the house. From long years of habit and many swats to his behind for doing the same thing, Nick hung his hat on the peg by the back door. He frowned as he listened to his mother's end of the conversation.

"This is serious, Rhy. You could lose the farm if you don't get yourself a good lawyer. I have no idea why they think they can sue us. I didn't know families did that to each other. They want SunStar Farms. That means the whole ball of wax. Get real, Rhy. How could I possibly know a lawyer in Virginia? I have to find one for Emmie and me. Ruby warned me right after the Belmont that she thought there was something wrong that day in the dining room. To this day, neither Emmie nor I have gotten one piece of paper from that lawyer. Do not use him, Rhy. Call me the minute you and Pyne get served. I'm going to call Ruby now. I'll call you back this evening. The only way you are going to lose that farm is over my dead body, and I have no intention of dying. You need to go through *his* papers again. You might have missed something the first time. Remember how *he* liked to hide stuff. I'm going to start looking for a slick lawyer. This definitely calls for slick. Good-bye, I'll talk to you tonight."

"Ma . . ."

"Not now, Nick. I have to call Ruby. Damn, she said something wasn't right."

"But Ma . . ."

"Eat without me, Nick. I'll eat later after I talk to Ruby."

"Kendrick Bell is here, Ma!" Nick shouted.

"Stop being so melodramatic. If that weasel ever shows up here, show him your boot and the road at the same time. Ruby, it's Nealy. Listen, I was just served papers for Emmie and me. The Colemans are suing us. So far my brothers haven't gotten their papers. I need to know if you can recommend a good lawyer. What do you mean what do they want? They want the goddamn farm. The whole thing, horses and all. You will? That's great, Ruby. I'll be waiting on the porch. I missed you from the moment you and Metaxas drove away. No, I haven't heard from him. Don't ever fix me up again. He stood me up. Apology my ass. How much time does it take to pick up the phone and say, sorry, I can't make it. I bought a new dress and shoes. I even put makeup on. And perfume. I'll see you later. Thanks, Ruby."

"Now you can talk, Nick," Nealy said, swinging around. Her back stiffened and her eyes narrowed at the sight of the tall man standing next to her son. She wanted to say a million different hurtful things. She wanted to sting his pride, make him feel ashamed for standing her up. Instead she said, "You were in the neighborhood and thought you would stop by for a cup of coffee, right?"

"No. I came here specifically to apologize. No gentleman ever stands up a lady. There were extenuating circumstances, but I don't suppose you want to hear them."

"Try me," Nealy said, walking over to the kitchen sink to wash her hands.

Kendrick grinned at Nick. "I had an accident and lost my memory, my mother lost her memory and I was trying to help her get it back, or I had a triple bypass."

"If you were me, which one would you go with?" Nealy asked quietly.

"The latter because it's true. I didn't know if I was going to make it or not, so dancing wasn't at the top of my priority list. In case you're interested, I'm okay now. Not a hundred percent, but I'm getting there. I thought about calling a hundred times. I'm sorry I didn't."

"Yeah, me too. Are you staying for lunch?" Nealy asked as she looked at the table setting.

"Your son invited me. I'd like to stay."

"By all means." Nealy squeezed her eyes shut as she tried to remember the week's menu Willow had given her to approve on Monday. "I think we're having smoked catfish with apple fennel salad and pickled onions. For dessert we're having rhubarb raspberry pie. We tend to eat light at lunchtime. In case your diet is restricted, you shouldn't have any problem with this lunch. By the way, a woman is cooking. In case you decide to stay for dinner we're having scallion chive soup, curried chicken patties with radish raita, purple potatoes, mango cucumber salsa, and a strawberry crème caramel tart for dessert. Do you think you can handle that?"

"I think so. Can you direct me to where I can wash up?"

"Second door on the left. Willow, where's Smitty?"

"She went into town and said not to wait for her."

"Strength in numbers, Ma?" Nick grinned. "I kind of like him. He doesn't look quite as robust as you said he was, but I guess his operation explains that."

"I wonder why Metaxas and Ruby didn't say anything to me about it. They just let me rant and rave."

"Probably because I asked them not to tell you," Kendrick said quietly. "I guess I should apologize for that, too. I couldn't help but hear you on the phone. Are they coming here?"

"Yes. They should be here around six, just in time for dinner. How long are you staying?"

"I have two weeks to go until the doctor gives the okay to return to work. I have a hotel room in town."

"That's silly. You can stay here if you like. I can have one of the men or even Nick go into town and fetch your things. I know Metaxas and Ruby will want to see you. We have plenty of room, as you can see, we have a wonderful *female* cook. Don't get any ideas about trying to steal her away either."

"I wouldn't dream of it. I might ask her for some of her recipes if you don't mind."

"I mind only if you don't pay her for them. That's assuming she wants to part with her creations. That's how she thinks of her recipes—creations."

Nealy's mind drifted to the summons lying on the kitchen counter while her son and Kendrick talked sports. Family suing family. It wasn't right. Blood was supposed to be thicker than water. She looked up from her reverie to see Kendrick Bell staring at her. He smiled.

She smiled.

At twenty minutes past six a shiny black limousine pulled alongside the front porch. Nealy ran down the steps, her arms outstretched to Ruby and Metaxas. She squeezed them both as hard as she could. "God, I am so glad to see you! Kendrick Bell is here sleeping on the front porch. I wish you had told me."

"I gave my word, Nealy," Metaxas said just as gently. "I want you to meet someone, Nealy. Nealy Clay, meet Clementine Fox, your new attorney!"

"Honey, it is my pleasure to shake your hand. Any woman who can do what you did at the Derby, the Preakness, and then the Belmont twice is my kind of woman," Clementine said.

The only word that came to Nealy's mind for a description of the attorney was spectacular. She was tall, five-ten or so with silver hair, exquisite makeup, designer suit, and a pair of legs that went all the way up to her neck. Clementine's handshake was every bit as hard and firm as her own. Nealy liked her immediately.

"Call her Clem, Nealy. We go way back, don't we Clem? In legal circles they call her the Silver Fox. What say we all have a drink?"

"Sounds good to me," Nealy said, linking her arm with Ruby's. "I missed you. I hope you can stay a little while."

"As long as you need us. This was just what Metaxas needed. He was starting to mope. That man has to be involved in thirty things at one time, or he isn't happy. The minute I told him he was on the phone to Clem. She's all yours for as long as you need her. You should see how many trunks and suitcases she has. She's the best, Nealy."

Kendrick Bell snapped to attention the minute he heard the

voices approaching the front porch. The handshakes and introductions over, Ruby took charge. "You all just sit here, and I'll
fetch us some drinks. What will you have, Clem?"

"How about some of that fine old Kentucky bourbon I hear
y'all talking about. A double on the rocks."

"I'll have a beer," Nealy said.

"Ice water with a twist of lemon," Kendrick said.

Nealy stared across at the attorney and felt a pang of jealousy.
She wasn't just spectacular, she was exquisitely spectacular. She
was lean and trim; obviously she worked out. Nealy just knew
there wasn't one ounce of fat on this woman. She probably spoke
seven or eight foreign languages, too. She absolutely *reeked* of
capability. The Prada purse said her bank account probably
wasn't just healthy, it was robust.

Clementine crossed her legs. Nealy felt smug when she recognized the shoes on the attorney's feet. "I have all night, talk to
me. Tell me everything you can think of."

Nealy talked. The others spoke softly of other things.

Clementine listened intently, her pen flying over the yellow
legal pad. "Look, don't be so crushed. Families sue each other
all the time. They sound like a sorry bunch of bastards. I know
how to play the game, and I know the *name* of the game. Let me
give it to you in clear, concise terms. The first rule in a case like
this is—if it looks like it's going to be a knock-down-drag-out,
you fuck them before they fuck you. Your estranged family, for
want of a better term, has hired themselves a barracuda of an attorney. They have to be paying her some big bucks to drag her
out of retirement. Valentine Mitchell is one kick-ass lawyer. We
both studied under the Devil himself. We're evenly matched. I
might have a bit of an edge since I'm still practicing and Val
isn't. I need to know something right now. Are we talking big-
bucks, whatever-it-takes, representation?"

"Whatever it takes. They only get that farm over my dead
body. I want you to file suits immediately for my brothers, my
daughter, my son, and myself. We are suing for our percentage
of Sunbridge, all that family's holdings. Every goddamn thing
they own. When you're done, don't bother telling me where the
dead bodies are either. Families shouldn't do this to each other,
but since they made the decision to file this suit, I am not going

to let them steal my brothers' home right out from under them. They worked all their lives for that spread, and no money-hungry person or persons are going to take it away. You just do whatever you have to do to make sure they don't lose the farm or the horses."

"I hear you, honey."

Nealy sighed. She knew she was in good hands.

In another state miles away, the weather was just as hot but dry, temperatures in the triple digits. Riley Coleman looked at his wife, then looked away. "There was no other way," he said.

"There's always another way. I cannot believe you . . . you and the others did what you did. How can you rip their home away from them? You didn't even talk to me about it. How could you do that, Riley? We've always shared the good and the bad. You did this without even consulting me. That's unforgivable."

"Jesus Christ, Ivy, if there was any other way, I would have taken it; so would the others. It came down to them or us. Since we don't really know *them*, I had no other choice but to opt for *us*. Us, Ivy. The family. This will all go to Moss someday," he said, waving his arms about. "No one is going to take this away from him."

"When he's old enough to understand, he won't want it knowing how it came to him. I rather think that other family is going to feel the exact same way you feel about their home. The only people who win in cases like this are the lawyers. You made the biggest mistake of your life, Riley. Undo it now before it's too late. Drop the case. You don't want this on your conscience," Ivy pleaded.

"It's too late, Ivy. I just heard from Val a little while ago. The papers were served on all of them today. It's going forward."

"It's never too late to do the right thing. Do you want to know something, Riley? That day we all met in Kentucky, when I looked into Nealy Coleman's eyes, I saw something that scared me. She's like your grandmother Billie. That is a good thing. She'll fight you till hell freezes over, and then she'll fight you on the ice. That's what Billie would do to protect her family. She did it so many times I lost count. She would be ashamed of you for what you're doing. I don't want any part of this. I *won't* be a part of this. I'm taking Moss, and we're going to my parents'. I am so disappointed in you, Riley, I could just bawl my eyes out. Damn you! Damn you for doing this!"

"Ivy . . . Wait!"

"No."

"Will you . . . will you call?"

"No."

"You can't take my son away from me. I won't allow it!"

"Why don't you sue me," Ivy said, stalking off, tears rolling down her cheeks.

Riley kicked at the parched ground he was standing on. A cloud of dust spiraled upward.

He hadn't lied to his wife. He'd begged, pleaded, and practically sold his soul to find another way. Now he was going to lose it all. He could feel it in his gut. His shoulders slumped. Losing it all because of drought and other terrible things was one thing, but losing it all in a court of law because he was greedy was something else. Ivy was right, how in the damn hell was he going to live with himself?

Riley headed for the house just as the Bronco roared past him. He was about to wave, but the cloud of dust settling over him made it impossible for Ivy to see him. He trudged into the house and picked up the phone. "Sawyer, it's Riley. Ivy just took Moss and left me. I don't know what to do. Val called and said the papers were served today. I feel like shit."

"You should feel like shit. This was all Cole's and your idea. Adam isn't speaking to me either. Does that make you feel any better? I tried to warn you. That woman is going to fight you to the death. She's like Billie, Riley. Even Maggie saw that. Ivy will come back. I don't know when, but she will."

"No, she won't. I committed the unconscionable sin of turning on family. You didn't have to vote with Cole and me. You have a mind of your own, Sawyer, and a mouth to match."

"I did what you and Cole wanted. I'm not happy, nor am I proud of it. Stop whining and let's see if there's a way to make this right. I'm going to call Maggie."

"Don't bother. I think she's washed her hands of us. She's sitting over there in her island paradise while we bust our asses so we can send her the checks she so graciously accepts." Bitterness rang in Riley's voice at his declaration.

"That's not fair, Riley. You take that back. My mother works just as hard as you do at Billie Limited. She offered to sell the company. For all I know she might have done it already. Billie Limited is the only thing that's solvent in this family, and those monies go into the Coleman coffers, so don't go blaming my mother. Look to yourself and Cole. You two are the problem, not us women. I'm going to hang up now before I say something I'll regret. I am sorry about Ivy leaving. You should have seen it coming. Good-bye, Riley."

Riley looked around the neat, tidy kitchen. It was so like Ivy, bright colors, green plants, colorful rag rugs on the floor. There was even a fresh pot of coffee waiting for him. His wife had just left him but she made a pot of coffee for him before closing the door behind her. It was so like Ivy. A sob caught in his throat.

He picked up the phone again to call Cole. He wasn't surprised to hear his cousin pick up on the first ring. He tried to calculate the time difference in Japan, but his brain was too numb to function. "It's Riley. Val called, and the papers were served today. Ivy just took Moss and left me. Sawyer said Adam isn't speaking to her, so there's trouble there. We need to get out of this. We never should have done it, Cole. Sawyer as much as said our brains were up our asses. Ivy said something that scared the living shit out of me. She said Nealy will fight us till hell freezes over, then she'll fight us on the ice. She said, and Sawyer and Maggie both agree, that Nealy Coleman is like Grandma Billie. If that's true, Cole, then we need to pack it in now and go back to scrounging for money. I cannot believe you let my grandfather's billions slip through your fingers!"

"You're blaming me for the fucking stock market! Get off it, Riley. We both know those black suits your grandfather had in place call the shots over here. They just let me think I'm doing it. Don't go down that road, cousin. You sound just like Sumi. She's ready to kick my ass back across the Pacific *and* the Atlantic. She's been out looking for a job! If that's all you called to tell me, then I'm going to hang up and go back to my doodling."

Riley slammed the phone back into the cradle. He poured himself a cup of coffee. Maybe he should take one more crack at the Thorntons.

The phone and Ivy's address book were in his hands a minute later. He punched in the number with shaking fingers and waited for Sage Thornton to come on the line. Sage was the one he'd felt a special affinity for, and they'd gotten on well the few times they'd met.

"This is Riley Coleman, Sage. I'm sorry it's not a social call. I need to ask one more time if your family can help us out of our present difficulties." He pressed the phone so tight against his ear he got an immediate headache.

"Riley, it's good to talk to you. I spoke to Mom and the others, and right now there is no way. We're mortgaged to the hilt ourselves with the new casino we're building. Our money is so tight at the present we're not taking salaries. I'd tell you to try Ruby and Metaxas, but they've aligned themselves with Nealy and her brothers. I heard about the suit. I wish you could have found another way. I'm really sorry, Riley. We'd help if we could. I want you to know that."

"Thanks, Sage. I sold off the last of the cattle yesterday."

"Jesus, that had to hurt. What about the horses?"

"They went last week. The money went to pay the back interest. I feel like bawling."

"Then do it. You might feel better. I'll put my ear to the ground and see if I can scare up some money for you. Whatever it is will only be a piss in the bucket, but I'll give it a try. Maybe you should rethink that lawsuit. My mother was really upset when she heard about it. If there was one thing she instilled in us as kids, it was this sense of family. She drilled it into us. I guess it rubbed off because all of us feel the same way. I'd hate like hell to be walking around in your shoes right now. I know where you're coming from, but Christ, Riley, wasn't there another way?"

"If there was, I would have taken it. What would you do if someone threatened to take away that mountain you live on? Would you just sit there and let it happen?"

"I honest to God don't know."

"I gotta go, Sage."

Riley stared at the phone until he felt his eyeballs would pop from his head.

"There's no other way," he mumbled. Maybe it was time for a trip up the hill.

24

"Is it really time for you to leave, Ken? It seems like you just got here. I've never seen two weeks go by so fast. So much has happened lately. Normally things are pretty quiet around here. I hope you call me from time to time. Are you sure you're feeling okay?" She was babbling and didn't know why.

"I feel fine, Nealy. I go in for my checkup Monday morning, and if everything is okay, and I think it is, then I can go back to working half days. According to my doctor, I won't be doing any extensive traveling for a while, though. I hope you can find the time to come to New York for a visit. I keep an apartment in the city and stay there during the week, but on the weekends I go to the Watchung Mountains in New Jersey. It's only fifty minutes from the city. I like to putter around outside, and it suits my needs for the great outdoors. I'm going to miss you, Nealy."

"I'm going to miss you, too. Right now I really can't make any plans to take trips. This lawsuit is consuming all my time. My brothers are beside themselves with worry. I imagine they view it as living with an ax hanging over their heads. I do plan on going to Virginia in a few weeks. I'm going to . . . pretty it up for them. It's time some sunshine entered their lives."

"Virginia isn't all that far from New York. Maybe I'll drive down to see you if you give me enough notice."

"I'd like that. I think you'll like my brothers. For a while I didn't like them, but I understand now what we all went through. I spent so many years being miserable and unhappy, and so did my brothers. Did you have a normal life, Ken?"

"Yes. Sometimes I almost feel like I should apologize for my life when people start talking about how miserable their own lives were."

"It's a beautiful night, isn't it? The sky looks like a big dark blanket with millions of sparkly diamonds lying on it. Oh, look, there's a shooting star. Quick, make a wish!" Nealy cried. "You can't tell what it is, or it won't come true."

"Okay. I made my wish. No, don't try weaseling it out of me. You said I can't tell. What did you wish for?" Ken asked.

"When I was a little girl I used to stand by the window at night when I was supposed to be asleep and stare at the stars. I don't know where I ever got the idea that my mother was a star up in the heavens. I probably made it up to make myself feel better. Little girls need a mother. I wanted a mother so desperately. Every time I saw a shooting star I thought it was my mother letting me know she could see me at the window. They're bringing her remains here next week. I thought my brothers would object, but they didn't. It's like my life now is coming full circle again. To answer your question, no, I'm not telling you what I wished for."

"Be like that then," Ken teased lightly as he reached for her hand. "What's that delightful smell?"

"It's either honeysuckle or confederate jasmine. They smell almost alike, and there's a lot of it creeping up and around the trees. When I first came here I used to prune the plants around the front porch for Maud. She always said it was intoxicating. She loved sitting on the porch in the evening. I did, too. I still do. You don't seem the homey type, Ken."

"I never had time to be the homey type. I was always on the go. Now, though, I'm enjoying it. I'm even giving some thought to retirement. I'm also thinking of getting myself a dog for companionship."

"For years now I've been saying I'm going to get another dog, but something always stopped me. When Charlie died, I was so devastated all I did was cry. I still cry when I think of him. Flyby knew he was gone, and he pitched a fit for months when that little dog didn't show up in the barn. I just can't put myself through that again. First it was Molly, and then Charlie. They are wonderful, though. I'm still not quite sure how Charlie ended up as my dog when I got him for Emmie. He used to sleep inside my pillowcase. Tell me that isn't amazing."

"It's amazing. Nealy, I think I'm falling in love with you."

"Please don't. I don't think . . . my life is . . . settled. I don't think I'm capable of loving a man the way he should be loved. It isn't you, it's me, so don't take that as a rejection. What I mean is, it is but it isn't. I hope that makes sense to you. I'm not marriage material, and I don't sleep around."

"Then let's be friends for now," Ken grinned.

"That I can handle."

Overhead the leaves in the trees rustled as the birds made ready for the night. Somewhere off in the distance an owl could be heard. Soft strains of music wafted up from one of the barns. Just the normal sounds she listened to every evening. Most times she wasn't even aware of them. Tonight was different for some strange reason. Was it Ken? Was it because he was leaving in the morning? Suddenly she felt jittery and out of sorts. He should have kissed her by now. Two weeks was a long time to spend in someone's company without some kind of overture. The closest he'd come to touching her was holding her hand on a walk. Mainly a walk around the house so Ken would sleep better at night. She liked the feel of his hand in hers.

"Have you ever been in love, Ken?" Nealy blurted.

"No. Well, maybe, but it was a temporary kind of feeling, and it certainly wasn't a feeling that I wanted to spend the rest of my life with that person. Hell, maybe it was lust, and I was too damn dumb to know the difference. I'm not a youngster, so it goes without saying that quite a few women have walked through my life. I used to wonder how I would know when the right one came along. Metaxas said I would know, that it's instinctive. That man has to be the happiest man in the whole world. He has it all. It means nothing to him. All he does is give, give, and give. Ruby is his reason for living. Do you ever watch him look at her or watch Ruby look at him? It's there for the whole world to see. Both of them are so incredibly grounded. I truly believe they could live together in a tent without a cent and be happy. When I first met him, he said something to me I've never forgotten. He said it doesn't matter where you've been, what matters is where you're going and how you get there."

"Ruby says that to me all the time." Nealy laughed. "I envy

their love, their closeness, and what they share, but most of all I envy their generosity. God blessed the two of them."

"Are we getting philosophical, Nealy?"

"No. Maybe. It's the end of the day," Nealy said, as if that explained everything.

"I always reflect on things before I go to bed. Doing that helps me make decisions on what to do the following day. I try never to dwell on the past. I never dwell too far into the future either. Works for me," Ken quipped. "What works for you?"

"Lately all I can think about is this lawsuit almost to the exclusion of all else. I don't understand how family can sue family."

"Money is a powerful incentive, Nealy. People murder for money. In the scheme of things a lawsuit isn't all that important."

"It is to me. Let's not talk about it. I regret that I wasn't able to teach you to ride while you're here. Perhaps another time."

"Does that mean at some point in time I can come back?"

"Absolutely. I'd be upset if you didn't. I do like you. I like you a lot. I never had friends. Believe it or not, Smitty was my first real friend. Back in Virginia there was no time for friends. Pa wouldn't allow it. Then when I came here, the horses became my friends. I'm trying to tell you something here, and it isn't coming out right. I'll never be glamorous or worldly. I'm probably always going to smell like horses no matter how much I shower and wash my hair. My hands will always be rough even though I use cream. I do dye my hair, though, because my son teased me to the point it was easier to do it than argue with him. He wants me to fix up and go dancing and take vacations. That's not what I'm about. I am what I am. I don't want to change, and I would never try to change to please someone else. I hope that all came out right."

"I think so. You just told me to take it or leave it. You are you, and you will never change for me or for anyone else. I respect that. The difference between you and me is I would try and probably not succeed, so in the end your way is probably better."

Nealy burst out laughing.

"Where do we go from here, Nealy?"

"I thought we agreed to be friends. It's a good place to start, don't you think?" She held out her hand for Ken to clasp in his.

"Friends."

Thunder rolled across the sky, ominous and chilling. An omen of some kind, Nealy thought as she tried to soothe Flyby, who was stomping about in his stall. Even the mints weren't calming him today. Lightning ricocheted overhead as another clap of thunder sounded. Nealy didn't know who hated storms more, she or the horses. Her biggest fear was a lightning strike to one of the barns. Even though she held regular fire drills, there was no guarantee everyone would perform the way they were supposed to. Maud always said her biggest fear was a fire in one of the barns.

It was only three o'clock in the afternoon, but it was midnight dark outside. Trees were doubled over as rain slashed downward and then sideways. It was just a wicked summer storm, Nealy reminded herself, no better or worse than hundreds of others she'd lived through.

An hour later, the horses calm, Nealy walked up to the house to find Clementine Fox waiting for her in the kitchen. She was dressed the way she would dress to go to a fancy office. Nealy thought it strange, since her office here at the house was a converted room that had been a pantry at one time. All hours of the day and evening the bells and whistles of the fax line, the telephone, and copy machine sounded. Clem was dressed in a raspberry-colored suit with a simple white-silk tee underneath. She wore panty hose and high heels and was exquisitely made up. The perfume she wore was absolutely sinful.

Nealy headed for the coffeepot. "What's for dinner?" she asked Willow.

"Shrimp-stuffed quail, twice-fried green plantains with garlic dipping sauce, and a crab salsa. For dessert, Miss Nealy, it is something you will savor, a sweet lemon tart with a marshmallow sauce. There will be extra for bedtime."

"Sounds scrumptious," Clem said, licking her lips. "If you have time, come into the office so we can talk. The Colemans' attorney called me a little while ago."

"Is it bad or good?" Nealy said, bringing the coffee mug to her lips.

Clem shrugged. "Our papers were served this morning. Cole Tanner's will be a few days late since he's in Japan. It doesn't really matter, he's part of the whole thing. It seems Valentine Mitchell is in the mood to talk. All I did was listen. What you don't know, nor did I know, is this. The Colemans are in serious financial difficulty. They're about to lose the ranch because of a severe drought. They've had to sell off the cattle and Thoroughbreds. There have been no new orders for planes for Coleman Aviation. No new oil gushers. The Japanese stock market, the Colemans' lifeline, is down so low it can't get any worse."

"Are you assuming I should care about this?" Nealy asked coldly.

"I'm obligated to tell you of any communication from opposing counsel. I'm telling you."

"I couldn't care less, Clem."

"Sunbridge is going to go on the auction block in the not-too-distant future. The banks holding the loans want their collateral."

"So what you're telling me is they are going to lose their home, so that's why they're trying to take SunStar away from my brothers. They don't care if my brothers are homeless. She called to tell you that. Why?"

Clem slapped her notepad down on her makeshift desk. "That sums it up pretty well, Nealy. As to the why of it, let's just say we lawyers don't ask questions like that. We fish and probe, trying to discover things without actually coming forward and asking. Maybe she's leading up to settlement talks. I let it all go over my head. Do not ever, under any circumstance, underestimate Valentine Mitchell. I've seen her go to court with *nothing* and win. She's a master at pulling rabbits out of hats."

Nealy digested the information. "What are you a master at?"

Clem laughed. "Skinning those rabbits."

"Do you know the name of the bank that holds the loans on Sunbridge?"

Clem shuffled the papers on her desk. "Yes, the Texas Savings and Loan."

Nealy shrugged as she walked away. In the kitchen she re-filled her coffee cup before she walked up the steps to her room. Inside, with the door closed and locked, Nealy yanked at the phone on the little desk under the window. The only people in the world that had this particular private number were Nick, Emmie, Ruby, and Kendrick Bell. She had no fear of Smitty, Clem, or any of the girls in the office picking up the phone. She dialed a number and waited for it to be picked up on the other end of the line. "This is Nealy Clay. I'd like to speak to Mr. Sloan, please."

"Nealy, what are you doing here? You weren't supposed to come till next week?" Pyne said as he reached out to hug her.

"I decided to come early so I could take Mama's remains with me when I leave. I thought it was the right thing to do. The truth is, I came to fix up this place. I'm going to bring some sunshine into your lives. I made a stop at High Point, North Carolina, and picked out new furniture. It's going to arrive tomorrow morning. I ordered curtains, carpets, everything I could find to lighten and brighten this place up. I even got you new dishes and silverware. And a ton of green plants. I want your promise to water them after I leave. Did you get a housekeeper?"

"Yep, and she's a whiz. She cooks like a dream, and the house is clean but shabby. How long are you staying?"

"Just a few days. Are you okay with the lawsuit and everything?"

"Hell no, we're not okay with it. I'll burn this place down before I turn it over to those . . . those people. I mean it."

"I don't think it's going to come to that, Pyne. I sure wish I knew what that family's reaction was to our court papers. They must be jumping out of their skin knowing the three of us are Seth Coleman's children with a claim to their precious Texas holdings. DNA is a wonderful thing. If we win this case, and Clem thinks we can win, how do you think you'll feel if we get the whole ball of wax?"

"Look, we didn't start all this legal crap, they did. We would have let sleeping dogs lie. All we want is this place. It's our home, and we aren't giving it up," Rhy said.

"I guess that's pretty much how they feel about their home.

Clem said their attorney wants to talk. We've been stalling. I'm not sure why. Probably to make them sweat would be my guess."

"Pyne and I would never rip anyone's home out from under them. When it looked like that was going to happen to us, we made the decision to pack up and go to work for one of the other farms. All we know is horses. They've been our life. This whole thing is making us crazy. We don't want to fight our relatives. All we want is to be left alone. Can't you undo this, Nealy?"

"I don't think so, Rhy. Clem said that paper Pa . . . Josh Coleman had—the one that said Seth Coleman signed off on the property for cash when he was in dire straits—was a forgery. If she knows it was a forgery, then the Colemans know it, too. Pa . . . Josh Coleman, rather, was tricky, just like his brother. They each tried to outsmart the other, and this is the result. We don't have any choice but to let the lawyers settle it for us. The only one in the whole clan who was decent was their sister Sallie. I keep meaning to hire a detective to find the other sister Peggy and her family, but something always comes up and I put it off. There were other sisters, too, but no one knows where they are. I'm hoping Peggy knows, and we can start searching for them. If we have more family, I want to know them. For all we know they might need our help. That's what families are supposed to do, help each other. I don't want to talk about this anymore. It's like beating a dead horse. What will be, will be."

Nealy stood back to admire her handiwork. She could hardly wait for her brothers to come up for supper so they could admire her decorating skills. Thank God for fast-drying paint, she chortled. She walked around the kitchen, the same kitchen that had once been her sanctuary when she lived here so long ago. Back then it had been dreary and dismal, with ancient appliances and dark woodwork. Now it glistened with fresh white paint and green-checkered curtains at the windows and door. State-of-the-art appliances graced both sides of the room. Underneath the cabinets a coffee machine, a stereo unit, and an electric can opener winked at her in the bright light overhead.

The table and matching chairs were pickled oak, almost white in color, with hunter green cushions and place mats. Overhead a multicolored Tiffany lamp gave off miniature rainbows in the late-afternoon sun. The new dishes had clusters of bright red cherries in the center. The silverware had scarlet handles that matched the cherries. The centerpiece was a bright red bowl full of Gerbera daisies. Everything looked warm and cozy, not to mention inviting. Delicious smells wafted toward her. Pot roast, potato pancakes, velvety gravy, emerald green snap peas, garden salad, and fresh homemade bread were on the dinner menu. Nealy eyed the luscious chocolate cake with thick frosting sitting on a rack on the counter.

Nealy looked down at her watch. She still had fifteen minutes until it was time for her brothers to wash up for dinner. She made good use of the time as she wandered from room to room, admiring her handiwork. It all looked light and inviting. She'd had to pay extra for the delivery people to cart off all the old stuff, but she didn't care. Her brothers didn't need any reminders of the past.

They were going to love the sixty-one-inch television set and the stereo unit tucked into one of the cabinets. Deep comfortable La-Z-Boy lounge chairs graced each side of the fireplace, whose mantel now held dried flowers, candles, and a photograph of herself and her brothers. A sofa, one shade darker than the loungers, took up the entire far wall. The old, dingy, smelly brown carpet was gone. In its place was light beige carpeting. Thick, luscious green plants filled out the corners, while a bowl of fresh flowers graced the light oak coffee table. Sheer curtains with hunter green draperies hanging at the sides finished off the room. A man's room. Comfortable and warm. Inviting. Homey. Tears burned Nealy's eyes as she stared around the room. If only it had been like this growing up. Once she'd seen a picture of a young girl lying on the floor in front of a fireplace, coloring in a book. She squeezed her eyes shut as she tried to conjure up the picture from her memory. There had been a fat little dog lying next to the little girl. She'd never had a coloring book or crayons or a fat little dog and if her father had caught her lying on the floor, he would have tanned her hide. She shook her head to drive away the memories. She turned just in time to see her brothers' faces as they stared about the room.

"God Almighty, is this the same room?" Rhy said, slapping at his head.

"Looks good enough to be in a magazine," Pyne said, flopping down on one of the lounge chairs. "Get a gander at that television set," he said in awe. "You're spoiling us, Nealy."

"That's what sisters are supposed to do. Now I can leave tomorrow and know you're living in a regular house that isn't dark like our past. Make sure you keep fresh flowers around. Flowers make all the difference. How did you like the kitchen?"

"It's too pretty to eat in," Rhy said. "We'll manage, though. You did good, sis. Real good."

Nealy beamed.

"We want to talk to you about something, Nealy."

"Spit it out. Did I do something wrong?"

"No, of course not. Rhy and I have been talking, and we'd like you to change your mind about . . . Ma. We'd like you to leave her here. It doesn't seem right to, you know, dig her up and move her. If you leave her here, you'll always be able to come back here and . . . you know, visit, talk, whatever people do in cemeteries. Rhy and I have always gone out there and mumbled and muttered when things go bad. It's important to us, Nealy."

"I thought . . . I didn't know . . . That's fine with me. I just didn't want her to be alone. We'll leave things as they are then. Do you take flowers to the grave? You're supposed to do that, you know."

"We do. We aren't *totally* ignorant, Nealy."

"I didn't say you were. It's just that men don't think about things like that. We don't know anything about our mother, and I find that very sad. We don't even know if she liked flowers. We don't know if she liked to read books or what her favorite color was. Did she like to bake cookies? Did she have a favorite dress, did she pray? We should know those things, but we don't. I'm going to make it my business to track down Mama's family. When I hire that detective to find our Aunt Peggy, I'm going to ask him to find out about Mama. Do you think that's a good idea? I bet we have *hundreds* of people out there that belong to us. People we don't even know about. I'm going to find them. Every single one."

"Attagirl, Nealy. Now can we eat?"

Nealy linked her arms with her brothers. "It's nice having a family, isn't it?"

25

Nealy stared at the calendar hanging on the kitchen wall. Where had the summer and autumn gone, she wondered. It all seemed like such a blur. Christmas and the New Year loomed ahead of her. Not that holidays meant much at the farm, they never had. Anything festive, anything out of the ordinary, had to be planned weeks, sometimes months in advance. The farm ran on a schedule that had to be adhered to regardless of social obligations and festivities. She grimaced when she likened the farm schedule to the United States Postal System. Mail had to be delivered regardless of the weather. These days they even delivered mail on holidays and weekends if one cared to pay for it.

This year Emmie and Buddy were going on a cruise for the holidays and Nick was going to try his hand at, or as he put it, his feet, skiing with Willow in Colorado. Clem was going to Vegas, and Smitty was heading for New York to do some heavy-duty shopping. Ruby had medical appointments scheduled at Johns Hopkins, and she and Metaxas would spend the holidays together and leave late Christmas Day. She'd assured Nealy they were just checkup appointments, but she had to keep them. With everyone gone, Nealy would be alone, without even a dog to keep her company.

Life, at that moment, Nealy decided, was at a standstill. There had been several glitches where the lawsuit and her family were concerned. Clem had suffered through a ruptured appendix and then peritonitis set in, laying her low for over a month. Within a week of Clem's return to work, Valentine Mitchell had been run off the road by a drunken driver. Her injuries were severe enough to put her in traction for five weeks. She, too, had recovered, and the suit was progressing. Interrogatories and depositions had been taken and filed, and a court date scheduled for

January 20, a little over a month away. Living with anxiety had become a way of life these past months. Nealy just knew in her gut the court date would be the day Misty Blue gave birth to the foal that was to go to Ruby. That was more important than any court date. She made a mental note to ask Clem about a possible postponement.

Nealy roll-called the list of things she'd taken care of during the summer months. She'd hired a private detective to track down her mother's people, with no results. The detective hadn't had any success finding her aunt Peggy's family either. Did they all drop off the face of the earth? Was it possible there wasn't any family? Maybe she should go to Austin, Texas, herself and start her own search. She could do the same thing in Las Vegas. Nick said the one-man detective agency was bleeding her dry, and she needed to get rid of him. He was probably right. Nick was right about most things.

Then there was Kendrick Bell. She realized just how much she cared about him the week he left to return to New York. He called daily, usually late at night, and they would talk for hours. These days she felt like she knew him as well as she knew herself. He hadn't insisted on visits, nor had he pushed himself on her. She thought he was waiting till he was fully recovered because he admitted to days that weren't as good as he would like. He'd gone from semiretirement to full retirement the first of October. At one point he had confessed to wishing he had done it sooner.

Just last night she'd asked him what he was going to do for the holidays, and he'd said he just wanted to sit by the fire and read some good books.

"Smitty," she bellowed at the top of her lungs.

"For God's sake, Nealy, what's wrong?" Smitty bellowed in return.

"I want you to make me a plane reservation. I'm going to New Jersey. The sooner the better. I'll need a rental car, too."

Smitty clapped her hands. "Well, good for you, Nealy! What date do you want on your return ticket?"

"Leave it open. Sometime after the New Year, I guess. I'm going to see Kendrick." The words rolled off her tongue as though she'd announced she was taking the first shuttle to the moon.

"Then I'd recommend you get yourself some new duds. Or were you planing on wearing that uniform of yours?"

"You mean my jeans and shirts?"

"Exactly. You know you could shop first. There's a very high-end shopping mall in New Jersey called the Short Hills Mall. Lots of designer, pricey shops. You could dude yourself up to look like a million bucks."

"Why would I want to do that, Smitty?"

Smitty rolled her eyes. "That's what women do when they want to snare a man. They start with underwear and work to the outside. I still can't believe you don't have pierced ears. Women get their belly buttons pierced, and you still don't have pierced ears. Having pierced ears is a good way to store diamonds. You know, if you have no more room for your *jools*," she drawled.

"First of all, I'm not trying to snare a man and my underwear is fine, thank you very much. Get me some maps and the directions to Watchung from the airport and to the mall. I might buy some perfume."

"Honey, you need more than perfume. Snazz up, blow his socks off. Be a goddamn woman for a change. You need *lessons.*"

"I do not! In case you forgot, *I was* married."

"All right, then, a refresher course. You need to go on the prowl, you need to strut and learn how to stalk a man. Sexily of course. You *clomp*, Nealy. It's those damn boots you wear all the time."

"What else is wrong with me?" Nealy demanded through clenched teeth.

"Other than all that, you're fine. Okay, okay, one open-ended ticket coming up. Tomorrow or late today?"

"Tomorrow will be fine. I think I'll go into town to have my hair done. Maybe I'll pick up something new to wear on the plane."

"Sounds like a plan to me," Smitty grinned.

"Sooner or later us late bloomers blossom up," Nealy said, tweaking Smitty's cheek.

Nealy stopped at a Mobil station to fill the tank of the rented Lincoln Town Car. According to the map Smitty had provided her with, she was now on Route 22 and about ten miles from

Kendrick's house. She allowed herself to look in the rearview mirror while the attendant filled her gas tank. The entire back-seat as well as the floor were filled with boxes and bags of new clothing, gifts, and Christmas decorations. But it was the front seat that held the most important gift. She bent over to peer inside. A wide smile stretched from ear to ear.

The back of the pickup truck waiting at the end of the lot held a twelve-foot Douglas fir and several evergreen wreaths that were completely decorated. By paying extra, the tree people had agreed to follow her and set up the tree in Kendrick's living room.

She felt excited as she paid for her gas and turned on the car's engine. Damn, it was cold. But it was supposed to be cold for Christmas, which was just days away. Now that she was just a spit away from Ken's house she wondered what she would do if he wasn't home. What if he had guests? What if? Surprises were just that, surprises. It was too late now to worry about what-ifs.

She thought about the first Christmas she'd spent with Hunt and how she'd cut the tree down herself. She'd ended up with a bush, but the kids loved it. So long ago. Another life.

Nealy turned on her right blinker. God, she'd almost missed the turnoff. She drove steadily for another fifteen minutes up steep, winding roads before she came to Lotus Crescent Drive, where she turned left. Ken had told her there were only three houses on the dead-end street, and his was the one in the middle.

It was a storybook house perched on the side of the mountain. Tudor in style with lots of gingerbread and diamond-paned windows. In the summer months the brown vines climbing the house would be green with shiny ivy. It looked like a house that cried for a family, not a solitary bachelor.

Inside the six-thousand-square-foot house, Kendrick Bell was adding another log to the fire when he heard the sound of a car. Probably the meter reader, he thought as he walked over to the front window. His eyebrows shot upward at the same moment his jaw dropped.

Nealy!

He watched her get out of the car and look around. He could feel his heart fluttering in his chest. She'd finally come to him.

"No, tell me about it."

They talked of the past, the present, and what the future might hold for hours and hours. They walked down their respective Memory Lanes, sharing and laughing.

"So you got married for all the wrong reasons, eh? At least you got married. I could never bring myself to take that step."

"It stopped working for us early on, but it was obvious neither one of us wanted to do anything about it. Hunt looked elsewhere. I pretended not to know. I had the kids and the horses. To this day I'm not sure if we loved each other."

"Too bad. One good thing came out of it, your son. He seems like a great young man."

"He is. He practically runs the farm. Emmie is a driving force, and so is Buddy. I find myself with time on my hands, but that will change next month with the court case and Misty Blue giving birth. This foal is for Ruby, so the next three years of my life are mapped out for me. To tell you the truth, Ken, I don't know if I have it in me at this point in time. I did promise Ruby, though. It's something she desperately wants for Metaxas, and I can't deny her that."

"Is there anything I can do to help out?"

"Oh, you bet. We can always use an extra hand. It might be good for you, Ken. You could see what my world is like. What it takes to train a winner. It's like no other feeling in the world. It's not something I can explain, it's something you have to be part of, something you have to experience. You're more than welcome to go back with me. Hell, I'll even pay you."

"An honest-to-God salary?" Ken said in pretended amazement.

"Yep."

"Are you worried about the lawsuit?"

"I'm not worried for myself, but I am worried about my brothers. I did a dumb stupid thing. Of course it didn't seem dumb or stupid at the time. I went back to fix up the house for them. It was drab and dingy, and they needed things to be warm and bright. At least I thought they did. I told myself I was letting the sunshine back into their lives. The courts could decide to rip the farm right out from under them. That hateful old man forged his brother's name to a document. The whole thing is just

Something he'd wished for, prayed for. *It is a season of miracles,* he thought happily. He noticed the truck, then, and the two men hefting a huge Christmas tree from the bed. Nealy was bringing him Christmas.

She was moving to the passenger side of the car, opening the door, reaching in for something. Probably her purse. And then he lost sight of her as the two men carrying the huge Douglas fir passed in front of her. The doorbell rang. He tripped over his feet in his haste to get to the door before it rang a second time. He pulled it open, stood back, and waited.

"Merry Christmas, Ken," Nealy said as she stood on her toes to kiss him lightly on the cheek. "I brought Christmas. This," she said, handing over a large basket, "is my gift to you. Good, you have a fire. Take it over there, and I'll close the door."

"Where do you want this, mister?"

His eyes on Nealy's, the basket in his hands, he turned. "Wherever you think it will look best. Any corner. The middle of the floor is good, too. Whatever."

Ken was all thumbs as he worked the top of the huge wicker basket. Two shiny, dark heads popped up. They yipped and wiggled to be free of their tight cocoon of warmth.

"This is Gracie and this one is Slick. They're shepherds. Six weeks and three days old. Merry Christmas, Ken. They come with a lot of gear and instructions. I think they're probably hungry and in need of some water."

Nealy looked around as she pretended not to see Ken's wet eyes as he cuddled both dogs against his chest. "Nice place you have here. It's almost too perfect. Uh-oh, looks like your tree is going in the middle of the floor."

"The middle is good. That way you can see it from all angles. Jesus, Nealy, I can't believe you're here. I can't believe you got me two dogs! I guess my next question should be *why?*"

"I hated the thought of you spending the holidays alone, and since I was going to be alone, too, it didn't make sense when we could be together. I wanted to surprise you, but on the way here I realized one should never do things like this. I think every scenario in the world flashed through my mind. You know, all the what-ifs."

"I'm so glad you came. I can't tell you how I dreaded these

holidays. Other years it wasn't so bad because I was working and there was always a Christmas party of some sort at one of the restaurants every single night. This is so much nicer. How long can you stay?"

"I'm yours till after the New Year. Do you think you can handle me that long?"

"Absolutely. I think you're going to have to help me with these dogs. As much as I've always wanted one, I don't have the first clue as to what to do with them."

"They're just like people, children in this case. The first thing you do is love them and then you feed them, see to their needs, love them even more, and they will love you unconditionally. It doesn't get any better than that."

"No, I guess it doesn't. Do you want to tip those guys, my hands are kind of full at the moment."

"I already did. Thanks," Nealy called to the men's retreating backs. "Oooh, it smells so good, doesn't it? I just love the smell of balsam. I brought some wreaths for your front door and windows. We can put them up later. Now we have to take care of these little guys."

Dinner over, the kitchen cleaned, and the tree decorated, Ken dusted his hands dramatically as the two pups chased each other around the living room. "I think we earned ourselves a nice nightcap and a comfortable spot on the couch in front of the fire."

"I think that's a great idea, Ken. The pups are wonderful, aren't they? Watch, in about five minutes one or the other is going to fizzle out, and then they'll curl up by the fire and sleep all cuddled up next to each other."

"We could do that, too."

"Yes, we could," Nealy said, flopping down on the sofa. She patted the space next to her. Ken eased himself down beside her. He reached for her hand.

"I'm so glad you came, Nealy. So, how do you like my place?"

"I think it's beautiful. I don't know why, but I thought it . . . you would have used a professional decorator. Men usually do. I guess I'm surprised at your good taste. It's obvious you like comfort," Nealy said, referring to the deep chocolate sofa and

equally deep, comfortable chairs scattered about the living room.

"Considering my circumstances, comfort was what I was looking forward to. My doctor is angry with me. He thinks I should be exercising, walking, doing activity things, and I try but . . ."

"You're afraid, is that it?"

"I'm ashamed to admit it, but yes, I am. There's something else I should tell you. You must be wondering . . . at least . . . damn, this isn't going to come out right. I'm just going to say it. In case you're wondering why I didn't . . . what's the expression the younger people use these days? Hit on you? I've been . . ."

"Afraid to have sex," Nealy said, finishing his sentence. "That's understandable. Tell me something. Is it your intention to hole up here for the rest of your life? Do you plan to read your life away? Television can kill you."

Ken laughed. "That's exactly what Metaxas said. When she was the sickest and undergoing her chemo, Ruby still made an effort to do things. He pointed that out to me daily. I feel like a slug, and I know it's something I have to work through. Until you stare at death you can't understand the fear. I know the cardiologist is right. I feel wonderful. I'm just afraid if I start doing things I won't feel this wonderful. I'll react to every little ache and pain with panic. I guess that's more than you wanted to know."

"We can work on that together starting tomorrow. You have two dogs now that will need to be walked. I love walking in the crisp, cold air. Doing it together will be good for both of us. Think how nice it will be when we get back. We'll have big cups of mulled cider while we curl up with the dogs and look at the beautiful tree. It really doesn't get much better than that, Ken. When you do things together it makes all the difference. Whatever will be will be. Do you remember when we first met, told you I wanted us to be friends. I still do. This is our jumping off place."

"Friends it is," Ken said, squeezing her shoulder.

"Did I ever tell you about my first experience cutting down a Christmas tree? Actually we now refer to it as our Christmas bush."

one damn big mess. It looks like the Colemans have a legitimate claim to SunStar Farms. We, on the other hand, have a claim on the whole ball of wax where they're concerned. Unfortunately, their holdings at the moment are worth zip. We had to give our samples for DNA. The Coleman lawyer laughed her head off when Clem told her we wanted DNA samples from Seth Coleman. Then the craziest thing happened a few weeks ago. It was a fluke to end all flukes. Ruby gave me a locket that Fanny Thornton had given to her a long time ago. For no reason other than she wanted Ruby to have it. When I told Ruby about the DNA she told me about the locket. In it was a lock of Seth Coleman's hair on one side and on the other side was a lock of Sallie's hair. Ruby said Sallie Thornton never gave up the search to find her siblings, and the one time Seth and his family went to her mountain in Las Vegas, she took a snip of it while he was sleeping. I don't know why she would do something like that, but I'm glad she did. I just don't know what's going to happen. It's a real mess. If I dwell on it, I make myself crazy."

"And the search for your other relatives, how's that going?"

"It isn't. Nick said the detective just took my money and didn't do anything. I'm beginning to think he's right. I have two choices. I either do the search myself, or I find another detective agency. I'd kind of like to do it myself. Once Misty Blue gives birth, I could take a few months to work on finding our people. Nick and Emmie can handle the foal for a little while. For the most part, it's just watching him to make sure he doesn't hurt himself. They're just so frisky at that age. Kind of like those two guys sleeping over there," Nealy said, pointing to the two sleeping puppies. "By the way, their names are Gracie and Slick. I forgot, I already told you that."

Ken roared with laughter. "Gracie and Slick. Perfect! For whatever good I'll be to you, I'd like to help, Nealy. Two heads are better than one."

"Do you mean that, Ken?"

"To coin a phrase from my good friend Nealy Clay, I never say anything I don't mean."

"I think we're going to have quite a few things to toast when we usher in the new year next week. I'm so glad I came up here."

"So am I." Ken sighed. "So am I. Our time will come, Nealy. I promise."

Nealy snuggled deeper into the crook of his arm. She smiled contentedly.

"I'm going to hold you to that promise, Ken."

"I never make promises I have no intention of honoring, Nealy."

Dear Reader,

I hope you enjoyed meeting Nealy Coleman Diamond between the pages of this first book in my new trilogy. I had a lot of fun developing Nealy and watching her grow so she could get ready to move into the second and third books—*Kentucky Heat* and *Kentucky Sunrise.* I believe she's every bit as wonderful and enticing as Billie Coleman and Fanny Thornton.

I don't know about you but I'm always sad when I turn the last page of a book. Inevitably, I want more. For that reason, I've included the first chapter of *Kentucky Heat* for your enjoyment.

I think all, or, at least, most of you know I love writing about women who become strong because they persevere and prevail. To me there is no greater entity than family. For that reason, I would like to share two poems, written by good friends about the meaning of family. On my best day I could never write a poem. Perhaps that's why I treasure these two, and want to share them with you.

There is something else I want to share with you. I'm taking cooking lessons! I have to tell you, it's hard giving up the pinch, the dab, just pour, don't measure, method of cooking. I don't know if I'll ever become a gourmet cook or not, but I'm enjoying the classes. Cooking kind of reminds me in a way of writing a book. You start with nothing and create something from that nothing. From me to you, I share this, my first culinary endeavor. I got an A on the dish.

Enjoy.

Fern Michaels

P.S. You can reach me through e-mail: *fernmichaels@fernmichaels.com* and you can also drop by my web page: *www.fernmichaels.com*. As always, I welcome your comments.

Family

～

The first breath of a newborn child a wonder of life to be shared
Proud parents hold tight their creation blessed by heaven this day
Tiny pure miracle of life from love, tenderness, passion and care
Souls bond joyously as family with the humbling of life to pray

Precious gentle and tender, a new generation miraculously formed
The wonderful gift of life bestowed to a pure and innocent heart
New beginnings welcomed and sweetly kissed by sacred dawn
Bonds of love bind tightly ensuring kith and kin not to easily part

Memories of childhood passing by momentarily without due cares
Children enveloped snugly within the protection of family womb
Together nurturing each moment thankful in unison with prayers
The harsh pendulum of time threatening adolescence all too soon

Teenage years beckon confusion presenting countless self-doubts
Self-discovery and unexplained emotions clambering each to sort
Young hearts impatiently seeking what the puzzle of life is about
Experiencing first love and firmly in the net of passion be caught

Loves found and loves lost each leaving incomprehensible pain
Finding emotions being repeated with lessons in life ever harsh
Comfort and protection from family bosom heals again and again
Until love finds a nest in the adult two lives sharing the same path

The gift of love to and from our family is nestled deep in all of us
Umbilical safe haven of sanctity, wherein secrets kept safe forever
Strong bonds impregnable knowingly secure in each other's trust
Our family, learns, laughs, cries, loves and happily lives together

Lee Minshull

FAMILY

Years ago
in some century past
one woman stepped forward
to take up the quest!
of creating the outlines of our family crest
one man joined her
in this holy deed
thus beginning the pages
of our family creed
two ribbons entwined
in this tapestry
forming the pattern
of our destiny
the fabric still unfolds
with each alteration
its design particular
to each generation
our family lives on
through struggle and strife
a tribute to those
who brought it
to life

Diane Daniels

Lime Chili Shrimp with Coriander and Avocado

1 pound large shrimp
clove garlic
3 tablespoons soy sauce
1 teaspoon chili powder
1 tablespoon brown sugar
2 teaspoons fresh lime juice
2 teaspoons fresh lemon juice
1/2 teaspoon hot chili peppers or flakes
4 to 5 teaspoons olive oil
1 solid but ripe avocado
2 tablespoons chopped fresh coriander leaves

Clean shrimp thoroughly. Chop garlic into fine bits. Mix in bowl brown sugar, garlic, chili powder, red pepper flakes, lime juice, soy sauce, and two to three teaspoons of olive oil. Add shrimp and be sure to coat each piece. Let marinate thirty minutes.

Preheat your broiler.

Cut and peel avocado. Cut into pieces (I like chunks). Remove shrimp from marinade and place in broiler pan in one layer only. Broil about 4 to 5 inches away from heat for app. two minutes. Turn shrimp at end of two minutes. Broil two more minutes. Transfer to another bowl. Add avocado and lemon juice, coriander, and rest of olive oil. Add salt and pepper to taste and gently toss in bowl.

Serves two nicely.

For a sneak preview of
the next novel in this series—
coming from Kensington in May, 2002—
just turn the page . . .

1

Nealy staggered to the corner of Misty Blue's birthing stall, leaned against the slatted wall, then slid to the ground. She wrapped her arms around her knees to stop the trembling in her arms and legs. She'd had no sleep at all for the past forty-eight hours and was operating on pure adrenaline. She wanted to sleep, needed to sleep, but she didn't dare close her eyes in case the fragile newborn colt needed her. A wan smile tugged at the corners of her mouth when she heard Flyby whicker softly. "I hear you, big guy. Your son is doing just fine, and so is his mama. It was touch-and-go there for a while, but then I guess you know that. I don't want you worrying one little bit." A second whicker, this one softer, echoed in Nealy's ears. "All's right with your world, eh, Flyby?"

As if in answer, Flyby whinnied.

"Everything is all right with his world, but it sure isn't right with mine right now. I think this straw has bugs in it."

"Ruby! Are you awake? Are you okay?"

"I'm as okay as I can be for going without sleep for forty-eight hours," Ruby said in a hoarse voice as she peeked through the slats into Misty Blue's stall. "Ah, look at him, Nealy, he's so gorgeous he takes my breath away." She gazed at the colt adoringly. "Metaxas is going to go over the moon when he gets here later today."

Nealy yawned. "I hope we're both awake to see his reaction." She groaned as she struggled to her feet. Every muscle in her body ached with the exertions of the last two days. She was getting too old to wrestle an eleven-hundred-pound mare to lie down or hold still. Even though she was still in good physical condition, it was too much. Still, it was the bed she'd chosen to lie in, so to speak, so lie in it she would, straw and all, for as long as she could.

Nealy raised her arm toward the light so she could read her watch. "When I get my hands on my two kids, I am going to strangle them," she said, stretching her aching back. "They know the first rule on this farm is someone is always here. I let them convince me that a week's vacation for everyone wasn't going to make the world come to an end. Yes, we have good help, yes, we left everything in capable hands, but there are always the what-ifs. What if I had decided to stay an extra few days with Ken? It's a damn good thing I didn't. I had this really weird feeling I should come home early. Don't ask me why because I can't explain it. Am I the only responsible family member around here? If I hadn't come back when I did, God only knows what would have happened. I'm so angry I could chew nails and spit rust. Not even a phone call from either of them. Two weeks, Ruby. They each took an extra week and didn't say boo to me. No calls, no nothing. It's unconscionable."

"I'm sure there's a good reason," Ruby said wearily. "Why don't you go up to the house and take a shower. I'll call you if anything goes wrong. Will you trust me with the colt, Nealy?"

"Of course I trust you. I would trust you with my life for God's sake." Nealy picked up her Stetson out of the straw and hit it against her leg to shake off the straw cleaving to the soft felt. Ruby was right. A shower was just what she needed. A long, hot, wonderful shower. She'd always thought she did some of her best thinking in the shower and right now there were some hard decisions she had to make. "The vet will be back in about an hour. Just talk to them, Ruby. Try not to fall asleep till I get back, then I'll spell you. This is the most crucial time for this little guy. God, we almost lost this beautiful baby." She straightened her hat. "Look at him, curious as all get-out. Okay, I'm outta here for some clean clothes and fresh coffee."

A voice boomed from the far end of the barn. "Ma! We're home!"

Nealy froze. *Not now,* she thought. *Not now. I need to think things through a little more to know what I need to do.*

Ruby dashed out into the breezeway and caught Nealy just as she was leaving Misty Blue's stall. "Ask questions before you say anything," she said, wiggling her finger in warning. "You might be surprised at the answers. That means take it easy, Nealy."

Nealy took a deep breath, exhaling it in an angry *swoosh.* She jammed her hands into her pockets so they would stop shaking.

"Ma . . ." His eyes took in the blood on Nealy's shirt. "What happened? Oh my God, the colt came early. Jeez, Ma, I'm sorry I wasn't here." He was tall, his lanky form casting a shadow in the breezeway, Willow at his side. Nealy saw him squeeze her hand and knew he knew he was in deep trouble. *Good,* she thought. His eyes took on a wary look as he shuffled his feet on the concrete.

"It's pretty obvious, isn't it, Nick? The colt came early, and we damn near lost him." She paused to let her words sink in before asking, "Where the hell have you been? You were supposed to be here a week ago. Wipe that sappy look off your face. This is a working farm in case you didn't know that. You have responsibilities like the rest of us. I let you talk me into a week, Nick. A week is seven days, not fourteen. You knew the deal. The workers who spelled us got their time off the day after New Year's. That left us shorthanded. Did you know and do you care? Bradley broke a leg on New Year's Eve. Donald is in the hospital undergoing an emergency gallbladder operation, and we have six men out with the flu as of yesterday. Everyone has been pulling double shifts, and they're tired. We all did your work while you frolicked in the snow and your sister is sunning herself on some luxury ocean liner God only knows where. If it wasn't for me and Ruby, this colt would be dead. Neither one of us has had any sleep for two days, and for days before that an hour here and there when we were able to snatch one. You were supposed to be here. I agreed to a week's vacation. You took two weeks. Why didn't you call me? This would be a very good time to offer up an explanation, Nick."

"I thought Emmie . . ."

"You thought Emmie would cover for you, I know. And she might have if she wasn't off sunning herself on some luxury cruise ship on God only knows what ocean." Her son's look of surprise told her he had thought Emmie was at the farm. It was no excuse.

Ruby had reached out to touch Nealy's shaking shoulder.

Nealy shrugged it off as she stalked toward her son. Willow, the household cook and Nick's skiing companion, cowered behind him as Nealy jabbed a finger into her son's chest, forcing him backward. Flyby snorted his displeasure. Ruby cringed against the stall. "Is there a reason why you didn't call, Nick?" She sounded angry even to her own ears. Angry, hurt, and disappointed. He wasn't the young man she thought he was. Maybe someday he would be, but not now.

Ruby's hand reached out again to touch Nealy's shaking shoulders, but again she shrugged it off and walked toward her son.

"I got married, Ma. Willow and I went to Vegas and tied the knot after our ski trip. That's why I'm late."

"You *what?*"

"We got married," Nick said, his eyes wary at the expression on his mother's face. Willow, his new bride, still cowered behind him.

Nealy closed her eyes to let his words sink in. If she'd been angry, hurt, and disappointed before, she was doubly so now. Stung to the quick by her son's words, she retaliated. "Pack your bags and get out. Now!"

Nick's gaze ricocheted first to Willow and then to his mother. "Ma! What the hell? Ruby, do something. Say something."

"You heard me. What part of pack your bags and get out don't you understand?" The only thing that could save her from breaking down was to walk away.

"You're fired, Willow," Nealy shot over her shoulder as she stalked out of the barn.

"Ruby . . ."

Ruby stared helplessly at the young man and his frightened bride. She shook her head as she tried to soothe Flyby, who was pawing the gate to his stall. She was only a few feet from his stall when he kicked the stall door so hard that splinters of wood flew in every direction. A second kick sent the door flying off its hinges. The big horse charged out into the breezeway, ears back, nostrils flaring.

Ruby screamed when she saw him heading for Nick. She'd learned enough about horses since coming here to Blue

Diamond Farms to know that stallions could be extremely dangerous.

"Flyby!" Nick shouted in an attempt to control the horse, but Flyby wasn't listening. Snorting and tossing his head, the stallion pushed Nick into the tack room opposite his stall, pushed him so hard that Nick lost his balance and fell.

Willow screamed.

Ruby gasped.

Satisfied that he'd had his say, Flyby whinnied before he ran after Nealy.

"Son of a bitch!" Nick groaned as he struggled to pick himself up off the floor. "I think that damn horse broke my ribs."

"Then you better see a doctor," Ruby said, not unkindly. "The vet is due any minute. He can look you over and maybe strap up your chest."

"Ruby . . ."

"No, Nick, I can't intervene. Nealy told me the first time I met her this farm, these horses, take precedence over everything. Maud and Jess instilled that creed in her, and she abides by it. Otherwise, it doesn't work. She was always so proud of the way you and Emmie adapted to it. Your mother was right, there are telephones. How could you have been so selfish, so uncaring? If I were you, I'd do what she says until she cools down."

Nick's eyes almost popped from their sockets. "Are you saying I should leave here? This is my home. Where am I supposed to go?"

"It *was* your home," Ruby said quietly.

"I . . . I . . . have a contract," Willow whispered.

Ruby guffawed as she offered up a withering look. "I would imagine, knowing Nealy, that when you go up to the house, there will be a check waiting and your pots and pans will be on the porch. I don't think this is a good time to try to negotiate. What were you thinking, Nick? You don't get married and *not* tell your mother."

"I guess I . . . come on, Willow, let's get your stuff and get out of here. Thanks for nothing, Ruby."

"Just a damn minute, Nick. You're the one at fault here, not me. Don't take your anger out on me. Like everyone else on this farm, I covered for you and Emmie. In case you haven't noticed, your mother and I both look like death warmed over, as does every other person working here. I haven't had any sleep either. Your mother and I did what the four of us should have done because that's what you do when a crisis arises. Look to yourself before you start blaming others."

"Bullshit!" Nick snapped.

"Wrong animal," Ruby snapped in return. She brought her hand up to shield her eyes from the bright morning sun invading the breezeway to see Nealy trying to soothe Flyby as he gently pushed her toward the back porch steps that would allow her the height to heft herself onto his back. She could only imagine what Nealy was saying to her prize stallion.

She continued to watch as a Dodge Durango, Emmie and Buddy's 4-by-4, skidded to a stop in the courtyard next to the back porch. She continued to watch as Nick wrapped his arms around his middle and hobbled over to Emmie's SUV, Willow close behind. And then all hell broke loose. Flyby reared up on his hind legs as Nealy grabbed his mane to secure her seat on the stallion. She could hear angry sounds but couldn't distinguish the words.

"I hope your excuse is a lot better than your brother's, Emmie. You're a week late. Misty Blue birthed early." She took a deep, sobering breath so she could say what she needed to say. "Make it good, girl, because you aren't going to get up to bat again. I can't believe how irresponsible the two of you are. I'm waiting, Emmie."

"Buddy left me. He went to Ohio. He left me stranded at the ship. Stranded, Mom."

Nealy clenched her teeth. "I gave you a week because you and your brother convinced me it would be okay. One week, not two. There are telephones. If you think so little of this farm and me, so be it. We have rules here, and you and your brother know what they are. You both broke those rules. If your husband left you, it is something you have to deal with. I have a farm to run here."

"Mom, didn't you hear what I just said? Buddy left me. He said I'm normal, and he can't handle it."

Nealy clenched and unclenched her teeth again. "When did this happen, Emmie?"

"Last week. I didn't know what to do," she said miserably.

Nealy nodded. Any other time she would have opened her arms to her daughter and offered comfort. Maybe that was part of the problem. Maybe she'd been too available through the years, offered a little too much comfort. "Last week, and you're just now getting around to coming here?" she forced herself to say, knowing where the question would lead, wishing there was another way. "Doesn't your telephone work?"

"I . . . I spent the whole week crying. I didn't see this coming, Mom."

"I'll leave it up to your brother and his new wife to explain things to you. Your services are no longer required, Emmie. That means you're fired and off the payroll. If I can't depend on you, what good are you to me? Now, you have something to cry about." Her heels kicked the stallion gently as she headed back toward the foaling barn and Ruby.

"Mom . . ." Emmie wailed after her.

Nick put his arm around his sister's shoulder. "Save your breath, Emmie, and go home. She just booted my ass out of here, too. We broke the cardinal rule. Now we have to stand up and take our punishment like the big boys and girls we're supposed to be. Do you mind if Willow and I bunk with you until I can find someplace for us to live?"

Emmie nodded, her face miserable. "I have to get her to listen to me," she said, starting after her mother.

Nick pulled her back. "Don't even *think* about it. Jesus! She sure can work fast when she wants to," he said, referring to Smitty standing on the back porch with two white envelopes in her hands. Within minutes Willow's pots and pans appeared in cardboard cartons as if by magic. "I'll drive, Emmie, but first I have to pack Willow's stuff in the cargo hold."

"What's wrong with her, Smitty?" Emmie sobbed.

Nick stopped long enough to hear the office manager's reply. "You both broke the rules. As far as I can see there is absolutely no excuse for your behavior. You're old enough to know better. There *are* telephones. If I were you, I wouldn't drag my feet," Smitty said coldly before she turned to enter the house.

"I don't understand," Willow said.

"With my mother there are no second chances when it comes to the horses. She gave us an inch and we took a yard. In plain English, we fucked up. She won't bend either. Let's get out of here. Stop bawling, Emmie. Life is going to go on whether Buddy left you or not."

"But not without Mom. I'm not going until I talk to her."

"It's too late for talking. You should have called. I should have called. We didn't. We're selfish bastards thinking only of ourselves. Look, we both know that is not acceptable on this farm or any other farm. She bent enough to give us a week. The horses always have to come first."

"Just like that, we're walking away?" Emmie sobbed.

"Unless you want to crawl. It's your call. Get in the truck, Emmie. We'll talk when we get to your house."

Her shoulders shaking with her sobs, Emmie climbed into the truck and buckled her seat belt. She turned to look out the back window to see her mother and Ruby staring at the truck. She cried harder.

Nealy watched her children drive away, a lump in her throat. Did she do the right thing? Only time would tell, she thought. Time had a way of dealing with everything. She slid off Flyby's back and led him to his stall.

"Nealy, are you sure you didn't overreact?" Ruby said, putting her arm around Nealy's shoulders.

Nealy's shoulders sagged. "To your way of thinking, I suppose I did. The farm runs as well as it does because of the rules. When Maud and Jess were alive, my ass would have been on the road in seconds if I had done what those two did. I accepted those rules going in, and I made damn sure I never broke them. Emmie and Nick learned that same rule from the minute they were able to walk and talk. I gave us all a week. I realize now I shouldn't even have done that."

"Is your heart breaking, Nealy?"

"No," Nealy lied. "I'm going up for that shower now. I won't be long."

"What will they do?"

Nealy stopped and stared down at the ground. "I have no idea. Don't ask me that again, Ruby."

"Okay. Don't forget the coffee when you come back."

"I'll remember."

In the kitchen, Nealy headed to Smitty, who held out her arms. She stepped into them as the tears started to flow. "Don't say it, okay, Smitty."

"You did what you had to do, Nealy. Now you have to live with it. I know what you're thinking and how hard it was for you to do what you did. This isn't like when you lit out with Emmie at the age of seventeen. There was no love there. You moved from darkness to sunshine. Don't start comparing. It's over, it's done with, and you don't look back. If you look back, Nealy, it's all over."

"It hurts, Smitty. I feel like those two ripped my heart out. Nick got married. He got married, Smitty, and he didn't think enough of me to invite me to his wedding or even call to tell me. I had no clue that he was serious about Willow. Flirting is one thing, marrying is something else entirely. And yes, I fired her. I had to. I sent my son packing, so how could I keep his wife around to cook for me? As for Emmie, we've always been so very close, and yet the one time when I could have consoled her, been with her, what does she do? She hangs me out to dry and stays home crying. I don't understand that either. I don't understand, Smitty, why she didn't come to me this time. At Thanksgiving they were talking about having a baby, they went on this second honeymoon cruise, and then he dumps her and leaves her stranded when they got off the ship. What's wrong with this picture, Smitty? Don't answer that. I probably couldn't handle it right now. I'd appreciate it if you would make some fresh coffee, and if you have time, call an agency and see about getting us a new cook. An all-round housekeeper might be better."

In the shower, with the water beating down on her weary body, Nealy cried, her tears mingled with the water cascading all about her. She'd broken one of Jess's rules, one of the rules he said it was okay to break from time to time: never let them see you sweat. She'd let Smitty and Ruby see her bruised heart, let them see her tears. *Well, that was then, and this is now.* She stepped from the shower, towel dried her hair, dressed in clean clothes, and was back in the kitchen just as the percolator made its last plopping sound. She filled a thermos for Ruby and one for herself. She was back in the barn in less than fifteen minutes.

"You okay, Nealy?" Ruby asked as she reached for her thermos.

"No. But I will be." The splintered door to Flyby's stall lay at her feet. "He really did a number on that stall, didn't he?"

"Yes he did. He didn't like your tone of voice, didn't like what was going on. And they say these guys are stupid lumps. Not this guy. You should have seen what he did, Nealy. He burst out of his stall and pushed Nick into the tack room. It was almost funny the way he did it, like he was trying to make your point for you. Nick said he hurt him, but I think he just scared the hell out of him. I know it scared the hell out of me, and he wasn't even after me."

"I know you might find this hard to believe, but that horse understands everything that goes on where I'm concerned. His daddy, Stardancer, was the same way." Nealy opened Misty Blue's stall door and smiled when she saw that the colt was nursing. "So, what do you think of our little Shufly?" she asked, shifting mental gears.

"Nealy, he is so gorgeous, he takes my breath away. He's just what Metaxas needs. I don't know how I can ever thank you for him. And for allowing me to be a part of all this. In my life, I've never been happier. I'm sorry about the kids. Things will get better."

Nealy waved her hand in dismissal. "Look, it's your turn to hit the shower. Take all the time you need. If you can, try to get a couple of hours' sleep. Be sure you take your medicine while you're up at the house. I'm okay, Ruby. Over the years I've learned how to sleep with one eye open. I mean it, I'm okay. I have to see about getting this gate fixed before Himself decides to pitch another fit."

"Okay, Nealy. Things will work out. I want to say just one thing before I go up to the house. I want you to listen to me, Nealy, and we will never talk about this again. It isn't all that hard to say those two little words, I'm sorry. But only if you are sorry in your heart. If you don't mean the words, don't say them. You are a mother. A mother is supposed to love and love and love. A mother will stand by her child even if he or she is an ax murderer. Never having been a mother, I can't know what you are feeling. To have a child must be the most wonderful thing in the world. I don't want to see you throw away the relationship you have with Nick and Emmie."

"I didn't throw it away, Ruby. They did. Maud and Jess used to say, for every action there is a reaction, and you go on from there. Let's not talk about this anymore."

"You got it. See you later."

"Yes, later," Nealy said, leaning over the door of Misty Blue's stall to watch the colt suckle from its mother.

"Make yourself at home, Nick. You've been here often enough to know where everything is. You, too, Willow. Take any room you want on the second floor. Before you can say it, Nick, Buddy must have had someone come in and move all his things out while we were on the cruise. It doesn't look like he ever lived here. I was so shocked, I just caved in. I wish you could have seen me. I was like a maniac going through everything for some little scrap of something that was left behind. There was nothing, not even an empty shaving-cream can. Not even a stray sock. I just don't understand how he could do this to me."

"Do you want me to go to Ohio and kill him?" Nick asked. He grimaced when Willow jerked her head sideways to indicate he should go upstairs while she talked to Emmie.

"He planned it very thoroughly," Emmie said, flopping down on the couch. "He let me talk and plan for a baby, he arranged the cruise, said it would be like a second honeymoon and then wham bam, he dumps me on the gangplank when the ship docked. He said he doesn't want anything. The house is mine, our joint bank account, everything. He just wanted out."

"I'm so sorry, Emmie. I wish there was something I could do for you. I need to ask, why did you wait so long to go to the farm and tell your mother?"

"I was too ashamed, Willow. Do you know what I did? Right there on the gangplank with people watching us, I begged him, I held on to his arm and tried to hang on to him. He shook me off like he would shake off a stray dog. And if that wasn't bad enough, I told him I would stop talking if that would make him stay. He laughed in my face. I was too ashamed to tell that to my mother. I just holed up here and cried all week. I didn't think about Mom, the farm, or the horses. All I thought about was Buddy. I turned on the computer and watched it until I thought my eyeballs would explode out of my head. I was so sure he would write me and tell me . . . something . . . anything. Today, I finally realized it wasn't going to happen. How could I have been so stupid? How, Willow?"

"You loved him. Love doesn't come with an intelligence degree."

"I feel terrible that you and Nick came home to such a mess. You just got married, and already there are problems. My brother is a great guy, but then I guess you already knew that or you wouldn't have married him. Mom won't bend. Things are either black or white with her. There are no gray areas anywhere in her life."

"I can't believe that, Emmie. Mothers are very forgiving. They love their children unconditionally. I'm sure you and Nick will be able to work things out with her once she calms down."

Emmie laughed, a bitter sound to Willow's ears. "Maybe other mothers are like that, but ours isn't. We learned early on, almost as soon as we could walk, that the horses always came first. We were raised that way. I'm not saying it's wrong, it's the way it is, and we knew that, accepted it. Mom is very loving, very generous and kind with us. As soon as we hit our teens she told us we could take care of ourselves. She stopped that motherly hovering thing all mothers do. I don't know how Nick is going to handle this. All he knows is horses, and yet I can't see him signing on with another farm. I'm glad he has you, Willow. I'm glad you're both here. I'm a terrible hostess. Would you like some coffee? I'll make some. Why don't you go upstairs and freshen up. I'll call you when the coffee is ready."

"That sounds like a splendid idea, Emmie."

"Yes."

"Would you really have stopped talking if Buddy agreed to stay with you?"

"I guess I meant it when I said it. I know that doesn't say

much for me, now does it? He dumped me because I'm normal. He hated it when people talked to me and I responded. He wanted me to keep signing. I got so used to talking I would forget to sign. Then he would grab my arm and swing me around and make me sign. I guess that should have been my first clue. I don't know what to do without him. All I do is walk around in circles."

"This is a pretty kitchen," Willow said, changing the subject.

"Mom helped me decorate it. The breakfast nook gets the full morning sun. I like to curl up in the wing chair in my pajamas on Sunday morning and read the paper and drink a whole pot of coffee. Nick and I used to alternate Sundays. I always looked forward to that time. It was special. I guess I can do that every day now for the rest of my life. Do you want to hear something strange, Willow? When my stepfather, Nick's dad, died, Mom never cried once. He was dead, and she didn't cry. Buddy leaves me, and I fall apart and can't stop crying. Can you explain that to me?"

"No, Emmie, I can't. Each of us grieves in our own way. I'm going to go upstairs and freshen up. I'll be down soon. Are you sure you're okay?"

Emmie nodded as she measured coffee into the silver basket.

Satisfied that the coffee was perking, Emmie curled up in the wing chair in the breakfast nook. Maybe she should have told Willow and Nick the rest of her sorry tale. To what end? Some things were just better left alone. She looked out the window to watch her two favorite squirrels that she'd named Lizzie and Dizzy scamper across the deck railing to the huge bowl of pecans she kept on the picnic table on the deck. She'd tamed them to a degree. Oftentimes when she sat out on the deck with a book they'd come right up to her chair and beg for the nuts. They always scampered away and watched from a distance when Buddy would join her. She wondered why that was. Did they sense something in him that wasn't right? Were squirrels like dogs, good judges of character? Did it matter? Right now, nothing mattered, not the loss of Buddy or her mother's ugly decision to banish her.

Lizzie and Dizzy scurried across the railing, hopped onto the back of one of the deck chairs, and then onto the windowsill outside the breakfast nook. Their eyes shiny bright, their bushy tails swinging from side to side, they watched the sleeping girl who fed them every day and changed their daily water bowl on the steps of the deck. They chattered to one another as their little paws tapped on the glass for recognition. When none was forthcoming, they scampered away.

Upstairs, Nick perched on the edge of the bed, his head between his hands. He wanted to bawl, to kick and scream the way he'd done when he was a little boy. Always be responsible for your own actions. Words his father had taught him early on. Words he'd always heeded. Until now. How could he make this all come out right? He couldn't.

His mother had looked so tired, so weary. Ruby, too. Ruby had undergone chemotherapy and radiation treatments for a whole year. On the road to recovery, she still had to take her meds, still had to get plenty of rest, and he'd failed her, too. He should have called. Why didn't he? Because he didn't want to hear a lecture, didn't want to hear his mother say he was too young to marry someone he barely knew. He knew what he felt, what Willow felt, and that was enough for him. If only Misty Blue hadn't foaled early. If only Buddy hadn't left Emmie. If only, if only, if only. One week, one miserable goddamn week, and his whole life changed in a matter of minutes. Did it matter that he'd never, ever, taken a vacation? Did it matter that up until now he'd given his life to Blue Diamond Farms and the horses? What mattered was the week he'd taken for himself to get married. No matter what, he should have called. Somewhere far back in his mind he'd had the thought that when he and Willow returned there would be a second marriage, like both his mother and Maud had, with a reception for the farm workers. A tradition of sorts. One stinking, lousy phone call, and he wouldn't be sitting here ready to bawl his head off.

Bottom line . . . he should have called.

"We'll work this out, Nick," Willow said, sitting down next to him on the bed. "I'm going to send the check back. Maybe I should take it back and try to talk to your mother. She used to like me. Maybe we can talk, woman to woman. It's worth a try, Nick. I hate seeing you so miserable."

"I'm not just miserable. I'm fucking miserable, and it's my

own fault. I'm in shock. I knew I should have called. Some small part of me wanted to, but the larger part of me said no, she'll demand I come home. Our trip was special in so many ways, my first-ever vacation, making love to you, getting married. I wanted to keep it close for as long as I could. I didn't want to share it with anyone but you. This is the result."

"You aren't selfish, honey. And you can't take all the blame. I should have insisted you call your mother. I know your mom. I should have known how she'd react." She cradled him against her. "First thing tomorrow, I'll take the check back and then drive into town and look for a job. There's that new hotel. They were advertising for a chef. We won't starve, Nick."

Nick flopped backward onto the bed and laughed bitterly. "Money is the least of my problems, Willow. I'm fixed financially for the rest of my life. Emmie is, too. Hell, between us we could buy and operate our own farm. Maybe that's what we'll do if Emmie is agreeable. I want your promise that you won't go to my mother. If you want to send the check back, that's okay, and it is your decision. Just so you know, my mother never backs down. Never."

"She's not like that, Nick. I used to talk to her for hours in the kitchen. It's like we're talking about two different people here. The woman I know is nothing like what you're describing."

"Don't delude yourself. I'm her son. I should know. Everyone wears two faces. There's the family side where it all hangs loose and you know someone inside and out, and then there is the public side, where that person lets you see only what they want you to see. You do it, I do it, everyone does it. Sometimes we do it consciously and sometimes we do it unconsciously. How is Emmie?"

"She's hurting, Nick. How do you expect her to feel? She said she didn't see it coming. What kind of man would do something like that? And in public." She told him about Emmie's confession.

"Jesus. I'm just spoiling for a fight. I should get on the next plane to Ohio and beat the crap out of that sorry son of a bitch. I don't care if he is deaf."

"That's not what you're going to do, Nick. This is Emmie's problem, and we aren't going to do anything unless she asks us to intervene, which she isn't going to do. Right now we are going to go downstairs and have some coffee and talk about our future. We have to start making plans."

"I don't know if I can leave here, Willow. I have to be around horses. It's my life. It's all I know."

"I didn't say anything about leaving or you not being around horses. I said we need to talk about what we're going to do. That includes Emmie."

"Okay. Listen, I just want to shower and change. I'll be down in a few minutes."

"Take your time. I'll unpack our suitcases and meet you downstairs."

In the bathroom with the door closed and locked, Nick broke down and sobbed, his shoulders shaking uncontrollably. "I'm sorry I let you down, *Dad.*"

In the foyer, Willow reached for her jacket. A breath of fresh air might be just what she needed. A walk around the yard might clear her head a little. She was on her second lap when she noticed the mailman trying to jam mail into Emmie's box and having a hard time of it. She jogged forward and held out her hands. The after-Christmas sale catalogs were heavy. She staggered under their weight and on into the house, where she shrugged out of her jacket, the huge pile of mail secure in her arms. She called out to Emmie as she entered the kitchen. "I brought your mail in. Nick seems to think you might have some bills that need to be paid. Oh, Emmie, I'm sorry. I didn't know you were asleep."

"I guess I dozed off. It's not a problem. Our coffee is ready. I've been meaning to go out and pick up the mail, but I simply didn't want to make the effort. I guess it did pile up. Two weeks' worth from the look of things. I'll go through it later."

"No, let's go through it now," Nick said, entering the kitchen. "I don't want to see you get a bad credit rating. You need to pay your bills on time. I would like some coffee, ladies."

"Oh yes, sir, kind sir, it will be my pleasure to serve you some coffee. Would you like me to whip up a double chocolate cake while I'm at it?" Willow teased.

"Nope. We ate too much rich food on vacation. Coffee will do just fine," Nick mumbled as he sorted through the first-class mail. "You have a certified letter one of your neighbors signed for. Guess they just stuck it back in your box. It came sometime last week. It's from Josh Coleman's lawyer, the one Mom sent packing. You remember, the ornery, dumb one who couldn't get anything right. Do you want me to open it?"

"Be my guest, then chuck it. I don't want anything to do with those people and all those crazy lawyers. All lawyers do is bleed you dry."

"Well, lookee here, Emmie. Don't be so quick to chuck this one. Seems that ornery old buzzard we all thought was on the dumb side is suffering from Alzheimer's. This letter is from his son informing us and apologizing at the same time for the mistakes his father made. Remember the day you signed off on SunStar Farms, Josh Coleman's farm in Virginia? You signed it over to Ma's brothers. Right?"

"Yes. So what?"

"So what is this. The filings were never made in the timely manner the courts require. They are now null and void, and you have to sign a new set that is enclosed. Do you want to sign these, Emmie? You don't have to, you know."

"Why wouldn't I want to sign them, Nick?"

"Think about it. Ma just booted our asses out of Blue Diamond Farms. You own a farm. We can go there and take it over. Between the two of us, we could bring that farm up to snuff."

"What about Uncle Rhy and Uncle Pyne?"

"What about them, Emmie?"

"If we take it over, even though it was willed to me, what will happen to them?"

"I don't know. I suppose they could work for us. I heard Ma say she would make them full partners at Blue Diamond Farms if they wanted to join her. I don't know how anyone in their right mind could turn down an offer like that."

"Isn't SunStar tied up in that legal mess Mom is dealing with?"

"I don't know, Emmie. Mom never said much about it to me. The lawyers are handling it all. Look, it's our answer to our futures. Do you want to stay here and cry yourself to death over Buddy and Mom, or do you want to get on with your life?"

"Don't we need a lawyer? We can't use the one Mom uses because it will be a conflict of interest. The whole thing is so messy I'm not sure I want to get involved. Can we think about it?"

"Hey, I know a lawyer. Dad had these two friends he went to law school with. They still call me on a regular basis. The one named Hatch is an Indian and bigger than life. According to Dad, his billable hours are in the millions. He loved that big guy. If he hadn't married Mom, he would have joined the firm. Another friend of Dad's is Bode Jessup. He's a full partner. Dad said if I ever needed a good lawyer, to call Hatch. According to Dad he's the best of the best. His first name is Shunpus. Guess it's an Indian name. He's our man. Dad used to talk about those guys all the time. Sometimes I think he thought he made a mistake by not going with them into the firm. What do you think, Emmie?"

"Mom . . ."

"Emmie, for God's sake, we aren't doing anything illegal. SunStar was left to you. It's yours. Where is it written you have to give it to Rhy and Pyne? Mom told you to sign off on it, and you did. Did you ever think about what you did and the why of it?"

"A few times," Emmie mumbled. "Buddy said I was stupid for doing it. He called Mom a dictator sometimes. Let's think about it before we make a decision. I don't see anything wrong with getting in touch with your father's friend. See what he thinks. If he thinks it's the right thing to do, we'll do it. You know, of course, that Mom will have a fit."

"That's a given. Guess we'll have to live with that, too. If you two fine young women think you can manage without me, I'd like to fly out to Santa Fe and talk to Hatch in person. I'm not comfortable discussing something like this on the phone. I could fly out early tomorrow, stay overnight, and be back the following morning. You okay with that?"

Willow nodded.

"Okay, Nick."

"Then it's a go. I'll go upstairs, pack, and make a reservation. An early dinner would be good, or I could take you ladies out to eat. Decide and tell me the verdict when I come back down."

"Okay, honey. We want to go out."

"That was quick."

"You know us women. We can make snap decisions. Right, Emmie?"

"You bet." Emmie smiled.